Hoover Institution Publications 119

# Trotskyism in Latin America

# TROTSKYISM IN LATIN AMERICA

Robert J. Alexander

Hoover Institution Press
Stanford University
Stanford, California

The Hoover Institution on War, Revolution and Peace, founded at Stanford University in 1919 by the late President Herbert Hoover, is a center for advanced study and research on public and international affairs in the twentieth century. The views expressed in its publications are entirely those of the authors and do not necessarily reflect the views of the Board of Overseers, officers, or staff of the Hoover Institution.

Alexander, Robert Jackson, 1918-
    Trotskyism in Latin America.

    (Hoover Institution publications, 119)
    Bibliography: p. 269
    1. Communism—Latin America.    I. Title.
II. Series: Stanford University. Hoover Institution
on War, Revolution, and Peace. Publications, 119.
HX110.5.A6A76        335.43'3'098        71-187262
ISBN 0-8179-1191-X

Hoover Institution Publications 119
Standard Book Number 8179-1191-X
Library of Congress Card Number 71-187262
© 1973 by the Board of Trustees of the
    Leland Stanford Junior University
All rights reserved
Printed in the United States of America

*To Meg*

# Contents

Preface   ix

1   The Rise and Development of International Trotskyism   3

2   Fourth Internationalism in Latin America   35

3   Trotskyism, Peronismo, and the National Revolution in Argentina   45

4   Brazilian Trotskyism, Getulio Vargas, and Luíz Carlos Prestes   69

5   Chilean Trotskyism   88

6   The Beginnings of Bolivian Trotskyism   111

7   Trotskyism and the Bolivian National Revolution   128

8   Peruvian Trotskyism   157

9   Leon Trotsky, Diego Rivera, and Mexican Trotskyism   179

10   Mexican Trotskyism After Trotsky   199

11   Cuban Trotskyism, the Fourth International, and the Castro Revolution   215

12   Trotskyism in Other Latin American Countries   236

Postscript   249

Notes   251

Bibliography   269

Index   281

# Preface

Trotskyism has been a small but persistent force in Latin American left-wing politics for over forty years, and Latin Americans have helped make Trotsky's Fourth International the most long-lived dissident group within international Communism. And yet very little serious history has been written about Trotskyism in any part of the world, and none about its place in the Latin American republics.

In a quarter of a century of wandering through Latin America I have met and talked with many believers in international Trotskyism; for an even longer period, I have known some of their counterparts in this country. Although I have often disagreed with these persons, I believe that Trotskyism is a serious political movement, worth careful study, and that the information they have given me, as well as the written material I have collected over several years, may qualify me to write a short history of the movement in Latin America.

One problem I faced in collecting data for this study was that much of the relevant written material was of an ephemeral nature—throwaways, mimeographed bulletins, or newspapers published in only a few copies—which most people would not think of collecting. Another obstacle was posed by the Fourth International's concern for secrecy. For one thing, the use of "party names" by Fourth Internationalists has been common. In the Argentine movement, to give only one example, Liborio Justo was known as "Bernal" or "Quebracho"; Homero Cristali was usually referred to in the 1930's and 1940's merely as "Homero," but after that he used the name "J. Posadas" exclusively. I also found it virtually impossible to get exact figures on party membership and the size of affiliated groups belonging to the movement, or even to get exact information concerning places, dates, and attendance at meetings. Fortunately, this part of the problem was largely solved for me by several non-Trotskyist friends who supplied me with relevant data in their possession, and by many members and ex-members of the Fourth International in several countries who submitted to interviewing and provided extensive documentary material.

One semantic issue is of importance in any book dealing with Trotskyism. The followers of Leon Trotsky refer to themselves as "Trotskyists," whereas their opponents on the left call them "Trotskyites." As an old Social Democrat, my natural proclivity would be to use the word "Trotskyite." In this volume, however, out of courtesy to the people with whom I am dealing, I have tried to effect a compromise: I have used both terms—sometimes one, sometimes the other, as seems appropriate in a given context.

In any work dealing with a highly controversial group, it behooves the author to state his own position. I have never been a Trotskyite, and for most of my adult life I have belonged to the Socialist Party and the Social Democratic Federation, organizations on the left which have opposed the Fourth Internationalists. I have tried to be as objective as possible in all matters, even though it may not be possible for me to be completely impartial.

Naturally, I am grateful to many persons who have helped me gather material and given me editorial advice. Some of these people are old friends: my colleague Professor Sam Baily, who provided much material on Argentina and put me in contact with old Trotskyists there; two former students of mine, Peter Lord and Irwin Rubinstein, now U.S. diplomats, who sent me invaluable (unclassified) information on the countries to which they were assigned at the time I wrote them; Dardo Cúneo, an Argentine friend who put me in touch with useful sources in his country; Rodrígo García Treviño of Mexico, who helped me obtain material on Trotskyism in his country and provided insights into Trotsky's stay in Mexico; and Carlos Manuel Pellecer, a one-time Communist leader in Guatemala, who provided interesting information about Trotskyism in Cuba and about the participation of Mexican Trotskyites in guerrilla movements in his native country. Finally, I must mention my good friend Max Shachtman, the former international Trotskyist leader and Trotsky's literary executor; he gave me extensive data for the first general chapter on the Fourth International movement, which he read and criticized, and also gave me valuable data on Mexican Trotskyism.

Then there are persons whom I came to know while writing this book. The young Cuban exile Nelson Valdés put me in touch with important sources of information concerning Trotskyism in Cuba; Liborio Justo, once a leading Argentine Trotskyist, sent me a priceless collection of his own pamphlets and books dealing with the movement in Argentina; and a Bolivian student at Rutgers University, Eduardo Michel, obtained for me a copy of Liborio Justo's study of Bolivian Trotskyism. Also exceedingly cooperative were Charles Curtiss, once a representative of the Fourth International in Mexico, who provided me, through letters and an interview, with important information about Trotsky's stay in Mexico and the schisms in Mexican Trotskyism, as well as putting me in touch with old-time leaders of the movement in Mexico. Félix Ibarra, a former Secretary-General of the Mexican Trotskyists, introduced me to a number of his former colleagues there; Octavio Fernández, another former leading Mexican Fourth Internationalist, submitted to several interviews and also allowed me to take notes on his invaluable archives of Mexican Trotskyism of the 1930's and 1940's.

I must also thank Joseph Hansen, editor of the *Intercontinental Press* and still a leading figure in the Socialist Workers Party of the United States; he granted me an interview, sent me material on the differences between the various factions of the Fourth International, and was kind enough to read and criticize the first draft of the introductory chapter on international Trotskyism. His wife Reba Hansen made available to me the files of several European periodicals published by affiliates of the United Secretariat of the Fourth International. Similarly, Lucy St. Johns of the Workers League allowed me to use the League's files of the publications of its British and French counterparts. Finally, Ronald Chilcote of the University of California at Riverside was kind enough to send me exceedingly useful material on Brazilian Trotskyism.

Needless to say, none of these persons bears any responsibility for what appears in this volume. Whatever errors there may be, and certainly the judgments and opinions offered (unless otherwise identified), are my own.

Finally, I must express my debt to my wife, Joan, and my two children, Tony and Meg, who endured my periods of preoccupation during the writing of this volume, when undoubtedly from their point of view I might have been doing things more interesting than knocking away at a typewriter with my thoughts far away from theirs. For their loving patience, my thanks.

Rutgers University                                                                          R.J.A.

New Brunswick, N.J.
September, 1972

# Trotskyism in Latin America

—1—

# The Rise and Development of
# International Trotskyism

Trotskyism as an international political movement had its origins in the struggle for power in the Communist Party of the Soviet Union (CPSU) in the late 1920's. Out of that bitter contest there developed three major factions, each having its counterparts outside the Union of Soviet Socialist Republics.

The victorious faction, gathered around and completely dominated by Stalin, kept control of the CPSU and the Communist International (the Third International or Comintern), which had been organized under Lenin's leadership in 1919. The so-called Right in the Soviet party, in which Nikolai Bukharin, Andrei Rykov, and Mikhail Tomsky were the most outstanding figures, had its counterpart abroad in the International Communist Opposition, although there seems to have been no direct contact between the Soviet right and the right opposition abroad. The most important Right Opposition groups outside the Soviet Union were the one in Germany, led by Heinrich Brandler and August Thalheimer, and the one in the United States, whose members were generally known as the Lovestoneites, after their leader Jay Lovestone, who had been expelled as Secretary-General of the U.S. Communist Party. The Right Opposition had disappeared as an international movement by the early part of World War II. The Brandler-Thalheimer exiles had dispersed and their principal Swiss leader, Jules Humbert-Droz, had entered the Swiss Social Democratic Party; the Lovestoneite group in the United States had opted for dissolution in 1939.

On the other side of the opposition, Leon Trotsky's followers abroad, grouped first in the International Left Communist Opposition and after 1938 in the Fourth International, were more significant and more persistent. They succeeded in bringing together small groups or parties in at least half a dozen Western European nations, in several Asian countries, and in at least ten nations in the Western Hemisphere. Two of their parties, those in Ceylon and Bolivia, became major forces in their respective countries' national politics for brief periods. Until the open break between the Soviet Union and China in the early 1960's, the Trotskyist opposition continued to be the most important dissident Communist element active on a worldwide scale.

3

## TROTSKY AND THE RUSSIAN REVOLUTION

Leon Trotsky was one of the principal leaders of the Bolshevik Revolution of November 1917. However, he had not joined the Bolshevik Party until August 1917, five months after the overthrow of the Tsar. Until then, he had maintained a more or less independent position between the Bolsheviks and their Menshevik opponents within Russian Marxist ranks, a fact which was later to be held against him in his struggles with Stalin, an Old Bolshevik.

A few weeks before the November Revolution, Trotsky was chosen to head the Revolutionary Military Committee of the All-Russian Soviet of Workers and Soldiers Deputies, in which the Bolsheviks had just achieved a majority. It was he who organized the Red Guard, which actually carried out the Bolshevik coup d'etat on November 7, 1917. He became Commissar of Foreign Affairs in the new Bolshevik-dominated government headed by Vladimir Ilyich Lenin.

During most of the period between November 7, 1917, and the death of Lenin in January 1924, Trotsky was generally regarded as the second most important figure in the Bolshevik regime. Although he resigned as Commissar of Foreign Affairs in March 1918 rather than sign the peace treaty with the Germans at Brest-Litovsk, he returned to the government a few months later as Commissar of War. It was he who organized the Red Army and led it to victory in the bitter two and a half year Civil War which finally established Bolshevik control over all of Russia.

Trotsky was a brilliant orator, a first-rate organizer in his tenure as Commissar of War, and a Marxist theoretician of first rank. However, he was badly out-maneuvered politically by Joseph Stalin after the death of Lenin, who had been the undisputed chief of the Bolshevik government. Between 1924 and 1927, when Trotsky carried on an unequal struggle for power with Stalin, ideological issues were hotly debated between the two factions. Trotsky argued that it was necessary to move quickly to incorporate the peasantry into the Socialist system established by the Bolsheviks by ending the pattern of small landholdings which had evolved in the early years of the Revolution, since the peasantry, as petty bourgeoisie, constituted a group potentially hostile to the building of Socialism. Stalin, on the other hand, argued that the peasantry were the allies of the Bolshevik-led proletariat, and that they should therefore be left alone, at least for the time being.

Trotsky also maintained that it was necessary to industrialize the Soviet Union as rapidly as possible, since the Russia of the early 1920's did not have the economic base necessary for a Socialist system, and that for this purpose it was necessary to end the semi-free enterprise system established by Lenin in the New Economic Policy, launched in 1921. Stalin, in contrast, maintained that there was no great urgency about the matter, that it was necessary rather to concentrate on restoring the economy to at least the level of 1913 (before World War I and the Civil War), and that for this purpose the New Economic Policy was proving effective.

Finally, Trotsky disagreed fundamentally with Stalin's argument that the Soviet Union should concentrate on the development of "socialism in one country." He argued that revolution was a continuing process; if it did not continue to deepen within the country in which it was already triumphant and expand geographically to other nations, it would come to a halt and be put on the defensive. Therefore, Trotsky maintained that the process of Socialist transformation in the Soviet Union had to be accompanied by continuing emphasis on extending the revolution to other countries.

On the basis of these three fundamental disagreements over revolutionary theory and practice, Trotsky had major criticisms of Stalin's foreign policy. He was strongly against the formation of the Anglo-Soviet Trade Union Committee, through which Stalin sought to use the Soviet trade unions as an instrument for gaining the support for the Soviet Union from the relatively conservative British labor movement. Trotsky also was highly critical of the policies followed by Stalin in China. There Stalin patronized the agreement by which the members of the fledgling Chinese Communist Party also became members of the Nationalist Party (Kuomintang) of Sun Yat Sen, the father of the Chinese Republic. This Communist-Kuomintang alliance proved disastrous for the Communists in May 1927, when Chiang Kai-shek, the successor to Sun Yat Sen, ordered the murder of virtually all of the country's leading Communists, which seemed to vindicate Trotsky's condemnation of Stalin's China policy.

Whatever the merits of the theoretical positions taken by the two sides, Stalin proved to be the better political maneuverer. By 1927 he had gained enough power to have Trotsky and his principal followers expelled from the Communist Party of the Soviet Union, and to have Trotsky forced into isolated residence in Siberia. In 1929, Stalin took the further step of deporting Trotsky across the Soviet border to Turkey.

By 1928 Stalin was adopting policies which were much closer to those which had been advocated by Trotsky than to those he himself had advocated earlier. These were the policies of collectivization of agriculture, forced draft industrialization through the Five Year Plans, and adoption of a "Third Period" super-revolutionary line for the Communist International. This shift drew opposition from many who had previously supported Stalin against Trotsky, but in 1929-30 Stalin liquidated this "Right Opposition" by expelling its principal leader, Nikolai Bukharin, and most of his closest associates from the Communist Party of the Soviet Union.

Upon being deported Trotsky settled in Prinkipo, Turkey, in 1929. Four years later he went to France, but in 1935 he was forced to migrate to Norway. Finally, as the result of continuing political pressure from the Soviet government on Norway, he was forced to leave there in 1937. This time only Mexico, under the reforming President Lázaro Cárdenas, was willing to give him asylum. He lived in Mexico until his murder at the hands of an agent of Stalin's secret police on August 21, 1940.

## ORIGINS OF TROTSKYISM OUTSIDE THE SOVIET UNION

The existence of the factional struggle for control of the Soviet Communist Party quickly became known to Communists outside the U.S.S.R., but until 1928—largely owing to Trotsky's own policy of keeping the conflict within the higher echelons of the party—most Communists outside the U.S.S.R. heard only the Stalinist side of the argument.* James Cannon, who became the most prominent leader of Trotskyism in the United States, described the situation in the following terms:

> The issues of the great struggle in the Russian Party were confined at the beginning to extremely complex Russian questions. Many of them were new and unfamiliar to us Americans, who knew very little about the internal problems of Russia. They were very difficult for us to understand because of their profound theoretical nature—after all, up to that time we had no really serious theoretical education—and the difficulty was increased by the fact that we were not presented with full information. We were not supplied with the documents of the Russian Left Opposition. Their arguments were concealed from us. We were not told the truth. On the contrary, we were systematically fed with misrepresentations, distortion, and one-sided documentation.[1]

Moreover, the Communist parties outside the Soviet Union were forced by the Comintern, on pain of disciplinary action, to support the positions of the victorious element in the Soviet party. Cannon has noted: "Campaigns against 'Trotskyism' were ordained from Moscow in all the parties of the world. The expulsion of Trotsky and Zinoviev [from the Communist Party of the Soviet Union] in the fall of 1927 were followed by demands that all the parties immediately take a position, with the implied threat of reprisals from Moscow against any individual or group failing to take a 'correct' position—that is, in favor of the expulsions. Campaigns of 'enlightenment' were carried on....Membership meetings, branch meetings, section meetings were held all over the party to which representatives of the Central Committee were sent in order to enlighten the membership on the necessity for the expulsions of the organizer of the Red Army and the Chairman of the Comintern."[2]

It was not until the Sixth Congress of the Communist International (July-September 1928) that the foreign parties were finally informed of Trotsky's

*Trotsky's followers still feel that he acted correctly in this early phase of the struggle with Stalin.

views in the Soviet dispute. Although he was in exile in Siberia at the time, Trotsky sent an appeal to the Congress against his expulsion from the Soviet part of what was theoretically a single international party. He also sent to the congress a document entitled "The Draft Program of the Communist International: A Criticism of Fundamentals," in which he commented on the Stalinist draft program for the Comintern.

Cannon describes how, despite Stalinist efforts to suppress Trotsky's views, this document found its way into the translating room established for the congress, and how, in the confusion that reigned there, it was translated and sent to the leaders of all national delegations attending the congress, as well as to the members of the program commission set up by the meeting.[3] Cannon does not mention that he had to turn in his own copy of the Trotsky document to the Secretariat, and that he succeeded in getting a copy to take back home only by getting Wilkinson, the Australian delegate, drunk and then stealing his copy.[4] Cannon began to distribute the document once he was out of the U.S.S.R.

As Trotsky's point of view concerning the various questions involved in his dispute with Stalin became more widely known outside the Soviet Union, small groups of people came forward to declare loyalty to Trotsky or sympathy with him. C. L. R. James has indicated the scope of this support: "The groups of the Left Opposition could not form a successful party . . . . In Germany there were only 750 strong in 1933, and were almost swept away in the debacle which followed the coming to power of Hitler. In Spanish America they had made considerable headway, and in Canada, Cuba, China, France, Spain, and Britain there were small or large groups, hounded always by the Stalinists, and unpopular in the working class movement generally, because their criticisms of Stalin seemed anti-Russian and formed a suitable background for the unending mud-stream of abuse against Trotskyism."[5]

After his deportation to Prinkipo in 1929, Leon Trotsky worked hard to organize his followers into a Communist faction that would have as its ultimate objective the reform of the CPSU and the Comintern. As Isaac Deutscher has noted, however: "The outcome of Trotsky's first attempts to organize his followers in the West was disappointing. He concentrated his attention on France where he had had a more influential following than elsewhere . . . in the hope of setting up there a strong base for the Opposition."[6] Trotsky's following in France proved too heterogeneous and quarrelsome to accept unification, but in at least one respect the venture did bear fruit. One of the principal Trotskyist leaders, Alfred Rosmer, "went on a tour of Germany and Belgium to inspect and rally groups of the Opposition there; and he established contact with Italian, Dutch, American, and other Trotskyists. In detailed reports he kept Trotsky informed about his findings."[7]

In 1930, with Trotsky's encouragement and approval, the first steps were taken toward giving an organizational structure to international Trotskyism. In April of that year an International Bureau was established at a conference attended by representatives from various nations. Named to the bureau were Alfred Rosmer of France, with Pierre Naville as his deputy; Max Shachtman of the United States; K. Landau of Germany and Andrés Nin of Spain; and Leon Sedov, Trotsky's son (serving under the name Markin) from Russia. This bureau was unable to function, however, because shortly after it was established Shachtman returned to the United States, Andrés Nin was jailed in Spain, and Sedov was unable to get out of Prinkipo.[8] In place of the bureau, therefore, an International Secretariat was established, consisting of Pierre Naville, an Italian known as Souzo, and Mill, a Russian Jewish émigré living in France, who was later discovered to be an agent of the Soviet secret police.[9] This body, too, was an ineffective coordinating force, and Trotsky reorganized it late in 1931.[10]

The goals of international Trotskyism in mid-1933 were summed up in an eleven-point program published in *The Militant* (New York) on September 30, 1933:

1. The independence of the proletarian party, always and under all conditions....

2. Recognition of the international, and thereby of the permanent, character of the proletarian revolution; rejection of the theory of socialism in one country....

3. Recognition of the Soviet state as a workers state in spite of the growing degeneration of the bureaucratic regime....

4. Condemnation of the economic policy of the Stalinist faction both in the stage of economic opportunism in 1923 to 1928...as well as its stage of economic adventurism in 1928 to 1932....

5. Recognition of the necessity for systematic Communist work in the proletarian mass organizations, particularly in the reformist trade unions....

6. Rejection of the formula of the "democratic dictatorship of the proletariat and peasantry" as a separate regime distinguished from the dictatorship of the proletariat....

7. Recognition of the necessity of mobilizing the masses under transitional slogans corresponding to the concrete situation in each country....

8. Recognition of the necessity of a developed united front policy with respect to the mass organizations of the working class both of trade union and political character....

9. Rejection of the theory of social fascism, and of the whole practice bound up with it, as serving fascism on the one hand and the Social Democracy on the other....*

---

*During the so-called "Third Period" of the Comintern, from 1928 to 1934, the Stalinists rather simplistically divided the political spectrum into "fascists" (anyone to the right of center), the "social fascists," consisting of the non-Communist left and particularly the Socialists, and the Communists. They argued that the principal enemies of the Communists were the "social fascists."

10. The struggle for the regrouping of the revolutionary forces of the world's working class, under the banner of international Communism. Recognition of the necessity for the creation of a genuine Communist International capable of applying the principles enumerated above.

11. Recognition of party democracy not only in words but in fact....

In June 1929, soon after arriving in Prinkipo, Trotsky had begun publication of a periodical, *Bulletin Oppositsii*. A few months later its publication was transferred to Paris, and in early 1931 an English language version, *International Bulletin of the Left Communist Opposition,* began to appear in the United States, under the patronage of the U.S. Trotskyist group, the Communist League of America (Opposition).

## COMMUNIST OPPOSITION OR NEW INTERNATIONAL?

For the first few years in the life of International Trotskyism, there was considerable discussion and controversy within its ranks as to the exact nature of the movement. Trotsky and most of his followers argued that it existed not to rival and supplant the Communist International, but rather to reform it. In this role, they contended, Trotskyism was an integral part of the Comintern. Isaac Deutscher has summed up Trotsky's position concerning the nature of international Trotskyism during its earliest years as follows: "He declared that he and his adherents owed their loyalty to the Communist International even though they had been expelled from it. They formed a school of thought struggling to regain its place within the general communist movement....Their sole purpose [according to Trotsky] was to influence communist opinion, to make it realize that usurpers had seized the reins of the Soviet Government and of the Comintern, and to induce it to strive for the restoration of pristine Marxism and Leninism."

In addition to stressing to his followers that it was wrong for them to forswear their basic loyalty to the Comintern, Trotsky pointed out that they were too weak to challenge the existing Second and Third Internationals. In the words of Deutscher, "Trotsky warned those who stood for a Fourth International that it was not enough for a group of dissidents to raise a new banner in order to become a real factor in politics. Revolutionary movements were not conjured up with banners and slogans, but rose and grew organically with the social class for which they spoke. Each of the Internationals represented a definite stage in the historic experience of the working class and in the struggle for socialism; and no one could ignore with impunity the ties the Second and Third Internationals had with the masses or the weight of their political traditions.[12] Trotsky and most of his followers continued to declare themselves an "opposition" within the Communist Third International until after the fall of the Weimar Republic and Hitler's rise to power in Germany on January 30, 1933.

During the years preceding Hitler's victory, when the Nazi party was moving from one gain to another, Trotsky repeatedly urged the formation of a united front between Germany's Communists and Social Democrats to confront the Hitlerite menace. But neither the Socialists nor the Communists were in a mood to pay heed to Trotsky's urgings, for during those years the Communists were pursuing a particularly violent vendetta against the "social fascist" Social Democrats, in conformity with the Third Period line of the Communist International. In pursuance of this policy, they allied themselves with the Nazis against the Social Democrats on various occasions.

This intransigency of the Communists was answered in kind by the groups which were attacked by them, principally the Social Democrats, and the element that gained in the long run from these struggles was the Nazi Party. Once Hitler came to power, both the Social Democratic and Communist Parties were helpless to resist the new regime he set up. Within a matter of weeks, both parties were outlawed and their organizations, which had once seemed almost invincible, were completely dismantled.

It was the rapid collapse of the German Communist Party that finally brought Trotsky around to the idea that he and his followers should establish a new, fourth, International. Deutscher has described the rationale behind this decision: "In these weeks Trotsky renounced his allegiance to the Third International. In an article under the title 'The Tragedy of the German Proletariat' (and the subtitle 'The German Workers Will Rise Again—Stalinism Never'), he thus summed up the situation: What the labor movement had suffered in Germany was not a temporary reverse or a tactical setback, but a decisive strategic defeat, which would leave the working class prostrated and paralyzed for a whole epoch.... He concluded that Stalinism had had its '4 August,' a collapse as ignominious as that which the Second International had suffered at the outbreak of the First World War."[13] Trotsky's first reaction was to call for the formation of a new Communist Party of Germany. Within a few weeks he had moved on to support the idea of a completely new International. Last of all, he began to urge the organization of a rival to the Communist Party of the Soviet Union, to work for a "political revolution" in that country.

## THE FORMATION OF THE FOURTH INTERNATIONAL

Although Trotsky was won over in 1933 to the idea of establishing the Fourth International as a rival to the Third rather than as a group trying to reform the Comintern, five more years passed before the existence of the Fourth International was actually proclaimed. Meanwhile, propaganda in favor of a new International became one of the major activities of Trotsky and his followers. Early in 1934 the International Left Opposition first signed a document supporting this idea; it was joined by representatives of the Socialist Workers Party (SAP) of Germany, the Independent Socialist Party of the Netherlands, and the Revolutionary Socialist Party of the Netherlands. Only the last of these national parties was in any sense a Trotskyist group.[14]

During the period preceding the proclamation of the Fourth International, Trotsky's followers also tested "the French turn" tactic, so named because it was in France that Trotsky's followers were first advised to enter the ranks of the Socialist Party of the Second International. Trotsky gave this advice "not in order to accept its ideas [the Socialist Party's], but on the contrary in order to defy reformism within its own stronghold and to 'carry their revolutionary program to the masses.' "[15] This tactic was hotly debated by all Trotskyist groups and accepted by most of them in 1934-35. However, with the possible exception of the Trotskyists of the United States, those who put the French turn into practice (including the Argentine group) did not succeed in substantially increasing membership through recruiting in Socialist ranks.

Trotsky and his closest associates nevertheless decided to launch the Fourth International officially in September 1938. The founding congress was held at the home of Alfred Rosmer in Perigny, a small town near Paris (although for years it was officially maintained that the conference had met "somewhere in Switzerland"). There were twenty-one delegates in attendance, who were said to represent organizations in eleven countries.

Because of fear of attacks by Stalinists—who had already murdered several of the conference planners and had stolen the draft of the statutes of the Fourth International, as well as some other documents—the meeting was completed in one day, September 3, 1938. It was chaired by Max Shachtman of the Socialist Workers Party of the United States. The meeting heard a progress report on Trotskyist groups in various parts of the world, and its formal agenda "was so crowded that it would have kept any normal congress busy for a week."[17] The major debate seems to have centered around the question of whether the new International should in fact be proclaimed. Two delegates from Poland were the principal opponents of the idea; Isaac Deutscher claimed that he had framed the position opposing foundation of the Fourth International which these two delegates presented.[18] A nineteen-to-three vote on the issue favored establishment of the Fourth International.[19] The conference then elected an Executive Committee to head the new organization, and this committee included at least one Latin American, Mario Pedrosa of Brazil.

The question obviously arises as to why Trotsky decided to establish the Fourth International at that particular moment. He certainly did not do so because international Trotskyism was making great progress. Within the Soviet Union his followers had been liquidated politically, and many of them physically. In Eastern and Southern Europe the labor movement and Marxist political groups had been suppressed by the fascist and semi-fascist regimes which dominated those countries. In Germany and Austria it was not possible for any opposition party to function in an organized way, and the same was to be true in Czechoslovakia after the Munich Agreement, which was reached less than a month after the Fourth International was founded.

Only in France and Britain in Europe were there Trotskyist groups which were functioning openly, and in France the demise of the Popular Front had brought deep gloom to the whole left. In Spain, fascism was within six months of winning total victory in the Civil War, and even in the remnants of Republican Spain, Trotskyism had been driven deeply underground by the Communist-influenced government. In Asia the only country in which there was any significant Trotskyist movement was Ceylon. In the New World, there were small Trotskyist groups in the United States, Canada, and half a dozen Latin American countries.[20]

Perhaps the only answer to the question of why Trotsky finally decided to formally establish a Fourth International was that by 1938 he had given up completely any hope that it was possible to reform the Communist International, and felt that it was therefore necessary to have an international movement which was committed, as he saw it, to the fulfillment of the international working-class revolution.

## THE CRISIS OF 1939-40

Within a year of its foundation, the Fourth International underwent its first major crisis. This arose from Trotsky's continued advocacy of "defense of the Soviet Union," even in the face of the events of the early years of the Second World War. These events—the Stalin-Hitler Pact, the partition of Poland between the Soviet Union and Nazi Germany, the absorption of other East European areas by the U.S.S.R., and the Soviet invasion of Finland—brought some of Trotsky's followers to question their leader's attitudes. They particularly took issue with his contention that while the U.S.S.R. was a "degenerated workers' state," it was still a workers' state and therefore the Fourth International was bound to defend it regardless of its actions.

"It is impossible to regard the Soviet Union as a workers' state in any sense whatsoever," declared James Burnham in a statement to the leadership of the U.S. Socialist Workers Party in September 1939. Shortly thereafter, Max Shachtman introduced a resolution to the SWP leadership calling the Soviet seizure of Eastern Poland "imperialist," and going on to deny that this action had any of the progressive consequences alleged by Trotsky. He urged the Socialist Workers Party to repudiate its pledge to defend the Soviet Union.[21] Trotsky remained adamant, however. He argued that the Soviet invasion was justified in order to defend Soviet frontiers, that any Soviet government would have had to act in much the same way that Stalin had done, and that the "strategic interest" of the workers' state took priority over Finland's right to self-determination.[22]

The majority of the leadership of the Socialist Workers Party sided with Trotsky, and against Shachtman and Burnham. Although Trotsky obviously was on the side of the majority in the intraparty struggle in the SWP, he advised the majority group, led by James Cannon, to avoid a showdown which would result in a split in the party. Nevertheless, such a schism did occur early in 1940, when the minority withdrew to form the Workers Party. This party remained a dissident Trotskyist group for a decade and a half; by the middle 1950's it had evolved in the direction of Social Democracy, and in mid-1958 the members of the Workers Party, by then known as the Independent Socialist League, were admitted to the Socialist Party of the United States.

The split in its largest affiliate had repercussions throughout the Fourth International, especially in France, where quite a few members accepted Burnham's or Shachtman's views.[23] In the Executive Committee of the Fourth International the only non-United States members who sided with Shachtman were the Brazilian Mario Pedrosa and C. R. L. James of Trinidad. (At that time both were active in the U.S. party.) A Spaniard then living in Mexico, Grandizo Muñis, later also sided with Shachtman.[24] This polemical struggle with the Shachtmanites was one of Trotsky's last political activities before he was brutally murdered on August 21, 1940.

## THE 1946 CONFERENCE OF THE FOURTH INTERNATIONAL

World War II interfered drastically with the functioning of the Fourth International. However, an Emergency Conference of the International was held between May 9 and May 16, 1940, to take stock of the situation provoked by the outbreak of the war. It adopted a "Manifesto on the Imperialist War and the Proletarian Revolution," written by Trotsky. This document looked forward to revolutionary upheaval coming in the wake of the world conflict, arguing that "in history war has not infrequently been the mother of revolution precisely because it rocks superannuated regimes to their foundation, weakens the ruling class, and hastens the growth of revolutionary indignation among the oppressed classes."[25]

The headquarters of the Fourth International was shifted to New York City, but while the war was still in progress an attempt was made to reestablish the International in Europe. A conference of European affiliates of the group was held at an undisclosed place in August 1943, with representatives reported as being present from the French, Belgian, Greek, Spanish, and German parties. It established a Provisional European Secretariat. It began to publish a periodical, *Quatrième Internationale,* which was first mimeographed but later printed. The Secretariat was reported to have helped to bring into existence a German section in exile in France.

In February 1944 a European Conference of the Fourth International was held. Delegations were present from the French, Belgian, Spanish, German, and Greek sections, and the meeting lasted six days. It chose a European Executive Committee and European Secretariat. Subsequently, the European Executive Committee was enlarged to include British, French, Belgian, Spanish, German,

Swiss, Greek, and Dutch representatives, as well as a delegate from a Trotskyist group among Indo-Chinese immigrants in France.[26]

The first postwar conference of the Fourth International was held in an unidentified place in Belgium in April 1946. There were apparently both majority and minority representatives present from several of the parties and groups attending the conference. The most important resolution of this meeting was one "to establish the authority of this Conference and of the Executive bodies elected by it." This motion read:

> This representative conference of mandated delegates from sections of the Fourth International, which is the first representative gathering since the Emergency Conference of 1940, having heard the organization report of the European Secretariat and taken cognizance of the opinion expressed by the members of the existing International Executive Committee, and with a full understanding of the difficulties in the preparation for the Conference, decides: (1) to sit as a world conference of the Fourth International and to take binding decisions on all questions that are on the agenda; and (2) to dissolve the existing IEC and IS and to elect from this Conference a new IEC and IS with full authority to act until the world congress."[27]

This conference laid down a twofold tactic for the affiliates of the Fourth International, particularly those in Europe. Because of supposed "crises" within the Socialist and Communist parties, Trotskyists should attempt to infiltrate both types of parties. In addition, however, they should promote "independent" development of the various Trotskyist parties. This dual policy was summed up thus: "In a general way, the road for the construction of our parties, particularly in continental Europe, leads at present through the combination of our independent work, guaranteed by our organizational and political autonomy, with patient, systematic, and sustained fraction work in reformist, centrist, and Stalinist organizations."[28]

## THE 1948 CONGRESS OF THE FOURTH INTERNATIONAL

The first full-fledged postwar congress of the International, the Second Congress, was held in Paris sometime between March and September 1948. Perhaps the outstanding characteristic of this congress was its extreme secrecy, apparently designed to protect it as much from attacks by Stalinists as from interruption by the police. Delegates who attended the meeting have testified that in spite of elaborate precautions, the police and foreign embassies were informed in detail about what occurred there.[29]

The congress was attended not only by representatives from regular sections of the International but by representatives from dissident Trotskyist elements in various countries. Max Shachtman has written: "The congress was undoubtedly the most numerously attended and representative of all the international meetings of the Trotskyist movement. Bourgeois or Stalinist repression and meagerness of financial resources prevented many sections from sending their representatives. Yet, as never before, delegates came to the meeting not only from Europe, but from Asia, South Africa, and several countries of the Western Hemisphere. Their presence was an earnest of the devotion of the Trotskyist movement to that socialist internationalism which has been abandoned by so many backsliders, cynics, and tired men."[30]

There were three major issues before the Second Congress: disunity in the French Trotskyist ranks, the so-called Russian question, and the idea of a new "French turn." The first issue arose from a split within the French movement over Trotskyist participation in the Resistance during World War II. One element had argued that Trotskyists should not participate because the Resistance served the ends of the "imperialist war." Other elements had supported the Resistance in some measure, and still others had been very active in the cause. As a result of this contention, there were perhaps five different groups calling themselves Trotskyist in France when the war ended in 1945. The Congress tried unsuccessfully to bring them together in a single organization.

The second issue arose over the way to categorize the Communist party-controlled regimes that had arisen in Eastern Europe since World War II. Joseph Hansen, of the Socialist Workers Party, in a letter to the author dated December 24, 1970, thus summed up the discussion among the delegates:

> At the time a division had occurred in the Trotskyist movement over how to characterize the state structures in Eastern Europe. A majority argued that they could not be designated as workers states, no matter what qualification might be placed upon this term. A minority held that they should be characterized as workers states, although certainly not of a kind in which any proletarian democracy reigned. The minority would have liked to have called them degenerated workers states, but could hardly do so in all consistency since they had originated under the bureaucratic military auspices of the Kremlin regime and therefore were "degenerated" to begin with. The minority therefore called them "deformed" workers states. The minority position, it should be added, eventually was adopted by the majority of all sectors of the world Trotskyist movement, becoming the official position of the Fourth International.

A third position on the issue was put forward by Max Shachtman, who as a representative of the Workers Party of the United States had the status of an observer, with the right to speak on the floor but not to vote. In a letter to the author dated December 7, 1970, Shachtman succinctly stated the position which he argued at that time:

> My argument was this: If Russia was a "degenerated workers state" — which I denied—then so were the new satellites, by virtue of the identity of socioeconomic and political structures and forms, which introduced into our "doctrine" the twin embarrassments that a proletarian revolution had taken place in the satellites without a proletariat or a revolutionary party; and that you could have a "degenerate

workers state'' before you ever had a non-degenerated workers state. I did not
say at all that on balance they were degenerated workers states, but that, like
Russia, they were reactionary, bureaucratic-collectivist states.

The majority at the Congress took the position that the East European regimes
were "capitalist," because "the state of the 'buffer' countries defends property
which, despite its diverse and hybrid forms, remains fundamentally bourgeois
in character." However, the resolution adopted by the congress also argued
that "the state of the 'buffer' countries represents at the same time *an extreme
form of Bonapartism*" [emphasis in the original], a declaration that was to
prove embarrassing once the Yugoslav leadership had broken with Stalin and
the Kremlin, and the Fourth International supported Tito's adherents.[31]

The third issue was presented by Max Shachtman's suggestion that all Trotskyist groups enter the Socialist parties. This suggestion differed from the
"French turn" of the 1930's in the sense that in 1948 it was proposed that
the Trotskyists enter the Social Democratic ranks with the intention of staying
there for a considerable period of time instead of making a species of "commando
raid" of the sort that was launched in France, the United States, Argentina,
and some other countries shortly before World War II. This notion was turned
down overwhelmingly by the Congress.[32]

## THE PABLOITE SCHISM IN THE FOURTH INTERNATIONAL

In the early 1950's a major schism developed within the Fourth International.
It arose over the new policy of "entrism" agreed upon by the Tenth Plenum
of the International Executive Committee of the International. The plenum was
held early in 1952 under the leadership of Michel Pablo, the Secretary-General
of the organization. The new policy recommended that affiliates of the International send their members into the Communist Party in those countries where
that was the principal working-class political group and into the Socialist Party
wherever it was predominant, while at the same time maintaining in each country
a small independent group outside of either party to carry on essential and
strictly Trotskyist tasks. Pablo himself appeared as the principal advocate of
this new entrist policy. He explained his position in the following terms:

> In these countries it is a question of putting into effect more and more a kind
> of entrist policy sui generis with relation to the organizations and workers influenced
> by the Stalinists. That means that, in proportion as we get closer to the war
> [the Third World War, which Pablo was predicting to be imminent] a more
> and more important part of our forces must be integrated into the various political
> and trade union organizations led or influenced by the Stalinists, including the
> CP, and remain and work there with tactics adapted to the nature of these organiza-
> tions and subordinated to the principle of long-term work."

In arguing against those who objected to seeking revolution through the Stalinist organizations which the Trotskyists had been opposing for almost twenty-five years, Pablo stressed that the policy he was advocating was a "long-term" one. He claimed: "People who despair of the fate of humanity because Stalinism continues to exist and even gains victories are shortening history to their measure. They would have liked the whole process of the transformation of capitalist society into socialism to be accomplished within the period of their brief life, so that they might be recompensed for their efforts on behalf of the revolution. As for ourselves we affirm what we wrote in the first article we devoted to the Yugoslav affair. This transformation will probably occupy an entire historical period of several centuries, which will be filled in between times by transitional forms and regimes between capitalism and socialism, necessarily remote from 'pure' forms and from norms. We know that this affirmation has shocked certain comrades and has served others as a springboard for attacking our 'revisionism.' But we are not disarming."[33]

As the dissident American Trotskyist periodical *Labor Action* reported it, the Pablo proposal would require keeping a number of Trotskyists out of either the Communist or Socialist parties, including "(1) those 'strictly necessary' to carry on...supplementary work—the skeleton crew; (2) those who can't get into the Stalinist organizations 'in spite of all our efforts'; and (3) those whom it is deemed advisable should get their Trotskyist training outside of CP ranks."[34]

Pablo's advocacy of entrism was sharply challenged in the Fourth International. Members of the French section were the first to oppose it, with the result that they were formally expelled from the International. Then, in November 1953, the Socialist Workers Party of the United States entered the battle with what it called an "Open Letter to all Trotskyist Organizations."

The SWP open letter first noted the expulsion of the majority of the French section of the Fourth International and expressed regret that the SWP itself had been remiss in not "taking more vigorous action" to protest this. It went on to warn: "A grave danger menaces the future and even the existence of the Fourth International. Revisionist conceptions, born of cowardice and petty bourgeois impressionism, have appeared within its leadership. The still great weakness of the International, cut off from the life of the sections, has momentarily facilitated the installation of a system of personal rule, basing itself and its anti-democratic methods on revisionism of and abandonment of the Marxist method."[35]

Subsequently, the Socialist Workers Party, the Socialist Labor League of Great Britain, the expelled French section, and several other groups joined forces to "reorganize" the Fourth International, establishing the International Committee of the Fourth International in opposition to the International Executive Committee controlled by Pablo. The Lanka Sama Samaja Party of Ceylon, the world's largest and most important Trotskyist party at that time, seems to have remained formally neutral in the dispute, although its leadership was more sympathetic to the International Committee than to Pablo.[36] However, the major Trotskyist groups in Italy, Belgium, and Latin America remained loyal to Pablo.

## UNIFICATION AND NEW DIVISION

The split in International Trotskyism that began in 1952-53 was to last a decade. One of the first attempts to bring about a reunification of the forces of the Fourth International took the form of a statement by the Political Committee of the Socialist Workers Party of the United States early in 1961, which set forth "the issues on which the two major factions in the world Trotskyist movement appear to be in agreement."[37] After active negotiations that extended over at least two years, the bulk of the parties affiliated with the International Committee and with the International Executive Committee were finally ready to declare themselves united once again. The supposed reunification of the Fourth International took place in a congress held at an undisclosed location in June 1963, and a new International Executive Committee and a United Secretariat were elected. It was reported that "delegates and observers were present from 26 countries and all continents."[38]

According to the New York Trotskyist newspaper *The Militant* (July 10, 1963), "the Reunification Congress followed two separate gatherings, one a conference held by delegates representing the majority of sections adhering to the International Committee (IC) of the Fourth International, the other the Seventh World Congress held by delegates from the sections adhering to the International Executive (IEC) of the Fourth International. At the Reunification Congress, common documents were adopted. The IEC delegates ratified the Reunification Congress at once; the delegates of the IC said that they would recommend early ratification by their respective organizations." In spite of this effort, true unity was not achieved. Rather, in place of two international groups, each claiming to be the "real" representative of the Trotskyist movement, there now appeared four, of which three had some international following. And as a result, there were soon four Fourth Internationals.

Michel Pablo, for one, refused to accept the "unity" decisions. He had been in a minority at the Seventh Congress of the IEC faction in 1963 over issues which "revolved around different estimates of how nuclear war will be prevented; the inter-relationship between various sectors of the world revolution; the significance of the Chinese-Soviet dispute and what the attitude of Trotskyists should be towards it; and the record of the outgoing leadership."[39] Subsequently, in 1965, he organized his own version of the Fourth International, but it seems to have rallied few if any national groups, although it still continues to put out a publication.[40] Michel Pablo was not the only source of resistance to the effort to unite world Trotskyism. Neither the British nor the French sections of the International Committee of the Fourth International (anti-Pablo) accepted unity. Neither did the Latin American Bureau of the Fourth International of the IEC of Michel Pablo.

As a result of the efforts in 1962-63 to form a single Fourth International, therefore, there emerged four groups claiming the name of the Fourth International. These were the following:

1. The so-called United Secretariat, centered on the Socialist Workers Party of the United States. The SWP officially did not belong to any international organization (this was in order to avoid compliance with the 1940 Voorhees or Foreign Agents Registration Act), but was in fact the principal associate of the United Secretariat.

2. Michel Pablo's organization, already mentioned.

3. The International Committee of the Fourth International, which had as its principal affiliates the Socialist Labor League of Great Britain and the Organization Communiste Internationaliste of France. This version of world Trotskyism was headed by Gerald Healy, and its members were commonly known as "Healyites." Its only affiliate in Latin America was the faction of Bolivian Trotskyism headed by Guillermo Lora.

4. The International Executive Committee headed by Secretary-General J. Posadas (Homero Cristali), an Argentine Trotskyist, which was organized by the Latin American Bureau of the pre-1963 Pablo group. Most of the older Latin American affiliates of the Fourth International had been associated with this Latin American Bureau, although by 1961 in Chile, Peru, Cuba, Argentina, and Mexico there were rival groups associated with the anti-Pablo faction; after 1963 these latter groups became part of the United Secretariat. When Posadas converted the Latin American Bureau into the fourth Fourth International, he by no means took all Latin American Trotskyists with him. Subsequently, Posadas succeeded in establishing small groups in several European countries.

## THE UNITED SECRETARIAT OF THE
## FOURTH INTERNATIONAL

The faction of International Trotskyism led by the United Secretariat held its first post-unity world congress in December 1965 at an unrevealed location. According to the editorial in the Spring 1966 issue of the Socialist Workers Party's *International Socialist Review*, "the Congress was attended by more than sixty delegates and fraternal observers, representing revolutionary Marxist organizations from almost all the countries of Western Europe, from numerous countries in Africa and Asia, as well as from North America and Latin America." This editorial went on to note: "the outgoing leadership reported that, despite... minor defections, in the two years since the last Congress numerous sections have been strengthened, new ones created, and the centrifugal tendencies of the past decade have been halted and reversed. The most significant and gratifying feature of the reinforced united movement has been the influx of recruits from the rising young generation of young revolutionists in numerous countries which was reflected in the considerably lowered age level of the delegates at the Congress itself.''

This congress adopted a series of resolutions which clearly presented the position of this faction on key questions facing international Trotskyism. The main resolution of the meeting was entitled ''The International Situation and the Tasks of Revolutionary Marxists.'' Others dealt with ''The Progress and Problems of the African Revolution,'' ''The Evolution of Capitalism in Western Europe,'' and ''The Sino-Soviet Conflict and the Crisis of the International Communist Movement.'' The basic resolution of the congress reiterated the classic position of orthodox Trotskyism when it listed, as the second of ''our tasks,'' ''the unconditional defense of all the workers states, beginning with the Soviet Union and the People's Republic of China, against imperialism. Of special concern in this field is the defense of revolutionary Cuba because of its exposed geographical position and the extreme measures taken by U.S. imperialism to crush it.''[41]

With regard to the Sino-Soviet split, the editorial in the Spring 1966 issue of the *International Socialist Review* summed up the United Secretariat's position in the following terms: ''The aim of the document is not to find 'reasons' for supporting one side or the other, but to ascertain the truth of the situation. In the process it emerges very clearly that the position of the Fourth International is independent. Nevertheless, as between Peking and Moscow, the Trotskyist movement leans to the side of the Chinese.''[42]

The major document of the 1965 Congress of the Fourth International of the United Secretariat indicated the group's support for the guerrilla war tactic that was then being vigorously prosecuted by Castroite elements in Latin America. This resolution stated: ''The victory of the Cuban Revolution touched off a movement among the revolutionary vanguard in Latin America essentially based on constructing small nuclei of guerrilla fighters, isolated from the masses, as a substitute for building a new revolutionary leadership. The vanguard paid a heavy price for these adventuristic experiences, which appeared in the Fidelist current itself, through the useless sacrifice of the most devoted and dynamic elements. But little by little a more mature conception of armed struggle displaced this putschist tendency, a conception fusing guerrilla struggle, armed mass struggle, and the organization of the masses in pursuit of economic demands.''[43]

This resolution obviously tried to play down the differences between this Fourth International's position on ''the road to power'' as stated in the resolution's last sentence, and the doctrine being propagated by the Castroite elements at that time. This Fidelista theoretical position was the so-called ''foco'' theory, which was elaborated first by Ernesto Ché Guevara and subsequently by Regis Debray; it was being put into practice by guerrilla groups in several countries at the time the resolution of the Fourth International was adopted, and soon afterwards it was to be applied by Guevara himself—unsuccessfully—in Bolivia. According to the ''foco'' theory, it was possible for a small group of young people from the city to go into an isolated rural area, from which it would first proceed to undermine the ability of the incumbent government to exercise its authority in that area. Once successful in establishing such a "foco," the revolutionaries would move on to establish a guerrilla army, and ultimately to carry the war to the cities.

Guevara and Debray broke with the traditional Marxist-Leninist position in arguing not only that the political and military leadership of the revolution should be unified in the "foco," but that there was no need for extensive political preparation of the populace in the area in which the revolutionary war was to be launched. Even more heretical was the argument that there was no need for a revolutionary Communist Party to exist before the revolution and to lead it—such a party would emerge out of the revolutionary army itself, this argument held.[44] The Trotskyists of the United Secretariat could not support the "foco" theory, no matter how strong their enthusiasm for Castro. They saw themselves as good Marxist-Leninists, and as such they could certainly not break with Lenin's key idea of the primary role in the revolution of the "vanguard" party.

The congress resolution dealing with Europe reflected a line being taken by the Trotskyists of the United Secretariat there, a line which apparently was also deemed applicable to at least a few of the group's affiliates in Latin America. Indicating that the "entrist" policy that had caused so much discussion in the ranks of the Fourth International in the years just after World War II had not been given up entirely, this resolution noted that "entrist work will continue to be applied in the CP's in France and Italy, in the Labor Party in Great Britain, in the SP in Austria, in the SFP in Denmark."[45]

Although we have found no published discussion on this point, the strategy of "entrism" was applied in the 1960's by at least two Latin American groups affiliated with the United Secretariat. In Chile, the party of the United Secretariat disappeared as an independent organization and its members became part of the pro-Castro Movimiento de Izquierda Revolucionaria (MIR). Similarly, in Cuba, the Trotskyists of the United Secretariat seem to have made no effort to maintain an independent organization after the formation by Castro and his associates of what became in 1965 the Partido Comunista de Cuba, but instead entered into the PCC.

During and after this congress the United Secretariat faction of international Trotskyism gave particular emphasis to support of the Vietcong and North Vietnamese side in the war then going on in Southeast Asia. Thus, a resolution adopted by a meeting of the International Executive Committee of the group, held in July 1966, proclaimed: "Our principal slogans today are: For the United Front on a World Scale of all Forces of the Workers and Anti-imperialist Movements Against United States Aggression in Vietnam. For the Defense of the Vietnam Revolution, and For the Maximum Aid to This Revolution."[46]

The most recent plenary meeting of the United Secretariat faction was its so-called Ninth World Congress, which met somewhere in Austria around Easter in 1969. That congress reportedly was attended by ninety-eight delegates and fraternal delegates, and observers from thirty countries. The main documents adopted by the meeting were a new thesis on the world revolution, and a resolution concerning the radicalization of youth around the world. The honorary presidents of the Ninth Congress included Hugo Blanco of Peru and Daniel Camejo and Carlos Sevilla of Mexico, all of whom were in jail in their native countries at the time.

Of particular interest is the Ninth Congress's resolution on Latin America. It stated: "The fundamental perspective, the only realistic one for Latin America, is that of an armed struggle likely to last many years. That is why the technical preparation cannot be conceived very simply as one of the aspects of revolutionary work, but as the fundamental aspect on a continental scale, and one of the fundamental aspects in the countries where the minimum conditions are not yet ready [for armed conflict]. It must not be forgotten that success in an armed struggle is, in the last analysis, possible only through a correct revolutionary orientation, or that to ignore the fact that the application of such a revolutionary struggle implies the gathering first of a minimum of organized and politically homogeneous forces."[47]

The United Secretariat faction of the Fourth International continues to be the strongest of the groups claiming to be the heirs of Leon Trotsky. It has in its ranks the most important Trotskyist elements of Europe, except for those in Great Britain, as well as parties in the United States and Canada, India, Ceylon, Australia, and New Zealand. However, this faction has not been predominant in Latin America, where throughout the 1960's the Posadas group had a larger number of parties than the United Secretariat.

## THE HEALYITE INTERNATIONAL COMMITTEE
## OF THE FOURTH INTERNATIONAL

Some elements of the anti-Pabloite International Committee of the Fourth International opposed the rapprochement of this group and the Pabloite faction of international Trotskyism, which gave rise in 1963 to the United Secretariat. Chief among these elements was the Socialist Labor League of Great Britain, whose most important leader was Gerald Healy. When unification of the International Committee and the Pabloite group was agreed upon, the SLL representatives and some others in the International Committee rejected unification and proclaimed the continued existence of the International Committee.

The first worldwide meeting of this rump International Committee—the so-called Third Conference of the International Committee of the Fourth International—was held in London in April 4-8, 1966. It was reported that "delegates and observers from ten countries attended. Delegates from two African countries were prevented from attending by passport difficulties."[48] Although no official record of just what groups and countries were represented seems to have been published, reports of the meeting indicate that Great Britain, France, Greece, Hungary, and the United States were among the countries from which delegates came. Presumably, the Hungarian representative was an exile.

This meeting adopted five major documents: "Rebuilding the Fourth International," "Report of the Commission on Rebuilding the Fourth International and the Tasks of the International Committee," "Report of the Conference American Commission," "Statement of the International Committee on Robertson and the Spartacist Delegation to the Conference," and "Manifesto of the International Conference." These documents give some indication of the differences that separated the International Committee from the United Secretariat.

One of the major differences concerned the issue of "entrism"—whether or not in some countries Trotskyist groups should seek to work within the Socialist and Communist parties. In this regard, the resolution on "Rebuilding the Fourth International" commented: "In the advanced countries, the revisionists who usurp the name of the Fourth International are prostrate before Social Democracy as well as before Stalinism. Here, too, the building of independent working-class parties is abandoned. Everything is concentrated on 'deep entry' and the encouragement of 'mass centrist' tendencies in the social democratic parties. In this way, the cadres of these sections are trained in opportunist adaptation to professional centrists and play their part in bolstering up the social-democratic bureaucracy."[49]

Another point at issue between the two groups was the International Committee's claim that the Trotskyists of the United Secretariat believed in "the 'theory' of the divison of the world into three sectors—'the socialist states' 'the advanced capitalist countries,' and 'the countries of the third world or the storm-center.'" In its resolution "Rebuilding the Fourth International" the London conference declared that "revisionism, which separates into distinct sectors the revolution in the advanced countries, the 'colonial revolution,' and the political revolution in the workers' states, is a most important cover for capitalist domination of the workers' movement and for obstructing the construction of revolutionary parties."[50]

The London conference was also highly critical of the attitude of the United Secretariat toward the Sino-Soviet split. Its resolution on "Rebuilding the Fourth International" commented: "The bankruptcy of this revisionism became particularly clear in the Pabloite evaluations of the split between the Russian and Chinese Communist parties. Instead of an objective analysis of the causes and consequences of this division as a way of strengthening the Fourth International in its struggle to defeat the bureaucracy, the Pabloites discussed at length the false problem of which line, the Chinese or the Russian, best expressed the needs of international socialism. The fact is that, although the Chinese make formally correct criticisms of the revisionist formulations of the CPSU, these are only a theoretical dressing for an empirical rejection of the consequences of the Soviet bureaucracy's attempted agreement with the American imperialists at

the expense of China. Correct formal criticisms of the role of the national
bourgeoisie and of the Soviet attitude towards them in the colonial countries
has not prevented the Chinese leaders from sabotaging the struggle of the workers,
for example in Indonesia and in North Africa, in accordance with the needs
of Chinese diplomacy."[51]

There was also fundamental disagreement over the attitude that Trotskyism
should adopt toward Castro's revolution in Cuba. The International Committee,
in the resolution "For the Rebuilding of the Fourth International," criticized
the position of the United Secretariat and indicated its own attitude on this
question: "Castro's regime in Cuba has been uncritically praised as a 'healthy
workers' state' and all independent working-class struggle, including the building
of a party, renounced. Even Castro's repressions of the Trotskyist party there
(part of the Posadas group which split from the Pabloites in 1962), has been
justified by the revisionists. The building of an independent workers party and
the establishment of workers' councils in Cuba as part of a proletarian internationalist orientation, with the extension of the revolution in Latin America and a revolutionary alliance with the workers of the U.S.A. and the rest of the world,
is completely abandoned. The 'aid' of the Soviet bureaucracy is not seen in the
content of the international class struggle, with the bureaucracy striving to trade
on the Cuban revolution for its own purposes, but as a 'progressive' assistance
to Cuba."[52]

After the invasion of Czechoslovakia by the Soviet Union in 1968, the
International Committee of the Fourth International issued a long document
attacking the United Secretariat. One paragraph said: "It all hangs together
and is absolutely coherent; having capitulated to the pressure of imperialism
and the Soviet bureaucracy, the renegades from the FI became the heralds
of the terrified petty bourgeoisie and the 'theoreticians' of fantasy. Their political
function from now on is to hinder the rebuilding of the FI by usurping its
name."[53]

By 1970 the International Committee of the Fourth International remained
one of the contenders for the position of heir to Leon Trotsky. However, its
adherents were largely confined to Europe and North America. The International
Committee had affiliates in Great Britain, the United States (where the Workers
League ostensibly was not an affiliate so as to avoid liability under the Voorhees
Act, but in fact participated in IC affairs), Canada, Hungary, Ireland, Greece,
and France. Only one Latin American group, the faction of the Bolivian Partido
Obrero Revolucionario led by Guillermo Lora, had relations with the International
Committee.[54]

Finally, the Healyites claimed as one of their affiliates a group that had
broken away from the Revolutionary Lanka Sama Samaja Party of Ceylon; the
RLSSP itself had been formed in 1964 by dissidents who regarded the parent
party's decision to join the cabinet of the then prime minister of Ceylon, Mrs.
S. Bandarinike, as "reformism." The Lanka Sama Samaja Party itself no longer

had affiliation with any of the contending international Trotskyist groups, although it still regarded itself as a Trotskyist organization.[55]

During the last months of 1971 a major split occured in the International Committee, headed on one side by the Socialist Labor League of Great Britain and on the other by the Organization Communiste Internationaliste of France. The immediate excuse for this split was a difference over the role which the IC's affiliate in Bolivia played in the events leading up to the overthrow of the leftist government of General Juan José Torres in August 1971. However, it appears that this controversy was the culmination of a divergence which had been developing for several years.

## THE POSADAS FACTION
## OF INTERNATIONAL TROTSKYISM

As in the anti-Pabloite factions, there were elements in the Pabloite group which were not in favor of the projected reunion of the ranks of world Trotskyism in the early 1960's. These were centered in the Latin American Bureau of the so-called International Executive Committee of the Fourth International, which was headed by the Argentine Trotskyist generally known as J. Posadas.

J. Posadas, whose real name is Homero Cristali, was the principal figure in a faction of Argentine Trotskyism which had delegates at the Second Congress of the Fourth International in 1948; these delegates were accepted as representing a "sympathizing organization." At the Third Congress, in 1951, the Posadas-led Argentine party was formally accepted into the International. From that date on, Posadista influence extended to other Latin American Trotskyist parties, and ultimately gained control first in the Uruguayan party and then in several others. After the 1953-54 split in the Fourth International, Posadas became the head of a newly established Latin American Bureau of the Pabloite faction.

At the end of 1959, Posadas and his friends began to express differences with the majority of the Pabloite Fourth International, and these continued during 1960 in the discussions preceding the Seventh World Congress of the Pablo faction. Posadas objected to the "European intellectual chiefs" of the Fourth International, whom he accused of concentrating too much on the problems of Europe; he himself insisted on the "primacy" of the "colonial revolution."

The dissidence of Posadas and his friends with the Pabloite Fourth International soon took organizational form. The first move in this direction was taken in October 1961 at a Latin American Conference organized by the Latin American Bureau.[56] Under the patronage of the Latin American Bureau, an Extraordinary Conference of the Fourth International was called to meet in an unnamed place in April 1962. Although published official records of the meeting give no indication of what parties and groups attended, the meeting was called by the Latin American Bureau and so it is reasonable to suppose that the great majority of the delegates present came from the Latin American affiliates of the Pabloite version of the Fourth International.

A "communique" issued by the April 1962 conference indicated the reasons for the quarrel between the Latin American Bureau and Pablo and other leaders of the Fourth International. It commented: "The former European intellectual leaders of the Fourth International compromised the Marxist revolutionary position of the Fourth International in the face of atomic world war, capitulating before petty bourgeois humanism and pacifisim, fighting the idea of the inevitability of war, of the need for preparing the masses for atomic world war, and falling into anti-Soviet positions, at the time of the reinitiation of the nuclear tests by the U.S.S.R."[57]

The organizational report to this Extraordinary Conference of the Fourth International was presented by L. Costa. This report was said to have made "an account of the entrist work, of the experience in constructing the parties," and a "summary of the activities of the Latin American Bureau and the plans proposed for the work of the International Executive Committee, and of the provisional International Secretariat, in preparation for the coming Extraordinary Congresses." The meeting elected a new Provisional International Executive Committee and an International Secretariat " to substitute for the previous ones which are paralyzed and disintegrated." The conference "resolved to work for the reconstruction of the sections of the Fourth International in Europe."[58]

The Posadista Fourth International held its first world meeting in March 1964. This meeting, held somewhere "in Europe," was dubbed the Seventh World Congress of the Fourth International. A communique issued by the Posadista International Secretariat after the congress noted: "Delegates attended representing thirteen countries of Africa, Europe, and Latin America. The delegation from the Cuban section could not attend because it was denied a visa to leave the country." In his organization report, Posadas noted that there were by then six European sections of the International.[59]

This same communique commented on the organizational activity of the Posadista groups which had been reported to the congress. It said: "The Congress became aware that after only a year and a half since the reorganization of the European and African sections, and the constitution of new sections, these have been strengthened and publish their fortnightly or monthly periodicals with regularity and have maintained dynamic activity and developed within the struggles of the European proletariat, gaining authority and positions in it. The Congress was particularly conscious of the activity of the Spanish section, which in spite of the repression of Franco, carries on regular and growing activity."[60]

The congress produced a number of documents, including the "Opening Speech of J. Posadas," which was adopted as a resolution. Others were "World Development of the Permanent Revolution"; "The Colonial Revolution in the Process of the World Permanent Revolution''; ''Development of the Political Revolution''; ''Chinese-Soviet Crisis''; and a ''Political Resolution.''

The Posadista faction of International Trotskyism held its third world meeting, which it dubbed the Eighth World Congress of the Fourth International, somewhere in Europe in April 1967. It was reported that forty-two delegates, representing thirteen of the seventeen affiliates of the faction, were present at the congress. Nine of these affiliates were in Latin America; six were in Europe and two in Africa. It was reported that before the meeting the International had published fifteen issues of the *Marxist Review,* in both a Latin American and an Italian version, as well as eighteen pamphlets ''on the principal problems of the socialist revolution.''

The Posadista faction had several characteristics that set it apart from other elements of international Trotskyism. One of these was the ''cult of personality'' around its principal leader, the Argentine J. Posadas. Every meeting of the International Secretariat was taken up largely with speeches by Posadas, which were then adopted as resolutions of the Secretariat. Even the resolutions of the Eighth Congress of the International consisted almost entirely of Posadas' speeches. Likewise, the content of the newspapers published by national affiliates of this Fourth International consisted largely of speeches by Posadas.

A ''theoretical'' justification for this cult of personality was provided by Posadas' interpretation of the old Bolshevik concept of ''democratic centralism,'' an interpretation which placed almost exclusive emphasis on ''centralism'' rather than ''democratic.'' Posadas developed this interpretation in a speech to members of the Brazilian section; it was later adopted as a resolution of the Plenum of the International Secretariat of the Fourth International in February 1966. This resolution is characteristic of the tortured, sometimes incomprehensible prose of Posadas.

In this document, Posadas commented that ''the organization of the Party and of the International must permit that the elements which are most capable, most developed, or which can develop themselves most, because this is the unequal and combined development of mankind, can influence the Party and carry it along, elevate it consciously to the objectives of the necessity of history, political program, the objective of overthrowing capitalism and constructing socialism, without all having to reach the same scientific comprehension of the whole of history, of society, and of socialism.''[61]

Posadas expounded upon this doctrine's specific application to the Fourth International that he headed. He said: ''The centralization of the International is, at the same time as being an historical organizational necessity, the means which permits the Party to be used instantaneously, from one moment to the next, to change from one moment to the other, to apply at any time. For example, the Party receives an article, reads it, discusses it, is harmonized.

It is thus around the world, in the face of any event. In the International, when Vietnam began, there were three interpretations, two of them erroneous. It was necessary to write immediately. An Italian comrade wrote an article, an Uruguayan another, and Comrade Posadas wrote another. The comrades needed to write, and they wrote. When they read the article by Posadas they fell into line, and activity went forward."[62]

Given this close association of the Posadista faction of the Fourth International with Posadas himself, the positions assumed by the group were those which its leader put forward. Many of these positions differed strongly from those assumed by other factions of international Trotskyism. One such position was the Posadas Fourth International's insistence on the inevitability of an atomic war and its view that victory for the workers and socialism would without question succeed such a conflict. A typical statement of this position was a manifesto written by Posadas that was adopted by the Amplified Meeting of the International Secretariat of the Fourth International of February 1966.

This manifesto, in discussing the Chinese situation, comments: "This signifies atomic war. The Chinese are conscious of the fact that atomic war is inevitable." But for Posadas, atomic war was not something to be feared: "After destruction commences, the masses are going to emerge in all countries—in a short time, in a few hours. Capitalism cannot defend itself in an atomic war except by putting itself in caves and attempting to destroy all that it can. The masses, in contrast, are going to come out, will have to come out, because it is the only way to survive, defeating the enemy. There is going to be a chain-like social reaction, and the preparation for the war, the days which precede it, will signify also a preparation for the masses. It is necessary to foresee that everywhere there will be a collapse of the power of capitalism. The apparatus of capitalism, police, army, will not be able to resist, will flee, will attempt to save themselves individually." The advent of an atomic war will thus be an opportunity for the workers. Posadas goes on: "It will be necessary to organize the workers' power immediately, even on a limited basis, without waiting to control a whole country or even all of a city. Committees, united fronts, Soviets, communes, must be formed and assume power. Not to impose themselves as a government on the masses, but to invite them to organize and to join forces....The bureaucratic trade union leaders will desert. It will be necessary to call together the unions, and get them to organize workers' power. To live in a democratic socialist regime, where everything is decided in common, with daily assemblies. And where social interest overcomes all individual interests through political life in assemblies, communes, and Soviets, and with armed support for all their actions."[63]

Posadas gives a slightly new twist to the traditional Trotskyist call for a political revolution in the Soviet Union. He argues that "the political revolution will be the result of the war in those Workers States in which the political power of the bureaucracy persists. The bureaucracy will put up fierce resistance, in the U.S.S.R. principally, where it is organized and has a political structure which is very differentiated from the masses."[64] The Posadista Trotskyites were also energetic supporters of the Chinese Communist regime, and were particularly enthusiastic in their endorsement of the Great Cultural Revolution. Thus, in a Resolution of the Eighth World Congress of the Fourth International entitled "Development of the Political Revolution in the Workers States," written by Posadas, it was asserted that "the political revolution in China is the center of the world revolution, because at the same time it is announcing in the midst of the political revolution in China the historical necessity for other revolutions, including the colonial revolution; the Chinese are rectifying their former position."[65]

Finally, a theoretical and tactical difference between the Posadista wing of international Trotskyism and the other Fourth Internationals was the Posadista call for an "Anti-imperialist United Front." Typical of this position was a passage in the May Day manifesto of 1970 of the Posadista Fourth International. This read: "The Fourth International calls upon all Communists, on all Communist masses, on the Communist leaders; on the Socialists, on the Christian Democrats, on the trade-union militants, on the trade-union leaderships, on the revolutionary nationalist militants and leaders; on the leadership and militants of the parties and unions of the Workers States, for unification, the world united front for the program of the Communist International of Masses, for the program of struggle to overthrow the remains of capitalism in the world, for the Anti-Imperialist United Front, for the organization of the preventive actions of the masses of the world against the atomic world war which imperialism is preparing, and which it is prepared to launch at any moment, even right now."[66]

Perhaps as a result of its being established by the Latin American Bureau of the Pabloite Fourth International, which included most of the original Trotskyist groups of that area, the Posadista faction of Trotskyism started with a relatively large following in Latin America. However, in addition, it has claimed sections in Italy, Great Britain, Belgium, France, Spain, Greece, and Algeria. Most of these parties have used the name Revolutionary Workers Party and each of them has published a periodical with some regularity. These publications have dutifully filled their pages with the long-winded proclamations and essays of J. Posadas, and have presented his version of the ideas of international Trotskyism.

Like all small political groups with a sense of destiny, the Posadas Fourth Internationalists have tended to exaggerate their own power and importance. However, they have gone farther than most in this direction. Typical was a statement by Posadas in a pamphlet dated April 1968, in which he wrote: "Since our separation and the expulsion of all of the other people from the

International, less than six years ago, we have progressed to such a degree that it is enough to measure the importance of the progress made in order to imagine the velocity of the future. In six years we are in sixteen countries, of which six are workers states. We are the constant concern of the leadership of six workers states, in six years. These other people, all of them, were incapable of having a cell and a section in Spain, incapable of maintaining a movement in North America, incapable of maintaining the movement in Cuba. And our sections have shown that they are already of transcendental importance, already considered by the masses as a responsible and capable leadership, which they follow from the beginning."[67]

This sanguine view of the Posadistas' significance is echoed in the opening speech given by "Horacio" at the Eighth Congress in April 1967: "Our sections are the instrument of human progress, which is today the struggle for Socialism. In Europe, as in Africa, as in Asia, as in Latin America, as in the Workers States, as in the United States, the masses show that they are ready for the development and affirmation of a world Trotskyist current. All the successes achieved by the International in this last period, among which are our publications, and all of the reports which have been given during the preparation for this Eighth World Congress, show the strengthening of this world current. The successes and the increasing importance that the world capitalist press gives to the articles and works of Comrade Posadas, as well as to the activity of the International, show that imperialism as well as the Soviet bureaucracy, as well as the reformist and conciliatory currents, now put us in our historical role and site."[68]


## THE INFLUENCE OF WORLD TROTSKYISM

Trotskyism is not, in fact, a major force in world politics. In the early 1970's no Trotskyite party is a serious contender for power in any country. The only party of Trotskyist origin that might perhaps be considered a significant political factor, the Lanka Sama Samaja of Ceylon, was repudiated by all factions of the Fourth International in the early 1960's when it accepted an invitation from Mrs. Bandarenike to enter her first government.

However, some Trotskyist parties are not without influence in the extreme Left in their respective countries. For example, parties associated with both the United Secretariat and the "Healyite" Internationals played a significant role, particularly among students, at the time of the upheavals in France in May 1968. The Socialist Labor League of Great Britain has the distinction of being the only Trotskyite group able to maintain a daily newspaper, *Workers Press*, which began publication in October 1969. In the United States the Socialist Workers Party, an affiliate of the United Secretariat, has for several years been the most significant influence on the extreme left within the movement organizing protests against the Vietnam war, and its youth group, the Young Socialist Alliance, became the most rapidly growing and largest left-wing student group in the United States in the late 1960's.

The long-time Secretary-General of the Fourth International, Michel Pablo, played a significant—and quite controversial—role in Algeria's affairs in the early years of that country's independence. *Workers Press*, the organ of the Healyite Socialist Labor League in Great Britain, noted in its edition of January 17, 1970, that Pablo "soon became an economic adviser of Ben Bella when he came to power." It added that "Algeria, after Ben Bella's accession to power, was proclaimed a 'workers state' by the revisionists, and Pablo, on Ben Bella's behalf, stomped Europe with bourgeois liberals to collect tinned milk for the starving Algerian masses, who hardly benefited from the meager reforms of Ben Bella's government." The article notes that when Ben Bella fell, Pablo escaped to Europe.

At least in terms of the geographical location of its affiliates, International Trotskyism is certainly a worldwide movement. One or another of the Fourth Internationals has affiliates in most countries of Western Europe, in the United States and Canada, in nine Latin American countries, in Algeria and South Africa, in Australia and New Zealand, and in Israel, India, Ceylon, and Japan, and there are sympathetic groups even in Poland and Czechoslovakia.

## INTERNATIONAL TROTSKYISM AND
## THE TRADITION OF LEON TROTSKY

It is perhaps inevitable, in connection with a movement originating so completely in the ideas and activities of one man, to ask whether, a generation after Trotsky's death, the movement bearing his name really continues to represent the ideas he espoused. Max Shachtman, a long-time participant in and subsequent acute observer of International Trotskyism, raised this question, in a letter to the author dated December 7, 1970, in the following terms:

There is an unmistakable continuity of the Trotskyist movement over the last forty to fifty years, represented in each of the three (or even four) Fourth Internationals. But there has ceased for some time to be a continuity in what may genuinely be called *Trotskyism*. As LT defined it between 1928 and 1932, particularly, it was based entirely on three propositions: Opposition to socialism in one country, to the policies of the Anglo-Russian Trade Union Unity Committee, and to the policies of Stalin-Bukharin in the Chinese Revolution ("bloc of our classes," etc.). All these were eventually "subsumed" in support of the theory and practices of the Permanent Revolution: only the proletariat ("supported by the peasantry")—and the proletariat only insofar as it is led by the

Bolshevik revolutionary party—can resolve all the problems of the democratic revolution *in the course* of establishing the socialist dictatorship of the proletariat. This basic and authentically Trotskyist proposition is nowhere represented or even reflected in any of the Fourth Internationals or in any of the separate neo-Trotskyist organizations. In this basic and all-important sense, Trotskyism died with Trotsky; the remains merely bear his name and honor (worship, venerate) his memory."

Perhaps the best short official Trotskyist answer to Shachtman's argument is found in the article by Joseph Hansen of the Socialist Workers Party of the United States, replying to the Cuban Communist leader Blas Roca's attack on Trotskyism. At one point Hansen writes: "Trotsky insisted that the defense of the Socialist achievements of the October Revolution required the extension of the revolution and its culmination in an international revolution which finally would establish socialism in the industrially advanced capitalist countries. The correctness of the position of Trotsky has been confirmed by reality: in the extension of the revolution to Eastern Europe, in the overthrow of the capitalists and landlords in China, and finally and no less importantly in the Cuban Revolution itself, only ninety miles from the greatest imperialist power."[69]

However, one may ask whether Leon Trotsky himself, shortly before his death, did not provide a rebuttal to his "orthodox" followers of a quarter of a century later. In an article which he published in the Mexican Trotskyist journal *Clave* in October 1939, there is a passage which raises grave doubts whether Trotsky himself would have remained an orthodox Trotskyist had he survived World War II. This passage is significant enough for the relevant parts of it to be reproduced completely. These read as follows:

If this war provokes, as we firmly believe, the proletarian revolution, it will inevitably lead to the fall of the bureaucracy in the USSR, and the regeneration of Soviet democracy, on an economic and cultural basis much higher than that of 1918. In this case, the question of whether the Stalinist bureaucracy is a "class" or an excrescence in a Workers State, will be resolved by itself. To all and to every one it will be clear that in the course of the development of the international revolution, the Soviet bureaucracy will not have been more than an *episode*.

If one admits, however, that the present war may not provoke the revolution, but rather the decline of the proletariat, then there remains the other aspect of the alternative: the subsequent putrefaction of monopolist capitalism, its merging with the State and the substitution of the bureaucracy by a totalitarian regime. The incapacity of the proletariat to take in its hands the direction of society would lead really, under these conditions, to the appearance of a new exploiting class, emerging from the Bonapartist and fascist bureaucracy. It would be, from all appearances, a declining regime which would signify the end of civilization.

The historical alternative is the following: either the Stalinist regime is a repugnant accident in the process of the transformation of the capitalist society into a socialist society, or the Stalinist regime is the first stage of a new exploitative society. If the second prediction proves to be correct, the bureaucracy will be converted, naturally into a new exploiting class. Hard as this second perspective is, if the world proletariat really proves incapable of carrying out the mission which events have placed upon it, we would have no alternative but to recognize that the socialist program, based on the internal contradictions of capitalist society, was a Utopia. There would be necessary, naturally, a new ''minimum'' program--for the defense of the interests of the slaves of the totalitarian bureaucratic society.

This quotation certainly seems to indicate that had he lived after World War II, Trotsky would no longer have argued that the Soviet Union was a ''workers state,'' and certainly he would not have maintained that the new Communist regimes set up after the war had this character. Some credence is given to this interpretation by the letter written by his widow, Natalia Sedova Trotsky, when she resigned from the Fourth International in 1951. She gave several reasons for her action: ''Obsessed by old and used-up formulas, you continue considering the Stalinist state as a Workers State. I cannot and don't wish to follow you in this....You maintain that the States of Eastern Europe, over which Stalinism has established dominion, during or since the war, are also Workers States. This is the equivalent of saying that Stalinism fulfills a revolutionary and socialist mission. I cannot and don't wish to follow you in this.''

She rejected the Fourth International's support of the Titoist regime in Yugoslavia, and wrote: ''You have until now supported the Stalinist armies in the war which they are making the tormented people of Korea suffer. I cannot and don't wish to follow you in this.'' She summed up her position with this statement: ''I know very well that you repeat frequently that you criticize and combat Stalinism. But in reality, your criticism and struggles lose their value, because they are determined by and subordinated to the position of defense of the Stalinist state, they cannot achieve any result.''[70]

## CONCLUSION

Trotskyism has thus been the most persistent of the opposition movements within International Communism. First appearing on the scene of world politics as a result of the struggle for power in the Soviet Union following the death of Lenin, Trotskyism gained adherents in many of the European countries, as well as in the United States and Canada and some of the Asian and Latin American nations.

Although the movement remained relatively united during Trotsky's lifetime, it has undergone a series of splits since his death. His heirs have differed considerably in the interpretation and application of the doctrines he developed. Struggles for power, both within national Trotskyist groups and within the Fourth International as a whole, have also not been absent. As a result, by the early 1960's world Trotskyism was divided into four competing Fourth Internationals, each of which claimed to be the true heir to the founder of the movement. This division continued to exist a decade later.

# —2—

# Fourth Internationalism
# in Latin America

Trotskyism has been a relatively minor element in the spectrum of leftist parties in Latin America. Fourth Internationalist groups have existed in only about half of the countries of the area, and with one or two exceptions they have never been major parties even in the left-wing politics of these nations. However, until the 1960's they were the principal Marxist-Leninist rivals of the Communists in the area, and their persistent efforts to become serious contenders for political power, in spite of continuing failure and lack of any substantial support from outside, are remarkable.

## TROTSKYISM IN THE LATIN AMERICAN
## MARXIST-LENINIST LEFT

Except in two or three countries, Marxist-Leninists have been minorities within those elements in Latin American politics which have been working for fundamental economic, social, and political change. In half a dozen nations the so-called national revolutionary parties (such as APRA in Peru and Acción Democrática in Venezuela) have been far more successful than Marxist-Leninists of any type; in a few cases the Christian Democrats have been more successful; and the Peronists in Argentina, the followers of Getulio Vargas in Brazil, and the Partido Colorado Batllista in Uruguay have all been much more important than the Marxist-Leninist parties. Only in Castro's Cuba and in Chile have Marxist-Leninists been major contenders for power.

Within the Marxist-Leninist camp, the orthodox Communist Parties (Stalinists until 1953, Khrushchevists and Brezhnevists since then) have constituted the oldest, most numerous, and strongest element. Some Communist parties antedated the Communist International itself, having been Socialist Parties which joined the Comintern in the early 1920's. By the late 1940's a Communist

Party existed in every Latin American republic. In the region as a whole they have persistently had extensive influence in organized labor and for most of the 1940's they were the dominant political force in the unions. They participated in the governments of General Fulgencio Batista in Cuba in the early 1940's, of José María Velasco Ibarra of Ecuador in 1944, and of Gabriel González Videla of Chile in 1946-47.

These orthodox Communist Parties remain today the largest and politically most significant Marxist-Leninist element in Latin America as a whole. In the Sino-Soviet split and in the quarrels between the Soviet leadership and Fidel Castro, they have remained steadfastly loyal to Moscow; indeed, they constitute one of the most significant groups of supporters of the CPSU leadership to be found anywhere outside the Soviet Union itself.

With the advent of the schism between the Soviet and Chinese Communist leaderships, there arose in Latin America a group of Communist Parties aligned with Peking. The Chinese themselves claim that there are ten such parties in the area. These generally arose as the result of schisms within the orthodox pro-Moscow Communist Parties, and they had a certain attraction for members of the youth groups associated with these parties. However, in no Latin American country have they been able to match the membership and influence of the pro-Russian party.

The 1960's also saw the appearance of a third kind of Marxist-Leninist group in Latin America, one looking principally to Havana for leadership and support. Generally drawing most of their membership and backing from middle-class and upper-class youths, these groups have grown up completely outside of the ranks of orthodox Communism. In several cases they were formed as the result of divisions within the national revolutionary parties. They have made the idea of the guerrilla road to power an absolute, and have adhered to the "foco" theory as developed by Ernesto Ché Guevara and Regis Debray. A few of these groups have turned to urban guerrilla activities, either when defeated in the countryside or when rural guerrilla activities were virtually impossible to organize. Nowhere has this element been able to develop a party with substantial popular backing.

Trotskyism has not been as significant as any of these other three versions of Marxism-Leninism. Fourth Internationalist parties have remained tiny in membership. Nowhere, except for a short while in Chile and Cuba in the 1930's and in Bolivia in the early 1950's, have they been able to gain substantial influence within organized labor. Nowhere have they been able to launch a guerrilla conflict, although for a time one faction of Trotskyism had some influence among the Guatemalan guerrillas.

## ORIGINS AND EXTENT OF TROTSKYISM IN LATIN AMERICA

Trotskyist parties or groups have existed, or now exist, in the following Latin American countries: Argentina, Uruguay, Brazil, Chile, Bolivia, Peru,

Ecuador, Colombia, Puerto Rico, Mexico, and Cuba. In most of these countries there are today at least two rival groups claiming to be adherents of the Fourth International. These parties have had diverse origins. In Argentina, Brazil, Chile, Mexico, Peru, and Cuba they originated as splits in the countries' Communist Parties. In Bolivia and Uruguay, they seem to have been established quite independently of the orthodox Communists, by people who had never belonged to the parties affiliated with the Comintern. In contrast to the situation of the parties associated with the Communist International, none of the Latin American parties affiliated with the Fourth International was established through the efforts of the worldwide Trotskyist organization. The Fourth International never had the kind of corps of paid organizers which the Comintern maintained for many years to help it set up several of the smaller Communist Parties of the area.

## RELATIONS OF LATIN AMERICAN PARTIES
## WITH THE FOURTH INTERNATIONAL

Generally, the Latin American Trotskyist parties have carried on their activities with relatively little interference—or help—from the Fourth International. The International has not been equipped to take an active role in the internal affairs of its Latin American affiliates in the way that the Comintern was in the 1930's. However, there have been some exceptions to this general situation.

The Founding Conference of the Fourth International in September 1938 confirmed the establishment of a Pan American and Pacific Bureau, which had been set up some months previously, to coordinate the activities of the affiliates in these areas. It seems to have had its headquarters from the beginning in New York. Even before the Founding Conference, a "Pre-Conference" for the Western Hemisphere had been held. It had adopted a number of resolutions dealing with the situation in Latin America, including two submitted by Diego Rivera, then a leading figure in Mexican Trotskyism; these were labeled "The Development of Latin America: Proposal for a Thesis on Latin America," and "The Class Struggle and the Indian Problem."[1]

In the early 1940's the Fourth International's headquarters, then located in New York, had a "representative" who was working in South America and became deeply involved in the internal quarrels of the Argentine and Chilean Fourth Internationalists. Two decades later, with the establishment of the "Posadista" version of the Fourth International headed by the Argentine J. Posadas, the International, and most particularly Posadas himself, interfered very actively in the internal affairs of the Latin American affiliates and even of those of other continents.

Soon after World War II an attempt was made to organize a conference of the Latin American affiliates of International Trotskyism. The Chilean Partido Obrero Revolucionario took the lead in this move, and received messages of support from its counterpart in Argentina.[2] However, nothing seems to have come of this move.

During the late 1950's and early 1960's the parties in southern South America affiliated with the anti-Pablo International Secretariat of the Fourth International maintained at least a skeleton organization on a regional basis; this was the Secretariado Latino Americano del Trotskismo Ortodoxo (Latin American Secretariat of Orthodox Trotskyism, or SLATO). The International Committee affiliates in Argentina, Chile, Bolivia, and Peru appear to have participated in this, and its principal organizer and inspirer was Nahuel Moreno, head of the International Committee affiliate in Argentina. It played a considerable role in the activities of the IC's Peruvian affiliate in the years 1961-63.[3] Finally, the Mexican Trotskyist movement experienced several periods of direct intervention by the U.S. Trotskyist organizations and the Fourth International.

Just as it has not interfered with them often, the Fourth International has given comparatively little help to its national parties. There is no indication that any of the Latin American Trotskyist parties has received any substantial amount of money from the Fourth International or from any other foreign source, although the International has published materials put out by national groups on behalf of the International as a whole. Again, this contrasts sharply with the Communist International, which heavily financed a number of its member parties in the Latin American area.

In recent years, the various versions of the Fourth International have carried on extensive publicity campaigns on behalf of certain of their Latin American members who found themselves in prison. For example, the Fourth International of the United Secretariat widely publicized the case of the imprisoned Peruvian leader Hugo Blanco, and the other Fourth Internationals also gave the case some notice. All the Fourth Internationals of the 1960's gave extensive publicity to the incarceration of Trotskyites and other leftists in Mexico after the student uprising in Mexico City in 1968. The Posadas version of the Fourth International publicized as widely as it could the fate of five of its comrades who were jailed by the Castro government in Cuba.

Individual Latin Americans have participated more or less extensively in the activities of the Fourth International. Latin American delegates were present at the founding congress of the International in Paris in 1938, and one of them, the Brazilian Mario Pedrosa, was elected to the International Executive Committee of the group. At least some Latin American affiliates had delegates present at the 1948 and 1951 congresses of the International. After the schisms in the International in the 1950's and 1960's, there also seem to have been at least a few Latin American representatives at the conferences and congresses of the various tendencies.

## THE LATIN AMERICAN PARTIES AND
## THE SCHISMS IN THE FOURTH INTERNATIONAL

Like the Trotskyist parties in other areas of the world, those of Latin America have had to choose between the rival factions into which International Trotskyism has been divided during the last two decades. At the time of the split between the adherents and the opponents of Michel Pablo in 1953-54, virtually all of the Latin American parties sided with Pablo and belonged to the Latin American Bureau which the Pabloite faction maintained. In Bolivia, differences over the issue of "Pabloism" were a contributing cause of the split which occurred in the Partido Obrero Revolucionario in 1956.

In the years following this split in the Fourth International in the early 1950's, the anti-Pablo faction gained considerable ground on its rival in Latin America. Joseph Hansen of the Socialist Workers Party of the United States (which was allied in the 1950's with the anti-Pablo elements), in a letter to the writer dated December 24, 1970, sketched the relative strength of the two groups a couple of years before the attempted unification of International Trotskyism. He commented: "First of all, when the 1953-54 split occurred, Pablo did not take everything in Latin America. I doubt that he even took a majority, although that would be very difficult to determine in view of the general conditions prevailing in Latin America at that time. There was some debate about this question within the Fourth International itself, and it was one of the questions I tried to determine during a trip I took in Latin America at the end of 1961. I talked with the leaders of the Posadas groups in Peru, Bolivia, Chile, and Argentina. I also checked with independent figures of the Left as well as with friends with whom I had been long acquainted."

Hansen described the situation in several of the countries he visited. Arguing that the Pablo group was a minority in Peru, he noted that 'in Peru the IEC grouping was far outweighed by the adherents of the International Committee. In addition, the IEC faction was undergoing a very sharp internal struggle." In neighboring Bolivia, he wrote, "it was difficult to ascertain the exact situation because of the repression and street fighting that was going on at the time. However, I talked with leaders of the International Executive Committee grouping there who likewise were struggling with the Posadas formation, and who, when Posadas staged his split, took everything outside of four or five persons. In addition, of course, Guillermo Lora headed still another grouping that had considerable prestige and had members not only in La Paz but in the mining areas."

Hansen commented that in Chile he "judged the International Committee group and the International Executive Committee forces to be not greatly different in size, but it appeared to me that the International Committee grouping had a much firmer base in the labor movement and also in Cuban defense work.'' He was apparently most impressed with his own party's counterpart in Argentina: ''In Argentina, where the Posadas group published a regular newspaper, participated in elections, and spoke as if there were no other Trotskyist grouping in that country, it turned out that their real strength was much less than that of the International Committee grouping. Although the IC contingents were partially underground, they had a functioning headquarters in Buenos Aires (the largest of any Trotskyist grouping in Latin America) and had sizeable, active groups in a number of other cities which I visited. It was very difficult to find the Posadistas, although it was easy to buy their paper.''

Hansen admitted that the International Committee faction of the Fourth International, with which he was associated, was the weaker of the two groups in 1961 in Uruguay and Brazil, having virtually no following at all in Brazil. Finally, insofar as Cuba was concerned, Hansen noted: ''The developments there were quite different. The International Committee forces were extremely sympathetic with the Castroist movement. They participated in its activities and were eventually absorbed by it. A rather old grouping around the city of Guantanamo stayed with the International Executive Committee and when Posadas split the IEC, they went with him.''

After the attempted reunification of the Fourth International in the early 1960's and the resultant split into four factions—the United Secretariat, the Healyite International Committee, the Posadistas, and also a separate group led by Michel Pablo—most of the older Latin American parties chose to go along with the Posadistas. That version of the Fourth International was in fact organized by the Latin American Bureau of the Pabloite International.

The major exception to Posadista influences among the older Latin American parties was the faction of the Bolivian Partido Obrero Revolucionario, which had been affiliated with the Pabloites. It supported the unification of the Pabloites and their opponents, and for some time it was the most important Latin American affiliate of the Fourth International of the United Secretariat. However, the United Secretariat actively sought to encourage the establishment of other rivals to the Posadista parties in a number of Latin American countries. As a result, the United Secretariat was able to acquire affiliates or sympathizing groups in Argentina, Brazil, Chile, Peru, Mexico, and Cuba. However, the Chilean and Cuban Trotskyists sympathetic to the United Secretariat did not form independent parties; they belonged to the pro-Castro Movimiento de Izquierda Revolucionaria and the Partido Comunista de Cuba, respectively. The Healyite element of the Fourth International was not able to win over any Latin American party, although the faction of the Bolivian POR led by Guillermo Lora was actively sympathetic with the Healyites. The small Fourth International established by Michel Pablo after his split with the United Secretariat does not seem to have won the backing of any Latin American group.

Thus, at least partly as a result of the schisms within the ranks of world Trotskyism, competing parties, affiliated with or sympathetic to rival Fourth Internationals, have developed in several Latin American countries. There are two Trotskyist parties or groups in Brazil, Argentina, Chile, and Mexico, and three in Bolivia and Peru. In the chapters that follow, we shall recount in more detail the origins and results of these schisms within the national Trotskyist movements.

## THE TROTSKYISTS AND FIDEL CASTRO

The establishment of the Castro regime in Cuba has had a significant impact on the Trotskyists, as it has on all political groups of the left in Latin America. The different factions of the Fourth International, and their parties in Latin America, have differed significantly in their assessments of the phenomenon of the Cuban Revolution.

The Fourth International of the United Secretariat has been the Trotskyist group which has been most enthusiastic to the Castro regime. It has regarded that government as a "workers state," and although it has been critical of Castro's vocal denunciation of Trotskyism, it has never wavered in its general support for his regime. In the United States, it was the principal political group participating in the Free Cuba Committee, which rallied support for the Castro government during the first half of the 1960's. Within Cuba itself, it has abandoned its own separate political organization and its followers have joined Fidel Castro's Communist Party of Cuba.

The Healyite Fourth International has taken quite a different position. It has continued to argue that the Castro regime is a "petty bourgeois" government and therefore not worthy of the kind of "unconditional support" which Trotskyists have traditionally given to "workers states," no matter how degenerate. Although they have had no affiliate in the island, the Healyites have protested strongly against the Castro government's action in suppressing the Partido Obrero Revolucionario (Trotskista), which is affiliated with the Posadista faction of international Trotskyism.

The Posadistas have taken still another position. They have declared their "unconditional" support for the Cuban revolution, but at the same time they have protested vigorously against the suppression of their party in the island and the jailing of some of its leaders by the Castro government, and they have continued to insist on the necessity of maintaining an independent Trotskyist party in Cuba.

For his part, Castro has paid virtually no attention to the Trotskyists elsewhere in Latin America. The only exception to this attitude was his denunciation early in 1966 of the activities of the Posadista Trotskyists in Guatemala and their association with the guerrilla group led by Lieutenant

Marco Antonio Yon Sosa. So far as we have been able to ascertain, no Trot-skyists were invited to the conference in Havana which established the Organización Latino Americana de Solidaridad (OLAS), the Castro equiva-lent of the Communist International. Nor has Castro extended any financial or other help to Trotskyists in other Latin American countries.

## CHARACTERISTICS OF LATIN AMERICAN
## TROTSKYIST PARTIES

The Latin American Trotskyist parties have all been small in membership. It is doubtful that the Partido Obrero Revolucionario of Bolivia, the most important of the Latin American Fourth Internationalist groups, ever had more than a few hundred members, even at the height of its influence in the early 1950's. None of the Trotskyist parties has shown the ability of the orthodox Communists to recruit large numbers of members at moments when the party's influence is growing and then later sift out these recruits through a process of purging.

Because of their small numbers, the Latin American Trotskyist parties have not generally been able to maintain nationwide organizations with grass-roots units throughout their countries. Usually their organizations have been confined largely to the national capitals and one or two other major cities. The Bolivian POR, and perhaps the Izquierda Comunista of Chile in the 1930's, have been the only parties able to maintain party units in most of the country's important cities as well as in the more important mining camps and a handful of rural areas. As a result of their weak organizations and inadequate finances, the Latin American Trotskyists have not generally been able to maintain party headquarters which could serve as centers of party activity. In most cases, the various national parties have at most been able to have a small national office, manned by volunteer labor of party leaders and rank and file members.

The Latin American Trotskyist parties have also not had the unity and discipline which has been such an outstanding characteristic of the orthodox Communists in the area. This relative lack of discipline is probably due to several factors. The Trotskyites have not had either the "carrots" or the "sticks" which the Moscow-oriented Communists have been able to provide. They have not had the substantial subsidies which the Communist Parties have enjoyed; nor have they been given the opportunities for "political tourism" to the Soviet Union, Eastern Europe, China, and elsewhere, which have been such an impor-tant aspect of orthodox Communist activities since World War II. Nor have the Trotskyists had the ability to punish those of their members who violate party discipline or defect. They have lacked the large press capable of destroying the reputations of those who break with their parties, and they have not had large payrolls for party and trade-union functionaries, which have given Communist Parties the ability to deprive of their livelihood those who differed publicly with the party leadership.

The upshot of this relative lack of discipline within the Latin American Trotskyist parties has been frequent dissension and factionalism. Internal bickering has been particularly notable in the Argentine, Bolivian, Chilean, and Mexican Trotskyist parties. As we have noted, quarrels between different factions of the Fourth International have tended to reinforce the tendency of the leaders of the individual parties to quarrel between themselves, often bitterly.

To a surprisingly large degree, the leadership of the Latin American Trotskyist parties has been of working-class origin. The earliest Trotskyists in Argentina, most of the more important figures in the Chilean party, most of the original Cuban Trotskyists and some in Peru, a considerable proportion of the Bolivian leadership, and many of the Mexican Trotskyist leaders have been manual workers. However, the Trotskyist parties have also been able to recruit leaders from other classes and groups. Thus artists and literary figures, most notably Diego Rivera, played an important part in the Mexican Trotskyist leadership; in Argentina the son of the president of the republic was among the Trotskyist leaders of the 1930's; and journalists, business people, teachers, and even leading art critics have been among the Brazilian Trotskyist chiefs.

The Latin American Trotskyites have had little experience in electoral politics. Only occasionally have the Chileans, the Bolivians, the Argentines, and the Uruguayans offered candidates for even the most humble public offices. The other parties have never done so. The political activity of these parties has been concentrated largely on attempts to penetrate the unions, to support regular periodicals, to publish occasional pamphlets, to hold infrequent public meetings, and in recent years to participate in guerrilla activity.

The Latin American Trotskyites have always tried to gain influence in the organized labor movements of the various Latin American countries. In those unions in which they have had members, the parties have organized factions which have sought to bring the organizations under party control, and to have them adopt Trotskyist political positions. On rare occasions there have been enough Trotskyite delegates to national trade union congresses to make possible the organization of party factions at those meetings as well.

However, in only a few cases have the Trotskyites had sufficient trade-union support to make such organizational activity possible. These cases involved the Chilean Trotskyists in the middle 1930's, the Cubans at about the same time, the Bolivians (particularly in the miners' organizations) for more than two decades, the Mexicans for short periods on several occasions, and the Brazilians in the cities in the 1930's and in the rural regions of the state of Pernambuco in the early 1960's.

Editing and distributing party periodicals has been an especially significant organizational activity for the Latin American Trotskyists. In some cases, particularly in some of the Posadista faction's parties in the 1960's, party activity has been largely concentrated on this. These periodicals have been important as a means of keeping the party members together, providing them with material for discussion and debate in their internal party meetings, and gaining at least some distribution of their ideas among the general public. Reports to congresses and other meetings of the individual parties and groups of the various Fourth Internationals have frequently reported on the number of periodicals issued and the frequency of their publication.

## CONCLUSION

The Trotskyists have had small parties in about half of the countries of Latin America. They have been persistent in their activities despite their small memberships and their small influence on the labor movements or general politics of their respective countries. They have not been able to match the discipline and organizational cohesiveness of the orthodox Communist Parties, but they have continued to be active and are a force of potential importance on the extreme left in Latin American politics.

# —3—

# Trotskyism, Peronismo, and the
# National Revolution in Argentina

At no time has Trotskyism been a really significant current in the Argentine labor movement or of any importance in general politics in the republic. However, in one form or another the Trotskyite movement has existed in Argentina for more than four decades, and some of the intellectuals associated with it have undoubtedly influenced the thinking of elements on the Argentine left which had no association with or loyalty to Leon Trotsky and his organized political followers. Perhaps more than in other Latin American countries, the Trotskyists of Argentina have long been torn by bitter factionalism and violent polemics. These internal conflicts help divide the movement's history into a number of more or less well-defined periods.

## THE FIRST PHASE OF ARGENTINE TROTSKYISM

The first Trotskyite group in Argentina was established in 1929 by three workers, Roberto Guinney, Camilo López, and M. Guinney. They had been members of the Communist Party of Argentina, and in 1927 had joined a dissident group under the leadership of the lone Communist member of the City Council of Buenos Aires, José Penelón; this group had taken the name Partido Comunista de la República Argentina.[1] Roberto Guinney served as the administrator of *Adelante*, the official organ of the PCRA, as well as secretary of its Russian-Ukrainian branch. Camilo López was a member of the Trade Union Commission of the party, and M. Guinney was the secretary of a party cell. All three were immigrants but had lived in Argentina for several decades.

In 1928 the two Guinneys and López had begun to defend the positions of the Trotskyist left opposition in the Soviet Union. In the following year, they withdrew entirely from the Partido Comunista de la República Argentina, which had little sympathy for Trotskyism, and established their own group, the Comité Comunista de Oposición (Communist Committee of Opposition). In March 1930 they published the first number of a periodical called *La Verdad*. In this they stated their reasons for forming the CCO, and published the famous "Testament of Lenin," which Trotsky had released but which was not recognized as authentic by the Stalinist Communists until Nikita Khrushchev's famous report on Stalin's crimes to the Twentieth Congress of the Communist Party of the Soviet Union in 1956.[2]

A later leader of Argentine Trotskyism, Liborio Justo, has verified that the Comité Comunista de Oposición was the first organized group of Trotsky supporters to be established in Latin America. Its members immediately established contact with their counterparts in the United States and elsewhere. *The Militant*, the organ of the Trotskyists' Communist League of America in the United States, published the following notice in its issue of December 21, 1929:

> Opposition Group formed in Argentina!
> The formation of the first South American group of the Opposition signifies a great step forward in the struggle for the regeneration of world Communism. This is another answer to those who talk about 'the failure of Trotsky.' The future will show very soon that the step taken by our comrades in Argentina will be imitated in all of the countries of South America. The Opposition of the United States salutes and desires victory to our comrades of the continent of the South."

Within a short time the three pioneer Trotskyists increased their number to eight. They also changed their name to Izquierda Comunista Argentina (Argentine Communist Left). In spite of their small number, they were violently attacked by the Communist Party's official organ *La Internacional* as being "police agents." They were also joined by a small group of Jewish Communists who withdrew from the official party; although most of these new recruits stayed for only a short time, those who remained published for a while a periodical in Yiddish entitled *Communist Tribune*. At the time of the military coup d'etat which overthrew the regime of President Hipólito Irigoyen on September 6, 1930, several of the Trotskyist workers were jailed.

In 1932 and 1933 the original Trotskyist group made contact with two other small groups which by that time had declared themselves supporters of the ideas of Leon Trotsky. The first of these was led by two Argentine students, R. Raurich and Antonio Gallo, who had met the founders of Spanish Trotskyism while studying in Spain. The Spanish Trotskyites had informed the Izquierda Comunista Argentina that these two young men were soon to return home, and suggested that they would make good recruits for the ICA. Raurich and Gallo made little effort to contact the ICA, however, and only after several invitations were the two elements brought together, largely through the efforts of a Spanish Trotskyite refugee, J. Ramos López. The last *Internal Bulletin* of the Izquierda Comunista Argentina, which appeared about the end of 1933, described the meeting of the ICA delegation with Gallo and Raurich thus:

> We attempted to have a general meeting together. In the course of this meeting, we believed that we were in accord on the principal points of our opposition, such as the condemnation of the policy followed by the Stalinists in the Anglo-Russian Committee; the adventures and massacres produced by the policy in China; the localization of socialism in one country; the subversion of Leninist methods of workers' democracy by the self-determination of upper bureaucracy, as well as condemnable dual unionism. This was sufficient to prove that we were in a meeting or assembly of true Communists of the left.
>
> In our first joint meeting a commission of both groups was named to draw up a thesis on the basis of which we could work together.

This early optimism proved to be unjustified, and the two groups finally pulled apart. The ICA attributed the failure to unify the country's self-proclaimed Trotskyists to the refusal of the Gallo-Raurich group to work with "ideologically unprepared" workers.[3]

The second group with which the original Trotskyites made contact was one led by Pedro Milesi, who also used the pseudonyms P. Maciel and Eduardo Islas. A municipal worker, he had been an anarchist in his youth and an early member of the Communist Party. He was expelled from the Communist ranks late in 1932, and during his "trial" in the party he had strongly denied any sympathies with Trotskyism. However, once outside of the Communist organization, he proclaimed his support for Trotsky and took a small group of followers out of the Communist Party with him.

Unlike the Gallo-Raurich group, the Milesi faction agreed to join the existing Izquierda Comunista Argentina. It was agreed that the ICA would publish an issue of *La Verdad* which would announce the newly achieved unity, and publish a statement by the Milesi group concerning why they were entering the ICA. Soon thereafter, a general assembly would be called to elect a new Central Committee and other officials.

This second move to unite the Argentine Trotskyites also failed. In February 1933 Camilo López, one of the original founders of the ICA, became seriously ill and Roberto Guinney died. This undoubtedly postponed fulfillment of the agreements which had been reached, and as a result the Milesi group took the initiative in calling the proposed general assembly of the Izquierda Comunista Argentina. Although annoyed by the move, the remaining founding members of the group agreed to participate in the meeting. The results of this general assembly were very disappointing for the original Trotskyists. The Milesi group was in the majority and they elected Pedro Milesi as Secretary-General of the Izquierda Comunista Argentina, and Milesi's wife as its secretary of organization. At the same time, they decided to send a delegation, headed by Milesi, to a Latin American antiwar congress which had been called under Communist auspices to meet later in the year in Montevideo. Shortly afterwards the new leaders of the ICA added the words "Section of the International Communist Left" to the organization's title.

Relations between the two elements in the ICA grew increasingly tense. The original Trotskyists protested when the first issue of the new periodical of the ICA did not contain the promised statement of the Milesi group concerning its motives for joining the Trotskyist movement. The founders also accused the Milesi group of not taking a correct position in its analysis of the situation in the Soviet Union. Finally, they objected to the change of the name of the ICA to "Liga Comunista Internacional, Sección Argentina," and insisted that they had not been informed that such an alteration was to take place.

As a result of continuing disagreement, the Milesi group moved to expel M. Guinney, one of the three founders of Argentine Trotskyism, from the ranks of the organization; it also expelled Guinney's wife Juana and suspended the treasurer of the group, C. C. Ostrobsky. When Milesi, as Secretary-General, failed to give what they considered an adequate explanation for these actions, the remaining members of the original Trotskyist nucleus withdrew from the Liga Comunista Internacional. They published one last issue of an *Internal Bulletin* of the Izquierda Comunista Argentina, at the end of 1933, and this virtually ended their political activity.[4]

## THE SECOND PHASE OF ARGENTINE TROTSKYISM

With the retirement from politics of the group of workers who had originally started the Trotskyist movement in Argentina, there remained two other elements who claimed to be loyal to the ideas of Leon Trotsky. These were the Raurich-Gallo faction and the Pedro Milesi faction. The first group seems to have called themselves Liga Comunista Internacionalista; for some time the Milesi faction bore the name Liga Comunista Internacional, Sección Argentina.

Both Raurich and Gallo were intellectuals. Raurich was accused by Liborio Justo of having "an intellectual production (which) did not go beyond cafe conversations." However, Justo admits that most other Trotskyites of the 1930's "considered themselves disciples of Raurich" and after Raurich's death in the 1960's two volumes of his work, one a study of Marxist esthetic criticism and the other on Hegel and Marx, were published.[5]

Antonio Gallo (who also used the pseudonym A. Ontiveros) had been a member of the Socialist Party as an adolescent, and by the time he was nineteen he had published a study entitled *An Esssay in Marxist Interpretation of the September Movement*, concerned with the Argentine military coup of September 1930. While continuing his studies in Spain, he had met the early Spanish followers of Trotsky, including the leading figure of that group, Andrés Nin, who was later murdered by the Stalinists during the Spanish Civil War.

When Raurich and Gallo returned from Spain they established what they called the Liga Comunista Internacionalista, of Trotskyist orientation, and gathered about them a small group of followers, mainly young intellectuals. They launched a periodical called *Nueva Etapa (New Phase)*. Liborio Justo later claimed that in 1933-34 they had no more than eight or ten members in their group.

Pedro Milesi's faction, which Justo later alleged had only ten or twelve members, published its own periodical, *Tribuna Leninista*, of which three or four numbers appeared in 1933 and 1934. They also put out a series of pamphlets through a publishing company, Editorial José Carlos Mariátegui, which they established. They had rather more contact with the labor movement than did the Raurich-Gallo group, but no appreciable influence in it.

During 1933 and most of 1934 these two groups carried on energetic polemics with one another, particularly over the proper attitude to be adopted toward the Radical Party, which made up the largest part of the opposition to the ruling military-Conservative Party dictatorship of President Agustín P. Justo. However, after the Liga Comunista Internacional, Sección Argentina had expelled its principal leader, Pedro Milesi, late in 1934, for reasons which remain obscure, the two groups decided to join forces. Together they established the Liga Comunista Internacionalista (Sección Argentina) and began publication of still another periodical, *IV Internacional*, the first issue of which appeared in April 1935. The first number of *IV Internacional* published a statement explaining the unification of the Trotskyist movement of Argentina in the following terms:

> The Bolshevik-Leninists of Argentina have united!...
> But in the way of our growing development was an obstacle in our own ranks; the existence of two groups instead of a single organization. Furthermore, these groups—*Nueva Etapa* and *Tribuna Leninista*—had divergent positions on important national and international problems. And those divergences created a factor of confusion for the Liga, keeping many sympathizers in a state of indecision and even inspiring a lack of confidence among them. This is not the moment to recount those divergences or the work carried out separately by each group. Those who are interested can refer to *Nueva Etapa* and *Tribuna Leninista*. The fundamental thing is that both, understanding the arduous and responsible task which rested upon them, have discussed these divergences, and have fused. This fusion, carried out on a programmatic basis—a basis which we shall publish soon—begins a new epoch for the Liga. We hope that it will be one of growth and improvement, although we are fully aware of our task.

Having opened the way for *IV Internacional, Nueva Etapa* and *Tribuna Leninista* will disappear. The new organ of the Bolshevik-Leninists will be augmented. The fusion of the groups of the Liga will certainly be a positive step. An advance for Marxism in our country. An advance toward the formation of a new Party and of the Fourth International which will give victory to the world proletariat.

We shall struggle for unity in action! For a new Communist Party! For the world revolution! Long live the fusion of the Bolshevik-Leninists!"[6]

The new Liga Comunista Internacionalista, Sección Argentina, lasted little more than two years. However, during its existence, it did succeed in establishing small groups in La Plata, Córdoba, and Santa Fé. The group in Córdoba published a review entitled *América Libre,* which had five issues and was directed by a Bolivian exile, Tristán Marof, and by Aquiles Garmendía. In Buenos Aires, a disciple of Raurich, C. Liacho, issued another periodical, *Transición.* A group of sympathizers led by L. Koiffman also published a short-lived magazine, *Visión.*

The Liga changed its name in 1936 to Partido Obrero, but a few months later returned to its original name. By the end of the year, the group was in difficulty again, and a new attempt was made to regroup the forces in a new organization, the Agrupación de Propaganda Marxista, organized by L. Koiffman. This new organization held only two or three meetings.

Early in 1937, faced with the disintegration of their own organization, the Trotskyists split over the issue of whether they should follow the line which Leon Trotsky had generally recommended to his followers—to enter the Socialist parties and attempt to bore from within them. One group of Argentine Trotskyites, led by C. Liacho and followed by the student nucleus in La Plata led by J. Lagos (later better known by his real name, Jorge Abelardo Ramos), took this line. They entered the Socialist Party and a left-wing group, the Partido Socialista Obrero, which had recently separated from the Socialist Party, taking with them a fair proportion of the Socialists' more youthful element. Antonio Gallo led the group which opposed this tactic.

This controversy over "entrism" was the final blow to the Liga Comunista Internacionalista. The last *Bulletin* of the Liga, which bore the Number 10 of Year II, was published in September 1937. The last few issues of the *Bulletin* were not printed but were reproduced on a mimeograph machine.[7]


## THE THIRD STAGE OF ARGENTINE TROTSKYISM


The Trotskyists were not able to exert much influence in either the Partido Socialista or the Partido Socialista Obrero. Most of the top leaders of the latter ultimately joined the Communist Party, and many of the rank and file members and lower level leaders rejoined the Socialist Party. A move soon developed among the Trotskyists to reestablish their own separate organization.

Within the ranks of the PSO those Trotskyists who joined it soon drew together to try to gain influence for their point of view within the party's ranks. From August to December 1937 a group under the leadership of C. Liacho published five issues of a mimeographed periodical entitled *Frente Proletario*, which bore the subtitle *Boletín del Marxismo Revolucionario*. The same group put out one issue of another publication, *Marxismo*, in August 1938. At the beginning of 1938 a national conference of Trotskyist members of the PSO was held in Córdoba, and was attended by delegates from that city and from Buenos Aires and La Plata. Liacho was again the major figure in this meeting.

The only local of the PSO over which the Trotskyists seem to have gained control was the small one in Liniers in the Province of Buenos Aires. That local published a small periodical called *Izquierda*, which was subtitled "Organ of Affiliates for Affiliates." Three numbers of the periodical appeared between February and August 1938.

Some of the Trotskyites had not entered the PSO, either because they were opposed to "entrism" or because the PSO would not admit them. These included Pedro Milesi, A. Garmendia of Córdoba, D. Siburu of Rosario, and a student group in Santa Fé led by V. Carbajal.

Meanwhile, a new recruit to Trotskyism, who was for a few years to be one of the most prominent members of the movement, had joined the forces of the anti-entrism faction. This was Liborio Justo, (who used the party names "Quebracho" and "Bernal"), the son of the then President of Argentina, General Agustín P. Justo (1932-38). Although a member of the generation which had carried out the University Reform after 1918, Justo had participated only tangentially in this important movement. Driven by a need to "find himself" and work out his own analysis of society and the world, he had traveled widely from one end of Argentina to the other, as well as making two trips to Europe and three to the United States in the 1920's and early 1930's.

Upon returning from his third voyage to the United States early in 1935 Justo became a "fellow traveler" of the Communist Party of Argentina, but he was alienated from the Stalinists by their persecution of other left-wing groups on the loyalist side in the Spanish Civil War, and in November 1936 he announced his split with them in an open letter which appeared in the Buenos Aires magazine *Claridad*. He had for some years been interested in the ideas of Trotsky, and after his split with the Stalinists he immediately gravitated toward Trotsky's professed Argentine followers.[8]

During 1937 Liborio Justo began issuing a mimeographed periodical of Trotskyist orientation, *Boletín de Información*. He also published one issue of a magazine entitled *España Obrera*, which dealt with the Spanish Civil War, and one issue of another periodical which he called *Piquete*.

Justo's formal entry into Trotskyist politics took the form of an invitation to the various factions to meet in Buenos Aires on November 7, 1937, to draw up a reply to a letter which had been received from Diego Rivera concerning a Latin American conference of Trotskyists which was being planned. Justo has listed those who accepted his invitation: "C. Liacho and G. [not otherwise identified] represented the 'entrists'; Miguel in representation of what was left of the L.C.I.; P. Milesi and some disciples of J.P. [not otherwise identified]; O. Rivas Rooney, and others."

Although most of the divided Argentine Trotskyist ranks were represented at the November 7 meeting, it did not result in reunification. Justo's suggestion that they join to establish a new periodical was not accepted by the "entrists," but the others agreed to the proposition. However, old quarrels between Antonio Gallo and Pedro Milesi interfered with the fulfillment of the plan. As a result, two periodicals of Trotskyist persuasion soon appeared.

The first of these periodicals was *Nuevo Curso*; it was put out by Justo together with Gallo and the remaining members of the LCI and supported by D. A. Siburu of Rosario and A. Garmendía of Córdoba. Only one number of *Nuevo Curso* appeared, and it consisted of articles which had already been published in the international Trotskyist press.[9] The second magazine was *Inicial*, put out by Milesi and J.P., five numbers of which appeared in 1938. In January 1939, after his efforts had not brought about unity in the Trotskyist movement of Argentina, Justo published a pamphlet entitled *Como Salir del Pántano: Hacia la Formación de la Sección Argentina del Partido Mundial de la Revolución Socialista (4a Internacional)*. In this, he discussed at some length the principal figures then active in the Trotskyist movement, and his sarcastic comments on them go far to explain why he aroused such antagonism among those who were supposed to be his fellows. At about the time this pamphlet appeared, the Trotskyists who had been members of the Partido Socialista Obrero were either expelled from it or withdrew voluntarily. Some of them associated with Pedro Milesi's group, around the magazine *Inicial,* while others were attracted to the group headed by Liborio Justo.

The Justo group, which soon took the name Grupo Obrero Revolucionario (GOR), published still another periodical, *La Internacional*, the first issue of which came out in April 1939, with 5,000 copies being printed. It had the collaboration of the Trotskyist groups in La Plata and Córdoba. Although the GOR continued to publish *La Internacional*, by February 1940 it was reduced to ten members, of whom four (Justo proudly boasted) were workers. Its affiliates outside of Buenos Aires withdrew, and in March 1940 a further split in the organization reduced it to "five or six members." However, Justo boasted that for the first time since the establishment of the first Trotskyist group in Argentina, a Trotskyist organization consisted in its majority of workers.

During 1940 and 1941 those who were left in the GOR were very active, and the organization grew somewhat. Justo described its activities in this period thus: "It continued publishing [as a periodical, rechristened] *La Nueva*

*Internacional* (June, July, August, and September—double number in homage to Trotsky, of which 10,000 copies were published, a number never before reached by any Argentine Trotskyist publication—and November-December). During all the year 1940, in constant activity, in permanent struggle against reaction and Stalinism (which resulted in various detentions of its members by police reaction), the GOR was strengthened, secured ample diffusion for its propaganda, carrying on intense labor—which was well mirrored in the attacks of the Stalinist press—and commenced again to grow, but now only in the workers area, where it attracted new elements."[10]

In May 1941 the Grupo Obrero Revolucionario changed its name to Liga Obrera Revolucionaria, an alteration which was supposed to reflect the organization's growth. It also altered the name of its periodical to *Lucha Obrera* instead of *La Nueva Internacional,* which it had been using until then. Liborio Justo boasted about this time that 90 per cent of the members of the LOR were workers.

In the meantime, the rival Trotskyist group headed by Pedro Milesi continued to publish *Inicial;* two issues came out in 1939. It sought to bring about a unification of Trotskyist ranks but failed. In September 1940 a group of new recruits to Trotskyism, who had left Communist circles in disillusionment over the Stalin-Hitler Pact of August 1939, sponsored another attempt to bring the splintered ranks of Trotskyism together. However, negotiations between the GOR, the *Inicial* group, and the remnants of the Liga Comunista Internacionalista who had adopted the name of their old publication *Nueva Etapa,* again failed, amid bitter polemics.

However, this unity effort brought together once again the groups associated with Antonio Gallo and Pedro Milesi. They formed a new organization, the Liga Obrera Socialista, which assumed the publication of *Inicial.* In the new version of their periodical, they referred to themselves as "the leaders of the Fourth International in Argentina." They were also able to attract many of those who had left the Grupo Obrero Revolucionario in 1939. The Liga Obrera Socialista wrote to the headquarters of the Fourth International in New York seeking recognition as the official representative of the International in Argentina.[11]

## THE FAILURE OF UNIFICATION AND THE END OF LOR

Bitter polemics continued between the Liga Obrera Revolucionaria and other Trotskyist groups. Aside from the Liga Obrera Socialista, these included a small circle in Córdoba, which after first joining the LOS declared itself independent. A leading figure in this Córdoba faction was a man who used the pseudonym "Homero" and later was to be better known by another pseudonym, "J. Posadas," although his real name was Homero Cristali. Even in the early 1940's Posadas was apparently adept at the sort of endless discourse which was later to distinguish his style as a leading figure in Latin American and world Trotskyism: Liborio Justo, in one of his numerous pamphlets, notes that Posadas carried on an attack against him, Justo, "for several hours" in one of the fruitless efforts to unite the various factions claiming adhesion to the Fourth International.[12]

Undoubtedly much of the dissidence in the various Trotskyist groups centered on personalities, as it had done since the birth of the movement in Argentina, but there were also ideological issues, which were to remain important for several decades in Argentine Trotskyism, that made their appearance in the early 1940's. Of particular importance was the issue of "national liberation." The Liga Obrera Revolucionaria maintained a position with nationalistic overtones which had been put forth by the LOR's principal leader, Liborio Justo, and which was in later years to be taken up by many who opposed it when it was first offered by Justo and his small group.

The "national liberation" position was argued in an issue of *La Nueva Internacional*, the organ of the LOR, early in 1940. After noting the conflict of rival imperialisms which it alleged was in progress during World War II, and the relative decline of British imperialism, this article continued:

> We must take advantage of the evident decline and possible definitive fall of English imperialism, which has imprisoned the country and paralyzes its progress, to accomplish our economic liberation. In no way is it possible to remain passive before the prospect that those English public utility companies, industrial firms, agricultural societies, and banks will change hands and as a heritage of war fall into the hands of the United States, as everything indicates that they will do. The same can be said of the territories which legitimately belong to Argentina, such as the Islas Malvinas [Falkland Islands]. The Argentine people must demand and take steps so that everything will be returned to it which belongs to it. . . .
>
> It is necessary that the Argentine people, and most of all the proletariat, understand the full significance and the tremendous gravity of the hour in which we live, the gigantic importance of the brusque and continuous changes which are being brought about by events; only energetic and decisive action of the proletariat in the interests of the whole country, and only the working class through a Proletarian United Front, stimulated by a revolutionary Marxist party and controlling the destinies of the republic, can prevent the entrance of Argentina into the killing and achieve national liberation, through the expropriation (without indemnization) and nationalizaton of the imperialist banks, firms, and properties, and latifundia, and the repudiation of the external debt and the monopoly of foreign trade.[13]

The Liga Obrera Socialista strongly opposed this position taken by Liborio Justo and the Liga Obrera Revolucionaria. In the April 1940 issue of its periodical, *Inicial,* the LOS wrote in part:

The Fourth International does not permit any slogan of 'national liberation' which tends to subordinate the proletariat to the dominant classes and, on the contrary, assures that the first step of proletarian national liberation is the struggle against these same classes. . . .

The Fourth International in Argentina has known how to analyze the reality of the country and develop its strategy. Nothing will force deviation from this except new events or new principles more correct than the former ones. 'National Liberation' has nothing to do with our movement. For the class struggle! For the Socialist revolution![14]

However, personalities remained as important as issues in the continued factionalism within Argentine Trotskyism, and no person was more controversial than Liborio Justo or ''Quebracho,'' the principal figure in the Liga Obrera Revolucionaria. He engaged in constant personal attacks on his opponents, whom he consistently accused of being ''centrists.'' Typical of the personal nature of his invective are the following characterizations of some of the principal figures of the rival group, contained in his pamphlet *Centrismo, Oportunismo y Bolchevismo* (p.3): ''Raurich, a Social Democrat of cheap bookish erudition...Gallo, a petty bourgeois climber...Milesi, a yellow trade-union leader...Liacho, a mediocre and failed literary man...Koiffman, also a Social Democrat by his position and his predilections.''

His opponents were no kinder to Quebracho than he was to them. In his book *Estrategia Revolucionaria,* Justo himself cites his enemies' charge that he was ''dictatorial, disloyal, undisciplined.'' The United States Trotskyist, Sherry Mangan, who used the pseudonym Terence Phelan, intervened in unity negotiations of the Argentine Trotskyists, and finally worked only with Justo's opponents. He once wrote: ''Quebracho is not so much vicious as mad. This is not merely a polemic epithet, or the fruit of personal indignation, but a carefully considered judgment. The man is without question mentally unbalanced, and lives in a world of his own.''[15]

In addition to irregular periodicals, both sides published various pamphlets as vehicles for their polemics against one another. In April 1939 Quebracho published a pamphlet entitled *Nuestras Perspectivas Políticas–Por una Fuerte Sección Argentina del Partido Mundial de la Revolución Socialista–4a Internacional.* In this, he proposed a congress to unite the various Argentine groups claiming adherence to the Fourth International, to be followed by a Latin American congress of all Trotskyist groups in the region. In another pamphlet, *Frente al Momento del Mundo–Que Quiere la Cuarta Internacional,* put out in October 1939, Liborio Justo first put forward in some detail his ideas on ''national liberation.'' in *Centrismo, Oportunismo y Bolchevismo,* published five months later, he continued his defense of these ideas and his polemics against those Trotskyists who opposed them.

Meanwhile, the Fourth International, whose headquarters had been moved from Paris to New York with the outbreak of the Second World War, was interested in trying to bring about the unification of the Argentine groups claiming to belong to the International. Their concern was expressed directly to the parties involved by Sherry Mangan (Terence Phelan).

Mangan-Phelan was a journalist in the employ of the *Time-Life-Fortune* combine, and he made it a policy of entering into contact with Trotskyist groups in whatever country he happened to be stationed in pursuit of his journalistic career.[16] According to a letter to Liborio Justo from Felix Morrow, a leading member of the Socialist Workers Party, the United States affiliate of the Fourth International: "The fact is that Comrade Phelan accepted his actual employment on our request. We wanted him to take this work so that he could get to South America. I repeat, his present employment is a designation of the Party."[17] Mangan-Phelan arrived in Argentina early in 1941 and began working to try to bring the various Trotskyist groups together. He soon ran afoul of Liborio Justo, who subsequently charged that since his arrival he had "put himself in close and assiduous relationship with the centrists of the LOS and had as his amanuensis a bizarre member of it, Jorge A. Ramos."[18]

Mangan-Phelan's own version of his activities was somewhat different. In a letter to his North American fellow party members, dated October 28, 1941, he wrote:

> Quebracho's initial ultimatum that the LOR would enter no unity negotiations unless the political difference was discussed at length, made me abandon the hope that the political accord could be reached solely within the Unification Committee. It was voted, as you remember, unanimously, including Q, that each organization should submit a thesis on the moot point. The other groups very wisely and correctly adopted the policy of putting their political cards on the table and asking Quebracho to do the same. They stated their political positions clearly and non-polemically in theses, and called on Quebracho to do as much. They furthermore stated in advance that they did not expect that the differences thus revealed would render unification impossible. Quebracho, whose opposition to unification of course has nothing political in it, but reflects only his desire to be left alone with his 'tame' group, which never talks back, naturally tried to avoid any presentation of proofs.[19]

Mangan-Phelan felt that the programmatic differences between the LOR and other Trotskyist groups were not sufficient to justify their staying apart. He suggested unification of their forces, and debate over the pending issues at the new party's first congress. Justo insisted that there be agreement on all pending issues before the establishment of a unified party. It proved impossible to reach any agreement, and polemics continued between the LOR on the one hand and the Liga Obrera Socialista and Terence Phelan on the other. Liborio Justo received considerable ammunition in the form of an article entitled "Report on Argentina," which appeared in the May 1941 issue of *Fortune* over the signature of Sherry Mangan, and which was written more in the spirit of *Fortune* than in that of a member of the Socialist Workers Party. The article discussed the penetration of Axis propaganda in South America and commented on the inadequacy of the United States' response to it.

A "corrected version" of this article appeared a few months later in *Claridad*, the left-wing monthly published in Buenos Aires, along with a hostile comment by its editor. The article was also attacked in the Socialist Workers Party newspaper *The Militant* of May 31, 1941, with no mention that this piece of "imperialist propaganda" had been written by an official delegate of the Fourth International. Justo used this incident to intensify his personal and political attacks on Mangan-Phelan.[20]

Other incidents contributed to the tension between the Liga Obrera Revolucionaria and the other Trotskyist groups in Argentina. One took place at a "reunification congress" of the Chilean Trotskyists, which was attended by Liborio Justo for the LOR and Terence Phelan for the Fourth International and the Unification Committee of Argentina. There Phelan read a letter of greeting from the Unification Committee and released a letter from Marc Loris, one of the secretaries of the Fourth International, which was critical of Quebracho. Liborio Justo soon issued a strong reply to Loris' epistle. In October 1941 the Unification Committee issued a bulletin which was quite critical of the LOR. In reply to this, Liborio Justo announced the withdrawal of the LOR from the committee, although saying that its representatives would continued to attend as "observers."[21]

Mangan-Phelan finally gave up hope of bringing the Liga Obrera Revolucionaria into the united Trotskyist party, at least at the time of its establishment. As a result, the Unification Committee, over which he presided, went ahead with its plans to merge most of the other groups existing in Buenos Aires and various interior provinces. Perhaps one reason for Phelan's attitude is indicated by his comment, in writing to his United States colleagues, that "there are limits beyond which concessions to Quebracho, representing his alleged 27, can wreck the new unity of the other nose-counted 75, and break down their new drive and optimism."

The unification brought into existence a new party, the Partido Obrero de la Revolución Socialista (PORS). It launched a new periodical, *Frente Obrero*, the first number of which was dated December 1941, and announced that "the Argentine proletariat now has its party." Among those who participated in the founding of the PORS were Carvajal (A. Narvaja), the party's new Secretary-General, and R. Frigerio (J. Lagos) of La Plata, J. Posadas, Jorge Abelardo Ramos, E. Rivera, Esteban Rey, E. Etkin, Miguel [or "Oscar," not otherwise identified], N. Moreno, and an Austrian refugee (a representative in Buenos Aires of the Overseas News Agency), Kurt Steinfeld.[22] The PORS was officially recognized by the Fourth International as its Argentine affiliate, apparently on the recommendation of Terence Phelan.

However, the establishment of the PORS did not bring about complete Trotskyist unity in Argentina and it was not very long-lasting. The Liga Obrera Revolucionaria continued to exist for about two years, and Quebracho (Liborio Justo) described its activities in this period as follows:

> It published 5,000 copies (once 10,000) of our organ *Lucha Obrera*, which we distributed in their totality with an unequalled effort, the few militants of the LOR going daily to union meetings and to the factories, workshops, and construction projects of Buenos Aires and the vicinity, where our periodical, generally, was distributed gratis for the purpose of getting a wide audience. Because the skepticism of the laboring masses, provoked by the reiterated betrayals of the parties of the left, was so great, when in one of the numbers of *Lucha Obrera* we offered to send without any cost any of our pamphlets, we received only one request![23]

The LOR also tried to establish contacts with Trotskyist groups in other Latin American countries, and to this end, it began publishing in February 1943 *Boletín Sudamericano (Por Una Cuarta Internacional Revolucionaria)* [*South American Bulletin (For a Revolutionary Fourth International)*]. Five numbers of this periodical appeared; they dealt with events in Brazil, Chile, Uruguay, Bolivia, Mexico, and Cuba as well as in Argentina.[24] The publication of this bulletin followed LOR's decision to break with the Fourth International. This decision was announced in a proclamation addressed to the Fourth International, signed by Quebracho and dated July 20, 1942, in which the Fourth International was accused of the same kind of bureaucratization which had long since characterized the Third International; the North American leaders of the Fourth International were in fact accused of being agents of U.S. imperialism. It concluded: "Comrades, I believe that the moment has come to demand of you: Who are you, gentlemen, to recognize us? Wouldn't it be more adequate to begin by asking us if we will recognize you? On this basis, isn't the time long overdue for us to deny you all authority for arrogating to yourselves the right to seat us before your bureaucratic desk, and instead to seat you before our revolutionary tribunal?"[25]

But in spite of its activities, the LOR was in decline. As Quebracho himself noted: it "began to suffer, nevertheless, a process of disintegration, which besides reflecting the adverse medium in which it had to operate also reflected the revolutionary retreat all over the world. Some active comrades of the interior stopped writing. Others became renegades to Marxism. The Spanish worker P. Varela. . . who had always given us decided moral support, died. Comrade Francisco A ... then a student of law and one of the activists in the LOR, announced that he wished to abandon activity ... Comrade Mateo Fossa disapproved of our break with New York, and finally, in spite of the high estimation he had always merited, we were obliged to continue without him."[26]

The final sad end of the LOR was described by Quebracho thus: "Finally, in Buenos Aires, we remained only two: Enrique Carmona (Santiago Escobar) and he who is writing. . . . We were writing almost for nobody but ourselves. And as generally happens in such circumstances, when forces cannot be developed outward they develop inward. With Comrade Enrique Carmona—whose intelligent and loyal adhesion and profound class sentiment (he was a food processing worker), and whose support had been essential for the action which we were able to carry out in the LOR—there arose some disagreements over silly matters. And the LOR ended by disintegrating forever."[27]

Liborio Justo never went back to Trotskyism. His criticism of the movement, which began with his quarrel with the leaders of the Socialist Workers Party of the United States, soon extended to Trotsky himself. In 1959 he published a book *Leon Trotsky y Wall Street*, in which he concluded that the founder of the Fourth International had in fact become an ally of U.S. imperialism during his last years in Mexico, and had supported policies which were a betrayal of true Marxist-Leninist revolution.

## ARGENTINE TROTSKYISM AND PERONISMO

The approach to Trotskyist unity represented by the establishment of the Partido Obrero de la Revolución Socialista was short-lived. By May 1942, only six months after it had been established, the PORS had begun to disintegrate under the pressure of personal feuds and ideological differences. One leading member, Nahuel Moreno, withdrew from the PORS and for a short while joined the Liga Obrera Revolucionaria, but within a few months he had also retired from Quebracho's faction. By June 1943 the PORS had decided to liquidate, and even to abandon farther efforts to publish its periodical *Frente Obrero*. However, in September and October 1945, two further issues of *Frente Obrero* appeared, and the periodical came out intermittently for some time thereafter. Finally, in March 1948, the remnants of the PORS, of which Carvajal remained the principal figure, once more decided to abandon all further political activity.[28]

Both ideological issues and personal differences caused the splintering of Argentine Trotskyism in the 1940's and thereafter. After the military coup d'etat of June 4, 1943, which ultimately resulted in Juan Perón coming to power, the most divisive ideological issue among Trotskyists was how to interpret the Peronista phenomenon and how to determine what attitude the Trotskyists should take toward it.

The way in which the various Trotskyist groups looked upon and reacted to Peronism was closely associated with their point of view on the issue of "national liberation." In spite of Liborio Justo's disappearance from Trotskyist politics, polemics over the issue continued. At the risk of greatly oversimplifying the issues involved in this long debate, one may say that it centered on the question of what group constituted the "principal enemy of the working class." One element argued that in the "semi-colonial" countries such as Argentina (and Latin America in general), as in the highly industrialized nations, the major struggle of the workers, and their vanguard party, must be against the native bourgeoisie. It denied that the national bourgeoisie had any significant revolutionary potential.

Those holding the opposing point of view argued that given the "semi-colonial" nature of such a country as Argentina, the major enemy was "imperialism." Since the interests of the national bourgeoisie were for a certain time in conflict with those of imperialism, there existed a basis of alliance for a certain period between the revolutionary workers movement and its vanguard party on the one hand, and the national bourgeoisie on the other. One advocate of this position summed up the idea thus: "The working class and its vanguard will march together with the national bourgeoisie, without ever becoming confused with it, to strike imperialism together."[29]

The attitude of the various Trotskyist groups toward the issue of "national liberation" influenced their response to the rise of Peronismo. Those who stressed the need to concentrate on the class struggle within the country tended to resist what they considered the bourgeois nationalism of Perón and his followers, and they only joined the Peronista ranks at the penultimate moment. Those who argued in favor of national class cooperation to fight imperialism came to Perón's support much earlier.

The position of the pro-Perón Argentine Trotskyists was attacked by both orthodox and dissident Trotskyists abroad. Thus, an article in the January 1948 issue of *The New International*, the organ of the "Shachtmanite" dissident Trotskyists in the United States, argued that "it should be evident now that the Argentine Trotskyists wish to be more Catholic than the Pope and more Peronista than Perón." Arguing the issues, this article commented: "The Argentine Octobrists confuse the phenomenon and relationships of modern imperialism with feudalism; the socialist with the bourgeois revolution; totalitarian Bonapartism with bourgeois democracy; and industrial development caused by the imperialist world crisis with the democratic industrial revolution. They make of Marxism, a scientific and international doctrine which seeks and finds the same phenomena in every part of the world, a native 'hash.' They proclaim the Perón reaction a bourgeois democratic revolution, and his inter-imperialist struggle for crumbs an anti-imperialist struggle which merits the support of the proletariat."

An early Trotskyist advocate of the anti-Peronista position was Mateo Fossa, who for a decade had been one of the principal trade unionists associated with Trotskyism. Apparently on his own initiative, he began in November 1946 to publish a periodical, *El Militante*, which he subtitled "In Defense of the Exploited and Oppressed! For the Fourth International!" In the first issue of this publication, Fossa published a long analysis addressed

"To the Argentine Workers," in which he described the Fourth International as having "the only revolutionary program of the present hour" and called for the establishment of a Fourth International party in Argentina. He also defined Peronismo as "nothing more than a bourgeois, or state, form of Stalinist and Socialist reformism."[30]

The group of Trotskyists who gathered around *El Militante* formed the principal group holding to the emphasis on the class struggle within Argentina. They formed the Partido Obrero Revolucionario, which was led by Nahuel Moreno. One of the leaders of this group has noted: "We were opponents of the Peronista government, implacable adversaries until 1954, when we saw the coming of an imperialist and anti-labor wave, and we reacted against it, although we engaged in extensive self-criticism of many sectarian errors which we may have committed in our work."[31]

In 1954 the Partido Obrero Revolucionario effectively dissolved as a separate party and its members entered as a group the new Partido Socialista de la Revolución Nacional (PSRN). This was a pro-Perón party established on the initiative of a group which had recently left the strongly anti-Peronista Partido Socialista. The best-known leaders of the PSRN were Enrique Dickmann, one of the earliest members of the Partido Socialista, and Carlos María Bravo, the son of Mario Bravo, another of the early members of the Socialist Party. Apparently an element in the POR, led by J. Posadas, refused to enter the PSRN and continued to maintain what was left of the Partido Obrero Revolucionario under the name Partido Obrero.

The Trotskyists of the former Partido Obrero Revolucionario soon came to control the Buenos Aires Provincial Federation of the new PSRN. They were responsible for publishing in 1954-55 that Federation's periodical, *La Verdad*.[32] It was probably not coincidental that the name of that publication was the same as that of the organ of the first Trotskyist group in Argentina, the Izquierda Comunista de Argentina.

The Partido Socialista de la Revolución Nacional was declared illegal soon after the overthrow of Perón in September 1955. As a result, *La Verdad* suspended publication, but soon afterwards the Trotskyists who had been associated with it began the publication of another periodical, *Unidad Obrera*.

## THE PALABRA OBRERA GROVE

When the first post-Perón trade-union elections were held late in 1956, the *Unidad Obrera* group began still another publication, *Tendencia*, and worked with some Peronistas to establish the Movimiento de Agrupaciones Obreras (MAO), which participated in these elections. The MAO soon began publication of another newspaper, *Palabra Obrera*, and those associated with the new periodical became a fraction within the so-called "62 Union Organizations," which was a kind of general staff of Peronismo in the Argentine labor movement.[33]

The *Palabra Obrera* group apparently gave their comrades abroad an exaggerated picture of their success in the 1956-57 trade-union elections. Thus the United States Trotskyist paper, *The Militant,* reported in its issue of June 17, 1957: "In Argentina, Trotskyists have established themselves as one of the strongest political tendencies among workers in the great industrial plants of Buenos Aires—the most powerful section of the Argentine working class. In the last union elections (September 1956), the Trotskyists won in more than 20 large factories and lost by a scant margin in as many others. In the metalworkers strike of January 1957, which involved 250,000 workers, the Trotskyists elected a number of militants to the national strike committee. Reflecting their growing influence, the Argentine Trotskyists now envisage publishing a weekly paper with a circulation of 10,000 to 15,000."

After the 1953 split in international Trotskyism the *Palabra Obrera* group was associated with the "anti-Pablo" element, of which the Socialist Workers Party of the United States was the most important segment. With the reunification of most of the "Pabloite" and "anti-Pablo" groups in 1963 to form the United Secretariat, the *Palabra Obrera* element became the United Secretariat's Argentine affiliate.[34]

The *Palabra Obrera* group was reported to have merged in January 1965 with another small faction, the Frente Revolucionario Indoamericanista Popular, "to constitute a new revolutionary organization." It was noted that "the two groups had previously participated together in many class-struggle actions."[35] This new organization was the Partido Revolucionario de los Trabajadores (Revolutionary Party of Workers). Although it had originally been agreed that the weekly *Palabra Obrera* and the biweekly *Norte Revolucionario* (the former organ of the Frente) would continue to be published as organs of the new party, by the late 1960's the party was publishing a single periodical, *La Verdad.*[36]

The Partido Revolucionario de Trabajadores held its Second National Congress in May 1966. With the establishment of the dictatorship of General Juan Carlos Onganía in the following month, the PRT's weekly newspaper *La Verdad* and its "theoretical organ," *Estrategia* (which had recently been launched), were forced to go underground, but were reported to have continued publishing.[37] By 1969 the name of the PRT paper had been changed to *El Combatiente.* The PRT Trotskyists accused the new Onganía regime of "classical Bonapartism," and noted that "even in its impotence, it is similar to De Gaulle, whose attempt to convert France into a great imperialist power is doomed to failure, as the plans of Onganía for this country."[38]

The Partido Revolucionario de los Trabajadores was violently opposed to the Onganía dictatorship. At the same time, it strongly denounced the trade-union leadership of the CGT (Confederación General del Trabajo), which it accused of having worked with the Onganía regime. A May Day proclamation in 1967 called upon the workers to repudiate their leadership and unite on a four-point program:

1. Total and absolute defeat of the military dictatorship at the service of the great monopolies and Yankee imperialism.

2. Establishment of a provisional government of the CGT and parties and organizations demanded by the labor movement, and the calling of a Constitutional Assembly to definitively organize the country.

3. Removal of the present trade-union leadership.

4. Development and deepening of the rank and file organizations through (a) factory and inter-factory commissions of resistance or defense, and (b) a great congress of rank and file with delegates elected directly in the factories with one for each thousand workers or fraction of five hundred.[39]

After the violent clashes between workers on the one hand and police and soldiers on the other in the cities of Rosario and Córdoba in May and June of 1969, the Partido Revolucionario de Trabajadores committed itself to launching an insurrection and organizing a revolutionary army. The issue of *El Combatiente* of June 11, 1969, proclaimed: "A mobilization is more educational than a hundred programs, and in the last resort the revolutionary army which it constructs must be really the army of the people, must arise from the struggles of the people and be nourished by them, since a revolutionary army must be formed from organizational operations and its own techniques differ from those which the people adopt spontaneously."[40]

The same issue of the PRT paper published a proposal to the two factions of the Confederación General del Trabajo, and to students and other groups, which included the following points:

1. A regional and national coordination of workers and student federations, developing and deepening the active resistance of workers, students, and other popular sectors.

2. The organization of commandos of resistance, of self-defense groups and armed detachments of militants, to protect popular demonstrations against the oppressive violence of the regime, to organize the violence of the people against the violence of the government, and to begin laying the foundation of the future revolutionary army.

3. A campaign of propaganda directed to the soldiers and noncommisioned officers of the organs of repression of the regime, the police and military forces, calling upon them to fraternize with the people and not to shoot at them.[41]

The PRT received little response to this appeal, but soon afterwards it organized its own paramilitary group, the Ejército Revolucionario del Pueblo. It carried out a number of impressive operations, the most spectacular of which was performed in early June of 1971, when they kidnapped the manager of the Swift & Co. packing house in Rosario and held him for ransom, the ransom being the rehiring of discharged workers and the distribution of food and clothing to the city's poor. Swift & Co. met the ERP's terms.[42]

An article in a January 1971 issue of *El Combatiente* explained the PRT's concept of the relationship between the party and the Ejército Revolucionario del Pueblo. It commented: "The Partido Revolucionario de los Trabajadores, representing the best traditions of Marxism, confirmed by the experiences of the proletarian revolutions triumphant in the world, supports as a question of principle the differentiation between party and army, and the direction of the army by the party. The party is a superior form of organization, the nucleus of the working-class vanguard, and the spokesman for revolutionary ideology. Its task is to direct the whole of the revolutionary process, through mass organizations, existing or to be created. The army is one mass organization for combat which must be created and directed by the party. The latter guarantees by its political work the proletarian character of the objectives of the army. This is what our party understands in creating and developing under its direction the Revolutionary Army of the People. To put to one side this party-army relationship is to open the door to all kinds of deviation."[43]

## THE "NATIONAL LEFT"

Probably the best-known leader of the "national liberation" element in Argentine Trotskyism has been Jorge Abelardo Ramos. After the dissolution of the PORS in the early 1940's, he had been associated with the publication of *Frente Obrero*, and in 1945 he became the principal editor of a new periodical called *Octubre*, of which five issues appeared in 1945 and 1946. In it, Ramos gave the first full exposition of his ideological position favoring the "national revolution" and offering "critical support" to the Peronista movement and government.

Subsequently, the Ramos faction, of which Jorge Spilimbergo emerged as one of the most prolific spokesmen, published a number of other periodicals, including *Izquierda* and *Política*. It also established a publishing house, Editorial Indoamérica, which put out Spanish editions of Trotsky's *History of the Russian Revolution*, as well as his *Life of Lenin* and *What Was the Russian Revolution?* Their publishing house also put out a number of books dealing with Latin America, and more specifically with Argentina. These included Juan Ramón Peñaloza's *Trotsky Ante la Revolución Nacional Latinoamericana*, which centered particularly on Trotsky's writings about Latin America when he was a refugee in Mexico; Jorge Abelardo Ramos' *América Latina: Un País* and his pamphlet about Manuel Ugarte entitled *La Revolución Nacional en Latinoamérica: Manuel Ugarte y la Lucha Antiimperialista,* in which he pictured that ex-Socialist turned nationalist as a predecessor of his faction of Argentine Trotskyism.

The Ramos faction of Argentine Trotskyism was much more frankly pro-

Peronista than its rivals were. This was reflected in the fact that the Peronista daily newspaper *Democracia* allowed Ramos himself to publish a number of articles in its pages. The group also became part of the Partido Socialista de la Revolución Nacional. Ramos himself has described his group's attitude toward Peronismo in the following terms: "With the 17th of October terminated the 'infamous decade' and the 'pink period.' From 1945 until 1955 we supported the historically progressive nature of Peronismo in two senses: as the first political experience of the new proletariat, and as a defensive bourgeois-nationalist movement facing foreign imperialism . . . . It is enough for us to indicate for now that in 1955, in *Lucha Obrera,* we defended the national conquests of the proletariat of 1945 in the face of the resurrected oligarchy."[44]

For some years after the suppression of the Partido Socialista de la Revolución Nacional in 1955, the Ramos group maintained its identity principally through the various periodicals which it issued. Although continuing to cite Trotsky extensively in their own writings, they tended to talk of themselves less as a Trotskyist group and more as the Izquierda Nacional (National Left).

Finally, in 1962 the Ramos group sought to give organic form to its views by establishing the Partido Socialista de la Izquierda Nacional. Although the new party remained small in numbers, and apparently did not engage independently in any electoral activity, its intellectual influence was considerably more extensive than the size of its membership would indicate. It published a more or less regular periodical, *Izquierda Nacional*, and was not affiliated with any of the tendencies of International Trotskyism.

José Luis Madariaga, in his pamphlet *¿Qué es la Izquierda Nacional?,* summed up the PSIN's program by stating that it "synthesizes its program, adding to the three banners of Peronismo—economic independence, political sovereignty, social justice—a fourth, a government of labor and the masses, a guarantee of the fulfillment of the other three."[45]

With the seizure of power by General Alejandro Lanusse in March 1971, and his promise to call new elections, the Partido Socialista de la Izquierda Nacional decided to orient its policy toward participating in these elections when the new government got around to organizing them. Jorge Abelardo Ramos, in reporting to the Nineteenth Plenum of his party, set forth its "fundamental tasks in the immediate future" as being:

1. To consolidate our penetration and influence in the working class.

2. To expand our work in the university and high-school student movement, the vanguard sector of the revolutionary petty bourgeoisie and natural ally of the working class.

3. To struggle for basic democratic liberties, the first of which at this moment is the return to the country of General Juan Perón and the immediate calling of elections without prohibitions or rigging.

4. To struggle for democratization of the unions, which are being choked by a frequently betraying and capitulating bureaucracy whose Peronista coloration doesn't offer any guarantee either to Peronismo or to the workers.

5. To extend the organization and influence of the PSIN to those provinces in which the party has not yet been established.

6. To enter directly into public political action, holding meetings, putting up posters, and speaking to the millions of Argentines who await knowledge of the way to lead Argentina to sovereignty, freedom, justice, and socialism, under a working-class and popular government, an Argentina confederated with the rest of the sister states of Socialist Latin America."[46]

In the same report, Ramos denounced violent revolutionary activity: "It is possible that general elections will be called. In these circumstances, individual terrorism, even though it reveals the self-sacrifice of many youngsters of the petty bourgeoisie who offer their lives for the revolution, cannot achieve the objectives it proclaims, separated from the mobilization of the masses. . . . The substitution of arms for politics or of the violence of a small action group for the collective violence of the masses has led and will lead to passivity, demoralization, and the loss of valuable energy and the sacrifice of militants to the forces of repression."[47]

In addition to the Trotskyists who participated in the Ramos group, and ultimately became members of the Partido Socialista de la Izquierda Nacional, there were various individuals who were critical of the "internationalist" positions of the official factions of world Trotskyism and were more sympathetic to the "national revolution" orientation of Ramos, although they disagreed with various aspects of his doctrine. Among them were Alberto Belloni, A. Perelman, and J. J. Hernandez Arregui, all of whom had been active in Trotskyism at least since the 1940's. Some of them published a periodical, *Programa Para los Estados Unidos Socialistas de América Latina,* the first issue of which appeared in July 1964.

Another group with Trotskyite leanings but no international affiliation has been the Movimiento Política Obrera, which publishes the weekly photo-offset periodical *Política Obrera*. Publication of this paper began in 1966; the issues we have seen deal principally with activities and problems of the organized labor movement, with relatively little strictly ideological discussion.

## THE POSADISTA TROTSKYISTS

The third major faction in Argentine Trotskyism in the 1950's and 1960's has been the Partido Obrero (Trostskista), associated with J. Posadas (Homero Cristali). Originating out of the confusion in Argentine Trotskyism in the late 1940's, the PO(T) was represented at the Second World Congress of the Fourth International, where it was seated as a "sympathizing organization." It was finally seated as a regular member of the Fourth International in the Third Congress in 1951.

This was the first national Trotskyist group in which Posadas achieved hegemony, and with it as a base, he reached out for influence in other member parties of the Fourth International in Latin America. It remained the smallest Trotskyist element in Argentina, but has been characterized by the particularly intense devotion of its small membership, which has permitted it over the years to publish on a more or less regular basis its monthly newspaper *Voz Proletaria*.

At the time of the split in the world Trotskyist movement in 1953, Posadas and the Partido Obrero (Trotskista) became the Argentine members of the so-called "Pabloite" faction. However, at the time of reunification of the Pabloite and anti-Pabloite factions, the Partido Obrero (Trotskista) of Argentina did not join the new United Secretariat. Instead, Posadas led in the formation of a rival Fourth International, to which the PO(T) became affiliated and of which he became Secretary-General.

The PO(T) has held congresses and other meetings periodically. These have usually been dominated by long discourses by Posadas, larded with quotes from Lenin and Trotsky and marked by the leader's own peculiar interpretations of history and predictions for the future. Perhaps typical is a passage from a speech by Posadas at a meeting of the Political Bureau of the PO(T) on November 15, 1964: "This meeting has very great importance. Since we have not had the opportunity and possibility to have a broader meeting, it is necessary that the whole party feel the impact of the present one, because we are preparing for the development of the party, to influence coming struggles and prepare for civil war. . . . The world is going to decide in a few years for revolution. Atomic war is going to bring revolution. The revolution is going to develop long before the atomic war."[48]

The PO(T), frequently referred to as the "Posadistas," took a somewhat unique position on national politics in the wake of the fall of the Perón dictatorship. It advocated general elections in which the country's central labor organization, the Confederación General del Trabajo (CGT), would offer its own candidates. It argued that this would be a first step toward organization of a new party based on the trade unions and the CGT.[49]

However, when the Posadistas' prescription for the post-Perón period found little support in the unions or anywhere else, they participated in elections on their own in the late 1950's and early 1960's. They claimed to have received 11,000 votes in the 1958 general election, and in the provincial election in the following year claimed 28,000 votes in the province of Buenos Aires, some 9,000 in Córdoba, 9,000 in Santa Fé, and a total of 52,000 in the country as a whole. In congressional elections in 1960, the PO(T) received 28,000 in Buenos Aires province, and in the 1962 congressional and provincial poll it won 11,000 votes in the same area. The Posadistas claimed that in the same election the rival Trotskyist group, headed by Nahuel Moreno and affiliated with the faction of international Trotskyism of which the Socialist Workers Party of the U.S. was the principal national affiliate, received only 400 votes in Buenos Aires.[50]

The PO(T) had very little influence in the labor movement after the fall of Perón. Whatever trade unionists the PO(T) had were aligned with the faction of the CGT known as the Movimiento de Unidad y Coordinación Sindical (MUCS), which was generally under Communist influence. The Posadista Trotskyists were generally committed to militant and political action by the unions. Thus in mid-1959, when a strike of sugar workers in the province of Tucumán led to a general walkout of the Confederación General del Trabajo in that province, the Political Bureau of the PO(T) called for the conversion of this provincial general strike into a nationwide one "to defeat the reactionary policy of the government" of President Arturo Frondizi.[51]

From time to time, the PO(T) held national meetings attended by representatives from various provincial groups. For example, in August 1962 a three-day Enlarged Central Committee meeting was held. In addition to the regular members of the Central Committee, delegates were said to be present from the capital and from Córdoba, Rosario, Tucumán, Salta, Santiago del Estero, San Juan, and Mendoza. The representatives from the interior were reported to be "politically mature" and imbued with "optimism." The meeting adopted resolutions in favor of "a workers party of the masses based on the unions and the installation of a workers government based on the unions."[52] In June 1967 another Enlarged Central Committee meeting was held. It was reported that there were delegates present at that meeting representing nineteen regional party groups in various parts of the country. No indication was given as to how many rank and file members these delegates represented.[53]

The "line" of the Posadista Trotskyists in Argentina was clearly put forth by Posadas himself in an open letter to the PO(T) dated October 1968. Posadas argued: "In Argentina it is necessary to prepare in the next period the development of our section as the essential base of the Labor Party based on the unions, to bring together and centralize the proletarian vanguard which exists in Peronismo, in the Communist Party, in Christian Democracy, in dispersed elements of the Socialists, and to organize them for the current task of developing the revolutionary leadership and in the struggle for power, for the Workers and Peasants Government in Argentina."[54]

## CONCLUSION

Trotskyism in Argentina has never become a major factor in the country's organized labor movement, and it has been even less important in general national politics. Although Trotskyism in Argentina began with a group of workers active in the trade-union movement, the movement has usually been led by middle-class intellectuals. Throughout its forty-year history it has been split into bitterly quarreling factions, which have made it impossible for all of the Trotskyist movements to work together in competition with other political tendencies on the Argentine left.

# — 4 —

# Brazilian Trotskyism, Getulio Vargas, and Luíz Carlos Prestes

Trotskyism has always been a splinter element in Brazilian politics. However, there were a few years in the early 1930's when it did represent one of the principal tendencies in the Brazilian left. Later, like other leftist groups, it suffered from the polarization of labor and radical politics in the country between the followers of Getulio Vargas and the supporters of the Communist Party, led for a generation by the almost mystical figure of Luís Carlos Prestes.

## THE ORIGINS AND EARLY HISTORY
## OF BRAZILIAN TROTSKYISM

Trotskyism first emerged in Brazil as the result of a split in the ranks of the Young Communist organization there. The leader of the dissident group was a student who had already achieved a position of considerable importance in Communist ranks, Mario Pedrosa. He had gone to Germany to study at the Economics Faculty of the University of Berlin in 1929. There, he first became acquainted with the split in the Communist International between the Stalinists and the Trotskyists. After studying the issue for some time, he decided to side with the Trotskyists and chose not to go on to Moscow to study in the Comintern's Marx-Engels-Lenin Institute, as he had originally planned.

Instead of going to Moscow, Pedrosa proceeded to Paris, where he became associated with the magazine *Clarte*, which was then being issued by the French Trotskyists. He sent various copies of it to his friends and associates among the Brazilian Young Communists; he also wrote them detailed letters about the struggle within the International and indicated his support for Trotskyism. He won over several of them to the Trotskyist point of view, including Livio Xavier, Aristides Lobo, and Hilcar Leite.

Meanwhile, Rodolfo Coutinho, who had traveled with the Brazilian delegation to the Sixth Congress of the Communist International, held in Moscow in 1928, at which the Stalin-Trotsky feud had generally been brought to the attention of Communists outside the Soviet Union, returned home sympathetic to the Trotskyist cause and withdrew from the Communist Party.

With Coutinho, a group of dissident Young Communists soon established the first Trotskyist group in the country, the Grupo Comunista Leninista. In 1931 they rechristened their organization the Liga dos Comunistas.[1]

Soon after the establishment of this first Trotskyist organization, one of its leading members, Aristides Lobo, was sent to Buenos Aires to meet an exiled young military man, Captain Luíz Carlos Prestes. Several years before, between 1924 and 1926, Captain Prestes had been one of the principal leaders of "Prestes' Column," a group of insurgent military men who had marched through much of the interior of Brazil attempting to arouse the rural inhabitants to revolt. During this guerrilla war, Prestes acquired a fabulous reputation as a military commander and a champion of the oppressed masses of Brazil; he came to be referred to as "the cavalier of hope." Most of the column had finally taken refuge in Bolivia, and from there Prestes and some others had gone to Buenos Aires, where they continued to carry on agitation against the Brazilian regime. Lobo went there to try to convert Prestes to the Trotskyist cause.

For a while, Lobo was moderately successful. He had gone to the Argentine capital armed with an introduction from a friend of Prestes in Río de Janeiro; Prestes seems to have accepted these credentials, and for some time Lobo worked closely with him and seems to have been one of his important political advisers.

The ex-military leader at that time headed his own political group, the Revolutionary League, composed principally of refugee members of his ill-fated column. He was generally regarded, both in Brazil and among the exiles, as the principal leader of and spokesman for the "Tenentes" (lieutenants), the name given to the young military men who had mounted the rebellion of 1924 in São Paulo and Río Grande do Sul, and had later made the long march through the Brazilian interior.

Lobo argued extensively with Prestes that he should give up his separate revolutionary organization and join the Communist movement. Of course, the Trotskyites at that time claimed that they were part of the Communist movement, its left wing, and so Lobo's argument was not a strange one. Lobo hoped that if Prestes did become a Communist, he would join the Trotskyist faction.

Prestes was still an amateur politician, and he apparently welcomed Lobo's relative sophistication and his ability to write public manifestos. Several of the documents which were signed by Prestes in 1929 and 1930 were in fact written by Aristides Lobo. These included a proclamation early in 1930 announcing that Prestes was dissolving the Revolutionary League.

With the beginning of the revolution of 1930, which brought Getulio Vargas to power in Brazil, the exiles felt that the rebellion would last at least six months before it succeeded. As a result, Lobo suggested to Prestes that the exiles take advantage of the situation to launch a new Prestes column in the interior of the country. Lobo's argument was that although the extreme leftists would probably not be able to come to power through such an adventure, they would probably be able to take advantage of the confusion resulting from the fighting provoked by the Vargas Revolution to establish nuclei of Marxist-Leninist revolutionaries in key positions throughout the interior of Brazil.

Prestes at least agreed to allow Lobo to go to the Brazilian border and survey the possibilities of forming such a new guerrilla group, and so the Trotskyite leader proceeded to the border town of Sant'Anna do Livramento, in the state of Río Grande do Sul, on the Uruguayan frontier. There he became impressed with the amount of control the Vargas revolutionaries had won over Río Grande do Sul, and reached the conclusion an effort such as he had proposed could hardly produce the results he had hoped for. He therefore returned to Buenos Aires.[2]

In the meantime, the Stalinist Communists had also been very busy proselytizing Luíz Carlos Prestes. Their efforts in this direction dated from shortly after Prestes had taken refuge in Bolivia, when Astrogildo Pereira, a leading figure in the Central Committee of the Communist Party, had gone to Bolivia to interview Prestes and try to win him over to the ideas and positions of the party.[3]

Subsequently, in July 1929, Leoncio Basbaum, a member of the Central Committee, went to Buenos Aires armed with credentials from the committee and a personal letter from Mauricio Lacerda, a prominent left-wing non-Communist politician with whom Prestes had had contacts. At this time, Basbaum met not only with Prestes but also with two other leading Tenente figures, Siqueira Campos and Juarez Távora. The Communist representative proposed that Luíz Carlos Prestes be a candidate in the forthcoming elections of 1930, and suggested a program upon which the Tenentes and the Communists might unite their forces behind Prestes. However, Prestes indicated that he did not intend to run for the presidency and that in any case the proposed program was too extreme.

Basbaum became convinced that Prestes and the other Tenente leaders were thinking more in terms of insurrection than of elections. As a result, the Communist Party established a Revolutionary Military Committee, of which Basbaum was a member, to attempt to maintain contacts with the Tenentes on that level. In the meanwhile, the principal job of trying to indoctrinate Prestes and win him over to the Communist point of view was placed in the hands of the South American Secretariat of the Communist International in Montevideo.[4]

By the time Aristides Lobo returned from his visit to Sant'Anna do Livramento, he was convinced that the Stalinists had been all too successful with their courting of Prestes. He therefore decided to return to Río de Janeiro, convinced that he had failed to recruit Prestes to the Trotskyist cause.[5] His estimate of the ideological position of Luíz Carlos Prestes proved to be correct. On

March 12, 1931, Prestes issued an "open letter" in which he announced his support of the Stalinists. This document contained a violent attack on the Trotskyists, which read as follows:

> Expelled from the party, they attack its leadership in every way, acting like Aristides Lobo, who has informed the police that there are close relations between me and the South American Secretariat of the Communist International, in spite of the attacks which the party has launched in attempting to remove 'Prestismo' from its midst. Naturally, they can even less understand that I, too, am now opposed to the petty bourgeois groups and that I accept the direction of the proletariat through its class party.
>
> "Trotskyism" in Brazil is one more form by which the petty bourgeoisie attempts to mislead the working masses, sneaking into the revolutionary movement and attempting to distract the proletariat with the opportunist and reformist slogan of the "Constituent Assembly" ... which is a natural consequence of the petty-bourgeois criteria with which the same "Trotskyists" evaluated the most recent inter-imperialist quarrel, which was really only a struggle of regional bourgeois groups, one with another, and which consciously or unconsciously serves one or another of the imperialisms. They rapidly pass to social fascism, as for instance in the trade unions organized by Plinio Melo.[6]

Plinio Melo, a former member of the Río Grande do Sul state committee of the Communist Party, was another important new recruit to Brazilian Trotskyism. He had been severely persecuted by the police and had fled to Uruguay, where he had participated in a meeting of Brazilian Communist Party leaders at the headquarters of the South American Secretariat of the Communist International in Montevideo. Among those who attended this meeting were Astrogildo Pereira, who had been the first Communist Party leader to suggest trying to recruit Luíz Carlos Prestes into the party, and who had been largely instrumental in winning him over; and Octavio Brandão, who led the faction of the party leadership which was most strongly opposed to Prestes.

This meeting took place in 1930, shortly before the outbreak of the Vargas revolution. On the insistence of the Secretariat, it was decided that the party should stop blindly opposing the Vargas movement and try instead to take advantage of the revolution to advance the fortunes of the party. At the same time, it agreed to admit Luíz Carlos Prestes to membership, although denying him a position in the leadership, at least until he had become better grounded in the philosophy and line of International Communism.

Soon afterwards, Melo returned to Brazil, landing in the port of Santos, where the Communists had a small nucleus. He soon moved to São Paulo, where he joined Josias Leão, Luíz de Barros , and several other in establishing a regional committee of the party.[7]

Once the Vargas Revolution had triumphed in São Paulo, the new regional committee of the Communist Party approached the "Interventor" (appointed state governor) named by Provisional President Getulio Vargas, for permission to carry on its activities legally in the state. The petition of the Communists was favored by the fact that one of them, Luíz de Barros, was a brother of the new Interventor, popularly known as João Alberto (his family name was de Barros). João Alberto finally issued a permit, which read: "This document grants Srs. Plinio Melo, Josias Carneiro Leão, and Luíz de Barros authorization, in the name of the Partido Comunista do Brasil, to establish its headquarters, carrying on whatever work of party organization, holding elections and propaganda or doctrinary meetings, and editing whatever publications of a political character. The aforesaid Srs. have, furthermore, entire responsibility for whatever material of a subversive character is promoted by that party."[8]

However, by the time Plinio Melo and his friends had received official permission from the São Paulo representative of the Vargas government to carry on their activities legally, they were ex-Communists. They had been expelled from the Communist Party by Octavio Brandão, Astrogildo Pereira, and the other national leaders of the party, who opposed their negotiations with João Alberto. Expulsion from the Stalinist Communist Party did not curb the activities of the São Paulo group. They sought to bring together all working-class groups in the city and state, for the purpose of establishing a "dual power," a kind of Soviet. However, the Anarchists, who still had considerable influence in the local labor movement, refused to have anything to do with the move, and it came to nothing. The São Paulo Communist faction headed by Plinio Melo and his friends soon joined the Trotskyist ranks.[9]

The São Paulo recruits to Trotskyism had considerably more influence in the state than did the orthodox Stalinist Communists. This is attested to by the following comment in the August 31, 1931, issue of the International Communist publication *R.I.L.U. Magazine*:

> In the first period the revolutionary trade unions made no unofficial attempts to win the right to legal existence, not in Río and not even in São Paulo, where there were favorable opportunities for this. We have already remarked upon the practically complete absence of the GCL in the big strike movement in São Paulo [GCL was the Communists' General Confederation of Labor]. The Trotskyists and Plinioites took successful advantage of this, seizing the leadership of several trade union—not only small unions, but also such important organizations as the newly formed union of workers in the electric power stations and tramways, numbering many thousands, and the old revolutionary printers' union, which commenced to collaborate with the police on the question of introducing a Sunday rest day.
>
> At the beginning the Plinioites also gained definite influence in the São Paulo textile workers' union, which arose spontaneously on a sort of trade unionist basis. Forming a bloc with the anarcho-syndicalists, they attempted to establish a new regional trade union centre, at first under the name of the São Paulo State Trade Union Reorganization Committee, and subsequently under the auspices of the old anarchist Labour Federation of São Paulo. They intended to use this federation for a well-thought-out splitting maneuvre, directed against the revolutio-

nary trade union movement and the GCL, preparing for the convocation in March of a national congress in São Paulo, at which was to be formed a new national trade union centre.''[10]

Throughout the first years of the Vargas administration, the Trotskyists continued to be a significant element in the Brazilian left. For some time, they controlled the printing trades workers and metallurgical workers unions in both Río de Janeiro and São Paulo, and they had some influence in other labor groups.[11]

The Trotskyists suffered from many attacks by their former Communist colleagues. Years later one of these early Trotskyists, writing under the pseudonym João Matheus, commented on this persecution: ''This struggle required personal sacrifices, ideological firmness, and physical courage to face the calumnies, provocations, and fascist methods of violence practiced by the Stalinist bureaucracy, both in the public plazas and in the prisons.''[12]

One can savor the nature of the verbal attacks made on the Trotskyists by the Stalinists from the following passage written by a Brazilian Communist leader, which appeared in a Communist International publication: ''It is not yet sufficiently clearly understood by all that Trotskyism is no longer a political current inside the working class, that the Trotskyites have become gangs of spies, assassins, terrorists, and are the bitterest enemies of democracy, the people, the working class....The Trotskyist provocateurs we shall unmask and ruthlessly drive out of our organizations, demanding that they be thrown out of every working class and people's organizations.''[13]

The Trotskyists also came into conflict with a fascist group which arose in the early 1930's, the Acão Integralista Brasileira. They participated in a violent clash between the Intergralistas and various left-wing groups in São Paulo on October 7, 1934. On that day, the Integralistas planned a march through the center of São Paulo, to be led by the party's ''fuehrer,'' Plinio Salgado. A united front of labor groups was organized to combat this demonstration. The counter-demonstration was led by the anarchist Grupos Libertarios and the Federacão Operaria de São Paulo, However, three working-class political groups also cooperated, the Partido Socialista, the Partido Comunista, and the Liga Comunista Internacionalista, the name which was by that time being used by the Trotskyists. Mario Pedrosa was a member of the united front committee which planned this counter-move to the Integralistas, and was the Liga's representative. The resulting clash between the Integralistas and left-wingers resulted in the death of two policemen, three Integralistas, and a student.[14]

The Trotskyists seem at first to have opposed the formation of the Aliança Nacional Libertadora (National Liberation Alliance), which was established by virtually all left-wing groups in 1935 to oppose the Vargas regime. The Communists charged: ''The Trotskyists attempted once again to prevent the formation of the national front. They attacked the National Liberation Alliance as a Communist organization in order to frighten away from it the masses of the people who are under the influence of the national-reformist bourgeoisie.... On the other hand, they designated the leadership of the Communist Party as opportunist because they 'formed a bloc with the enemies of the working people.' With this accusation they endeavoured to split away from the National Liberation movement and from the Communist Party leadership those elements which were still influenced by the false sectarian ideas regarding the present stage of the revolution in Brazil."[15] Later, however, the Trotskyites seem to have changed their minds. One former Trotskyist informed the author that they were finally allowed to form part of the committees of the Alliance which were established in virtually all of the country's cities and towns, in spite of the opposition of the Communists.[16]

Ironically, the Communists later blamed the Trotskyites for the failure of the ANL, and particularly for its ill-fated resort to violence. Thus Fernando Lacerda wrote in *International Press Correspondence,* the Communist International's periodical: "The Trotskyites helped Vargas to split the national front and to provoke them to precipitate action like that of November 1935, in which he was able cruelly to defeat and crush the heroic fighters for the independence of our country and our people."[17]

The irony of this allegation lay in the fact that the catastrophic military uprising carried out in the name of the ANL in November 1935 was in fact organized and carried out by the Stalinist Communist Party. This is attested to by Agildo Barata, one of the Communist military men who led the uprising,[18] and by Roberto Sisson, the Secretary of the ANL, who alleged that the Communists called for the revolt against the wishes of the non-Communist officials of the Aliança.[19]

## THE TROTSKYITES DURING THE ESTADO NOVO

The Liga Comunista Internacionalista suffered along with the rest of the Brazilian left from the establishment by President Getulio Vargas of a semi-fascist dictatorship, known as the Estado Novo, in November 1937. The Trotskyist group was driven underground, many of its leaders were jailed, and some were driven into exile.[20] In the underground, the Trotskyist organization went through certain changes. Those members of the Liga Comunista Internacionalista who remained out of jail renamed their organization the Bolshevik-Leninist Group (Grupo Bolchevique-Leninista). Subsequently, they joined with a small left-oppositionist group from the Communist Party to form the Partido Leninista Operario, which was accepted as the Brazilian section of the Fourth International.[21]

Mario Pedrosa, the leading figure in the Liga Comunista Internacionalista, went abroad. He attended the founding congress of the Fourth International near Paris in September 1938. At that meeting, he was elected to the International

Executive Committee of the Trotskyist world organization, and was apparently the only Latin American representative on that body. After the founding congress of the International, he went to the United States, where he stayed for about a year. He was in the United States at the time of the first split in the ranks of the Fourth International, in 1940, when the Socialist Workers Party of the United States underwent a schism over the issue of the Soviet invasion of Finland. A majority of the SWP supported Leon Trotsky's endorsement of the Soviet invasion, but the minority led by Max Shachtman opposed Trotsky's position. The minority withdrew to form a new Workers Party. Shachtman took the issue to the International Executive Committee of the Fourth International, and one of the few non-United States members of that body who supported his position was Mario Pedrosa.[22]

In 1940 Pedrosa returned to Brazil, but his life there was harrowing, and in 1941 he fled the country again, one step ahead of the police. He returned to the United States and stayed there until 1945. During this period of residence abroad, he abandoned his belief in Trotskyism, establishing friendly relations with several leaders of the Socialist Party of the United States, the party led by Norman Thomas. When Pedrosa once again went back to Brazil in the closing months of the Vargas dictatorship, he was a democratic Socialist and wanted nothing more to do with Trotskyism.[23]

The position which Pedrosa took on the Finnish issue reflected a split which seems already to have occurred within the Brazilian Trotskyist ranks. The Partido Leninista Operario split in 1939 over the issue of whether or not the Soviet Union was a "workers' state." Pedrosa's position in the 1940 split in the Fourth International—in the process of which the Shachtmanite faction soon developed the thesis that the U.S.S.R. had ceased to be a workers' state and was governed by a new bureaucratic ruling class—reflected the stand which a faction of the Brazilian Trotskyists had already adopted. Most of those who agreed with Pedrosa's position seem to have withdrawn from the party's ranks in 1939.[24]

Meanwhile, Brazilian Trotskyism had received new recruits from the Communist Party. In 1936 a split occurred in the Communist ranks over the question of what attitude to take toward the presidential election campaign which was then beginning. One faction wanted to support José Américo, a literary figure and politician from the state of Paraíba, who was the official "government" candidate. This group was headed by Laudo Reginaldo de Rocha, known popularly as Bangú. The other faction suggested instead that the Communists launch the symbolic candidacy of Luíz Carlos Prestes, who was then in jail for his part in the November 1935 National Liberation Alliance uprising, during which he had been proclaimed "President" by the rebels.

During discussions over this issue, the group opposed to the candidacy of José Americo embraced the majority of the party's leadership. However, the Moscow headquarters of the Communist International intervened, and what had been the majority was converted into the minority by edict of the International. The opponents of the José Americo candidacy remained in control of the Communist Party's regional committee in the state of São Paulo, as well as the regional committee in the state of Parana and part of the party in Minas Gerais, Río Grande do Sul, and Pernambuco. After some months, they withdrew from or were thrown out of the Communist Party and began to move in the direction of Trotskyism. In 1937 they reorganized under the name of the Partido Socialista Revolucionario, which launched a semi-legal paper called *Orientacão Socialista*.

During the period of this split in the Communist Party, the Liga Comunista Internacionalista had little contact with the dissidents. Subsequently, the Liga (by then rechristened the Partido Leninista Operario) and the new recruits to Trotskyism sought recognition as the Brazilian affiliate of the Fourth International. Hilcar Leite, a leading figure in the PLO, participated in the Partido Socialista Revolucionario for a short while, but subsequently withdrew.[25]

The election in which José Americo was supposed to be the government's candidate did not take place, as a result of President Getulio Vargas' coup d'etat of November 10, 1937, which established the semi-fascist Estado Novo (New State). As a result of the establishment of this dictatorship, many of the leaders of the Trotskyists were arrested by the regime and were shipped to the mid-Atlantic island of Fernando de Noronha, where Vargas had established a huge political prison.[26]

After the Communist Party's Regional Committee in São Paulo split with the Stalinist party, the party it established, the Partido Socialista Revolucionario, issued a call for unity among all elements in the country sympathetic to Trotskyism. It included in this invitation the Partido Leninista Obrero, the Brazilian section of the Fourth International.[27] This meeting, labeled the First National Conference of Brazilian Fourth Internationalists, took place in August 1939. Included at the meeting, which met under "precarious conditions of illegality," were delegates of the old Partido Leninista Operario, the PSR, and "elements linked to the labor movement." It named as honorary chairman not only Leon Trotsky but also a number of the Trotskyists jailed at Fernando de Noronha.

The delegates conducted a long debate "on the international situation" and finally agreed to unite "around the program of the Fourth International." They sent greetings to Trotsky, then living in Mexico. Finally, they decided that the name of the party established at the conference would be Partido Socialista Revolucionario.[28]

For some time, at least, the Trotskyists were able to publish underground periodicals. The March 1939 issue of *Clave*, the Mexican Trotskyist publication, listed two of these, *A Luta de Classe (Class Struggle)* and *Sob Nova Bandeira (Under A New Banner)*. Subsequently, although the Trotskyites were severely persecuted—as was all of the opposition—during the Estado Novo dictatorship, they were able to publish *Class Struggle* from time to time throughout the period. Sometimes it was printed, but usually it came out in mimeographed form. However, the party never developed any real influence in the government-controlled labor movement, and it is said never to have had more than two hundred members.[29]

The effect of the persecution of the Trotskyists by the Vargas dictatorship was reflected in a letter written by "L. Rodríguez" to Liborio Justo, then a Trotskyist leader in Argentina. Rodríguez wrote: "After almost seven years of ferocious reaction, the Brazilian 'Fourth International movement' ... is now entirely anemic, and no pardons are given to those who escape or to those who succeed in returning from somber prisons, nor are they given a chance to begin their lives again. We are thus entirely fragmented, and struggling with even more difficulty since the frightful resistance of the Russians to Hitler has brought about the rebirth of a certain confidence in Stalinism."[30]

## TROTSKYISM AFTER THE ESTADO NOVO PERIOD

In 1944 the Partido Socialista Revolucionario was one of the first political groups to advocate the calling of a constitutional assembly to end the Vargas Estado Novo and establish a new regime. During the rapid disintegration of the Vargas dictatorship in the following months, the PSR took no side in the ensuing presidential election campaign. The former Trotskyists led by Mario Pedrosa threw their meager support behind the candidacy of the anti-Vargas nominee, Brigadeiro Eduardo Gomes, but the PSR refused to do so. Herminio Saccheta explained the PSR position thus: "For our part, we prefer to be internationalists and remain loyal to the class struggle. We prefer to say to those who can or wish to hear, that the Trotskyists refuse to support bourgeois candidacies for the presidency of the Republic. The class instincts of the bourgeoisie are never wrong in choosing rulers, and the rulers, no matter how 'saintly' they may be, are never more than mere executives of the political groups which support them."[31]

The Trotskyites of the Partido Socialista Revolucionario were credited by their critics on Mario Pedrosa's *Vanguarda Socialista* with having "some trade-union positions" and were said to control "posts of importance in one organization." However, these same ex-Trotskyist opponents claimed that the PSR trade unionists did not make use of the influence they did have to fight actively for the freeing of the labor movement from the stringent controls established under Estado Novo legislation.[32]

The Trotskyites were not able to extend their influence in the organized labor movement or to establish a base in general Brazilian politics. The trade unions after 1945 were almost completely dominated by the Communists and the followers of Getulio Vargas. (Vargas was once again elected President at the end of 1950; he committed suicide in August 1954 when presented with an ultimatum to resign by the military high command.) The Partido Socialista

Revolucionario apparently did not offer candidates in any elections during the 1950's, and such influence as it had was centered largely in São Paulo.

During the 1960's the Brazilian Trotskyites were divided into two different groups, which were aligned with some of the different factions into which the international Trotskyist movement was by then split. The successor to the Partido Socialista Revolucionario, the Partido Operario Revolucionario (Trotskista), was until 1963 part of the Pablo Faction, the International Secretariat of the Fourth International. After moves toward unity of the Pabloites with their opponents were started, and most Latin American affiliates broke away to form a rival International Secretariat headed by J. Posadas, the POR(T) joined the Posadista faction of international Trotskyism. The other group, aligned with the anti-Pabloites, and ultimately with the United Secretariat of the Fourth International established in 1963, was the Organizacão Revolucionaria Marxista Política Operaria, which in 1968 was converted into the Partido Operario Comunista.

## THE PARTIDO OPERARIO
## REVOLUCIONARIO (TROTSKISTA)

The Partido Operario Revolucionario (Trotskista) is reported to have held its first congress in São Paulo in February 1963. The Central Committee was established in São Paulo, and a Northeastern Regional Committee was set up in Recife. The party decided to concentrate particular attention on work in urban unions and in the peasant movement.[33] The POR(T) had some minor success in the peasant unions of the northeastern state of Pernambuco. Cynthia Hewitt describes their activities in this area as follows:

> At the extreme left of the political spectrum in Pernambuco were the Trotskyites, whose base of operations was the municipio of També. Although the Trotskyites were few in number, they were extremely vocal. *Frente Operaria*, published in Rio, attacked the church-sponsored Federation as "un orgão puramente formal, paralizado, que so intervem para conciliar, sempre gerando a revolta dos camponeses...." And the First Peasant Congress, held in També on September 7, 1963, recommended a united front of all workers in Pernambuco, a general strike, and a popular tribunal to try *patroes*. The manifesto of the Congress ended with the phrases "Nenhuma conciliacao com o governo o os patroes," and "Avante trabalhadores contra o capitalismo e o latifundio." The Trotskyites were equally as opposed to the Chinese communists as to the Russian communists. They formed alliances with no other groups and remained confined to the municipio of Tambe until October, 1963, when their sindicato was the object of intervention by the Delegado Regional do Trabalho.[34]

Miss Hewitt also noted in another article: "A small band of Trotskyites, with headquarters in the northern municipio of També, issued the most explicit denunciations of the existing social system. Their newspaper, *Frente Operaria*, published in São Paulo, spoke of the need for a popular tribunal to try those associated with 'capitalism and the latifundio.' "[35]

Trotskyite influence in the Pernambuco peasant movement had been established by Paulo Roberto Pinto (whose party name was Jeremias), a twenty-two year old member of the Central Committee and Political Bureau of the POR(T), and a former secretary-general of the printers union in Mogi dos Cruzes in the state of São Paulo. Pinto had been dispatched by the leadership of the POR(T) to work among the peasants in Pernambuco. He became secretary of the party's Regional Committee in the state, which began to issue a periodical called *Terra e Socialismo (Land and Socialism)*.

Pinto was assassinated while leading a demonstration of a group of workers of the També sindicato who were demanding of the Oriente sugar mill the payment of a year-end bonus and the establishment of a minimum wage. The POR(T) accused "a band of latifundists and gangsters" of murdering Jermias. Both the Political Bureau of the POR(T) and the International Secretariat of the Posadista Fourth International issued statements denouncing the assassination of Pinto in the latter part of 1963.[36]

The Trotskyists of the POR(T) were the smallest of the political groups which were participating in the early 1960's in the establishment of a peasant movement in northeastern Brazil. Other elements included the Peasant Leagues organized by Socialist deputy Francisco Julião, the pro-Moscow Communists of the Partido Comunista Brasileiro, the pro-Chinese Communists of the Partido Comunista do Brasil, the Catholic Church groups led by Padres Paulo Crespo and Antonio Melo, and the personal followers of President João Goulart and Pernambuco Governor Miguel Araes.

In spite of (or perhaps because of) their relatively small influence in the peasant movement of the northeast, the Trotskyists were the most extreme in their militancy. The newspaper *O Estado de São Paulo*, in its issue of August 15, 1963, noted that the POR(T) argued that "to accomplish the agrarian reform, the peasants must invade and stay on the land, defending themselves with all of the arms at their disposal.... The land must be taken by force. The rural workers must go on strike to support the occupation of lands and prevent the police from putting an end to the peasant movement. The workers must agree to hold a general strike, to occupy the sugar mills and rural properties and establish popular tribunals to kill the assassins of the people. This is the path of the agrarian revolution and of the Socialist revolution in Brazil."[37]

As a result of their extremism, the members of the POR(T) came into conflict with other political groups and with the national and state governments. We have already noted that the federal government's regional labor delegate deprived the Trotskyite-controlled union in També of its legal standing in October 1963. At the same time, three of the Trotskyist leaders in the area were arrested by the state government of Governor Miguel Araes of Pernambuco. These were Carlos Montarroyos, Aybire Sá, and Claudio Cavalcanti.

The POR(T) attempted to make a cause celebre out of the arrest of their party members in Pernambuco. They organized a meeting in Recife, which they claimed was attended by 1,000 peasants, and peasant strikers at Serinhaem were convinced to go on record in favor of the freedom of the Trotskyite peasant leaders. Whether as a result of the Trotskyites' agitation or for other reasons, Montarroyos, Sá, and Cavalcanti were released after two months in prison. The Political Bureau of the POR(T) took advantage of this event to insist once again on their extremist position with regard to the peasant movement. A statement of the Bureau, published in the party newspaper *Frente Operaria* on December 29, 1963, included the following passage: "At the moment when our comrades obtain their liberty, the Trotskyists reassert their firm disposition to maintain and apply the program and the action which brought these comrades to prison: for the occupation of lands, for the Central Peasant Organization of Pernambuco and of the nation, for the organization of peasant militia and of peasant committees on the plantations, for the Congress of Workers, Peasants, and Soldiers, and for the Regional and National Labor Confederation. Out with Lacerda! Out with Imperialism! For the Workers and Peasants' Government!"

This statement by the Political Bureau of the POR(T) indicated that the Trotskyites shared the political euphoria felt by the left at this time—the belief that revolution was about to occur and that power was about to fall into their hands. The POR(T) declaration commented that "the objectively revolutionary conditions, the immense crisis of the regime, and absolute confidence in the fighting spirit of the masses are the bases of our disposition to carry forward this struggle."

The position of the Trotskyites of the POR(T) in favor of violent action in the last months of the regime of President João Goulart is demonstrated by another article in the December 29, 1963, issue of *Frente Operaria,* entitled "In the Midst of Crises, Coups, and Civil Wars the Road is Open for the Revolutionary Way: Worker-Peasant Government." It said: "But the coup is inevitable. It is impossible to continue to govern with the parliament, and with Lacerda and Adhemar de Barros conspiring continually. If they had more force, Goulart would go immediately and would leave them in power.... But it is evident that they don't have the force or the capacity to do anything, in spite of the ostentatious support of imperialism, in spite of the protection of Goulart, in spite of everything.... The inevitability of the coup by Goulart or by another reformist, civil or military, arises from all of this. There is no other way out of the situation."

With the overthrow of the government of President João Goulart, the POR(T) was driven underground, along with all other extreme leftist groups in Brazilian politics. J. Posadas, however, called upon his colleagues in Brazil to continue their activities. Posadas indicated that he thought the party should work toward a general strike against the military government of Marshal Castelo Branco, which took over after the ouster of Goulart; but he stressed that a general strike would not be possible for some time, and suggested that the party's agitation in the labor movement should center on "elimination of legal control of unions, against the law on strikes, for the increase of wages, and democratic liberties." He also urged that the party work with Leonel Brizola, the leftist brother-in-law of Goulart, "but go much further." Posadas also warned that the POR(T) could expect attacks from the Communist Party, "which will seek to ally itself with Castelo Branco and anyone else who attempts to make any reform or concession."[38]

Sometime later the POR(T) was reported to have joined a Frente Popular de Libertacão, in a pact signed in Montevideo with the pro-Soviet and pro-Chinese Communist Parties. However, Ronald Chilcote has noted that "this alliance did not preclude POR(T) criticism of the PCB and PC do B."[39]

The POR(T) was persecuted by the police of the military dictatorship. In May 1970 Olavo Hansen, a POR(T) member and leader of the Metal Workers Union of São Paulo, was killed by the police, and a leading lawyer submitted evidence to the courts that he had been tortured extensively before being killed. At that time, seventeen other POR(T) members were reported to be in jail. The Posadista Fourth International mounted a considerable campaign on their behalf and received support from non-Trotskyists in a number of countries.[40] Late in 1970 it was reported that the Brazilian Posadista group had split, with a majority of the POR(T) breaking with the Posadas leadership.[41]

## THE POLÍTICA OPERARIA

The Trotskyite group associated with the anti-Pabloite faction of the Fourth International from the early 1960's was the Organizacão Revolucionaria Marxista Política Operaria, established in 1961. According to its own account, this group "was formed to fill a vacuum, the lack of a Marxist vanguard among us." Its self-proclaimed objective was "the formation of a revolutionary Marxist party ... a prerequisite of the Socialist revolution in the country."[42] Soon after the establishment of the Organizacão Revolucionaria Marxista Política Operaria, the group began publishing a periodical, *Política Operaria,* under the editor ship of Luís Alberto Días Lima.

The Second Congress of the Política Operaria group took place early in 1963. At that meeting they passed a number of resolutions dealing with various aspects of national and international problems. No mention of Trotskyism or of the Fourth International appeared in any of these resolutions, although they contain frequent criticisms of the Communists, particularly of the pro-Moscow Partido Comunista Brasileiro.

One of the most important theses presented at this congress of the Organizacão Revolucionaria Marxista Política Operaria dealt with the problems of organized labor. After noting that the existing system of trade-union organization had

had its origins in the corporate Estado Novo set up by Getulio Vargas during his 1937-45 dictatorship, the resolution suggested the following "immediate demands":

> Abolition of the Trade Union Fund and transfer of all of these moneys to the treasuries of the unions, federations, and confederations, in proportions to be fixed by the Central Labor Organization;
> Abolition of control over trade-union budgets by the Ministry of Labor through the Bank of Brazil. The administration of trade-union funds is the business of the trade-union organizations themselves;
> Abolition of the Commission of Trade Union Jurisdiction. The jurisdiction over crafts and industrial sectors is in the competence of the trade-union organizations;
> Abolition of the Standard Trade Union Statute elaborated by the Ministry of Labor. Trade-union statutes should be elaborated by the workers' organizations;
> Abolition of the power of recognition and dissolution of trade-union organizations by the Ministry of Labor. This power must rest exclusively with the federations, confederations, and the Central Labor Organization;
> Repeal of Decree 9070. For defense of the unlimited right to strike.[43]

At the time this resolution was adopted, there was no Central Labor Organization, and the proposal to establish one was forbidden by existing legislation on labor relations.

The Organizacão Revolucionaria Marxista Política Operaria also passed an extensive resolution with regard to the peasant movement, which was then beginning to be established in various parts of the country. This resolution commented: "The task of organizing the peasantry divides into two parts: (a) that of mass associations, where, working together with the other leftist forces, Política Operaria will attempt to restructure and expand the associations, leagues, and unions on a local plane, and orient these organisms toward integration of the federative type, crowned by a national confederation; and (b) that of party organization, which requires the creation of conditions in the countryside for the establishment of the future revolutionary Party, beginning with a systematic policy of forming Marxist-Leninist nuclei and the politicalization of the masses."[44]

Even before its Second Congress, the Política Operaria had been active in the peasant movement. There does not seem to be any evidence of its influence in the northeastern states, where the most dramatic development of the peasant movement took place, but an editorial entitled "Os Aventureiros," in *Política Operaria* for January-February 1963, notes that the group was "participating actively in the organization of the peasant movement in the south of the country." This same editorial stressed the importance which it placed on the organization of rural wage workers, as opposed to tenants, squatters, and other propertyless agriculturalists.

The political position adopted by Política Operaria placed it on the extreme left of the political spectrum of the early 1960's. It was opposed to collaborating with or supporting Goulart, in contrast to the position of the pro-Moscow Communists, Socialists, and left-wing Trabalhistas. Its position on Goulart was set forth in an article entitled "Novo Plan Cohen" in the January-February 1963 issue of *Política Operaria*. It said: "In strengthening João Goulart in the struggle against the rightist group, the reformist left commits two fundamental errors. In the first place, they leave intact the force of the rightist group, since the center only wishes to defeat it, not destroy it, as the interests of the proletariat would demand.... In the second place, the eternal idea of strengthening one group in order to defeat another always leads to its own weakening. Thus in strengthening the center the left weakens itself by permitting Jango and his helpers to turn against it.... The true role of the left at this moment is to take an independent position, strengthening itself organically and preparing the masses to combat with their own forces the strongholds of both the right and the center with its subtleties."

In this vein, the Política Operaria refused to join the campaign to restore the presidential system of government—which had been replaced by a parliamentary system in September 1961 as the price exacted by the military leaders for permitting Goulart to assume the presidency. A national plebiscite on the question was held by the government in January 1963, and the great majority of the Brazilian left enthusiastically supported restoration of the presidential system. However, *Política Operaria* of January-February 1963 carried an unsigned article entitled "The Plebiscite: A 'No' to the Left," in which its attitude was spelled out thus: "Exactly the need to stimulate development of the self-consciousness and organization of the proletariat is what brings *Política Operaria* to undertake the task of repudiating the option presented by the plebiscite.... Parliamentarianism or presidentialism in a society of oppressed and oppressors always represents the domination of the powerful, and points out the true problems of the Brazilian people. The appropriate policy of the working class today is, fundamentally, to show that there is a socialist solution for Brazil."

Instead of an alliance with such elements as João Goulart and Leonel Brizola, the principal leader of the left wing of the Partido Trabalhista, the Política Operaria sought to bring about the formation of a leftist front embracing all or most of the extreme leftist groups. It was for this reason that it supported the gubernatorial candidacy of Socialist Party (PSB) nominee Cid Franco, in the state of São Paulo, in the October 1962 elections. The October 1962 issue of *Política Operaria* argued that "the candidacy of Cid Franco was born of the attempt launched by the PSB to promote a campaign led by a front of the left, which would carry on propaganda, agitation, and organization around a socialist program which went beyond the electoral episode."[45] Throughout the rest of the Goulart period, the Política Operaria sought to bring about the formation of such a leftist front. In mid-1963 the organization issued a document entitled "Por Uma Frente da Esquerda Revolucionaria," which was directed to "all the sectors which propose the revolutionary transformation of Brazil, on the road of Socialism." This document set forth suggestions for a basic "platform of struggle," which included sections on the cost of living, trade-union autonomy and freedom, peasant demands, political freedoms, the anti-imperialist struggle, and foreign policy.[46]

It is not clear what parties the Política Operaria leaders expected to be incorporated in such a front of the revolutionary left. However, from the occasional friendly references in *Política Operaria* during 1963 to the pro-Peking Partido Comunista do Brazil and the Movimiento Revolucionario Tiradentes (a peasant-based extreme leftist group), it would seem likely that they saw these two as possible partners in such a front, together with the Socialist Party.

With the overthrow of the government of President João Goulart on April 1, 1964, Política Operaria suffered a severe blow, as did all of the Brazilian left. Regular publication of its periodicals was suspended. It would appear that it was June 1965 before *Política Operaria* began to appear once again; and although it was supposed to appear on a monthly basis, it was three months later before the next issue of the publication came out.[47] In November 1965 the Organizacão Revolucionaria Marxista Política Operaria began putting out a mimeographed bulletin, *Informe Nacional,* on a weekly basis. The fourteenth issue of this periodical, dated February 5, 1966, noted that for three months it had appeared regularly. It also noted that it was being distributed in six states, and that a separate publication was being put out by the party organization in the state of Baia. Finally, it announced that there would soon appear a monthly supplement which would go more deeply into current problems, as well as a series of monographs dealing with particular issues.[48]

The position of Política Operaria concerning the way to fight the military dictatorship established with the overthrow of João Goulart was somewhat equivocal. The group threw its support behind the candidacy of General Henrique Teixeira Lott for governor of the state of Guanabara, when he was nominated by the Social Democratic and Trabalhista Parties in August 1965. Their explanation for this attitude was that "the revolutionary left gave its support to the Lott candidacy, in spite of its conservatism and his strict legalism, exactly because this legalism has turned out to be impermissible for the dominant classes." It also argued that "if the candidacy of Lott was a banner of struggle for the masses it was exactly because it constituted a clear opposition to the regime of April."[49]

However, once the government of President Castelo Branco vetoed the candidacy of General Lott, the *Política Operaria* group refused to support the nominee put in place of Lott by the Social Democrats and Trabalhistas, and took a position in favor of a vote in blank. This was summed up in a throwaway issued by the group, which concluded: "How to confront the problem politically? Since we defend the point of view—and we are profoundly convinced of its correctness—that the militarist coup can only be overthrown by violent action of the working masses, we must know how to tailor our electoral tactics to this strategy. We cannot accept the battlefield prepared by the system and reinforce it. Since there is no candidate in Guanabara capable of mobilizing and giving consciousness to the masses under an objectively revolutionary banner, we cannot repeat the tactic of the 'lesser evil' which brought us the defeat of April. We must denounce the electoral farce, take our objectives to the masses, and call for a vote of protest."[50]

The *Política Operaria* group continued to agitate in favor of a front of the revolutionary left. In its weekly bulletin *Informe Nacional* at the end of 1966 it issued another call for such a front: "More than ever, *Política Operaria* is dedicated now to forming this front, from which could come the perspective of Marxist-revolutionary unification, as well as for the independent mobilization of the workers. The revolutionary forces which are carrying on an internal struggle in the Partido Comunista Brasileiro, the Brizolistas, the various groups of dissident revolutionary Communists, independent revolutionary elements of the labor, peasant, student movements and the clandestine movement of the noncommissioned officers and sailors, are raw material for a united front of the revolutionary left."[51]

At least a step toward unity among pro-Trotskyist groups was the establishment in April 1968 of a new party, the Partido Operario Comunista, through the merger of the Organazacão Revolucionaria Marxista Política Operaria with a group known as the Oposicão Leninista, which had broken away from the pro-Moscow Partido Comunista Brasileiro.

An article which appeared in *Informe Nacional*, the new party's periodical, on the first anniversary of the establishment of the Partido Operario Comunista, summed up what it considered the significance of the establishment of the group:

In the first place, the founding of our party was a reaffirmation of the Leninist principle of a proletarian party against both the revisionist party that was in chaos and the Debrayists who were trying to substitute 'a unified political-military command in the mountains for the party....

In the second place, the formation of the POC reflected a determination to consolidate firm and cohesive minorities instead of trying to create fictitiously broad aggregations lacking in ideological unity. We said in our call for the formation of the party that quality would produce quantity....

In the third place, the constitution of the POC expressed the victory of a concept of proletarian revolution. While the Left was immersed in a conflict between reformism and *foquismo* (the theory of the guerrilla nucleus), we held very clearly to our program of proletarian revolution and the practical consequences this program entailed....

In the fourth place, the POC held the banner of ideological struggle very high. It held high the banner of intransigent opposition to a tradition of compromising principles developed during the years of reformist deformation, a tradition that was responsible for disorienting the masses. From the universities to the factories, we kept up a campaign of agitation and propaganda for anti-capitalist struggle and proletarian hegemony, for the socialist revolution.[52]

The new party claimed that it was making particular gains in the student movement. Early in 1969 it was reported that in the student movement there had been "a decline in the influence of AP [Acão Popular, Popular Action ] and a corresponding increase in that of the opposition currents, in the CP youth and the POC."[53]

Although the POC maintained friendly relations with the Fourth International of the United Secretariat, it did not affiliate with it. As time went on, that Fourth International became increasingly critical of the Partido Operario Comunista. An article by Eduardo Pinheiro and J. Mattos, "La Gauche Revolutionaire au Brésil," in *Quatrième Internationale* of May 1971, noted that "the important weaknesses and deviations have resulted in the POC not becoming the *practical* alternative that it wished to become, and one can doubt that it had ever been or will be the *theoretical* alternative."

This same article says that the former leaders of the Política Operaria withdrew from the POC, and reformed the Política Operaria at the end of 1969. It commented: "The new leadership of the POC, the former leadership of the opposition tendency, has begun to make a balance sheet of the Brazilian revolutionary left, which is also a balance sheet of self-criticism, which is a correct method. Under the pressure of certain militants who do not hide their Trotskyist sympathies and influence, an attempt at tactical elaboration assimilating the concept of a program of transition seems to have been made. But it is clear that the political and organizational questions which would permit a development of the influence of the POC in the labor movement, which it judges to have priority, are far from being resolved."[54]

CONCLUSION

Trotskyism has consistently been a minority element within the leftist minority in Brazilian politics. Except for a few short years in the 1930's the Trotskyists have had no significant influence in organized labor. As elsewhere in Latin America, Trotskyism has been split in recent years between adherents or sympathizers of quarreling factions of the Fourth International. However, as a movement which has existed for more than forty years, Trotskyism is one of the oldest political currents in the republic. Its persistence is worthy of note, even though it has never become a major current in Brazilian public affairs.

# Chilean Trotskyism

Chilean Trotskyism began as the result of factional fighting within the ranks of the Chilean Communist Party just before and during the dictatorship of General Carlos Ibañez del Campo (1927-31). Since the South American Secretariat of the Comintern became involved early in support of one of the contending factional groups, the schism over national leadership had international repercussions from the beginning.

## THE DIVISION OF THE CHILEAN COMMUNIST PARTY

The schism within Chilean Communist ranks, which gave rise to the Trotskyist movement there, had its origins in a struggle for leadership after the death of the party's founder and first leader, Luis Emilio Recabarren, who committed suicide in December 1924. It was intensified by the persecution of the Communists by the Ibañez dictatorship.[1]

The two principal figures contending to succeed to the position of undisputed leadership which Recabarren had held were Manuel Hidalgo, a lawyer and head of the Communist Party in the region of Santiago, the national capital; and Elías Lafferte, who took over Recabarren's position as head of the Communist-controlled labor group, the Federación Obrera de Chile (FOCh). Understandably, the strength of the Hidalgo faction (which ultimately became Trotskyist) tended to be centered in the Santiago region, because of Hidalgo's importance in that area, whereas the Lafferte group (which became Stalinist) drew its strength from the copper and nitrate mining regions of the north and in the coal mining areas near Concepción some three hundred miles south of Santiago.

Hildalgo and Lafferte were very different personalities. Hidalgo was of pure Indian ancestry and was known among his friends as "El Indio"; he had been a worker and a trade-union organizer in his youth, but by the middle

1920's he was a lawyer. He had a strong personality and aroused strong loyalties among his supporters. Lafferte, by contrast, was largely self-educated, spent most of his life as a trade-union and party bureaucrat, and had a retiring personality; he was more of a prestigious figure who could serve as a rallying point for those opposed to Hidalgo's influence than a charismatic leader in his own right.

In the years between Recabarren's death and the establishment of the Ibañez dictatorship in May 1927, Hidalgo and Lafferte had more or less amicably divided the labors of leadership; Hidalgo was the Communist Party's principal political spokesman, and Lafferte directed the FOCh, which was then a major factor in the national labor movement. With the establishment of the Ibañez dictatorship, however, the FOCh was virtually destroyed and Lafferte himself was deported, along with many other Communist figures, to a mid-Pacific island prison camp. The party itself found it very difficult to function. Although Manuel Hidalgo was also exiled for a while early in the dictatorship, he was never officially removed from his post in the Senate, and this position gave him a certain immunity from persecution.

Differences of opinion had developed between Manuel Hidalgo and the South American Secretariat of the Communist International even before the full establishment of the Ibañez dictatorship. Hidalgo had urged that the headquarters of the Secretariat be transferred to Santiago, on the grounds that Chile was the most industrialized and advanced of the South American countries. However, for their own reasons, the Comintern leaders did not want to do so, and the seat of the South American Secretariat remained in Montevideo.[2]

The last open congress of the party to be held in several years (officially the party's Eighth Congress), took place in December 1926 and January 1927. A month later, even before Ibañez had formally assumed the presidency, the persecution of the Communists began. By May 1927 almost all members of the party's Central Committee had been arrested, the only ones escaping being López P., Jose R. Bascuñan, Donoso, and Iriarte. The last three of these constituted themselves a new Central Committee, which remained in control of the party's affairs until August 1928.

Thereafter, the Central Committee was reorganized once again, with the addition of people released from prison and returning from exile, owing to a temporary relaxation of rigor in the dictatorship. Among the members of this new group were Bascuñan, Galdames, Donoso, Iriarte, J. S. Zavala, and Rosas. It was this group which undertook to reorganize the structure of the party on the basis of three-member local groups, which were apparently to have no contact among themselves, and were to maintain their liaison with the rest of the party only through higher levels of the party hierarchy.[3]

This new method of organization appears to have been the first issue around which dissension arose within the Communist ranks. It provoked a conflict between the national leadership and the local committee of the party in the city of Santiago. Later, the members of the Santiago group were to describe the three-man type of party organization as "perhaps a good system for conspiracy but in no case good for giving the party the firm and strong organization which is the basis of its role as the revolutionary vanguard of the proletariat."[4]

The local committee of the Communist Party in Santiago was composed of M. Contreras, E. Torres, Humberto Mendoza, H. Godoy, M. Araya, A. González, and O. Moreno (who was later replaced by D. Barrios). It was very active, publishing a mimeographed bulletin and establishing local party units in various neighborhoods of the city. However, when it sought to extend its activities from the city into the surrounding province of Santiago, the newly enlarged Central Committee blocked these efforts, on the grounds that the local committee was opposed to the three-man unit type of organization.

In January 1929 the local committee of the Communist Party in Santiago was reorganized, with H. Godoy, G. Valdés, J. Chacón, and D. Cáceres being its members. It succeeded in establishing cells in various parts of the city until the third wave of persecution by the Ibañez government, a few months later. At this time every member of the Central Committee was arrested; two of its members, Rosas and Galdames, were turned into the police by a third, J.S. Zavala. Several of the arrested Central Committee members, led by Bascuñan, wrote a letter to President Ibañez asking for their freedom. Those who later became Trotskyists described this plea as showing "a complete lack of Communist conscience and of the most elemental obligations of the vanguard revolutionists that Communists are."[5]

Because of the arrest of the whole Central Committee, a new provisional one was formed by the party leaders in Santiago on April 20, 1929. Consisting of H. Godoy, E. Figueroa, Manuel Hidalgo, G. Valdés, and Humberto Mendoza, the new committee was recognized by the South American Secretariat of the Communist International, located in Montevideo. It sent delegations to the northern and southern parts of the republic, and "began once more the reconstruction of the party, which until that moment had not been able to make a reality of the cellular type of organization."[6]

In spite of recognition by the South American headquarters of the Comintern, the Provisional Central Committee began to have increasingly strained relations with Montevideo. Requests by the Chileans for financial aid to send delegates to Montevideo and Moscow were not acted upon; and the South American Secretariat insisted on maintaining direct contacts with local party groups in various Chilean cities, instead of dealing with them through the Central Committee in Santiago, a procedure which drew several protests from the Central Committee.

Finally, a break occured when the Central Committee sent a young comrade named Sotelo to Montevideo to inform the South American Secretariat of the activities of the Chilean party. Although he was given credentials by the Chilean Central Committee, he was not authorized to be more than an informant. However, he was sent back by the South American Secretariat with full authority to summon an "Ampleado" of the Central Committee—a meeting of Central Committee members plus leading figures from provincial organizations—to decide upon the party's future.

Meanwhile, the South American Secretariat had entered into direct contact with Bascuñan and other party leaders, who were being released from prison camp, in spite of objections of the Chilean Provisional Central Committee. As a result of these disagreements, Sotelo called together the Central Committee and announced that with full authorization of the South American Secretariat he was taking over full direction of the Chilean Communist Party, since the Provisional Central Committee no longer enjoyed the confidence of the Secretariat.

The Provisional Central Committee countered by summoning the scheduled Ampleado, without waiting for the instructions regarding time and place which were to be sent to it by the South American Secretariat. Pending the meeting of the Ampleado, the Provisional Central Committee expelled Sotelo from the party.[7]

The Ampleado of the Chilean Communist Party met in January 1930. It elected still another Central Committee, composed of H. Godoy, Humberto Mendoza, H. Figueroa, Carlos Contreras Labarca, Elías Lafferte, Maclovio Galdames, and R. Rosas, with Manuel Hidalgo, Luis Cruz, M. Araya, Braulio Leon Peña, and Luis Peña being chosen as alternate CC members. However, this new committee was unable to function because Rosas, Lafferte, and Galdames were absent and Contreras Labarca could not be located. As a result, a new meeting was held in one of the offices of the National Congress, in which Manuel Hidalgo, Luis Cruz, and M. Araya assumed the role of a new Provisional Central Committee. This new arrangement did not work either, because of the fourth persecution of the party by the Ibañez dictatorship; a new Ampleado of the party held in August 1930 resulted in the arrest of all of those participating.

Later in the year, at a meeting in Valparaíso, party members from various parts of the country elected still another Central Commitee, composed of Braulio Leon Peña, Galo González, José Vega, and Carlos Contreras Labarca. According to the Hidalgo faction, this group, which was recognized by the South American Secretariat of the Comintern, "proceeded bureaucratically in dealing with a series of problems, particularly in reference to discipline." The local committee of the party in Santiago was reorganized by the new Central Committee; it consisted of men who had not formerly served in the leadership.[8] Because of this dissidence in the leadership, and the periodical persecution of the Communists by the Ibañez regime, the ranks of the Communist Party had been much thinned by the end of the dictatorship in July 1931. The Hidalgoites reported that by that time "an enormous percentage" of old-time members were outside the party,and that the party had lost most of its influence over the masses.[9]

At the time of the calling of their first separate national congress, the Secretary-

General of the Hidalgo faction of the Chilean Communists, Jorge Lavín (the pseudonym by then adopted by Humberto Mendoza), listed eight reasons for the dispute between them and the South American Secretariat:

1. The South American Secretariat kept up constant correspondence with local party groups in spite of protests from the Central Committee.

2. The South American Secretariat refused the Central Committee the right to establish a "legal" party, which could have functioned in the open, although being controlled by the underground Communist apparatus, and gave no reasons for its refusal.

3. The Central Committee asked the Secretariat to send two members to sit as part of the Central Committee and give technical advice, but the Secretariat never did so.

4. The Secretariat sent Sotelo with full powers to discipline the Central Committee because it would not follow the bureaucratic mandates from Montevideo.

5. The Secretariat failed to maintain adequate contact; for example, it gave the Chileans notice of a Comintern meeting only ten days before the meeting was scheduled.

6. The South American Secretariat often virtually served as the Central Committee of the Chilean Party, "against all the dispositions of the program of the Comintern."

7. The methods of attesting to the authenticity of correspondence going from the Secretariat to the Chilean party, and vice versa, were confused.

8. During and after the Ibáñez dictatorship, the Secretariat refused to call a congress of the Chilean party.[10]

During this period, the principal contact between the Chilean party and the South American Secretariat in Montevideo was Rodolfo Ghioldi, one of the two principal leaders of the Argentine party. He traveled back and forth frequently, and undoubtedly had much to do with determining the policy of the South American Comintern headquarters towards its Chilean affiliate.[11]

## THE EMERGENCE OF TWO COMMUNIST PARTIES

With the end of the Ibáñez dictatorship, the schism within the Chilean Communist Party became an open split, and two rival parties were formed. At first both called themselves Partido Comunista (Sección Chilena de la Internacional Comunista).

The Central Committee which had been operating for some months with the blessings of the South American Secretariat of the Comintern met soon after the fall of Ibáñez, and expelled a number of leading members of the opposition faction. These included Manuel Hidalgo, as well as Carlos Acuña, Roberto Pinto, and various others who were to become leading figures in the

Trotskyist Communist Party. A request for reinstatement by certain expelled Communists, who had been thrown out of the party while incarcerated in a prison camp on Mas Afuera Island, was not accepted.[12] The Central Committee also refused to call a party congress, to which representatives of both factions would be invited, a move which was also being demanded by the opposition.[13]

As a result of these rebuffs, those members of the opposition who had belonged to one or another of the Central Committees of the party during the Ibáñez regime, together with the members of the local committee of Santiago, established a new Provisional Central Committee and proceeded to speak in the name of the Communist Party. Part of the statement announcing the establishment of this new body read thus:

> We stand against this policy of audacious abuses, of a dirty camarilla, and of intolerable personalism. We wish that all comrades against whom charges have been made be called to explain themselves; that punishments and measures be applied in conformity with true justice, as is appropriate for us proletarians. No one who is a true Communist runs away from his responsibilities, and those who are guilty will be energetically punished.
>
> You should know, esteemed comrade, that the party, now in our hands, will recover its initial pure impulse, and that upon taking into our hands the reorganization of our ranks, we feel ourselves equal to the responsibilities assumed, and feel ever more our Communist ideology.
>
> The moments which are approaching are of incalculable value for the success of the proletarian struggle. The need to present ourselves strongly united is imperious. At a time which we shall soon announce, the Communists will have to meet in a national conference to ascertain responsibilities and complete the organization of our ranks. There we shall give an account of all of our activities.[14]

The new Central Committee had seven members at its inception, but the number was later expanded to fifteen. Humberto Mendoza, who used the name Jorge Lavín, was named Secretary-General. It was decided that the Secretary-General of the party organization in Santiago as well as the party's members of Congress would regularly attend Central Committee meetings. Various subsidiary bodies were established by the Central Committee, including an Organization Commission, an agitprop group, and trade-union and political committees.

The new leadership undertook an energetic campaign to reestablish the party organization. Units were set up in Puente Alto, in San Bernardo, and in the capital city itself in the Santiago region; units were also formed in Viña del Mar, Quilpue, Valparaíso, Talcahuano, Talca, Antofagasta, Tocopilla, Curepto, Coquimbo, Parhuano, San Rosende, San Antonio, Llolleo, Peñaflor, and Talagante. A Communist Youth organization was also established.[15]

The new party leadership was immediatley faced with the question of what attitude to adopt toward a mutiny which occurred in the Chilean navy in September 1931. The opposition Communists formed a Revolutionary Committee of the

Workers United Front, which was joined by the Anarchists, the Renters League, "isolated labor organizations," and the Marxist Socialist Party; it sought to launch a general strike in support of the insurrection, but very few workers responded to the Committee's appeal. The party sought to organize united action with the official Laffertista Communist faction, but the Laffertistas did not respond to their overtures. In spite of this, the opposition Communists supported a demonstration organized by the Lafferte group on the Alameda in the center of Santiago, with members of the opposition Central Committee walking at the head of a column organized to participate in this meeting. This demonstration, which was organized by the Lafferte Communists against the advice of the oppositionists, was not a success, largely because the police broke up the various columns converging toward the Alameda.

An official report to a regional party congress of the opposition party in Aconcagua and Santiago summed up the opposition Communists' experience in the naval mutiny as follows: "This movement of the navy has resulted in the following experiences: lack of a base of the party in the most important zones of production (nitrates, copper, transport, the food industry, agriculture), and the concrete need to carry out the penetration of the party in the ranks of the army, navy, and carabineros."[16]

While the opposition Communists were trying to organize support for rebellious navy men in the streets, the leader of their party, Senator Manuel Hidalgo, sought to give support to the uprising in a speech in Congress. He was not given the floor, however, until September 16, after the mutiny had been suppressed. He then focused his attack on the civilians and high-ranking officers of the armed forces who had brought the Ibáñez dictatorship to power. He condemned demands that the navy mutineers be severely punished; he pointed out that the officers who had overthrown the government in September 1924 and January 1925 had been pardoned, and thus demanded that the enlisted men and junior officers involved in the September 1931 naval mutiny receive the same treatment.[17]

The naval mutiny took place during a campaign to elect a successor to the fallen dictator Carlos Ibáñez. As one of their first acts after Ibáñez' fall, the Lafferte Communists had nominated Elías Lafferte for president. The oppositionists would not accept this, however, and when they formed a separate Provisional Central Committee it nominated Manuel Hidalgo. During the election campaign the opposition Communists found their campaign for Hidalgo considerably hampered by rumors spread and published by supporters of both of the major candidates, Juan Esteban Montero and Arturo Alessandri, to the effect that Hidalgo had withdrawn from the contest.[18] It was also hindered by the state of martial law which had been proclaimed at the time of the naval mutiny and was continued during the election campaign. Under the martial law regulations, three provincial newspapers, in Illapel, Ovalle, and Mulchen, which were supporting Hidalgo's candidacy, were closed, and a sizable number of opposition Communists were jailed.[19]

Before Arturo Alessandri entered the election, some foreign observers gave Hidalgo a serious chance of being elected President. The New York *Herald Tribune* on September 6, 1931, published a United Press dispatch which said that "many observers believe that unless there is a serious rift in the ranks of the 'Left' group, Senator Hidalgo will stand a very good chance of winning the election." This dispatch discussed Hidalgo's campaign program in the following somewhat naïve terms:

His platform, adopted at the Communist party convention here a week ago, embodies principles strikingly similar to the lines on which Soviet Russia is now governed. Included in his platform are proposals for government control of house rents, a moratorium on rents of private dwellings during the depression, confiscation of public lands, the lands to be turned over to the workers to be farmed on a partnership basis, the return to Chilean Indians of land seized from them by the government, equal social and legal rights for men and women, and equal salaries for both sexes among government employees.

Senator Hidalgo told the United Press in an interview that if he were elected he would advocate having laborers farm confiscated lands, with the farmers retaining 75 per cent of the produce and giving 25 per cent to the state. Taxes on incomes of less than $45 a month should be abolished, the Communist leader said, and heavier taxes placed on people earning higher salaries.

Ill-feeling was strong between the two Communist parties. The group backed by the Comintern focused much of its attack on Manuel Hidalgo. It officially charged him with having said that "the regulatory action of the state over all the social forces reflects perfectly our Communist doctrines," and that he would not oppose "progressive" capitalist penetration in Chile. They also alleged that he had said he would die as a "Republican," and had called Carlos Ibañez "the first Republican," and had voted for the Law on the Internal Security of the State, opposing Communist orders to oppose it.[20]

A bit later, the Lafferte faction raised the slogan "Out with Hidalgo, the renegade and traitor to the working class!"; it called the party headed by Hidalgo "a bourgeois-agent in the heart of the working class,"[21] and labeled Hidalgo himself "a professional collaborator with the bourgeoisie, a professional traitor."[22]

The Hidalgoites replied with equal vigor, if not vituperation, to the Lafferte group. In its report to the first congress of the opposition Communist Party, the Hidalgoite Central Committee attacked a disastrous attempt which occurred on Christmas Eve 1931 by members of the Lafferte group to seize military barracks in Copiapó and Vallenar as an "adventurist attempt, characteristic of petty bourgeois infantile leftist mentalities." It characterized the attack as "forming part of the long series of blunders committed by Lafferteism (a faction systematically assassinating the revolution)," and as "aiding the bourgeoisie by provocative actions." It also accused the Lafferte group of killing a leading young opposition Communist, Luis López Cáceres, Secretary-General of the Central Construction Workers Committee, "and menacing others."[23]

In spite of this ill-feeling, the oppositionists supported the campaign of Elías Lafferte for the Senate in a bye election in the northern provinces of Antofagasta and Tarapacá, late in 1931. The oppositionists claimed that this gesture on their part helped them to gain sympathizers among the Lafferte followers.[24]

The struggle between the Hidalgo and Lafferte Communist factions was reflected in different policies in the labor movement. With the fall of Ibañez, the Laffertistas immediately reestablished the Federación Obrera de Chile (FOCh), which had been the Communist-controlled labor group before the Ibañez dictatorship, and of which Elías Lafferte had been Secretary-General. Lafferte, writing in the September-October 1931 issue of the Latin American Communist periodical *El Trabajador Latino Americano*, claimed that the meeting which reconstituted the FOCh was attended by delegates from the Lota and Coronel coal mines, from the nitrate pampas of Tarapacá and Antofagasta, as well as construction workers, food processing workers, and transport workers from Coquimbo, Valparaíso, Santiago, and Concepción, and agricultural workers from some provinces.

However, the opposition Communists strongly opposed the reestablishment of the Federación Obrera de Chile. In the "trade-union report" to the first congress of the Hidalgo party, Emilio Lobos commented: "The Lafferte sect did not hesitate to use the swindle of a supposed trade-union organization, as they did not hesitate later to transfer divisionism from the party to the terrain of labor organization. The bureaucracy has always looked more to its own stability than to the general interests of the workers. Before analyzing whether it was convenient to resuscitate the FOCh, before organizing a sole basic unit, they thought that they would gain control of its executive. Lafferte, returning from seclusion, presided over a meeting of less than a hundred comrades in the headquarters of the Trolley-car Workers, and established a Directive Board, including among others Contreras Labarca, Secretary-General of the Laffertistas. Thus they intensified the role of the FOCh as the anteroom of the party and made impossible any chance of its rebirth."[25]

In spite of their opposition to the reestablishment of the FOCh, many members of the opposition Communist Party helped to reestablish some basic units of the Federación. These included Roberto Pinto, Secretary-General of the Council of Unemployed Workers; Pablo López, Secretary-General of the Council of Construction Workers; and Emilio Zapata, leader of the Painters Union.

However, the Lafferte faction had no intention of sharing power with the opposition Communists within the FOCh. They indicated this in the FOCh convention in Valparaíso in September 1931, which "expelled" Manuel Hidalgo from the organization in spite of the fact that he did not claim to belong to it. A short time later, the Executive Committee of the FOCh expelled other opposition Communists, including Pablo López, Roberto Pinto, Manuel González, Francisco Martínez, Emilio Zapata, and other members of the Hidalgo group. The opposition Communists, on the other hand, took the position that it was necessary to form a new "revolutionary" central labor organization, which would group together all the unions under official Communist, opposition Communist, and Anarchist control, and which did not have official government recognition. They never succeeded in bringing about the establishment of such a group, however.

The Hidalgoites were strongest in the construction unions. In September 1931 they led construction workers to victory in a strike on government building projects in Santiago; Senator Manuel Hidalgo was the official representative of the strikers. Soon afterwards, they succeeded in establishing a Unified Construction Committee, which soon had affiliates not only in Santiago but also in nearby Puente Alto and in San Antonio, Talca, and San Bernardo. This committee published fourteen issues of a journal, eight of which appeared illegally. The Hidalgoites brought into the Committee a number of unions in which they had influence, but which were not composed of construction workers. These included groups of municipal workers in Santiago and agricultural workers in Puente Alto.[26]

## OPPOSITION COMMUNISTS AND THE "SOCIALIST REPUBLIC"

On June 4, 1932, a coup d'etat established a "Socialist Republic of Chile." This coup was carried out by part of the military with support from a number of small Socialist parties which had appeared after the fall of the Ibañez dictatorship, and help from supporters of ex-dictator Carlos Ibañez. The prime mover in the army was Colonel Marmaduque Grove, founder of the Chilean Air Force; the two most important civilian leaders of the movement were Eugenio Matte, head of the country's Masons and of the Socialist group called Nueva Acción Política, and Carlos Dávila, an Ibañista, former editor of the government newspaper *La Nación,* and a once Ambassador to the United States.

The proclamation of the new Junta del Gobierno, addressed to the people of Chile and issued the day after the coup, said in part: "The proletariat of the productive classes, the whole nation, has suffered from the effects of an economic and social regime which permitted the exploitation of labor, speculation without restraint, and the existence of irritating privileges. The increasing disorganization of the economy, the increasingly more absolute control of foreign interests, raised and managed by the plutocracy and the oligarchy, the negligence and inefficiency of the Governments, have accentuated in a tragic manner the misery of the people and the agony of the nation."[27]

In a thirty-point program the new Junta del Gobierno announced what it intended to do with power. The points included increased taxation of the rich, expropriation of all reserves of gold and foreign currency, colonization of the unemployed on state lands and unused private lands, ending of the eviction of renters by landlords, exploitation of gold mining by the state, establishment of state firms in nitrates, oil, phosphorus, tobacco, alcohol, and sugar, establishment of a government monopoly of foreign trade, improvement and extension of public education, and the establishment of a Ministry of Public Health.[28]

The attitude of the two Communist groups toward the new Socialist Republic, the effective leader of which was Colonel Marmaduque Grove, was quite different. Immediately after the coup, the Federación de Estudiantes took over the University of Chile, and Oscar Waiss, a member of the Hidalgo group, and Tómas Chadwick, then a Lafferte Communist (although he later joined the Socialist Party), became the semi-official controllers of university property. A representative of the Communist International, a Rumanian, arrived in Chile the day after the Grove revolt and met with Waiss and Pedro López, also a student Hidalguista leader; he proposed that the Hidalgo party members reenter the Communist Party and confess their errors publicly. The Hidalgoites refused.[29]

Both factions of the Communists took part in the establishment of a Revolutionary Council of Workers, Peasants, Soldiers, and Sailors, which met in a building of the university. However, the two groups wanted the Revolutionary Council to adopt different positions toward the new regime. The official Communists of Lafferte wanted it to declare open and complete opposition to the Grove government; the opposition Communists wanted the Council to give qualified support to the regime, arguing that it was good as far as it went, but that the ideas presented by the government could only be carried out if there existed a strong Communist Party. The opposition Communists also launched a seven-point program, the key item of which was a demand for the arming of the proletariat.[30]

Differences of opinion resulted in the withdrawal of the oppositionists from the Revolutionary Council, which was dominated by the Laffertistas. Thereupon the Hidalgo Communists joined with the Partido Socialista Marxista, led by Eliodoro Dominguez, to organize the Alianza Socialista Revolucionaria, which set up local groups in various parts of the country. The Alianza declared its tentative support of the Grove regime but continued to demand the arming of the country's workers.[31]

Meanwhile, the government was anxious to get both groups of Communists out of the University of Chile, and so it offered each the use of other buildings in Santiago. The coincidence that the Lafferte group was given a Methodist church building earned them the nickname of "chaplains" for some time thereafter.[32]

With the ouster of Grove and the installation of Carlos Dávila as the principal leader of the "Socialist Republic," twelve days after the first coup, the Alianza Socialista Revolucionaria, dominated by the Hidalgo Communists, launched a revolutionary general strike. This lasted for three days, during which the stoppage on the railroads was virtually complete, and many construction workers, factory employees, taxi drivers, trolley and bus drivers, bakers, and other workers participated.[33]

After the failure of the revolutionary general strike, the Hidalgo Communists were driven underground, but they continued to seek ways to participate in the country's open political life. In preparation for elections for a constitutional assembly, which the Grove regime had first proposed and the Dávila one continued to prepare for, the Hidalgo group entered into what was called the Cartel Socialista. This was an alliance of the opposition Communist Party with two of the small Socialist groups which had appeared at the end of the Ibañez regime, the Partido Socialista Unificado and the Orden Socialista.[34] Its purposes were not only to present a slate of candidates in the constitutional assembly elections but also to promote the "conspiracy which would be carried on among officers, non-commissioned officers, and revolutionary organizations."[35]

The government of Carlos Dávila was overthrown before the constitutional assembly elections were held. His ouster was followed within a few weeks by new presidential and congressional elections. The elements which had supported the Grove government rallied around his candidacy for president. Among these groups was the opposition Communist Party. In a public statement, it explained: "The C.P. does not fight in any way for the person of Grove, it fights for the unification of the proletariat and for unified revolutionary action by it, and in these moments Grove constitutes, in spite of the comrades of infantile leftism, a strong center of possible political union which may be transformed into effective revolutionary action for the seizure of power."[36]

At the same time, the opposition Communists ran candidates of their own for Congress. However, it was able to elect only two men: Manuel Hidalgo to the Senate, in a coalition with the Radical Socialist Party, and Emilio Zapata to the Chamber of Deputies, in an alliance with the Partido Socialista Unificado.[37]

By early 1933 the Hidalgo party had virtually given up all hope of bringing about the unification of all Communists in Chile. As a result, it called a national congress to establish the separate party on a permanent basis. However, it called this meeting an "amplified National Congress (Congress of Communist unification) of the Communist Party."[38]

## THE MOVEMENT OF OPPOSITION
## COMMUNISTS TO TROTSKYISM

The struggle for power within the Communist ranks in Chile drove both factions to seek allies within the international Communist movement. Quite logically, the Lafferte group, which had the support of the South American Secretariat of the Communist International, stayed with the majority which came under the control of Joseph Stalin and his associates in the leadership of the

Communist Party of the Soviet Union. With equal logic, the Hidalgo group, which constituted the opposition within Chilean Communism, allied itself with the international left opposition, headed by Leon Trotsky. But the logic behind opposing the thoroughly Stalinist Lafferte faction was not the only factor which influenced the Hidalgoites to evolve toward Trotskyism. The influence of Spanish Trotskyist literature, particularly the writings of Andrés Nin, one of the founders of Spanish Trotskyism, helped convince them of the correctness of Trotsky's analysis of the ills of the Communist International.

By the time of the first congress of the Hidalgo-led party, this alignment on an international plane was clear. The "Report and Political Thesis" offered to this congress by Jorge Norte noted the connection between what had happened in Chile and the split in the Communist International when it said: "The strident verbiage of the bureaucracy of Contreras Labarca and Company can be nothing less than a consequential reflection of erroneous direction and of an erroneous international policy which has provoked a decline in revolutionary tension."[39]

The same report adopted the Trotskyist analysis of the international situation: "The process of bureaucratic subordination based on the system of bribes and arbitrary exclusions was soon extended from the central organs of the Communist International and the Russian Communist Party to all of the sections of the International. The struggle against the CP's consequently acquired international characteristics and shapes; the struggle of factions within communism, born throughout the world from similar reasons, also acquired similar aspects, and there soon appeared face to face two Communist bands, separated theoretically, although agreeing on the revolutionary objective—these were the Communist International and its official sections, and the International Opposition, or the left wing of the Communist movement, which has sections in almost all countries and is on an accelerated road of growth."[40] The report then went on to criticize four different theoretical "deviations" of the Stalinists. These were its advocacy of "Socialism in one country," its characterization of Social Democracy as "objectively the moderate wing of Fascism," the substitution of advocacy of a "government of workers and peasants" for "the dictatorship of the proletariat," and the "adventurism" of the Communist International during its "Third Period."

Jorge Norte's analysis summed up the relevance of all this to Chile as follows: "The division of the Communist Party of Chile is nothing more than a reflection of the worldwide split, and since it developed from similar causes it must exhibit similar aspects....The conscientiously tenacious and revolutionary struggle against the bureaucracy of Contreras, Lafferte, Rosas, Chamudez, and the intellectuals and company, is the same struggle which without quarter and in spite of all obstacles sustained by opposition factions throughout the world. Only the fervent desire for unity has retarded the Party from taking this position."[41] Aligning itself firmly with the Trotskyists, this document concluded: "The official alignment with the International Communist Opposition signifies the termination of an absurd isolation which subjected the party to the greatest dangers, and the strengthening of an heroically defended position."[42]

Thus by early 1933 the Hidalgo faction of Chilean Communism had officially decided to join forces with the international Trotskyist movement. As a result, the International Communist Opposition acquired what was for the time being at least, its largest and most important party in Latin America.

## THE IZQUIERDA COMUNISTA

The first congress of the opposition Communists made several important decisions. For one thing, it voted to change the party's name from Partido Comunista to Izquierda Comunista (Communist Left). Second, it decided to affiliate with the International Left Opposition, the world Trotskyist organization. For some years thereafter it was without doubt the most influential of the Latin American affiliates of the International Left Opposition.

The Izquierda Comunista continued to have basic programmatic and ideological differences with the Chilean Stalinist Communists. One of the areas in which these differences were most obvious and important was that of the labor movement. For some years, the Trotskyist and Stalinist Communists had at least two major quarrels about trade-union policy; these concerned the attitude to be adopted toward the so-called "legal" unions, and the importance of a united labor movement.

The "legal" unions were the most important single element in organized labor after the fall of the dictatorship of General Ibañez. They had originated as a result of the laws passed in September 1924, during the crisis which finally resulted in the first overthrow of President Arturo Alessandri. One of these statutes provided for legal recognition of unions, laid down provisions for the kind of jurisdiction individual labor groups could have, and established certain controls by the Ministry of Labor over union elections and finances. This law also provided that employers could not refuse to negotiate with duly recognized unions, and that after certain procedures had been followed unions could engage in legal strikes.[43]

The labor laws passed in September 1924 were finally put into effect during the Ibañez dictatorship. Sizable numbers of unions sought and were granted legal recognition. By the time of the fall of Ibañez, there were 549 legal unions with 68,132 members. They constituted the majority of the country's organized labor movement.[44]

The different political groups which had a following among the organized workers took different attitudes toward the "legal" unions. The Anarchists and Lafferte Communists rejected the legally recognized organizations out of hand, arguing that when a workers' group obtained legal recognition it submitted to an unacceptable degree of government control. In contrast, most of the new

Socialist parties which arose after the Ibañez dictatorship turned to the workers belonging to these new organizations for the bulk of their support.

The Izquierda Comunista took a somewhat intermediary position. They were active in the predominantly ''non-legal'' unions in the construction industry, as well as among the municipal workers and other groups which were not authorized under the 1924 law to obtain legal recognition for their organizations. On the other hand, they also worked among the unions which had obtained legal sanction from the government. In 1934 they aided in the formation of the Confederación Nacional de Sindicatos Legales (CNSL), which brought together most of the legal unions. Oscar Waiss and several other Trotskyists helped write a famous speech delivered by Luis Solís Solís, the Secretary-General of the CNSL, at the First Inter-American Conference of the International Labor Organization in Santiago in 1936.[45]

There was also a strong difference of opinion for several years between the Stalinist Communists and the Izquierda Comunista concerning the issue of trade-union unity. We have already noted that one of the first acts of the Lafferte group after the fall of Ibañez was to revive the Federación Obrera de Chile, under strict Communist Party control. Likewise, we have seen that the Hidalgo faction immediately urged the establishment of a unified ''revolutionary'' central labor organization, to include union groups controlled by both Communist factions, the Socialists, and the Anarchists.

The Izquierda Comunista continued to support the idea of overall unity of the organized labor movement. This was a contributing factor in their backing of the Confederación Nacional de Sindicatos Legales. Within that group as well as in the Comité Único de la Construcción, which was under their influence, they continued to urge the unification of all Chilean unions. The Comité Único de la Construcción was one of the groups which sent delegates to the founding Congress in December 1936 of the Confederación de Trabajadores de Chile (CTCh), an organization that brought together virtually all of the country's unions except those dominated by the Anarchists, who continued to have their own Confederación General de Trabajadores.[46]

For about four years after its first congress, the Izquierda Comunista was a kind of ''third force'' on the Chilean left. During this period, Stephen Naft, who was then well informed about most Marxist groups and parties in Latin America, believed that the Izquierda Comunista was probably ''more influential'' than the Stalinist Communist Party.[47]

However, the Izquierda Comunista was by no means as important as the new Socialist Party, organized early in 1933. This party, the Partido Socialista de Chile, was established by a merger of small parties which had been established in the wake of the Ibañez dictatorship. Among these were the Partido Socialista Marxista, Orden Socialista, Partido Socialista Unificado, Partido Social Republicano, Partido Social Democrata, Nueva Acción Politica, Partido Socialista de Chile, Partido Socialista Internacional, Partido Laborista, and Acción Socialista.[48] These parties had supported the Grove regime in June of 1932. They had also rallied around Grove's candidacy for president in November of 1932, forming part of the Alianza Socialista Revolucionaria. Most of them merged with the Socialist Party when it was formed early in 1933, under the leadership of Marmaduque Grove and Eugenio Matte, who had been the two major figures in the first phase of the "Socialist Republic" of June 1932.

At the time of the establishment of the Socialist Party, the attitude of the opposition Communists toward the "Grovistas" was quite hostile. Although they had supported Grove's candidacy in the 1932 election, they did so, as we have noted earlier, largely on the grounds that the great majority of the workers were backing him, and if the opposition Communists were to influence the workers, they had to be aligned with them. A few months later, Izquierda Comunista's Secretary-General Jorge Lavín, in his political report to the party's first congress (which took place almost simultaneously with the founding congress of the Socialist Party), assessed the Grovista movement as follows: "At the present time, Grovism is tending to demonstrate what it really is, and is thus beginning to die as a movement of the masses, to be transformed into a simple means of reinforcing a particular political tendency."[49]

However, this hostility toward the Socialists was later modified. By 1935 the Izquierda Comunista joined in the formation of the Bloc de Izquierda (Left Bloc), along with the Socialists, the Partido Democrático, and the Partido Radical Socialista. This alliance proved to be a forerunner to the organization of the Popular Front.[50] Finally, in 1937, the majority of the Izquierda Comunista decided to dissolve their party and enter as a group into the Partido Socialista de Chile. There were undoubtedly several reasons for this decision. One was that the Izquierda Comunista was losing its enthusiasm for international Trotskyism, and had come to the conclusion that the Fourth International was more fictitious than real. Another was that they had concluded that there was no room on the Chilean left for a third party standing between the Communists and the Socialists, and that the masses were with these two groups. The members of Izquierda Comunista decided that if they wanted to represent a trend in politics, they could do it better within the Socialist Party than by trying to maintain their own organization.

There seems to be little indication that the entry of the Izquierda Comunista into the Socialist ranks was the result of the so-called "French turn," Trotsky's recommendation that his followers enter the Socialist parties to try to win supporters there, and if possible take them over. The Chilean Trotskyists carried out the "turn" at exactly the moment when other Trotskyist groups which had taken it—such as those in France and the United States—were abandoning the idea. Furthermore, there is little indication that the Izquierda Comunista people continued to operate as an organized and disciplined faction within the Socialist Party, as their opposite numbers did in the United States, for instance.

## THE EX-TROTSKYISTS IN THE SOCIALIST PARTY

The ex-members of the Izquierda Comunista were generally integrated into the Socialist Party. Some of them became leading figures in the party's trade-union apparatus, while others assumed positions of importance in the general leadership of the party. Manuel Hidalgo himself became the Chilean Ambassador in Mexico, as a Socialist nominee, during the Popular Front government of President Pedro Aguirre Cerda, in 1939.[51]

The entry of the Trotskyites into the Socialist Party tended to make the relations between the Socialists and the Communist Party more difficult. During the 1930's and 1940's the Communists of Chile, like their colleagues in other countries, had a virtual phobia against Trotskyism, and they strongly attacked what they thought to be the influence of the Trotskyists in the Socialist ranks. Typical was an attack in a speech by Galo González Díaz, one of the principal Communist leaders, who later became Secretary-General of that party: "The fight against Trotskyism was referred to, and he said that it is necessary to win over one by one the men of the left who are influenced by Trotskyism and to aid the Socialists to free themselves from this gangrene. He thought the struggle against these elements had been weak in Chile. 'Trotskyism has ceased to be a political current and now consists of a band of spies and assassins at the service of international fascism.' "[52]

The ex-Trotskyites played an important role in a split in the Socialist Party which took place in 1940. Under the leadership of deputy Cesar Godoy Urrutia, who had never been a Trotskyite, a sizable group broke away from the Socialist Party to establish the Partido Socialista de Trabajadores (PST). Emilio Zapata, a former member of Izquierda Comunista, became Sub-Secretary-General of the new party. Among the other important ex-Trotskyists who joined the PST were Carlos Acuña and Carlos Videla, who were Socialist members of the Executive of the Confederación de Trabajadores de Chile (CTCh) before the split, and Ramón Sepúlveda Leal, who was a member of the executive of the Santiago branch of the CTCh. All three of these trade unionists were removed from their positions in the Confederación after the formation of the PST, as a result of the cooperation of the Socialist Party and Communist members of the CTCh leadership.[53]

In spite of early attacks by the Communists on the PST, these two parties joined with the Partido Radical Socialista and the Partido Democrático to run a list of candidates in the 1941 congressional elections. Among those ex-members of the Izquierda Comunista who were on this list were Emilio Zapata, Carlos Acuña, and José Santiago.[54] Santiago ultimately rejoined the Trotskyite movement as a leader of the Partido Obrero Revolucionario. Although most of the PST leaders who had not been Trotskyites finally joined the Communist Party, the ex-Trotskyists ultimately returned to the Socialist Party. Among those who returned were Ramón Sepúlveda, Carlos Acuña and Emilio Zapata.[55] By the late 1940's, the ex-Trotskyites had lost all separate identity within the Socialist Party.

## THE PARTIDO OBRERO REVOLUCIONARIO

Although the great majority of the leaders and members of the Izquierda Comunista entered the Socialist Party, a minority did not. As the Izquierda Comunista moved increasingly away from Trotskyism, those who were still loyal to the International Left Opposition broke away to form separate organizations.

Late in 1935 the Santiago Regional Committee of the Izquierda Comunista broke with the body of the party and established a new group, the Group Bolchevique-Leninista, which declared its loyalty to the International Left Opposition. Two years later, the Grupo Bolchevique-Leninista changed its name to Partido Obrero Revolucionario and became an official affiliate of the International Left Opposition.[56] In the meantime, a second new group declaring loyalty to Trotskyism was established. This had its origins among dissident members of the Juventud Socialista, the youth group of the Socialist Party.[57] It first adopted the name Grupo Internacionalista Obrero (GIO), but in 1940 changed this to Partido Obrero Internacionalista.[58]

For some time the two new Trotskyist groups adopted quite different policies, and perhaps fought one another as much as they struggled against anti-Trotskyist elements. Their differences were evident, for instance, in the 1938 election, which brought the Popular Front to power. The POR named the Socialist leader Marmaduque Grove as their candidate for president, supporting him because they regarded him as a "working-class" representative. The GIO, on the hand, supported Pedro Aguirre Cerda, the nominee of the Popular Front. Sometimes, in spite of their enmity toward one another, the rival Trotskyist groups were able to cooperate. Thus early in 1939 the POR and the Grupo Internacionalista held a joint meeting in a small I.W.W. hall in Santiago "to commemorate those who had fallen under the Fascists' bullets." More than one hundred workers were reported to have attended this meeting.[59]

Typical of the polemics between the two groups was an attack on the GIO in the November 1939 issue of the Partido Obrero Revolucionario's periodical *Alianza Obrera*. The POR organ attacked "the authors of the policy of the so-called GIO, who first vacillated before breaking, who supported traitors like Cerda, who sold out to the reformist Masonic bureaucracy of the Socialist Party, who sustain a capitulating position of betrayal of Marxism in the face of the fascist Vanguardia Popular Socialista, and who only yesterday served as 'leftist' stooges of the rotten democracy of the Popular Front."[60]

In spite of the hostility between the two Trotskyist factions, they were finally brought together in 1941. Although the leaders of the POR had apparently been quite critical of the Fourth International headquarters in New York City, accusing it of siding with the Partido Obrero Internacionalista, the Fourth International played a key role in the unification of Chilean Trotskyism.[61]

Negotiations for unity began in 1940, and the unity convention met in Santiago in June 1941. Among those attending as fraternal delegates were Terence Phelan, representing the Fourth International, and Liborio Justo, of the Liga Obrera Revolucionaria of Argentina, who was then engaged in a polemic with Phelan. Whatever may have been the earlier attitude of the Fourth International toward the two Chilean groups claiming to be its affiliates, there seems to have been no objection on Phelan's part to the predominant position which the POR representatives had in the unity congress: the POR representatives had to admit certain ideological errors of the past; they also had to accept Partido Obrero Revolucionario as the name for the united group, and the election of Diego Henriquez, Secretary-General of the old POR, as Secretary-General of the new one.[62]

During the 1940's the Partido Obrero Revolucionario was active in the trade unions and in the general political arena. For example, in 1946 it claimed to have members in executive committees of the Unión de Obreros Municipales (Union of Municipal Workers), several construction workers' unions, the railroad workers' union in the San Bernardo marshalling yards, in the textile union of Bella Vista, and in the anarcho-syndicalist Leather Workers Federation and Printing Trades Union. They operated in the unions as "fractions" of party members and sympathizers.[63] However, Eduardo Ibarra, President of the Unión de Obreros Municipales de Chile, told the writer early in 1947 that although the Trotskyists had once been a group of considerable influence in his union, they no longer had enough strength to elect union officers on either a national or a regional level.[64]

The POR, which had about 300 members in 1946, participated in the elections of 1942 and 1946. In the presidential election of 1942, it presented its own candidate, Humberto Valenzuela, against the major nominees, Juan Antonio Ríos and Carlos Ibañez del Campo, but the number of votes he received does not seem to have been recorded. In 1945 the POR had several candidates for deputy, who in all received about 1,000 votes. No Trotskyists were elected to office.[65]

Meanwhile, the Chilean Trotskyists underwent further splits. In 1942 the Partido Obrero Revolucionario suffered a division, with a group of dissidents establishing the Liga Revolucionaria Leninista. The questions at issue seem to have been concerned more with organization than with doctrine.[66]

When this split took place, there was established a "Central Provisional Committee for the Formation of a Revolutionary Vanguard, Chilean Section of the Fourth International." This body issued a periodical, *Boletín Leninista*, which attacked the "flabby" policies of the POR and criticized the expulsion of "old militants and Fourth Internationalists." Three leaders of the POR,

Srs. Henriquez, Suarez, and Silva (the first two apparently being Diego Henriquez, former Secretary-General, and Ismael Suarez, also one of the founders of the POR), were said to be the "minority" of its executive body and were apparently the prime movers in the establishment of the dissident group.[67]

Another unification of Trotskyist forces took place in 1946. At the Fourth Ordinary Congress of the POR, held early in the year, representatives of the Liga Obrera Leninista attended and the issue of unification was taken up. The congress proposed unification on the basis "of the program and internal democracy, based on Leninist democratic centralism, of the Partido Obrero Revolucionario." The Central Committee of the Liga agreed to merge, because there were no differences in principle between the two groups, the issue of "national liberation" having been resolved in the POR's document "Nuestra Revolución." The LOL agreed to a merger if all LOL members were taken into the new organization and if it was given proportional representation in the leadership.

The POR congress responded by saying that it would accept everyone in the LOL leadership except Pedro Isla, and that his admission would be determined by the new Central Committee of the reunited POR. It also agreed that if its terms were accepted by the LOL while the POR congress was still in session, the LOL would be given representation on the new Central Committee. The Liga Obrera Leninista rejected this, after the POR congress had ended; it announced that it had no "political confidence" in the new Central Committee of the POR. However, in August 1946 the First Extraordinary Conference of the Partido Obrero Revolucionario was held, and it named a completely new Central Committee. This conference also agreed to admit all LOL members, and so the split which had dated from 1942 was healed.[68]

## THE RECENT HISTORY OF CHILEAN TROTSKYISM

By the early 1950's the Trotskyites were once again divided. One of the groups had its principal stronghold in the Municipal Workers Union, and it was in opposition to the Partido Obrero Revolucionario. In the Santiago regional congress of the Central Única de Trabajadores de Chile (the country's central labor organization) held early in 1953, the Trotskyist group in the Municipal Workers Union joined with the Anarchists and the Partido Socialista Popular to put up a "list three" of candidates for the regional executive. This bloc won four seats on that body. The Trotskyists of the Partido Obrero Revolucionario presented "list two," which failed to win any posts in the regional labor directorate.[69]

In 1957 the Partido Obrero Revolucionario called for a general reorganization of the structure of the labor movement. An article in the May 20, 1957, issue of *The Militant*, the organ of the Socialist Workers Party of the United States,

noted: "What is now of primary importance is to reorganize the workers movement. The Revolutionary Workers Party (POR ) calls for the formation of reor-
ganizing committees by trades or by industries and of inter-industry committees
of all the unions, whether they belong to the CUT or not. This process should
culminate in trade-wide and industry-wide congresses and in a general congress
of all workers which should form a powerful workers center." This article
also provided information about the Trotskyists' own work in the unions: "The
Chilean Trotskyists are fighting to establish a left wing in the trade unions
which would champion unity among the most class-conscious workers in order
to struggle against the reformists and bureaucrats in the labor movement."

At the same time, the POR was calling for the labor movement to run
its own candidate in the elections scheduled for 1958, a candidate "who comes
from the ranks of the workers' movement and is chosen by a national convention
of trade unions of workers and of farmers." The POR's advice was ignored
by the labor movement; most union leaders, who were Socialists and Communists,
supported the candidacy of Socialist Senator Salvador Allende.

During the 1960's the Chilean Trotskyites remained divided into two groups.
One of these was the Partido Obrero Revolucionario, which had been associated
with the "anti-Pablo" faction of the international Trotskyist movement, of which
the Socialist Workers Party was the leading group; after the reunification of
most of the Pabloites and most of the anti-Pablo group, it was the Chilean
representative of the new "united" international group. The other group, the
Partido Obrero Revolucionario (Trotskista), was at first part of the Pabloite
faction of international Trotskyism and later became the Chilean affiliate of
the "Posadista" Fourth International, headed by the Argentine leader J. Posadas.

The principal figure in the Partido Obrero Revolucionario was Luis Vitale.
A man of Argentine birth who had been given Chilean citizenship, he was
described by the left-wing daily *El Clarín,* in its issue of July 3, 1969, in
the following terms: "Vitale was active in the Central Única de Trabajadores
de Chile, where he was a national leader side by side with Clotario Blest.
He has written books showing considerable learning and careful historical and
sociological research."[70]

The POR joined with three other groups in 1964 to establish a new extremist
left-wing party, which seems at first to have been called the Partido Socialista
Popular, but ultimately became the Movimiento de la Izquierda Revolucionaria
(MIR). The elements joining to form this group were the Movimiento
Revolucionario Comunista, which was composed of persons who had split away
from the Communist Party; the *Polémica* group, which according to Trotskyist
sources "was made up of members who had left the organized Trotskyist movement for one reason or another and by others who had left the Communist
and Socialist parties"; and the followers of Clotario Blest, who for a decade
had been Secretary-General of the Central Única de Trabajadores de Chile,
but had been expelled from that post when he was deemed by the Communists
to be too extreme.[71]

At the beginning, the most important leaders of the MIR were Blest and Oscar Waiss. Waiss was a one-time secondary figure in the Izquierda Comunista, had joined the Socialist Party with the Izquierda Comunista, and had belonged to the Partido Socialista de Trabajadores in the early 1940's. In the 1950's he had been one of the principal figures in the Partido Socialista Popular (PSP). The PSP united in 1957 with another Socialist group to form the Partido Socialista de Chile (PSCh); Waiss was expelled from the PSCh as a result of a disagreement with its Secretary-General, Raúl Ampuero.[72]

However, these older leaders soon lost control of the Movimiento de la Izquierda Revolucionaria. The party had some influence in the student movement, winning control of the Students Federation at the University of Concepción, and it was these younger elements which took control of the party. Although Waiss continued to consider himself a member of the party, he admitted to the author in 1968 that he had no influence in the organization.[73] In 1971 he rejoined the Socialist Party.

Luis Vitale continued for some time to be one of the principal leaders of the MIR. However, because of the party's advocacy of the "violent road to power," and its terrorist activities, it frequently clashed with the authorities. In 1964 Vitale was sent away by the police to Curepto, a town of 2,000 inhabitants in the south of Chile.[74] In 1969 he was again being sought by the police and was officially deprived of his Chilean citizenship, an action which brought wide protests from the nation's press, including some relatively conservative periodicals.[75]

The MIR adopted an equivocal position toward the Popular Unity government of President Salvador Allende, which came to power as a result of the September 1970 presidential election. One element backed the new regime, and some of its members were part of the new presidential guard organized by Allende; another element was hostile toward it. Meanwhile, the Trotskyist element seems to have retained little visible influence in the organization.

The other Trotskyist group, the Partido Obrero Revolucionario (Trotskista) continued its independent existence. It had some minor influence in the organized labor movement, at least in the early 1960's. The magazine *Cuarta Internacional,* the organ of the Posadista faction of the international Trotskyist movement, reported in its issue of September 1962 that there were ten members of the party who were delegates to the Third Congress of the Central Única de Trabajadores de Chile. It named René Pérez Baz, Abel González, and Ramón Ibabaca as leading POR(T) spokesmen at this meeting; these three were representatives of the union of workers at the Huachipato steel plant. The periodical notes that during the CUTCh congress, the Political Bureau of the POR(T) "published and distributed profusely a manifesto directed to the delegates."[76]

The POR(T) supported the Allende regime. The April 1971 issue of the party newspaper *Lucha Obrera,* in commenting on the Popular Unity gains in the March municipal elections, noted that "the larger number of votes of the PS [Socialist Party] is explained by the need of important sectors of the masses to give Comrade President Allende more direct support through the party to which he belongs.'' The same article directed an appeal ''to the Communist Party and its Central Committee, and militants in general, to discuss the need for affirming in their party the revolutionary Communist positions, of pushing with all power this process in Chile of development toward a workers state, in preparing to confront the last efforts of capitalism, an inevitable process of civil war ... to deepen the methods, the policy, and the revolutionary program of which the Trotskyists of the Fourth International are a part, together with the Socialist and Communist comrades.''

The editorial on the front page of *Lucha Obrera* of the first fortnight of July 1971 called among other things for ''committees of vigilance and self-defense in each work place and neighborhood to sustain and support the revolutionary state and the popular government, and to control the economic, social, and political functioning of the country.'' It also called for establishment of ''The Single Marxist Party of the Masses,'' through a merger of Socialists, Communists, and the POR(T).


## CONCLUSION

Chile was the first country in Latin America in which the Trotskyists became a factor of some significance in national politics. The Hidalgista Partido Comunista, which in 1933 became the Izquierda Comunista, was an important force in the Chilean left for some years, but after the entry of most members and leaders of the Izquierda into the Partido Socialista de Chile in 1937, the influence of Trotskyism in Chilean politics declined sharply. Those who entered the Socialist Party ranks lost all identity as Trotskyists after a few years; those who chose to stay out of the Partido Socialista had relatively little influence in the labor movement and virtually none in national politics, and were plagued by a series of splits which did not serve to increase their general prestige or influence. By the late 1960's the Chilean Trotskyites were still sharply divided, along the lines of division of Trotskyism internationally, and although individual Trotskyists had some importance in the far-leftist Movimiento de Izquierda Revolucionaria, Trotskyism in general had virtually no significance in Chilean political life.

# — 6 —

# The Beginnings of
# Bolivian Trotskyism

Bolivia is the only country in Latin America in which Trotskyism became a major force in national politics, albeit for a very short while. In fact, Bolivia and the Asian island nation of Ceylon are the only countries on the globe in which Trotskyism has ever acquired this degree of importance. Bolivian Trotskyism is also distinctive in at least two other ways: it came into existence independently, and considerably before the founding of the Communist Party of Bolivia, as did the Ceylonese Fourth Internationalists;[1] and Bolivia is one of only two Latin American countries in which all three major contending factions of the Fourth International had affiliated groups in the late 1960's.

## TRISTÁN MAROF AND THE ORIGINS
## OF TROTSKYISM IN BOLIVIA

The first figure of major significance in Bolivian Trotskyism was Gustavo Navarro. As a young man he served in the Bolivian diplomatic corps and was stationed in Paris, where he became sympathetic with the revolutionary agitation which followed the end of World War I. He wrote his first book about this time, *El Ingenuo Continente Americano*, which advocated revolutionary changes in Latin America; as a member of the Bolivian diplomatic corps, he could not publish this work under his own name, so he chose the pseudonym "Tristán Marof."

Marof gave up his diplomatic career and returned to Bolivia in 1926. There he took the lead in organizing a Socialist Party, which although not belonging to any international group, had a general sympathy for the Soviet Union and the Comintern. The party was severely persecuted, and Marof was forced into exile in 1928. The Partido Socialista did not survive the Chaco War between Bolivia and Paraguay, which began at the end of 1932 and continued until the beginning of 1936.[2]

Marof spent most of his exile in Argentina. There he took the lead in organizing a new revolutionary group, the Grupo Tupac Amarú, in which Luis Peñaloza (later to be a founder of the Movimiento Nacionalista Revolucionario) and Alipio Valencia were also leading figures. The Grupo Tupac Amarú did not take on any clear political coloration, and maintained more or less friendly relations with both the Socialists and Communists of Argentina. It was during this period that Marof published what was probably his major work, *La Tragedia del Altiplano*.[3]

In December 1934 the Grupo Tupac Amarú joined with two other Bolivian exile groups, the Izquierda Boliviana, with headquarters in Chile, and Exilados en el Peru, composed of Bolivian refugees in Peru, to hold a congress in Córdoba, Argentina. Out of this meeting came the Partido Obrero Revolucionario (POR).[4] Among the principal figures in the POR at its inception were Tristán Marof, José Aguirre Gainsborg, Alipio Valencia, Tomás Gwarkey, Lucio Mendívil, and Ernesto Ayala Mercado.[5]

Of all of the founders of the POR, Tristán Marof was certainly the oldest and best known, and he became the group's principal spokesman. A future leader of Bolivian Trotskyism, Guillermo Lora, commented in this regard many years later that "The monstrous error of the young Aguirre was to put at the head of the new party Tristán Marof, with the strange idea of capitalizing on his prestige as a 'fearful revolutionary.' "[6]

At its founding congress, the POR decided to align itself with the International Left Opposition headed by Leon Trotsky. The principal advocate of the Trotskyist line among the founders of the party seems to have been José Aguirre Gainsborg. The congress is reported to have discussed "all Bolivian problems: mining, agrarian, the Oriente, the national political situation, party organization, etc.," and on each of these matters theses and other documents were presented, extensive discussions took place, and resolutions were adopted.[7] The Bolivian Trotskyists of the POR collaborated with some of their Argentine comrades to publish a periodical in Córdoba which they entitled *América Libre*. The editor of this review was Tristán Marof, and its first number appeared in June 1935.[8]

With the end of the Chaco War early in 1936, control of the government was seized by Colonel David Toro, who established what he called a "Socialist Republic." Some of the POR exiles, including Aguirre Gainsborg and Arze Loureiro, returned to Bolivia, where they joined the young sociologist José Antonio Arze and the economist Ricardo Anaya to form a group known as the Bloque de Izquierda Boliviana. The Bloque entered the Partido Socialista del Estado, established by Colonel Toro to support his regime. The Partido Socialista del Estado was headed by Toro's vice-president, Enrique Baldivieso, and José Tamayo, who later became a member of the Movimiento Nacionalista Revolucionario. Toro sent Arze Loureiro to Cochabamba, with adequate funds to organize a rural union in Cleza, on an estate owned by the Church. However, Aguirre Gainsborg was persecuted by the Toro regime, took refuge in the Chilean Embassy, and returned to exile in Chile.[9]

Early in 1938 Colonel Toro was overthrown by Colonel Germán Busch, one of the few Bolivian heroes of the Chaco War. With Busch's accession to power, virtually all of the exiled leaders of the POR returned home, including Tristán Marof. Soon after his arrival in Bolivia, Marof went to see President Busch. It was reported that Busch began the interview by saying "I'm not afraid of you, you know," to which Marof is said to have replied "Nor I of you, Mr. President." From then on, Busch and Marof were good friends, and Marof had considerable influence in the administration. Marof had been greeted virtually as a returning prophet by the small labor movement then existing in the country, and for the next two years he and his followers dominated the country's principal trade-union group, the Confederación Sindical de Trabajadores de Bolivia.[10]

Meanwhile, the Partido Obrero Revolucionario held its second congress, this time on Bolivian soil, in October 1938. At this meeting the first split developed within the POR, with the two factions lead by Aguirre Gainsborg and Tristán Marof. Gainsborg's position was more or less in the orthodox line of Trotskyism. He favored a tightly organized, well indoctrinated revolutionary party. The majority of the congress endorsed this position, with the result that the Trotskyist nature of the party was confirmed, and Tristán Marof was expelled from the POR.

Marof advocated the formation of a broad mass party of generally Socialist orientation, which would seek legalization and would not have official commitments to Trotskyism. According to Marof, "many years of exile" had made him and his supporters "understand that it was necessary to organize a strong Socialist Party and not place themselves in an extremist position, building in the air a theory which did not coincide with a backward society."[11]

## THE PARTIDO SOCIALISTA OBRERO DE BOLIVIA

Although expelled by the POR, Tristán Marof continued his political activities. He was elected to Congress in 1938 as an independent. Two years later he and his followers established a rival to the POR, the Partido Socialista Obrero de Bolivia (PSOB). In the year of its foundation, the PSOB succeeded in electing four deputies, including Marof, to Congress.[12]

One of the strongest Trotskyist opponents of the PSOB, Guillermo Lora, admitted that the Partido Socialista Obrero de Bolivia "was in its time a party with a large membership and succeeded in achieving national proportions."[13] One of the centers of strength for Marof and his followers was the tin miners. In August 1939, during the friendly administration of President Germán Busch, they succeeded in establishing the country's first Miners Federation at a congress in Oruro. Hernán Sánchez Fernández, a leading member of the PSOB, was the principal figure in setting up this first organization among the country's most strategic group of workers. The federation was destroyed after the death of President Busch, which occurred a few weeks after the miners' group was established.[14]

During the administration of General Enrique Peñaranda, who was elected President in 1940, the PSOB was accused of supporting this essentially conservative regime. This charge was later denied by Tristán Marof and his associates. They cited, for example, an article in the PSOB weekly paper *Batalla* of August 16, 1943, which attacked the Peñaranda government's role in the massacre of a group of miners in Catavi in the previous December. The article called the incident "the ruthless massacre of hundreds of strikers, a mass assassination, cold and barbarous, which will remain the outstanding deed of the Peñaranda government."

In this period the PSOB continued to have some influence in the organized labor movement. Thus, the Confederación Sindical de Trabajadores Bolivianos (CSTB), the nation's only central labor group, which was by then controlled by the pro-Stalinist Partido de Izquierda Revolucionaria (PIR), split during its second congress in 1942. The regional federations of Santa Cruz, Oruro, Sucre, and La Paz withdrew and formed a rival CSTB dominated by the Partido Socialista Obrero. However, by the middle of 1943 the two factions of the CSTB had reunited under PIR leadership, largely because of the hostility of the Villarroel government to both factions of the confederation.[15]

With the overthrow of Peñaranda by a coup d'etat of junior Army officers and the nationalist party, Movimiento Nacionalista Revolucionario, and the establishment of the government of Major Gualberto Villarroel, the PSOB was strongly persecuted. *La Batalla* was suppressed, and the party did not succeed in electing any members of Congress. Tristán Marof himself was said to have narrowly escaped with his life from an attack upon his house.[16]

The Villarroel government was ousted by a popular uprising and military coup d'etat on July 20, 1946, and the Partido Socialista Obrero Boliviano resumed public activity. It began to publish *Batalla* again, and it ran candidates in the December 1946 election for Congress, with Carlos Salazar, the editor of *Batalla*, and Alipio Valencia Vega as its nominees in the La Paz area.[17] Their chances of election, which the PSOB apparently believed to be good, were destroyed when the Partido Obrero Revolucionario ran opposing candidates.[18] In at least some parts of the country, PSOB candidates seem to have run on the "Proletarian Front" ticket, backed by the Movimiento Nacionalista Revolucionario and the Partido Obrero Revolucionario. One of these was Lucio Mendívil, Secretary-General of the PSOB in the Department of Pososí, who was elected senator from that part of the country. However, after the election, Mendívil appears to have abandoned the PSOB and joined the POR.[20]

The ideology of the Partido Socialista Obrero de Bolivia was somewhat imprecise. Certainly some of its members and leaders considered themselves to be Trotskyist. This was demonstrated by an article in the January 4, 1947, issue of *Batalla*, which compared "Trotskyism" and "Stalinism" to the complete advantage of the former. Trotskyism was referred to as (among other things) "the doctrine of Marx and Engels, which had its historical fulfillment on the political level with the Russian Revolution of October 1917." However, Tristán Marof himself argued that events "have repudiated the thesis of the 'fourths' (Fourth Internationalists), which do not exist solidly anywhere or have any world influence."[21] By 1947 at least, Marof had few pretensions of being a Trotskyist. He professed to see the left-wing group of the French Socialist Party led by Marceau Pivert as the nearest foreign counterpart to the PSOB.[22]

During the years following the overthrow of Villarroel, the PSOB, which Marof claimed had 2,000 members in early 1947, went out of existence. The principal reason for this was undoubtedly the fact that Tristán Marof accepted the post of private secretary to President Enrique Hertzog (elected at the beginning of 1947), who was widely regarded by workers as a representative par excellence of the traditional ruling oligarchy.[23] Alberto Cornejo reported that the PSOB was "defunct" by 1949.[24] As Guillermo Lora correctly reported some years later, the PSOB "disappeared without a trace."[25]

## THE PROGRAM AND STATUTES OF THE POR

Meanwhile, the Partido Obrero Revolucionario had become the recognized representative in Bolivia of orthodox Trotskyism. Only two months after the congress which had expelled Tristán Marof, the POR held another conference, in Cochabamba, where it adopted a program, statutes, and a series of "national theses," which came to be the basic statements of the party's political position.[26]

The POR program began with a description of the "extreme sharpening" of the "contradictions" of imperialism, which, after Lenin, it characterized as "the last stage of capitalism." The program proclaimed that "imperialism—full of internal and external contradictions—must fatally provoke a world war for a new division of the globe, and in consequence will also provoke the world proletarian revolution."[27] Within this context of the coming crisis of capitalist imperialism, the POR program proclaimed that "Bolivia has and will have its part in this process of universal dimensions." Furthermore, "The POR, the party of the revolutionary proletariat of Bolivia, must prepare itself constantly to lead the proletariat along the most just road, that is to say, along the most revolutionary road against the feudal-bourgeoisie, which has sold out to imperialism."[28]

The program goes on to note that within this revolutionary process there will be periods of progress and retreat. During the former, the POR will be called upon to lead the workers in their revolutionary mission, by helping in the organization of workers councils which will challenge the bourgeois parliament for power; and once successful the councils will set about to establish a "socialist organization of the economy," which is described as the process by which "the workers will take into their hands the affairs of the state, the direction of the mines, factories, and other enterprises seized from their exploiters, insofar as the progress of the world revolution does not push us and aid us to enter into the phase of integral socialism."[29]

The POR program argued that the revolution in Bolivia would take on special characteristics appropriate to the country's semicolonial position. The description of this as "a revolution of a combined type" is underscored in the program, by which is meant "there will be combined the democratic-bourgeois revolution—characterized by the war and an uprising of the peasants—and the proletarian socialist revolution, characterized by working-class insurrection."[30]

The Marxist-Leninist orthodoxy of the POR's position was underscored by its insistence on the primacy of the urban proletariat—this in a country in which 80 per cent of the population was composed of Indian peasants. The program phrased the idea thus: "We see then, that the principal role falls to the proletariat, which in its capacity as leader of the oppressed nation in general and of its peasant masses in particular (who today are vilely oppressed and miserably expolited by their agrarian masters) *will carry out the fundamental objectives of democracy,* while at the same time establishing its dictatorship." This position was buttressed by the statement that "the peasant either follows the worker or follows the imperialist feudal-bourgeoisie, and if we lead him along the right path he will have to follow us by force of circumstances."[31]

This insistence on the essential role of the urban proletariat in Bolivia was emphasized again in a later part of the program: "We deduce that bipartite (worker-peasant) parties are impossible because the interests of the two groups are different, because if they were the same, there would be no need for the alliance of which we have always talked and still talk, and both groups would simply fight together for the same objectives. The problems of the proletariat are found in industry and those of the serf (Indian) on the land. The resolution of the problems of the former carry with them perforce the resolution of the problems of the latter; but the resolution of the problems of the latter does not involve the resolution of the problems of the former. For this reason, the only thing which will resolve and help to resolve social problems in our day is the proletariat."[32]

The POR likewise rejected even the idea of an alliance with the national bourgeoisie. The program states: "We do not accept that argument which says that because of the oppressive and exploitative character of the imperialist yoke, the feudal-bourgeoisie is revolutionary and wants to get rid of that yoke. The feudal-bourgeoisie has always gone with financial capital.... Bolivia is a milk cow, imperialism its owner, and the native bourgeoisie the milkmaid."[33]

The POR's Trotskyist orthodoxy is shown in its endorsement of the concept of "permanent revolution." The program argued that "the triumph of the Socialist revolution in Bolivia must not and cannot terminate within our national frontiers,'' and adds that "the revolution which might begin in our country, or in other words on the national stage, will be completed on the world stage, whereupon the revolution will have become permanent (in the international sense) in that the revolution will only be consumated with the victory of the new socialist society on the whole planet."[34]

The POR program ended with an affirmation of the Leninist concept of "democratic centralism" insofar as the party's own organization was concerned. This concept was described as implying "the absolute possibility for the party to discuss, criticize, express its discontent, depose, elect; while at the same time having an iron discipline in action, directed with full powers by the elected and deposable directing organs."[35]

The statutes of the POR, adopted by the same national conference which ratified the program, began with the statement that "The POR as an organization is subject to the fundamental principles of democratic centralism of the Fourth International (without yet being a national section of this organization, becoming so only when its organic growth and political influence have increased)."[36] The statutes sketch the "Bolshevik" type of party which was provided for in the first three congresses of the Communist International, while Lenin was still alive, and before the split between Stalinists and Trotskyists. It called for the establishment of "cells" as the basic unit of party organization, with the member's type of employment rather than the area in which he lived being the preferred basis for the establishment of a cell. It also called for party members in unions to form "fractions" through which PORistas would work in an organized form within the various labor organizations. They provided for the national congress of the party, which was to meet at least once a year, to be its highest authority, and for the Central Committee to be in charge of activities between congresses. A Secretary-General was to be elected from the members of the Central Committee, to be "the member of the POR with greatest responsibility."[37]

Thus, by the end of 1938 the Bolivian Partido Obrero Revolucionario had acquired the formal characteristics of an orthodox member of the international Trotskyist movement. However, it still remained a very minor element in national politics.

## THE EARLY GROWTH OF THE POR

A few weeks after the December 1938 congress of the POR, the party suffered a severe blow. Its principal ideologist and political leader, José Aguirre Gainsborg, was killed in what Liborio Justo has called "a stupid accident."[38] With his death, leadership of the party passed into the hands of what Justo calls "petty bourgeois centrist leaders, with their headquarters in Cochabamba."[39]

For several years, the Partido Obrero Revolucionario remained a very minor force in national politics. The PSOB was a great deal more significant between 1938 and 1940; and later the Partido de Izquierda Revolucionaria (PIR), which proclaimed itself to be of "independent Marxist" persuasion but had within its ranks those elements who were loyal to Stalinism, emerged as the largest and most important of the country's left-wing parties, largely as a result of the candidacy of its chief leader, José Antonio Arze, against the government's candidate in the 1940 election, General Enrique Peñaranda. In the process of a presidential election, the PIR won in a majority of the country's principal cities, although it lost the election. The POR meanwhile remained illegal, though it published a periodical, *Pucara,* from time to time.[40]

During this early period, the Bolivian POR maintained some contact with the international Trotskyist movement, particularly through other Latin American parties of the Fourth International. It had particularly close contacts with the POR of Chile; in addition, Mario Pedrosa, a Brazilian member of the Executive Committee of the Fourth International and an exile from his own country, was resident in Bolivia for some time.[41] Bolivian Trotskyites also had contact with some dissident elements within the international Trotskyist movement. For instance, the Oruro a Liga Obrera Marxista, which proclaimed itself Trotskyist but apparently did not belong to the POR, and which had contacts with Liborio Justo, harbored a dissident Argentine Trotskyist. Likewise, the Centro Obrero Revolucionario, which was affiliated with the POR, wrote Justo for advice concerning the position it should take at a meeting of the POR to be held some time after February 1943. Justo sent a long letter of advice to the COR.[42]

During the early 1940's a new figure appeared in the leadership of the Partido Obrero Revolucionario—Guillermo Lora. Lora came from the Cochabamba area and even before going to the university he had had some contact with persons of Trotskyist persuasion. While a university student, he read the works of Leon Trotsky and became one of his fervent followers. At the same time, he carried on agitation for the POR among the tin miners, an activity which brought about his arrest in December 1942 and resulted in his exile on an island in Lake Titicaca.[43]

The mines were the first area in which the Partido Obrero Revolucionario succeeded in gaining some trade-union influence. The miners, who were the major proletarian group in Bolivia, had had virtually no union organization until the advent of the regime of Colonel Germán Busch (1937-39), when with the blessing of the government, Tristán Marof and his followers first succeeded in setting up miners' unions. In the conservative reaction following the death of Busch, the Miners Federation established in August 1939 became inactive. It was not revived until after the coup of December 1943, which brought to power the government of Major Gualberto Villarroel.

The Miners Federation was reestablished under Villarroel. In 1945 Juan

Lechín, a member of the Movimiento Nacionalista Revolucionario, and a white collar employee of Patiño Mines—who had gained wide popularity for his refusal to accept "supplements" to his salary from Patiño when he had been named Sub-Prefect of Catavi by the Villarroel government—was chosen as Executive Secretary of the Federación Sindical de Trabajadores Mineros (FSTM).[44]

It was in the next congress of the FSTM, its third, held in Catavi in March 1946, that the Trotskyists, under the leadership of Guillermo Lora, first gained public notice for their role in the miners' union. The conservative newspapers *La Razón* of La Paz and *Los Tiempos* of Cochabamba both wrote that "the Trotskyists have been the sensation and revelation of the Miners Congress."[45] The Trotskyists themselves described their role in the Third Miners Congress in the following terms: "It was the Trotskyist militants—headed by Guillermo Lora—who inflicted the greatest political defeat that the MNR has suffered, in the Third Congress of Miners in Llallagua.... The Movimientistas, accustomed to having no serious competitors, believed that this Congress, like the former ones, would allow them an easy and secure victory. They believed that with some demagogic speeches, the mass of miners would applaud them. But it did not happen that way. The Third Miners Congress was a stunning defeat for the MNR. It was enough for the Trotskyist workers to express their revolutionary opposition for the working masses to follow them, and a program of revolutionary struggle was approved, the points of which were: a wage escalator clause, a working hours escalator clause, formation of an anti-capitalist workers bloc (proletarian united front), and so on. The Minister of Labor, Monroy Boock, was defeated in a debate with Guillermo Lora, a young POR militant, who was carried out on the shoulders of the workers representatives at the Congress."[46] In spite of this glowing account by the Trotskyists, their influence in the Third Miners Congress was something less than absolute. Alberto Cornejo has noted that the meeting was under "official control," meaning the control of the Movimiento Nacionalista Revolucionario (MNR).[47]

During the period of the Villarroel regime (December 1943 until July 1946), the Partido Obrero Revolucionario generally fought against the influence of the MNR in the miners' unions. For instance, one of the throwaways distributed by the party in the mining areas attacked "all servants of the Rosca, the fascist ones of the MNR and the democratic ones of the PIR." (The term "the Rosca" was an epithet frequently used for the ruling economic and social group in Bolivia before 1952.) Labor leaders of the POR suffered some persecution during the Villarroel regime, in which the MNR had ministers part of the time. For instance, Nelson Capelino, the first PORista to achieve an official position in the Miners Federation in 1945, was jailed on several occasions. Guillermo Lora was also jailed and exiled several times under Villarroel.[48]

However, in spite of competition and hostility between elements of the POR and those of the MNR in the miners' unions, the PORistas' attitude toward Juan Lechín was substantially different from its attitude toward most of the "Movimientistas." The Trotskyists regarded Juan Lechín as being considerably to the left of most MNR trade unionists, and only occasionally during the Villarroel period were POR attacks on the MNR extended to include Lechín. Lechín had fought in the Chaco War, and during the administration of Germán Busch he had been active in the war veterans' organization, the Legión de Ex-Combatientes, which was one of the principal supporters of the Busch government and out of which later came many of the leaders of the MNR. He worked for a time for the Patiño Mines in a white collar position, and he became a star on the company's soccer team, which gained him wide recognition and popularity. In 1945 he succeeded another MNR member, Emilio Carvajal, as the top official of the Miners Federation.[49]

Although it was sometimes charged by his political opponents that Juan Lechín was a member of the Partido Obrero Revolucionario during his early years as leader of the Mine Workers Federation, there is no truth in this. Certainly, all of the Trotskyists with whom the author talked in La Paz in 1947 regarded Lechín as a Movimientista, albeit a friendly one; Lechín himself told the author that he was a Movimientista. Nevertheless, during these early years a rather special relationship was established, in spite of political differences, between the Trotskyites—particularly those active in the mining unions—and Juan Lechín; and this relationship was to have a considerable impact on the future of the Partido Obrero Revolucionario.

## THE POR AND THE PULACAYO THESIS

The relatively close relationship between the POR and Juan Lechín had an important political effect after the overthrow of the government of President Gualberto Villarroel on July 20, 1946. After that date, Bolivian politicians and parties tended to be sharply divided between the MNR and those aligned with it on the one hand, and those opposed to the MNR on the other. The two traditional parties, the Partido Liberal and the Partido Unión Republicana Socialista, together with the Stalinist-influenced Partido de Izquierda Revolucionaria and the segment of the labor movement under its control, were grouped together in the anti-MNR camp. They collaborated in the provisional government which followed the overthrow of Villarroel; and although they opposed one another in the election of January 1947, they joined once again in the government set up under the victor, President Enrique Hertzog.

The Partido Obrero Revolucionario did not join this anti-MNR group. On the contrary, a somewhat precarious and fragile alliance was established between the POR and the left-wing of the MNR—and hence to some degree with the MNR as a whole—through the vehicle of their "competitive cooperation" in the Miners Federation and in the politics of the mining regions.

The Miners Federation held an extraordinary congress in the town of Pulacayo in November 1946, less than four months after the overthrow of Villarroel. The two significant political forces represented in this congress were the MNR and the POR. Although Lechín and his associates had sufficient influence in the congress to maintain majority control of the Executive Committee of the Federation, they did agree to the adoption of what came to be known as the "Pulacayo thesis," introduced by the Trotskyite delegates, as a basic statement of the political philosophy and position of the Miners Federation.

The Pulacayo thesis was reportedly written by Guillermo Lora,[50] and is certainly a Trotskyite document in its orientation. It returned to plague Juan Lechín in later years, as one of the principal bases for the charges that he was a Trotskyist himself. However, what seems to have been the case at the Pulacayo congress was that Lechín, a man who at that point knew a good deal more about the rough and tumble of trade-union politics than he did about revolutionary ideology and political philosophy, acquiesced in allowing the PORistas, who were much more expert than he in these fields, to elaborate a document setting forth the philosophical stand of the Federación Sindical de Trabajadores Mineros.

The Pulacayo thesis began with this statement: "The proletariat, even in Bolivia, constitutes the revolutionary social class par excellence. The workers of the mines, the most advanced and combative sector of the national proletariat, define the nature of the struggle of the FSTMB."[51] It went on to describe Bolivia as "a backward capitalist country" which was "only a link in the world capitalist chain." The country was said to be characterized by having a bourgeoisie unable "to liquidate latifundia and (carry out) other pre-capitalist reforms."[52]

The Pulacayo thesis presents a simple catechism of the Marxist faith. One section reads: "The class struggle is, in the last analysis, the struggle for the appropriation of surplus value. The proletarians, who sell their labor power, struggle to do so under better conditions, and the owners of the means of production (capitalists), who struggle to continue usurping the product of unpaid labor, follow contrary objectives, which results in irreconcilable interests. We cannot close our eyes to the evidence that our struggle against the employers is a struggle to the death, because in that struggle there is at stake the destiny of private property. We cannot recognize, in the same way as our enemies, a truce in the class struggle. The present historical phase, which is a period of shame for humanity, can only be surpassed when social classes disappear, when there no longer exist exploited and exploiters."[53] The thesis concludes with a series of slogans: "War to the death against capitalism! War to the death against reformist collaborationism! By the road of the class struggle to the destruction of capitalist society!"[54]

Following the concepts of the POR's own program, the Pulacayo thesis asserts that "the proletariat of backward countries is obliged to combine the struggle for bourgeois-democratic objectives with the struggle for socialist demands." In doing so it is faced with a latifundista ruling group which has aligned itself with imperialism and has submitted the country as a whole to "imperialist domination."[55] Like the POR program, too, the Pulacayo thesis lays great stress on the leading role of the urban proletariat, and on its having "the force necessary to carry out its own objectives as well as those of other groups." It proclaims the Bolivian working class movement to be "one of the most advanced in Latin America."[56]

This same theme is continued in section two of the thesis, entitled "The Type of Revolution Which Must Be Realized." Here the thesis proclaims: "We clearly state that the revolution will be bourgeois-democratic in its objectives, and only an episode in the proletarian revolution for the social class which leads it. The proletarian revolution in Bolivia does not mean the exclusion of other exploited segments of the nation, but a revolutionary alliance of the proletariat with the peasants, the artisans, and other sectors of the petty bourgeoisie.... The dictatorship of the Proletariat is a projection of this alliance in terms of the state. The slogan of proletarian revolution and dictatorship makes clear the fact that it will be the working class which is the directing nucleus of this transformation and this state."[57]

In its exclusion of any idea of cooperation with the "national bourgeoisie" the Pulacayo thesis reflects its Trotskyist origins. These roots are also demonstrated clearly in the statement that "the workers once in power cannot remain indefinitely within bourgeois-democratic limits, and will find themselves obliged, each day more urgently, to invade always more profoundly the regime of private property, and in this way the revolution will acquire a permanent character."[58]

The Pulacayo thesis goes on with a series of so-called "transitory demands." These include the demand for a "basic living wage and escalator wage clause," including the elimination of low-priced company stores; a "forty-hour week and escalator working time clause"; a policy of sit-in strikes in the mines; collective instead of individual contracts; and trade unionism independent of the government.

The final sections of the thesis call for union participation in elections and the formation of a parliamentary bloc of workers' representatives; and they propose the establishment of a "proletarian united front," to consist of "the revolutionary elements which identify with our fundamental declarations, and proletarian organizations such as those of the railroaders, factory workers, printing tradesmen, chauffeurs, and so on." They also call for the formation of a new central labor organization, to take the place of the Confederación Sindical de Trabajadores Bolivianos, which they argue is dominated by artisans and reformists. Finally, the thesis calls for a revolutionary alliance of the mine workers and peasants.[59]

## POR-MNR COLLABORATION IN
## THE POST-VILLARROEL PERIOD

During the immediate post-Villarroel period, there was extensive cooperation between the Partido Obrero Revolucionario and the Movimento Nacionalista Revolucionario in both the electoral and trade-union fields. In the predominantly mining areas the two parties supported joint lists of candidates, with the result that the mining bloc elected two senators and seven members of the Chamber of Deputies in the January 1947 election. The two senators were Lucio Mendívil of the POR and Juan Lechín of the MNR; the deputies consisted of four Movimientistas and three members of the POR, including Guillermo Lora.[60]

The trade unionists of the two parties also collaborated in an attempt during 1947 to establish a new central labor organization as a competitor to the Confederación Sindical de Trabajadores Bolivianos, which was controlled by the pro-Stalinist Partido de Izquierda Revolucionaria. They established the Central Obrera Nacional (CON), to which affiliated the Federación Sindical de Trabajadores Mineros and the Unión de Fabriles, the organization to which most factory workers unions were affiliated. The CON also had among its members a group of peasant unions under the control of the MNR.[61] Some unions affiliated with the CSTB were reported to have retired from that organization to join the CON, including local federations in Cochabamba and Sucre and printing trades unions in La Paz and Oruro.[62]

In the years that followed, both the MNR and the POR were severely persecuted by the governments of Presidents Hertzog and Mamerto Urriolagoitia (who succeeded Hertzog when he fell ill and resigned). They cooperated in early 1949 in a virtual insurrection in the mining camps of Siglo XX and Catavi. Likewise, the POR appears to have supported the MNR in a civil war it launched late in 1949; this movement succeeded for a time in gaining control of Cochabamba, Potosí, Sucre, and Santa Cruz, but was ultimately defeated by the Army.[63]

The Trotskyists also played a significant role in a general strike which took place under predomiantly MNR leadership in May 1950. Edwin Moller has described this strike as a "rehearsal" for the April 9, 1952, revolution. PORista trade unionists, including Moller, were an important element in an Emergency Committee which was set up by a group of the smaller unions, including the bank clerks, commercial and industrial white collar workers, and printing trades workers. It was this Emergency Committee which finally spurred the much larger Coordinating Committee, which included most of the country's unions, into taking strike action which was openly intended to bring down the government (though it failed to do so).[64]

## PERSECUTION OF THE PNR AND POR IN THE SEXENIO

Guillermo Lora himself has described the nature of effects of the government's persecution of the MNR during the 1946-52 period, which came to be known as the "Sexenio." He has noted: "The Sexenio signified the martyrology of the MNR and from it there arose its idols and its caudillos. The stupidity and the abuses of the authorities contributed to creating the legend of an invincible MNR. No one can deny that the history of the Movimiento of this period is fascinating, since it is full of incredible sacrifices and the human quality of many heroes.... Contrary to what was expected, this ruthless persecution marked by useless terror was one of the fundamental causes which contributed to converting the MNR—the defeated, disorganized, and almost disbanded party—into the undoubted leader of the opposition. The excesses of repression contributed also to make the MNR appear as the revolutionary party par excellence and as the one nearest to power."[65]

The POR found its principal enemy in the Partido de Izquierda Revolucionaria (PIR), which contained the country's Stalinists, and which was in the government during much of the Sexenio. In its congress of October 1947, the PIR stressed the need "to unmask the Trotsky-Movimiento agitators who, in seeming to carry on an anti-employer struggle in favor of the mine workers, seek only favorable slogans." The PIR also noted that among the factory workers, particularly in La Paz, there had been "Trotsky-Movimientista proselytism," and that "the Trotsky-Movimientistas have succeeded also in taking advantage of the discontent of the Indians against landlordism to bring about uprisings or participate in them." Finally, argued the PIR, "with regard to the POR, our party cannot take any other position than that of the most irreconcilable antagonism," because the POR "misleads the workers with illusory prescriptions for social revolution, unrealizable from the sociological-historical point of view." The party's resolution declared that "the PIR is the most solid guarantee against the subversive attempts of the Trotsky-Movimientistas."[66]

In spite of persecution, the POR was able to hold its eighth national congress in March 1951. This meeting decided to run Trotskyist candidates in the elections scheduled for May of the same year.[67] However, there were no Trotskyist candidates for president or vice-president in this election; the POR apparently supported Víctor Paz Estenssoro and Hernán Siles, the MNR nominees, who won a plurality if not a majority, thus precipitating the establishment of a military government under General Hugo Ballivián, a few days after the elections.

The Eighth Congress of the POR voted to continue the tactic of seeking to establish "a united front of all working-class organizations." It also was reported to have adopted "a strong resolution of support for the oppressed Korean people in their revolutionary struggle," and to have voted to back "the Yugoslav workers against both 'Wall Street and the Kremlin,' " but to have "criticized the foreign policy of the Yugoslav government."[68]

## REASONS FOR POR FAILURE TO ASSUME LEFT LEADERSHIP IN THE SEXENIO

In the alliance between the POR and the MNR during the Sexenio, the POR remained the junior partner. The reasons for this puzzled the Trotskyites and their friends, both inside Bolivia and abroad. For instance, the Argentine ex-Trotskyite Liborio Justo has asked: "How and why had the MNR returned, displacing the POR from the direction of affairs, when it appeared that the latter was destined finally to give a revolutionary way out to the workers of the high plateau, which had followed fruitlessly the banners of other parties?"[69]

We have already noted the importance of the martyrdom of the MNR during these years in rehabilitating its prestige among the workers and the lower middle class. But there were a number of other factors which contributed to the fact that the MNR rather than the POR emerged from the Sexenio as the major mass party of Bolivia.

Guillermo Lora, who during this period emerged as the POR's principal leader, attributed the failure of the POR to assume the major role in the revolutionary struggle against the conservative regime in power after 1946 to the party's inability to build an organization which was equal to the opportunities afforded it. Lora noted that the events of the Villarroel period, and immediately thereafter, had brought about a growth of the party which was "fantastic and exceptional" and "permitted it to become a mass party." However, this rapid growth "could not help but aggravate and put in relief our organizational weakness. Internally, there continued to be applied the norms learned in a reading club, or in the best of cases, in a propaganda circle.... A chasm yawned between the goals of the party and its primitive work methods. This was a typical case of growing pains. Exceptionally favorable circumstances had placed us at the head of the masses.... We were converted into a powerful party, but in spite of all this, organizationally we had many of the characteristics of a circle of friends. The most intelligent of the Bolivian youth entered the POR. We had a magnificent group of agitators, many of whom believed that their mission consisted also in theorizing. But we lacked and still lack organizers."[70] Lora indicates more precisely what he considered the weakness of the POR, in this period, from an organizational point of view: "The penetration of the masses was not accompanied by the formation of cells in factories or in streets, and their labor was confined to the propagation of revolutionary principles ... whereas the extreme weakness of the party was expressed in its rudimentary organization."[71]

Another reason for the subordinate position of the POR in the MNR-POR relationship seems to have been the secondary role which the Trotskyists assigned themselves during this period. The Bolivian correspondent of the dissident Trotskyist newspaper *Labor Action* of New York City, Juan Rey, discussed this issue thus: "In the Internal Bulletin of the Fourth International Secretariat, we read a proud confirmation of the Bolivian POR's policy of supporting the Nationalists and Peronism. One of the old militants of the POR told us, likewise with pride, that the MNR *has offered two ministries* to the POR. The Internal Bulletin stated that the POR will proclaim the 'creation of the workers' and peasants' government formed by the two parties (the MNR and POR), based on the aforesaid program (of the POR) and supported by the workers' committees, peasants' committees, and the revolutionary elements of the petty bourgeoisie of the cities.' "

Juan Rey also noted the POR's theoretical justification for its subordinate relationship with the MNR. He writes: "Behind this policy is its corresponding 'theory': 'The program of the revolutionary party,' the Internal Bulletin says, 'must be built by a combination of the anti-imperialists, anti-capitalists, and democratic and Nationalist spokesmen,' and 'this broad conception of the program must be manifested practically by participation and activity, without any sectarianism, in all organizations and all movements of the masses which can express, even if indirectly, the aspirations and feelings of the masses.' "

The implications of this line of the Bolivian Trotskyites are spelled out by Juan Rey. He notes that they supported the efforts of the Peronistas of Argentina to establish a hemispheric trade-union group, in opposition to the Confederación de Trabajadores de América Latina (CTAL), which was controlled by the Communists, and the Organización Regional Interamericana de Trabajadores (ORIT), to which the AFL and CIO were affiliated. Juan Rey notes that the leaders of the POR were "backing the Peronist Congress of Workers Unions; this outfit was organized by Perón's agents in Asunción, Paraguay, with the aim of winning the support of Latin American workers to Perón, not only against 'Yankee imperialism' but also against his own Argentine opposition, that is, the workers' opposition in Argentina.... The Bolivian 'official Trotskyists' uncritically support the move by the Peronistas and greet it as the 'process of the unification of the Latin American workers'; they assert that it is breaking out of the 'narrow aims of the Peronist bureaucrats' and that it is at bottom an 'anti-capitalist and anti-Stalinist movement!'"[72]

Most important of all in determining the secondary position of the POR vis-à-vis the MNR by the end of the Sexenio was undoubtedly the fact that the MNR had both a program and a history which was more adjusted to the realities of Bolivian politics at that time than did the POR. The MNR advocated a program of nationalism and basic economic and social reform which could appeal to wide segments of the population. By the end of the Sexenio, it had come out strongly in favor of expropriating the Big Three tin mining companies, so as to put the industry which was the source of most of the country's foreign exchange in the hands of the nation; a policy which was supported not only by the mine workers and other trade unionists, but also by large segments of the middle classes. It also advocated a thorough agrarian reform, which potentially at least would rally the support of the landless peasants who made up the substantial majority of the population.

Unlike the POR, whose ideas and program were embedded in Marxism-Leninism-Trotskyism, with their emphasis on the primacy of the proletariat and the vanguard role of the POR itself within the urban working class, the MNR did not make a one-class or exclusivist appeal. On the contrary, it was frankly a multiclass party, seeking to unite the interests of urban workers, the peasantry, and sizable segments of the middle class. In contrast to the POR, which sought to get the peasantry and middle class to help implant a "dictatorship of the proletariat," which would function primarily in the interests of the urban workers, and would have the avowed objective of abolishing not only the private property of the "oligarchs" but that of the small farmers and merchants as well, the MNR promised a regime which would seek to conciliate the interests of those elements which made up the great majority of the population.

Furthermore, the experience which the MNR had gained in the government of President Villarroel had already indicated the direction an MNR regime would be likely to take. MNR members of his government had taken the first steps toward establishing a nationwide organization of the Indian peasantry and toward seeking to find out and deal with the grievances of this majority group.

As a result of the events of the Sexenio, as a former PORista commented, "It was not the POR which became the leader of the proletariat, but the MNR, nourished by a numerous middle class, which adjusted its slogans of struggle to the anxieties of the masses."[73]

# —7—

# Trotskyism and the
# Bolivian National Revolution

Between April 9 and 11, 1952, the Movimiento Nacionalista Revolucionario seized power. Armed workers with the support of the military police, the carabineros, overcame the resistance of the Army in La Paz. In the mining town such as Oruro and Potosí, miners armed with dynamite seized control in the name of the revolution.

The revolutionary movement was led on the spot by Hernán Siles, who had been the MNR candidate for Vice-President of the Republic in the May 1951 election, and Juan Lechín, the leader of the Miners Federation. Upon the victory of the revolution, Siles and Lechín declared Víctor Paz Estenssoro to be Constitutional President of the Republic, in conformity with the MNR's claim that it had won the 1951 election. Paz Estenssoro returned from exile in Argentina at the end of April.[1]

General Antonio Selemé, head of the carabineros and first choice to be head of the new government, had taken refuge in the Chilean Embassy during the fighting, when he thought that the insurrection was lost, and thus forfeited his leadership of the movement; because of this, and because of the total defeat of the Army, the April 1952 revolution put power completely in the hands of the MNR. To strengthen its position the MNR government dissolved the existing Army (which was not reconstituted until more than a year after the April 1952 events) and distributed the military's weapons to the MNR working-class and peasant supporters.

In the years that followed April 9, 1952, the MNR government brought about fundamental changes in the economy, society, and political life of Bolivia. Among its other accomplishments, it gave the vote to all illiterates, meaning principally the Indian peasants; distributed most of the country's agricultural land among the Indians; nationalized the Big Three mining companies; launched a major economic development program in the eastern part of the country; and politicized the hitherto apathetic rural masses to a degree never before known.

128

Most of its accomplishments were irreversible by the time it was forced out of office again in November 1964.[2]

## THE ATTITUDE OF POR TO THE APRIL 1952 REVOLUTION

The Partido Obrero Revolucionario supported the Bolivian National Revolution from the beginning. The New York Trotskyite newspaper *The Militant* reported: "The Revolutionary Workers Party (POR), Bolivian section of the Fourth International, issued a declaration calling for participation in the revolution, investing it with a program expressing the aspirations of all the people: nationalization, wage increases, etc. The members of the POR played a leading role on the barricades which they transformed into centers of armed resistance and into forums for revolutionary propaganda. To be sure, control over the masses was exercised completely by the MNR, with whom the masses identified themselves, but the political action of the POR had the effect of further radicalizing these masses by setting concrete objectives of struggle before them."[3]

More details on PORista participation in the events of April 9-11, 1952, were given by Juan Rey, the South American correspondent of *Labor Action*, a dissident Trotskyist publication in New York City. Rey wrote: "The Bolivian POR (Trotskyists) supported the MNR; the militants of the POR fought under the leadership of the nationalists, in Lechín's groups on the streets, as this writer was able to see personally. They fought in the hope that the MNR would start the democratic revolution in Bolivia and that 'then we (the POR) will come.' "[4]

The POR undoubtedly sought to take advantage of the revolution to advance its own interests. However, there seems to have been some considerable disagreement within the party concerning the nature of its support of the new MNR regime, and how far this support should go. Guillermo Lora has written: "Immediately after the 9th of April there arose within the POR a series of misguided theories. Some maintained that the MNR had practically come to occupy the position of the POR as the proletarian vanguard; others insinuated that the POR was only a branch of the MNR and that its role was to support in unconditionally, avoiding all criticisms.... All these theories were the product of desperation and of fear."[5]

Those outside of the POR recognized that there was a certain difference of opinion among the Trotskyites with regard to the position they ought to adopt toward the MNR government. In an interview with the author on August 14, 1952, Juan Lechín noted that the POR had no influence in the government but that it was working with the MNR trade unionists in the new COB (Central Obrera Boliviana, Bolivian Central Labor Union), and that the general attitude of the PORistas seemed to be one of cooperation with the new regime. But he added that he did not think all the Trotskyites favored such cooperation.

In spite of whatever dissidence may have existed within the ranks of the POR, the general attitude of the party in the first months of the Bolivian National Revolution seemed to be roughly that of the Bolshevik Party in Russia between March and November 1917. They gave "critical support" to the MNR government, defending it against the opponents from the right, but thought of themselves as more or less inevitably destined to take over control of the revolution from the "petty bourgeois" MNR.

This attitude was expressed soon after the April 9 uprising by Guillermo Lora. He was in Europe at the time, after escaping from jail in Bolivia some months before the revolution. Interviewed by the French Trotskyist paper *La Verité*, he expressed support for the movement. He then added: "In reality, the MNR is a petty bourgeois party which bases itself on the organizations of the masses. We do not believe at all that it can fulfill the fundamental task of the bourgeois democratic revolution (destruction of large landed property and national liberation) and our program states that these tasks are the tasks of the proletarian revolution in the present stage. The daily struggle now allows us to forge a common front with all the exploited of all political tendencies, among them the MNR. Our aim is to liberate the workers from their petty bourgeois leadership. We do not believe this can be done by slander and falsification."[6]

Lora went on to explain that "the essential mission of the POR is to assume the role of a vigilant guide to prevent the aspirations of the workers from being diluted by vague promises or by maneuvers of right-wing elements." He ended his interview by saying that "today, far from succumbing to the hysteria of a struggle against the MNR, whom the pro-imperialists have dubbed 'fascists,' we are marching with the masses to make the April 9th movement the prelude to the triumph of the workers' and peasants' government."[7]

The same line of argument was given to the writer in La Paz in August 1952 by Jorge Salazar, former manager of the Railroad Workers Social Security Fund, who was then a leading figure in the POR. He argued that the "normal and natural" evolution of the revolution would be for the POR to grow rapidly and join with left-wing elements of the MNR to convert the revolution into a "proletarian" one.[8]

Soon after the April 9 insurrection, the POR published an eleven-point "program of the exploited," which stated its position vis-à-vis the revolution at that time. The program was set forth thus:

1. Prevent the strangling of the April 9 revolution within a bourgeois and bureaucratic framework.
2. Strengthening of the working class, consolidation of the COB, [Central Obrera Boliviana].
3. Mobilization of the peasants under the slogan of nationalization of the land and expropriation of the latifundia without indemnization, to permit the revolutionary process to culminate in victory.
4. Conquest of democratic guarantees for the exploited. Development of the

unions within trade-union democracy. Freedom of propaganda for the revolutionary parties. Cancellation of all privileges of the counter-revolutionary 'rosca.'

5. Armed workers militia as a substitute for the regular army.

6. Better conditions of life and labor. Basic living wage with an escalator clause. Collective contracts.

7. Nationalization of mines and railroads, without indemnization and with workers control.

8. Expulsion of imperialism. Repudiation of all international treaties which submit the country to imperialism. Rejection of the agreement for technical aid with the U.N.

9. General amnesty for all workers and peasants jailed for trade-union activities.

10. Workers control of the YPFB [government oil firm] and the San José mine.

11. Strengthening of the POR, as the inevitable condition for the victory of the revolution.[9]

In one of the first issues of the POR paper in which this "program of the exploited" appeared, there was an editorial entitled "What Revolution?" Its last paragraph emphasized the attitude of the POR toward the national revolution which we have been stressing: "The events which have had the virtue of arousing the masses demonstrate that democracy for them cannot exist within bourgeois-democratic limits—there is neither time nor material possibility for this democracy to be realized—and it will come in the form of the dictatorship of the proletariat, supported by the peasants and the most exploited sectors of the petty bourgeoisie of the cities."[10]

The Trotskyites tended to look upon the new central labor organization established a few days after the victory of the revolution, the Central Obrera Boliviana (COB), as the Bolivian equivalent of the Soviets of the Russian Revolution. Guillermo Lora made this clear when he wrote, some years later: "The birth of the COB demonstrated that the proletariat, through its daily activity, was marching toward state control....One could not apply to the COB the traditional concept of trade unionism. In the first stage of the revolution, under pressure of circumstances, it broke out of the framework of purely trade union concerns and brashly entered the political sphere....In the first months of the revolution, the COB had armed forces, the militia of the workers and peasants."[11]

The Trotskyites' equation of the COB with the Russian Soviets of 1917 was demonstrated in the August 5, 1952, issue of *Lucha Obrera*, the party paper. It discussed the announcement of the intention to hold under COB auspices "the first national congress of Bolivian workers and peasants." *Lucha Obrera* commented: "We say to the workers: Vigilance! Expropriate your revolution from the hands of those who have promised you to expropriate the expropriators! The National Labor Congress is the road that will lead you to avoid all violations of your interests. The Workers' Parliament, or the General Congress of the Toilers, will be a reality, as will the Workers and Peasants Government, provided that the three million workers, peasants, soldiers, and layers of the exploited petty bourgeoisie decide to put an end to a society of exploitation and misery.''[12]

While thus tending to picture themselves as playing the role of Bolsheviks to Víctor Paz Estenssoro's Kerensky, the PORistas sought to encourage what they conceived to be fissions within both the MNR and the government. Guillermo Lora stressed these divisions in his interview with *La Verité*. There he commented that the POR ''supports the left-wing faction of the new cabinet,'' and went on to say that ''the Paz Estenssoro government, dominated by its reactionary wing, shows all the characteristc features of 'Bonapartism,' operating between the proletariat and imperialism. The declarations of the new president leave no doubt as to his decision to capitulate to the Yankees and to win their confidence by presenting himself as the only one capable of controlling the masses. One cannot exclude the possibility that the right wing, faced with the sharpening of the mass struggle against it, will ally itself with imperialism in order to crush the so-called 'communist' danger.''[13]

Typical, too, of this hope of profiting from divisions within the MNR was an article in the June 12, 1952, issue of the POR newspaper *Lucha Obrera*, entitled ''Prisoner of the Palace,'' which commented: ''It should not surprise anyone, least of all members of the Cabinet, to know that [different] tendencies exist and are clearly definable: the left represented by Lechín, Butrón, and Chávez; the center characterized by Paz Estenssoro and some others; and the right headed by Guevara, Siles, Barrenechea, and others, who have until now directed the acts of the government.''

This attempt to encourage and exploit dissidence within the victorious MNR was undoubtedly one of the tactical mistakes made by the POR during the early months of the revolution. Prisoners of their own doctrinal conviction that a left, right, and center *must* exist, and that the left *must* associate itself in short order with the ''real'' revolutionaries congregated in the POR, the Trotskyist leaders greatly underestimated the loyalty to the MNR of the left-wing MNR leaders, including Lechín, Germán Butrón, and the ex-Trotskyite Ñuflo Chávez. Although difference of opinion did exist within the MNR leadership (in a few years they were to come out into the open, violently), during the early months of the revolution all factions, including the left-wing MNR labor leaders, were anxious to play down these differences; certainly the left-wingers had no intention of having their disagreements with other Movimientistas play into the hands of a rival party, the POR. The net result, within a few months of the April 1952 uprising, was to bring about a split in the POR rather than within the MNR.


## THE POR AND THE LABOR MOVEMENT


Some substance seemed to be given to the PORistas' belief that they would ultimately ''inherit'' the Bolivian National Revolution from the MNR because of the role they played in the labor movement during the first few months of the revolution. They emerged from the events of April 9-11 with considerably more influence in the unions than they had had previously.

The POR claimed to control the Unión de Fabriles, the organization of factory workers in La Paz. A member of the party was president of the group right after the revolution, and although he was expelled from the POR soon thereafter, the Trotskyites continued to control a number of the affiliates of the Unión de Fabriles for some time. It also controlled the Federación de Empleados Particulares, the union of white collar workers, and continued to have considerable influence in a number of the important mine workers local unions. Finally, the POR had considerable power in the new provincial Peasants Federation organized in Cochabamba soon after April 9.[14] The party also succeeded in capturing control of the Cochabamba Departmental Federation of Labor, which had been part of the Confederación Sindical de Trabajadores Bolivianos (CSTB), dominated by the pro-Stalinist Partido de Izquierda Revolucionaria, and promptly switched its affiliation from the CSTB to the new Central Obrera Boliviana.[15]

The Trotskyites also played a very important role in the Central Obrera Boliviana (COB), the new central labor organization established immediately after the victory of the revolution. Edwin Moller, a leader of the Federación de Empleados Particulares and the principal trade-union figure of the POR in this period, was chosen as a member of the first Executive Committee of the POR. At the same time, José Zegada, who had belonged to the POR until 1951, was chosen Recording Secretary of the COB and editor of its newspaper, *Rebelión*. In the first issue of the newspaper, on May 1, 1952, a special tribute was paid to Guillermo Lora, who was praised as "an authentic hero of our aspirations."[16]

However, Trotskyite influence in the Central Obrera Boliviana went far beyond the minority representation in the COB Executive. POR influence was secured in these early months in large part as a result of the peculiar manner in which delegates to the organization were selected. The COB held meetings once a week, or even more often. As a result, it was virtually impossible for provincial organizations affiliated with the COB to send regular delegates from their own membership to these meetings. The COB therefore adopted a procedure by which provincial affiliates could select permanent delegates to the COB from among people who were resident in La Paz.

During the first months after the revolution, the POR succeeded in having many provincial groups choose PORistas as their permanent delegates to the COB. The Trotskyites were thus represented in the central labor organization out of all proportion to their membership or actual influence in the country's trade unions. Juan Rey reported in *Labor Action* of October 27, 1952, that within the COB "the largest fraction is that of the POR; next comes the group of Lechín and Torres, that is, the nationalist wing of the unions; and the Stalinists are in third place with scarcely five votes."

This importance of the Trotskyists in the COB was facilitated by the fact that the principal leaders of the COB were preoccupied with activities elsewhere and had little time to devote to the COB. The main officers of the organization were the Executive Secretary, Juan Lechín; the Secretary-General, Germán Butrón; and Mario Torres, Secretary of Public Relations, all Movimientistas. However, after April 11, Juan Lechín was Minister of Mines and Petroleum, Germán Butrón was Minister of Labor, and Mario Torres was the effective head of the Mine Workers Federation.

The result of this situation, for the first six months the COB was practically in the hands of the Trotskyists. This fact was particularly serious because during the first Paz Estenssoro administration the revolutionary government was officially a "bipartisan" regime, in which the organized labor movement was recognized as having the right to name three representatives in the government along with others chosen officially by the MNR. In the first months of the revolution, these ministers were Juan Lechín, Germán Butrón, and Ñuflo Chávez, the Minister of Peasant Affairs. In theory at least, although all three of these men belonged to the MNR, they were responsible to the COB, and upon its demand could be forced to withdraw from the cabinet.

On various occasions during the first months of the Revolution, the Trotskyists used their control of the COB to put it into more or less open conflict with the government and the MNR. At one point, they put the COB on record as demanding the resignation of the labor ministers from the cabinet, as a result of which "the government of Paz Estenssoro then solemnly promised to nationalize the mines, and the Central Obrera authorized the 'labor ministers' to stay in the cabinet."

On another occasion, the COB organ *Rebelión* published a document entitled "The Ideological Position of the Bolivian Working Class," which was certainly influenced by the ideology of the POR rather than by that of the MNR. For example: "The Bolivian revolution must have the character of a combined revolution—bourgeois-democratic in its immediate objectives and socialist in its uninterrupted results. It is quite impossible to separate the two phases of the revolution; that means the workers in power must not halt at bourgeois-democratic limits but must strike ever more deeply at the rights of private property, going over to socialist methods and in this way giving the revolution a permanent character."

The publication of this document provoked a group of MNR leaders to publish a "Manifesto Against Communism," whereupon President Paz Estenssoro announced that no political statement could be made in the name of the MNR except by its Political Committee, consisting of Paz Estenssoro, Hernán Siles, and Julio Álvarez Plata. At the same time, Juan Lechín announced that the statement published in *Rebelión* was "only a private draft and not a definitive program and that such a definitive program would be adopted by the workers congress in January.'' Juan Rey reported that ''thus the conflict between the government and the Central Obrera was smoothed over this time.''[17]

The anomalous situation in the COB finally caused a crisis for the government in October 1952, and brought a showdown between the MNR and the POR. At that time, the Paz Estenssoro government was about to issue its decree nationalizing the property of the three major tin mining companies, Patiño, Aramayo, and Hochschild, and providing (in vague but unequivocal terms) that the companies would be compensated ultimately for what was being taken from them. This ran completely counter to the Trotskyist demand that the mines be confiscated, with the companies receiving no compensation.

The PORistas used their control of the COB to publish in the COB's name an ''Open Letter to President Víctor Paz Estenssoro'' on the mining issue. The result of the letter, which Juan Rey described as ''calling for nationalization without compensation, and workers' control and administration,'' was that ''A session of the Central was thereupon organized with a strong turnout by the nationalists (who ordinarily do not participate in the sessions); and at this meeting they revoked and condemned the position on nationalization. . . . They then formed a new commission to draw up a new open letter to the president, with a nationalist majority on it.'' Rey summed up the incident by saying that ''the government, with the help of Lechín, has administered a setback to the POR fraction in the Central Obrera.''[18]

The degree to which the POR had lost out in the COB was shown a few weeks later, when the POR faction introduced a motion to direct the labor ministers once again to resign for the cabinet. According to Juan Rey, ''Lechín, Butrón, and Chávez (the peasant minister) have consolidated support for their policy as against the POR's attack, and with the support of the Stalinists of the PIR and the CP have conquered a majority of 23 against 4 in favor of their participation in the government.''[19]

What had happened was that the MNR trade unionists no longer took the COB for granted. Lechín, Butrón, and Chávez began attending all of its meetings. They had also persuaded the regional labor groups, which were generally under MNR control, to name new delegates to the COB. They were particularly urged to name officials of the various government ministries as their delegates; by the middle of 1953 there were six ''oficiales mayors'' (the second-ranking officials of the various ministries) among these provincial delegates. In July 1953, the leading Trotskyist trade unionist, Edwin Moller, claimed that about 50 per cent of the delegates who regularly attended meetings of the COB were government officials of one kind or another;[20] in an interview on July 11, 1953, Guillermo Limpias Villegas, the head of the Bank Workers Union and an MNR member, put the estimate at the more modest figure of 25 to 28 per cent.

Although no longer in control of the COB, the Trotskyite trade unionists continued to participate in its deliberations. A more or less typical session of the COB in this period was attended by the writer on July 9, 1953. The subject under discussion at the meeting, which was presided over by Juan Lechín, and attended by Minister of Labor Germán Butrón and Minister of Peasant Affairs Ñuflo Chávez, was the forthcoming agrarian reform decree.

The first person to speak was Dr. Hugo López Ávila, the COB's representative on the Agrarian Reform Commission, which had been set up to draft a land distribution decree. He described the basic features of the decree, and discussion then proceeded along purely partisan lines. Ñuflo Chávez presented the MNR's position, which generally supported the proposed agrarian reform. José Pereira, the Communist Party's representative, then read a document signed by the head of the Communist Party, Sergio Almaraz; Ñuflo Chávez later said that it read like the Chinese Agrarian Reform Law of 1950, and had little relevance to the actual situation in rural Bolivia. Edwin Moller then presented the POR's draft. It urged confiscation of land without compensation. (The government proposed to offer compensation in bonds, but given the inflation already rampant in Bolivia, this amounted to almost the same thing.) Moller also urged that the peasants occupy the land themselves, and decide among themselves how it should be distributed. He stressed that in law the land should be nationalized, with the peasants being given use-rights to it but not freehold titles. Moller stressed the importance of using the existing Indian communities in the agrarian reform process; he also urged that the land redistribution program not be looked upon as one step in the long process of capitalist evolution but rather as a step toward "a higher form of economic organization."

All three points of view found some support from the floor, but control of the meeting was clearly in the hands of the three MNR government ministers seated at the head table. Ñuflo Chávez was particularly biting in his criticisms of the draft legislation offered by the Communists and Trotskyites, and was especially sarcastic in his references to the Communist document.

Trotskyite influence in various local and industrial labor groups declined in the year or so following their loss of control over the COB. They lost most of their considerable influence in the labor and peasant movement in the Cochabamba area. Whereas the POR had had one-third to one-half of the delegates to the COB departmental affiliate there during the early months of the revolution, by 1954 it had no more than 10 per cent of them. The peasants, in particular, had been largely won over to the MNR by the government's agrarian reform program.[21] The Trotskyists also lost out in the unions in the La Paz area. Germán Butrón, the head of the Confederación General de Trabajadores Fabriles, informed the author on July 11, 1953, that the PORistas no longer controlled a single union among the factory workers of La Paz, whereas a year before they had had considerable influence.

However, the PORistas continued to have some strength in the mining regions. Juan Lechín told the author in an interview on July 30, 1957, that the POR only had at that time one member of the Miners Federation Executive; but Edwin Moller, who by then had quit the POR and joined the MNR, where he was an important Lechín lieutenant, maintained that five of the ten members of the Miners Federation Executive were Trotskyists, principally of the González Moscoso faction of the POR.[22] We have no way of checking the accuracy of either of these versions, but both indicate that POR influence among the miners was by no means completely destroyed either by the growing hostility between the Trotskyists and the MNR or by the split within the POR ranks which had taken place by 1957.

## THE GROWING HOSTILITY OF POR TO REVOLUTIONARY GOVERNMENT

With the loss of control of the Central Obrera Boliviana, the POR became stronger in its criticisms of the Paz Estenssoro government. In mid-November of 1952 *Lucha Obrera* questioned the usefulness of having labor ministers in the cabinet: "The revolution cannot be given an impulse from cabinet posts which the government graciously grants us in order to permit them to reestablish their own political equilibrium, later to kick out without the slightest consideration all those who have served them so abjectly." The same issue attacked the government itself: "The road chosen by the government leads to the strengthening of the capitalist class, to the submission of the country to Yankee imperialism. Our road, the road of the proletariat, the road of our party, leads to the reinforcement of the revolutionary and anti-imperialist political consciousness of the exploited, oppressed peoples of our Latin American colonies and thereby effectively helps to deepen, extend, and generalize the revolution."[23]

The POR continued to picture the COB as the possible "dual power" sharing control with the government as the Soviets did in Russia between March and November 1917. The January 1953 issue of *Lucha Obrera* noted: "In embryonic form the elements of power are stirring within it and are consciously expressed by the POR's fraction. The development of these tendencies will profoundly transform the structure of the COB and will convert it into a workers' parliament, which will have executive attributes." However, the POR no longer thought that the development of the COB into a dual power would be more or less automatic. First, it required "complete independence of the workers organizations from government institutions," and in the second place, *Lucha Obrera* argued that "the future of the COB depends upon its strengthening itself, converting itself into a form of proletarian power, and following the course indicated by the Revolutionary Workers Party."[24]

The Trotskyites strongly criticized the Paz Estenssoro administration's willingness to negotiate with the United States for U.S. purchases of tin from the nationalized mines. The February 1953 issue of *Lucha Obrera* claimed that the Bolivian government "overestimates the imperialist power" and that in fact the general world situation had "created an unfavorable relation of forces for imperialism." It argued that "tin is a strategic material which all nations need and which must be purchased no matter what." The Trotskyites argued that if the United States would not buy Bolivia's tin, it should be "placed on the free world market and sold to the highest bidder, whether Chinese, English, Russian, or Japanese." *Lucha Obrera* argued that the workers "should demand the breaking of the imperialist encirclement blocking trade relations between the countries of Western and Eastern Europe, the China of Mao Tsetung, the U.S.S.R., and full interchange among Latin American nations."[25]

Relations with the government became increasingly difficult. The POR claimed late in 1953 that the administration was seeking to suppress publication of the Trotskyist newspaper *Lucha Obrera*. However, it was still appearing; according to the New York *New Militant*, its December 20, 1953, issue "savagely criticized the Estenssoro regime for betraying the Bolivian revolution, bowing to the U.S. State Department, and making it possible for fascist-like forces to grow in strength in Bolivia."[26]

The Trotskyists also claimed that members of their party were being jailed unjustly by the MNR government. Thus José Bonetti wrote in early 1954: "A militant of the Partido Obrero Revolucionario (Trotskyist), Henríquez, a health worker, has been in prison for several months. Chura, a peasant leader from Potosí, and a member of the POR, was jailed two months ago. Forty peasants from the region of Taraco have been jailed for occupying with thousands of others the lands which the government had decided to cede to a Yankee mission, but the troops were not able to dislodge them. Five militants of the POR, miners from Llallagua, have been detained and brought to La Paz."[27]

The fact the Trotskyists had lost out almost completely to the MNR in the Central Obrera Boliviana was shown by the First National Congress of the COB, which met in La Paz between October 30 and November 16, 1954. The congress, which was presided over by Juan Lechín and attended by 310 delegates, was addressed by Víctor Paz Estenssoro on its opening day.[28] Juan Rey described this first labor congress in the following terms: "In spite of attacks by the CP and the POR, the congress was so organized and prepared by the Lechín caucus that opposition was absolutely eliminated, and the MNR controlled the discussion and all resolutions. Thus the congress demonstrated the nationalists' stability in the control of state power and the workers' movement."[29]

The POR's loss of influence was reflected in the poor showing that the party made in the 1956 general election, the first held under the MNR regime. The MNR nominees for President and Vice-President, Hernán Siles and Ñuflo Chávez, received 786,729 votes; the candidates of the Falange Socialista Boliviana got 130,494; the candidates Iñiguez and Lara, backed by the Communist Party and the PIR, received 12,273 votes. In contrast, the Trotskyist nominees, Hugo González Moscoso and F. Bravo, obtained only 2,239 votes.[30]

However, the leaders of the Pabloite Fourth International did not admit that the vote received by the POR was a defeat for the Trotskyists. A pamphlet published by the Latin American Secretariat of the International reported that "those votes coming from the important worker and peasant centers of the country constitute an enormous force and a solid base for the task of pushing the revolution through the COB, where the great masses are located."[31]

## SPLITS IN THE POR

The POR's decline of influence in the labor movement and the growing friction between the POR and the MNR and government played an important part in bringing about two serious splits in the POR, and these largely eliminated the Trotskyites as a significant force in national politics. Factionalism within the Fourth International also played a role in the divisions within the POR.

The two contending groups which first appeared within the POR centered around Guillermo Lora and the party's principal trade unionists led by Edwin Moller on the one hand, and Hugo González Moscoso on the other. The Lora-Moller group favored a policy of cooperation with the left-wing of the MNR, particularly with Juan Lechín and other MNR trade unionists. They felt that the long-range task of the POR was one of political education among the country's workers, rather than one of seeking power in the fairly near future. By 1954 they did not feel that the POR had any appreciable chance of coming to power, and that given the international circumstances of the period, a POR government would not be able to stay in power for more than a few days.

The González Moscoso faction of the POR took a much harder line towards the Bolivian national revolution. They were for breaking any kind of political relations with the MNR or any of its factions, and seeking to push the revolution which had begun in April 1952 as rapidly as possible toward the establishment of a dictatorship of the proletariat—a dictatorship, that is, of the POR.

Problems within the Fourth International played a role in the internal struggle within the Bolivian POR. By the time the conflict between the Lora-Moller and González factions became apparent, there already existed within the POR a group which aligned itself with the Socialist Workers Party of the United States in its opposition to the line of the Secretary of the Fourth International, Michel Pablo, in favor of entering Communist parties. In the first alignment of factions, the González Moscoso group and the pro-SWP elements made common cause against the Lora-Moller leadership. However, this alliance soon broke down.

The Lora-Moller faction became critical of the leadership of Michel Pablo within the Fourth International. They accused Pablo of trying to force the POR into an outright confrontation with the Paz Estenssoro government, and they were opposed to any kind of a reconciliation with international Stalinism. However, the Lora-Moller faction did not completely align itself with the Socialist

Workers Party, and they felt that the SWP did not give enough attention to the problems of underdeveloped countries. Guillermo Lora went to the Paris Congress of the Fourth International which ratified the split within international Trotskyist ranks. Meanwhile, the pro-SWP faction in the POR joined forces with the Lora-Moller group.[32]

The internal fighting in the POR took public form in November 1954. At that time, Guillermo Lora, still using the name of the POR, launched his own party newspaper, *Masas*, in competition with *Lucha Obrera*, the control of which had come into the hands of Hugo González Moscoso.[33] However, it seems that the formal separation into two parties (both with the name Partido Obrero Revolucionario) did not take place until May 1956.[34]

In *Masas* of August 18, 1956, edited by Guillermo Lora and subtitled "Official Organ of the Partido Obrero Revolucionario, published by its Central Committee," the Lora faction presented the basis of some of its grievances against the González Moscoso group which held a majority of seats on the POR Central Committee. This periodical said: "In our conception of democratic centralism we assume the defense of the purest tradition of our international and national movement. The 'majority,' in this matter, is going along the road of revisionism. . . . One comes to the conclusion that the usurpers of the Political Bureau have acted and are acting in flagrant violation of the fundamental organizational norms of the International and of the POR. We could launch against them accusations against these norms; but this involves not isolated cases of a disciplinary character, but a system of thought and action which seeks to strangle the party with the aid of Stalinist methods."[35]

*Masas*, in its issue of October 1956, discussed the origins and development of the split in the POR. It said: "The factional struggle began over the characterization of the Bolivian revolution, over the evolution of the consciousness of the masses and over the attitude which should be assumed toward the Movimiento Nacionalista Revolucionario, the only party of the masses in Bolivia. On the basis of differences concerning these central points of revolutionary politics, there were elaborated two criteria on the structure of the party. In the process of the struggle there appeared the so-called Internationalist Proletarian Faction; it adopted this name to underscore its unconditional submission to the Stalinist conception of the party and used typically Stalinist methods. The Leninist Workers Faction—the term Leninist was used in opposition to the Stalinist deviations of what was then considered the majority—defended the Leninist concept of the party and it was converted into the defender of the Trotskyist traditions of the Partido Obrero Revolucionario."[36]

This article goes on to note that the Leninist Workers Faction took form around the political thesis approved by the POR's Tenth Conference, (held in La Paz in June 1953), which began to be attacked by the party leadership, on instructions from the Fourth International's Latin American Bureau. This thesis had argued that the revolution was passing through "a stage of momentary depression'' which was due to ''bureaucratization of the trade-union movement, weakening of its combativity, and also organizational decadence of the Party.'' The document had argued: ''The immediate task was not the seizure of power, but winning over a majority of the working class and the peasants for the positions of the Partido Obrero Revolucionario. We reiterated over and over that there was no other path toward a worker-peasant government.''

The Lora faction's periodical argued that the rival group ''appeared to be trying to revise the political positions approved by the Tenth Conference, which they labeled pessimistic and capitulating.'' The Lora group charged that its opponents argued as follows: ''The masses have conserved all their vitality of attack and are marching rapidly toward power. In consequence, the slogan of worker-peasant government must be transformed into agitation, because it will be immediately carried out. The Movimiento Nacionalista Revolucionario ... has ceased to be a Party of the masses, who are rapidly abandoning petty bourgeois leadership.''

The Lora group argued that this analysis was wrong, and that the first job of the POR was ''strengthening the party, both organizationally and ideologically.'' The period was opening, it said, in which the POR could be transformed into a party of the masses, which would be essential if the masses were to come to power; the central problem was removing the masses from Movimientista control.

In contrast, the González group argued that there was no time for the POR to become a mass party, because the masses were already on the march and would take control of the state with or without POR leadership. They pictured the POR's main job as being that of ''satisfactorily organizing the left-wing of the MNR'' to bring about the seizure of power.

The Michel Pablo faction of the Fourth International accepted the González Moscoso group as its affiliate in Bolivia. In a message directed to the Lora group, the International Secretariat said: ''At the base of your attitude is a concept which is bad for our movement in Bolivia, and which today, happily, the POR has overcome. You no longer represent Trotskyism in Bolivia.''[37] This position conformed to a passage in the political resolution of the Fourth Congress of the Pabloite Fourth International, which had been held in Italy in June 1954. The principal authors of this part of the resolution had been M. Arroyo and J. Posadas, and it had said: ''The right-wing and even reactionary deviation of the government of the MNR in conformity with the pressure of imperialism and native reaction, makes more necessary than ever a frank denunciation of this by the Partido Obrero Revolucionario, which must dissipate all traces of sympathy for this government, including its 'labor ministers.' '' It urged that the POR support the idea of the election of a Constituent Assembly, in which election the COB would present its own candidates.[38]

In the long run, what was more serious for the POR than this split was the abandonment of Trotskyism by some of the POR's principal trade-union figures, led by Edwin Moller. In 1954 they quit the POR and joined the MNR, in which they became regular members of the MNR left wing led by Juan Lechín. Moller was a victorious MNR candidate for the Chamber of Deputies in the 1956 general election, and was named Secretary of Organization of the COB and editor of its newspaper *Rebelión*.[39] *Rebelión*, under Moller's editorship, had the following to say about the general elections of June 17, 1956: "The masses will vote today with all their power for the MNR, for the red ticket, for the first color in the national flag, which signifies the sacrifice and the blood spilt by the oppressed along the difficult road of anti-imperialism and anti-feudalism."[40] As editor of *Rebelión*, Moller accepted articles contributed by Trotskyites in other countries who had taken more or less his own path. Thus, Jorge Abelardo Ramos and Enrique Rivera (who wrote under the pseudonym Juan Ramón Peñaloza), both Argentine Trotskyites who had come around to support of Perón, had a number of articles published in the COB newspaper.[41]

It became apparent in 1957 that the ex-Trotskyists were to play an important part in the Lechín-led faction of the MNR. The government of Hernán Siles, Paz Estenssoro's successor, launched a drastic program of price stabilization, which aroused considerable opposition in the labor movement, opposition which was led by Juan Lechín, in spite of the fact that he had originally endorsed the stabilization effort.[42] This led to a showdown between the Lechín forces and the President, when Lechín got the COB to call a general strike against the Siles program. Siles was able to thwart the strike by an appeal over the heads of the union leaders to the rank and file workers. Once the threat of a general strike had passed, President Siles and his supporters in the MNR and the unions took some retaliatory measures against the Lechín faction, particularly that part of it which had formerly been Trotskyist. Thus, Edwin Moller was temporarily expelled from the MNR and forced to resign from his leading position in the Confederación de Trabajadores Particulares.[43]

One interesting aspect of this 1957 crisis within the government, the MNR, and the labor movement was the fact that those Movimientistas in organized labor who had belonged to the pro-Stalinist PIR before the April 1952 uprising generally sided with President Siles, while those Movimientista trade unionists who until 1954 had been Trotskyists were aligned firmly with Juan Lechín. The old enmities between pro-Stalinists and Trotskyists thus continued even though both groups had abandoned their former affiliations and were members of the MNR.

Although there were attempts to remove Lechín and his associates from the leadership of the COB and the Miners Federation, these efforts apparently did not receive the wholehearted support of President Siles. As a result, the Lechinistas remained the dominant element in the labor movement, and among them, Edwin Moller continued to be an important figure in the COB. In 1960 he was head of the Department of Cooperatives of the Ministry of Peasant

Affairs.[44] Three years later, when Juan Lechín broke with the MNR because he was denied its presidential nomination, Moller joined Lechín's new party, the Partido Revolucionario de la Izquierda Nacionalista (PRIN).

## THE PORS AFTER THE SPLIT

By the middle of 1957 the split of the POR into two distinct parties, one led by Guillermo Lora and the other by Hugo González Moscoso, was clear. The González Moscoso faction held what it called the Fourteenth Conference of the POR early in 1957; González Moscoso was elected Secretary-General, and the conference adopted a political resolution, an "Open Letter to the Second COB Congress," and a "Manifesto to the Masses of Bolivia."[45] For its part, the Lora faction established a leaders school, which met between January and July, 1957, the purpose of which was reported to be "to create secondary leaders who can win new members and train them in an efficient manner."[46]

Both POR factions took a strong anti-MNR position during the Second COB Congress, which was responsible for calling the anti-Siles general strike of July 1, 1957. The González faction presented a document entitled "Tasks and Program of the Proletariat to Defend the Bolivian Revolution," written by Fernando Bravo, and a "Workers Plan for Stabilization and Development of the Economy," written by Jesus Muriel, a miners' delegate affiliated with the party. As *Lucha Obrera* reported, "The Trotskyist theses presented the need for ending the co-government [MNR and COB] not for the purpose of giving up positions which had been won, but to advance the revolution, freeing the COB from its dependence upon the bourgeois government, and fighting for *power for the COB*, for *the Workers-Peasants Government*."[47]

The Lora faction was equally opposed to the Siles government. It proclaimed that the "Program of National Liberation" of the MNR had been "thrown in the wastebasket by President Siles." The solution to the situation, said the Lora Trotskyists, was easy: "the MNR must leave power." They added: "The MNR stays in power only because no one dares to give it a push. . . . This position supposes that the Partido Obrero Revolucionario sought to take power. Then we will have at the head of the government workers and peasants as a class, and not adventurers and traitors occupying ministries under the title of 'workers.' "[48] A clearer attack on the Lechinistas would be difficult to imagine.

The Bolivian Trotskyists continued to be divided into two violently conflicting parties, both called Partido Obrero Revolucionario until 1963, when the González Moscoso faction split, with its dissident element taking the name Partido Obrero Revolucionario (Trotskista), or POR(T). This further schism of Bolivian Trotskyism was precipitated in large part by the shifting politics of the Fourth International.

When the Fourth International faction led by Michel Pablo decided to merge with the Trotskyist groups associated with the Socialist Workers Party of the United States, a segment of the González Moscoso POR, which had been aligned with the Pablo Fourth International, refused to go along with the merger. Instead, it joined the secessionist forces led by the Argentine Trotskyist J. Posadas, which set up their own Fourth International, based largely on the Latin American Bureau of the Pabloite International.

The Posadista element in the POR held what it called the Eighteenth Conference of the party in the mining town of Huanuni. It proceeded to expel "Mr. Lawyer González and his gangsters and servants Guzman and Sánchez." It sent greetings to the Posadista International Secretariat, "to the Cuban masses, the Cuban POR, and all the sections of the Fourth International and particularly to the Peruvian comrades." It also sent greetings to "Comrade Posadas for his activity in the political organization of the International, and in solidarity with him in the face of the attacks to which he has been subjected by the capitulators."

The POR(T) aligned itself strongly with the ideas of Posadas. Thus the conference accepted "the policy of the Fourth International based on the conception that imperialism is preparing counter-revolutionary atomic war, that war is inevitable, and that it will not be the destruction of humanity but instead will be followed by immediate revolution and the triumph of Communism." The Posadista POR(T), in its first conference, foresaw the possibility of a Marxist-Leninist-Trotskyist revolution in Bolivia in the near future: "The Movimientista bureaucracy has restrained the functioning of some organisms of dual power, but has not been able to destroy them or to turn back the masses. These remain full of vigor and revolutionary spirit. In the stage which has begun with the struggles of the miners and peasants, of the poor petty bourgeoisie, there exist the conditions for a real functioning of those organisms, for a confrontation which will impel a working-class solution to the duality of power." To this end, "the party of the Fourth International in Bolivia analyzed the tactics for intervening in the mobilization which is now occurring and the preparation of the general strike of indefinite duration, in the development of which is the struggle for workers' power and for the workers and peasants government."[49]

An unsuccessful attempt was made in the late 1960's to unify the two most important factions of Bolivian Trotskyism, the POR factions led by Guillermo Lora and Hugo González Moscoso. On February 17, 1966, an agreement was signed between the two parties. It provided for the establishment of a "unified directorate, centralized, composed of a Central Committee and of a Political Bureau; Comrades Guillermo Lora and Hugo González Moscoso will compose the National Secretariat." It was also provided that *Lucha Obrera,* the former organ of the González Moscoso faction, would continue to be published as "a review of education and theoretical orientation," while Guillermo Lora's newspaper *Masas* would be put out as the united party's "political periodical." The united party was committed "to fight with all possible means against the military junta,'' which had seized power from the MNR in November 1964. The announcement of the unification of the two PORs was signed by Hugo González Moscoso on behalf of his group and Filemon Escobar for the POR headed by Guillermo Lora.[50]

The leaders of the united POR expressed considerable optimism about the role the party could play in national politics. González Moscoso was interviewed shortly before the election which made General René Barrientos President of the Republic early in 1967; he commented that ''whereas the bourgeois and reformist parties have fallen into a historical and programmatic crisis, the POR, whose principles have been confirmed by reality, is on the verge of implanting itself as the definitive alternative for the Bolivian masses.''

González was critical of the reelection of Juan Lechín as head of the Miners Federation, which had occurred at a congress of the Federation shortly before the interview. He explained this in terms of the unrepresentative nature of the Federation's convention, and added that ''the bureaucracy thus supplanted the wishes of the masses.''[51] This unification of two groups which had been bitter enemies for a decade was not destined to last very long. Gerry Foley, writing in the Socialist Workers Party (U.S.A.) periodical *Intercontinental Press* for December 15, 1964, explained the new division in the POR ranks in the following terms: ''On February 17, 1966, the two tendencies in the Bolivian Trotskyist movement united. Guillermo Lora, who is a well-known parliamentary figure, approved the unification although he was out of the country. When he returned, however, he refused to work in the united organization. He formed a personal grouping which eventually called itself by the same name as the organization it split from.'' As we shall see, the Lora and González Moscoso groups continued to have basic differences of opinion and perspective. The Lora group came to align itself with the Healyite faction of international Trotskyism, becoming the only Latin American group to do so.

## THE GUILLERMO LORA POR

The Lora faction maintained an independent position in Bolivian politics. Although a Round Table of the Opposition was established at the time of the 1962 parliamentary election, in an attempt to offer a united front to the MNR government, no faction of the POR seems to have collaborated in this effort.[52] The Lora faction of the POR continued to have some influence in the mining areas, but it received a severe blow on July 20, 1965, when César Lora, a brother of the POR leader and its principal figure in the mining regions, was arrested by the Army in the Department of Potosí and was murdered on the spot.[53]

The Lora faction apparently did not cooperate with the guerrilla movement, which gained international prominence during 1966 and 1967, when Ernesto Guevara was leading it, but which continued on a more modest scale even after Guevara's death. As early as 1963 Lora was quoted as calling any guerrilla attempt in Bolivia "adventurous rebellion." He continued: "Partisans who rebel against the will of the people and look out for goals that obviously are in contrast to the interests of the majority have no chance to operate successfully, to consolidate themselves and to survive." He argued that guerrilla war must remain subordinate to "the political strategy of the revolutionary class," and that it was not the only strategy for the war of the masses, "as some Marxists of the latest hour seem to suppose."[54] In the middle of 1967 Régis Debray, a publicizer of the "foco"theory of guerrilla war favored by the Castro regime, was arrested while trying to get out of Bolivia after spending time with the Guevara guerrillas; the Lora POR called him "an adventurer." Lora commented that political nuclei were more important than militaristic ones.[55]

In 1969 the Lora POR strongly denounced the campaign carried on by the United Secretariat of the Fourth International (the group with which the United States Socialist Workers Party was associated) in favor of raising funds for the defense of arrested guerrillas. Guillermo Lora published a letter to *Informations Ouvrières*, the organ of the French affiliate of the Healyite Fourth International, in which he charged that this campaign was "an operation with all the signs of a fraud." He then went on to make a charge which the Socialist Workers Party's *Intercontinental Press* translated as follows: "Serious suspicions exist today that Mr. González Moscoso in person is working in the pay of the Bolivian government."[56]

*Workers Press*, the organ of the Healyite Socialist Labour League of Great Britain, in its issue of January 17, 1970, claimed that Lora's charge against González Moscoso had been mistranslated by the American magazine, that what he had really said was that González Moscoso "would work on behalf of the Bolivian government," and added that Lora "has stated his willingness to appear before any tribunal of the working class to prove his charges."

Alberto Sáenz, another leader of the Lora POR, also charged that the United Secretariat campaign was a "fraud." In a press release dated November 8, 1969, he charged that some of the PORistas of the González Moscoso faction had been accused by the guerrilla groups of being "informers and confidants of the Ministry of the Interior."

Guillermo Lora later issued a statement in *Informations Ouvrières* in which he declared, "I am in complete solidarity with the communique that was written by my party in order to unmask the adventurers who have turned revolutionary involvement into a business proposition designed to satisfy their personal needs."[57] The Lora group thus associated itself internationally with the Healyite faction in international Trotskyism, although it is not clear whether it was ever officially affiliated with it.

Lora was violently denounced by the González Moscoso faction and its international associates, as in the *Intercontinental Press* of April 13, 1970: "As for the Lora splinter group, which has been an instrument of provocation for years, it is devoting itself, as it has in the past, to discrediting the guerrillas. During the repression that started in July, this bourgeois poltroon spent his time condemning the guerrillas in little communiques, which the papers published for him, and in giving lectures ridiculing the heroic and valiant conduct of the ELN fighters. In reality, the behavior of this yellow exrevolutionary is gratifying to the counter-revolutionaries. Claiming to 'evaluate' the guerrilla movement, he always tried to discredit it before the masses. His present position, as in the past, is politically yellow and cowardly and confined to mere syndicalist and economist activism. He continues spinning theories about a 'mass insurrection' in the abstract and for a vague far-off time. . . .For this ex-Marxist, ex-internationalist, and ex-Trotskyist, the conditions never exist. As a bourgeois poltroon, Lora is frightened by revolution and still more by the noise of arms that the guerrillas make.''

The Lora party declared that it did not support the government of General Alfredo Ovando, which came to power in a coup d'etat late in 1969, but it was apparently more sympathetic to it then other Trotskyist factions. Alberto Sáenz issued a communique in the name of the POR in which he said that the POR "has not come to the support nor will it come to the support of the present military government." It also denounced the backing which certain unidentified "left-wing nationalists" had offered the government as "simple opportunism." However, the Sáenz communique said that the dilemma of the moment was "to direct our efforts toward the perfecting of petty bourgeois democracy," and that it was necessary "to become the left of the government so as to march toward the consummation of the socialist revolution, headed by the proletariat."[58] Soon after Ovando's professedly left-wing nationalist government seized power, *Masas* defined the POR attitude toward the regime thus: "To speak of the limitations of the present government, to indicate that it is condemned to stop half way and to capitulate to imperialism, is equivalent to teaching the masses not to have confidence in it, and that constitutes one of the most important tasks of the moment."[59]

Further indication of the way in which the POR of Guillermo Lora saw its role in Bolivia and in Latin America was given in an article entitled "Amérique Latine: Le Proletariat Occupe la Scène Politique" in the January 28-February 4, 1970, issue of *Informations Ouvrières*. It commented that "the capacity of the POR to impose itself as the pole for regrouping the Latin American militants who search for a new orientation must result first of all from intervention in the course of current political crises in Bolivia." Lora's POR still concentrated much of its attention on the tin miners. That it continued to maintain some influence among them is indicated by the fact that Lora himself sat prominently in the front row of the congress of the Miners Federation held in late 1970.[60]

During the Ovando regime the Lora POR continued to hold regular party organizational meetings. Thus the January 28, 1970, issue of *Masas* reported that on January 18 a plenum of party cadres of the La Paz region had been held. It approved the political line of the party, and answered an attack on it by the Ovando government by labeling that regime an "agent of imperialism and of the old local oligarchy."[61]

The POR of Lora continued to be active during the short regime of General Juan José Torres (November 1970 to August 1971). It had members in the "Popular Assembly" organized by Juan Lechín, some labor groups, and various radical parties as an embryo "soviet." In the Assembly, PORistas expressed "critical support" for the Torres regime, and called upon it to arm the workers so that they could defend themselves against those who were plotting to overthrow Torres.

Lora himself explained his party's position during the Torres period: "The ultra-lefts and the Pabloites forget the teachings of Lenin and Trotsky: they draw up their 'documents' in a simple-minded way and place Torres and Ovando-Banzer on the same level. These people refuse to understand the various shades that bourgeois nationalism can take in underdeveloped countries. . . . Revolutionary tactics must begin with this difference. It is not a question of supporting Torres but of crushing fascism to impose a workers' government."[62]

After the overthrow of the Torres regime by a military coup, headed by Colonel Hugo Banzer and supported by the MNR and the Falange Socialista Boliviana, the issue of the Lora POR's behavior during the regime provoked a split in the ranks of the International Committee of the Fourth International, of which the party had been a member. Lora's opponents criticized him and his party bitterly for not having armed the workers and for being dupes of Torres. Lora himself commented on the debacle of August 1971 that "everybody thought—including we Marxists—that the arms would be given by the government military team, which would consider that only through resting on the masses and giving them adequate firepower could they at least neutralize the 'gorilla' [reactionary militarist] right." His supporters in the French Organization Communiste Internationaliste defended Lora by arguing that "at every stage in the process, the political fight waged by the POR has enabled the masses to preserve their class independence vis-à-vis Torres and to frustrate the maneuvers aimed at subordinating them once again to bourgeois and petty bourgeois nationalism."[63]

## THE GONZÁLEZ MOSCOSO POR

The González Moscoso POR, affiliated with the United Secretariat of the Fourth International, at first supported the coup of generals René Barrientos and Alfredo Ovando in November 1964, which overthrew the MNR government of President Víctor Paz Estenssoro. A correspondent of the New York Trotskyist newspaper *The Militant* reported: "At present there is the most complete liberty since the Paz apparatus was dismantled. There is a veritable flowering of newspapers, and each class, each social layer, each party, group, and political tendency is freely expressing itself and advancing its own demands. Thus, one can read the program of the extreme right and, at the other pole, the program of the COB . . . which shows the evident influence of the Trotskyists.''

At first the González Moscoso Trotskyites seemed enthusiastic about General Barrientos, the apparent leader of the new military government. Thus *The Militant's* correspondent wrote: "Barrientos is not playing the role of the typical 'gorilla' (reactionary militarist). On the contrary. He is promising everything to everybody, visiting the mines, etc. He has made overtures about reestablishing workers control, his Minister of Labor coming out flatly in favor of it.'' *The Militant's* correspondent also had a word to say about the position of the Trotskyists in the situation: "I should add that the Trotskyists, whose ranks are recruited from the poorest levels of the population, are completely out of funds. This greatly handicaps them in presenting their program in this promising situation.''[64]

About this same time, Livio Maitan, the principal Italian leader of the Fourth International of the United Secretariat, commented that "Barrientos and those with him are compelled to operate in a context characterized by the fact that all the anti-MNR currents developed a convergent action, symbolized by the establishment of the Revolutionary Committee of the People, which includes all political formations from the extreme right to Lechín's PRIN, only the Trotskyist POR . . . and the Communist Party being excluded.'' Maitan said of the González Moscoso party that "the POR, despite its important ties and its degree of influence in the decision-making sectors, has not yet had the opportunity of proceeding as the actual direct leadership on a national scale.''[65]

But the González Moscoso POR did not support the military regime for long. Writing soon after the election of General René Barrientos as "constitutional" president in July 1966, Hugo González Moscoso himself said, "Before the fraudulent elections of the 3rd of July, we affirmed that the Barrientos-Siles government* would be nothing more than the 'legalized' continuation of the military dictatorship. The actions of the government have clearly confirmed this assertion.'' González Moscoso went on to endorse revolt against the regime: "To prepare and organize seriously and responsibly insurrection and the seizing of power to replace this anti-national, anti-worker, and anti-democratic government is the minimum obligation which the workers and leftist parties, the trade-union leaders and the leftist intellectuals have.'' Within this context, he said, the POR should "demonstrate in practice that the *ideological vanguard* of the proletariat is in the condition to become the *political leader* of the nation.''

By the early months of 1967 the Barrientos government was rounding up leftists of every stripe. These included members of the MNR, Juan Lechín's PRIN, the pro-Chinese Communist party, and the various factions of the POR. PORistas jailed included Guillermo Lora, Miguel Lora, Víctor Sosa, and Oscar

---

*Luis Adolfo Siles, leader of the conservative Social Democratic Party and half-brother of MNR President Hernán Siles, was elected as Barrientos' Vice-President and succeeded to the presidency in 1969, when Barrientos died.

Sanjines.[66] On April 11, 1967, the POR of González Moscoso was outlawed by the government, together with the pro-Moscow and pro-Peking Communist Parties.[67]

The opposition of the González Moscoso POR to the Barrientos regime was underscored again in an article written by González early in 1967, in which he said that "the military regime, first under the military junta and later under the Barrientos presidency, carried forward the work left unfinished by the MNR of dismantling all the conquests of the masses, destroying the unions, cutting wages, attacking nationalized property and converting the country into a Yankee colony." In this article, written before the Ché Guevara guerrilla action became generally known, González Moscoso went on to endorse the guerrilla road to power as applied to Bolivia. He wrote: "In Bolivia, for example, an agrarian reform has already been carried through which, although limited, has solved the basic land problem. However, guerrilla warfare is still the necessary road to defeat the military dictatorship. In our case, the mines, the slums around the cities, as well as certain agricultural zones where the conditions of life are very difficult, will be fertile fields for the development of guerrilla groups."[68]

Even after the catastrophic defeat of Guevara's guerrilla movement, culminating in Ché's death, the González Moscoso POR reiterated its faith in guerrilla war. This was indicated in an article in *Perspectiva Mundial*, of January 1968, which said in part: "But the guerrilla struggle in Bolivia, in spite of the death of Comandante Guevara, in spite of the blows, continues to be the only way out of the economic and political crisis of the country. It is the duty of the revolutionaries in Bolivia and in Latin America, as the POR sees it, to support the present guerrilla struggle, strengthening it, making it come out of its isolation, joining it to the movement of the masses in the cities and the mines, and bringing about the participation of the peasantry as a fighting force." But there is no indication that Guevara had entered into contact with the González Moscoso group or any other Trotskyist faction in Bolivia. Nor is there evidence that any members of the Trotskyist groups actually participated in his guerrilla forces.[69]

An article by a Bolivian correspondent in the New York Trotskyist periodical *Intercontinental Press* of June 10, 1968, described the position of the González Moscoso party in the wake of the Guevara disaster. Commenting on the illegal opposition to the Barrientos regime, this article said that the opposition "is made up of the ELN (Ejército de Liberación Nacional, National Liberation Army), fiercely persecuted since the start of the armed struggle in Nanchauazu, the POR, and the pro-Chinese Communist Party. These parties have all been outlawed, subjected to persecution and driven completely underground. Warrants are out for the arrest of Hugo González Moscoso and Oscar Zamora, respectively the leaders of the POR and the pro-Chinese party. . . . These political forces are identitified as supporting armed struggle (guerrilla warfare), and their influence over the masses can be measured by the general sympathy existing for guerrilla warfare. Their perspectives are likewise bound up with the fight for power by means of armed struggle.''

For many months after the death of Ché Guevara in October 1967, guerrilla warfare subsided in Bolivia. However, in July 1969 there were clashes in various parts of the country between police and soldiers on the one hand and urban guerrillas, including members of the González Moscoso POR, on the other. As a result, PORistas Antonio Moreno and Víctor Córdova were arrested in Cochabamba after a street fight; in Oruro, Felipe and Elio Vázquez, both PORistas and leaders of unions in nearby mines, were picked up; in La Paz other PORistas were jailed. After these events, it was reported that the Trotskyists of the González Moscoso POR "have begun to reorganize among the workers, peasants, and students, above all with the aim of starting a campaign of solidarity with those imprisoned.''[70]

With the seizure of power by General Alfredo Ovando in September 1969, the POR of González Moscoso gave the new regime tentative sympathy. It greeted the new government's decision to expropriate the Gulf Oil Co. as a "popular victory" and expressed support for it. But it added, ''We Trotskyists remind the people that this anti-imperialist triumph is bound up with the struggle of the Nancahuazu guerrillas, with Ché Guevara, Inti Peredo, and their comrades.'' This statement urged ''unconditional release'' for political prisoners, including not only Trotskyists but Régis Debray and the Argentine aide of Guevara, C. Bustos.[71]

In November 1969 the national committee of the POR again issued a statement headed ''An Unconditional General Amnesty and Freedom for the Revolutionists Accused of Being Guerrillas.'' It named many persons whom it demanded be freed and ended, ''Stop the manhunt; civil rights for the Secretary-General of the POR, Hugo González Moscoso.''[72]

However, the POR did not give general political backing to the Ovando government. At a special meeting of the POR in November 1969, a resolution was adopted which labeled Ovando ''a representative of the bourgeoisie'' and stated that ''it is naïve, if not stupid, to appeal to him to accomplish tasks which belong to the revolutionary proletariat and its vanguard. . . . Calling on Ovando to give the workers a share in the government amounts to a betrayal because it would subject them to bourgeois control and leadership.''

The POR further declared that ''the principled and revolutionary position we proclaim before the masses is *independent action and no political confidence in the Ovando government,* its bourgeois program, or the army-party and its operation to rescue the capitalist system.'' It reasserted its faith in guerrilla war: ''Guerrilla warfare is still a valid method. The blows suffered and the losses of men and equipment are not important. However painful, all these losses can be repaired. The important thing is to be clear on the fact that there is no other path for real revolutionists. The illusions conjured up by Ovando will quickly vanish and be dissipated by the crack of the army's guns firing on the masses. The process is heading toward a confrontation."[73]

By the middle of 1970, after clashes between troops and students, the González Moscoso POR issued a statement calling for wide protests against the treatment of the students. It said in part: "We call on the students and workers organizations to suspend all dialogue with the government until the political prisoners are released, until the tortures and persecutions are stopped, and until the terrorist organizations which operate under government protection are broken up. While such crimes abound and while our rights are being violated, talking with the government would be tantamount to sanctioning this situation and accepting it."[74]

When still another turn of the wheel of Bolivian military politics brought about the downfall of General Ovando and the placing of General Juan Torres in the presidency, the POR issued a manifesto signed by Hugo González Moscoso, E. Sánchez, and Elisco Aldana. This statement argued: "The crisis of the military and of the regime, which culminated in the replacement of Ovando, was a mere manifestation of the erosion of the capitalist system and the party-army of the bourgeoisie in face of the ripening revolutionary process. The impetus in this development comes from the guerrillas of Teoponte, the workers' struggles, and the battles in the cities."

The POR manifesto went on to argue: "No social revolution has occurred. The crisis was resolved within the framework of the military circles themselves. . . . The army, the armed party of the bourgeoisie, still controls the state. In the presidency General Torres has not taken a single social or political measure that would identify him as a revolutionary. . . . His concepts on structural change and the so-called 'strategy of development' place him within the context of 'desarrollismo' [the policy of limited industrialization and modernization] which imperialism is advancing for the semicolonial countries."

The POR added: "The intervention of the worker, student, and popular masses which benefited General Torres, does not change the picture. It is important to be able to distinguish this military tendency from the living process taking place in the masses." It described this process as "ripening in the vitals of the people, in the depths of the mines, in the factories and universities, on the former haciendas and in the communal villages, the process which has its fullest expression in armed struggle and guerrilla warfare, with the conflicts that periodically arise, under the pressure of this process, in the ranks of the military."

The POR proclamation ended with the call for "organizing a Revolutionary Command, including all political tendencies that favor a socialist solution to the country's present situation and support the armed struggle for power"; for "creating a Revolutionary Workers and Peoples' Army"; and for "developing a body representative of the masses, through which they can express all their revolutionary power, initiative, worries, and determination to transform society."[75]

However, in spite of the González Moscoso POR's skeptical attitude toward the government of General Torres, its own situation during that government was considerably different from what it had been during the two previous regimes. In an interview which appeared in the June 14, 1971, issue of *Rouge*, the organ of the Ligue Communiste, the French affiliate of the United Secretariat, González Moscoso himself noted that under Ovando the party was outlawed and had concentrated all of its efforts on "armed work," but that under Torres the party was once again legal. He pointed out that the party was concentrating its work on the workers and peasants unions and the university. He said that they had won control of a number of small unions of urban workers, and that in the December 1970 congress of unions of La Paz, the party's program had been accepted. He also said that the party had "acquired an important audience in the universities."

González Moscoso also commented that the party's newspaper *Combate* was being put out regularly each month, that it was also publishing a monthly student journal, and that it was proposing soon to issue a theoretical review. He said that the POR had been part of the left in the "Popular Assembly" and had argued that it should be "an organism which discusses national problems, their solutions, and pushes them, but which leaves power in the mass organizations (unions and popular militia or popular army)." González Moscoso insisted that the party had representatives in the Assembly not only representing the party itself but also "representing this or that union."

## THE POSADISTA POR(T)

The Posadista Partido Obrero Revolucionario (Trotskista), headed by Amadeo Vargas, has certainly been the smallest and least important of the three Trotskyist organizations in Bolivia. The González Moscoso POR charged that it "has no life but that breathed into it and allowed it by the military establishment,"[76] and although this may be an exaggeration and a libel, it is certainly true that the Posadista faction has been less important than either the Lora or González Moscoso group. It continued to publish an illegal periodical, *Voz Obrera*.

The POR(T) was said to have issued "solidarity proclamations" of support for the guerrilla movement in Bolivia headed by Ché Guevara.[77] However, it was also quite critical of the Guevara effort: the Argentine-Cuban leader was accused of not using "the revolutionary experience of the masses" and of lacking "a revolutionary program."[78] Their opponents in the rival González Moscoso POR accused the Amadeo Vargas POR(T) of having "stood up to openly support and glorify the military caste and Ovando," when General Ovando was in power. Vargas was alleged to have called these "part of the world revolutionary current."[79]

But the publications of the Vargas group did not indicate quite so much enthusiasm for Ovando as their POR rivals asserted. The issue of the POR(T)'s mimeographed newspaper *Voz Obrera* for October 1969, referring to the advent of the Ovando regime, said: "The movement in Bolivia is an anti-imperialist nationalistic movement, as yet unstructured, without full consciousness, full of contradictions, more contradictions than the nationalist movement in Peru, but which because of the historic, political, and revolutionary conditions of Bolivia, in a very short period, very short, is going to take giant steps and experience internal struggles which will permit the Fourth International to be at the head of large mobilizations." This same statement proclaimed, "Today there exist the conditions for the mining, industrial, peasant, and student vanguards to begin organizing on the basis of the program of revolutionary agrarian reform, of aid and credits, price stabilization and marketing of all agricultural products, of technicial aid, of the miner-peasant alliance." It added: "This is the task of the proletarian miner vanguard, and it is the task of the Bolivian section of the Fourth International. That is the center of the activities of the section—to reorganize itself, while at the same time attacking immediate problems, such as forming democratic trade unions, securing political rights, and cementing the alliance of workers, miners, and peasants. This will bring in its train the petty bourgeoisie and the intellectuals, and will push the anti-imperialist nationalist sectors of the army itself to go forward. One should not discount the possiblity of gaining sectors of the army, even such an officially chosen one as the Bolivian army. On that issue Ovando must respond also."

## WHY THE DECLINE OF BOLIVIAN TROTSKYISM?

The Trotskyites of Bolivia have been the only Fourth Internationalist group in Latin America ever to play a significant role in national politics. But they did so only briefly, and by the late 1960's had been reduced to a marginal and sharply divided group of little more than nuisance value on the Bolivian political scene. How does one explain this reversal of fortune?

The Argentine ex-Trotskyite, Liborio Justo, has explained the failure of the Bolivian Trotskyists in terms of doctrinal deficiencies on their part. He has argued that they failed because they did not, in good Bolshevik fashion, use their control of the Central Obrera Boliviana in the early months of the National Revolution (beginning in April 1952) to convert the COB into an equivalent of the Russian Soviets of 1917, to make it a "dual power" that could challenge and seize power from the MNR government of Víctor Paz Estenssoro. Instead, argues Justo, the POR supported the MNR, and particularly its left wing, and thus threw away its chance of setting up a proletarian dictatorship under POR control.

In our view, however, the failure of the POR was caused by mistakes of exactly the opposite kind. To begin with, it is true that the Bolivian Trotskyites had succeeded in gaining a minority influence in the country's tin miners' unions during the Villarroel administration of 1943-46; but it was able to maintain this influence, and to gain some support in other segments of the labor movement during the Sexenio, largely because of its alliance with Juan Lechín and the MNR faction in the trade unions.

It was the Movimiento Nacionalista Revolucionario which during the Sexenio became by far the country's most popular party. It was the MNR which launched several revolts against the unpopular governments of this period. It was Víctor Paz Estenssoro, the exiled leader of the MNR, who won the largest number of votes in the 1951 election. It was the MNR which organized the revolt of April 9, 1952, and thus began the process of the Bolivian National Revolution. And it was the MNR which came to power in that revolution.

The great majority of the workers of Bolivia were supporters of the Movimiento Nacionalista Revolucionario in the period immediately following April 9, 1952. Those who had backed the pro-Stalinist Partido de Izquierda Revolucionaria before the overthrow of President Villarroel had been alienated from the PIR by its support of the governments of the Sexenio, and had joined the ranks of the MNR.

The POR, in contrast to the PIR, had aligned itself during the Sexenio with Juan Lechín and the MNR. It had supported the MNR's revolutionary attempts during that period, and its members had fought in the streets alongside militants of the MNR during the events of April 9-11, 1952. As a result, the POR shared, as a junior partner, in the popularity of the MNR.

The MNR, however, was always the senior partner in this relationship. The POR's rank and file support in the labor movement in the first months of the Bolivian national revolution was limited to some local unions of the Federación Sindical de Trabajadores Mineros, some locals of the Factory Workers Union, the Confederation of White Collar Workers, and the urban and rural unions in the Department of Cochabamba. The POR had influence in the newly established Central Obrera Boliviana during the first months of the revolution almost completely because Guillermo Lora, Edwin Moller, and other Trotskyist leaders were on more or less friendly terms with Juan Lechín and other MNR trade unionists, and because the MNR labor leaders were preoccupied with their new activities in the government and the various national labor federations. These leaders allowed Trotskyites to run the Central Obrera Boliviana so long as they did not create really serious problems for the MNR government.

The Trotskyists, then, were in no position from April to October of 1952 to convert the COB into the equivalent of the Russian Soviets of 1917. Their influence in the COB was a result of the tolerance of the MNR labor leaders, not a reflection of rank and file support of the POR in the labor movement. Furthermore, Lechín and other MNR labor leaders were loyal to their own party, and were not ready to see its leadership of the revolution challenged by the POR or any other competing party.

The Trotskyites were thus mistaken in thinking they could play the Bolsheviks to Víctor Paz Estenssoro's Kerensky. This became clear when they made their first serious challenge to the MNR government, on the mine nationalization issue: in the process of one COB meeting Trotskyist control of the Central Obrera Boliviana was ended, never again to be restored. Thereafter, the position of the Trotskyites in the labor movement and elsewhere was further undermined by splits within the POR's ranks. The party split into two rival factions, each using the same name, and many of the leading Trotskyite trade unionists withdrew from the party altogether and joined the MNR. The dissidence within PORista ranks was encouraged by the split within the Fourth International.

In sum, it was the POR's dogmatic adherence to the model of the Bolshevik Revolution, rather than their failure to follow that model, which led to their downfall in Bolivia. Once they had ceased to be a really significant factor in the trade union movement and the general revolutionary process going on in Bolivia in the 1950's, factionalism within their own ranks reduced them to a group of quarreling sects.

# — 8 —

## Peruvian Trotskyism

Popular and left-wing politics in Peru has been dominated since 1930 by the Partido Aprista Peruano. The Apristas, headed by Víctor Raúl Haya de la Torre, have been the leading advocates in Latin America of a multiclass party dedicated to bringing about basic social change and economic development through political democracy. Since its establishment, the party has had the support of the great majority of politically active workers and lower middle-class elements in Peru. The Communists of all kinds have traditionally been a minority element on the Peruvian left, and within this Marxist-Leninist segment of the left, the Peruvian Trotskyists have themselves been a relatively small minority.

### THE EARLY YEARS OF TROTSKYISM

The Trotskyist movement in Peru began in 1944 as a result of the merger of two groups. One of these consisted of intellectuals, of whom the most important were Francisco Abríl de Vivero, Emilio Adolfo Bestfalling, and Rafael Méndez Dorch. The other element was made up of textile workers who had left the Communist Party because they felt that it had betrayed a textile workers strike, in conformity with their current line of "national union." The most important of these workers were Félix Zevallos and Leoncio Bueno.

Together these two pioneer Trotskyist elements began to publish a paper called *Cara y Sello* (*Facade and Reality*). In August 1946 they formed the Grupo Obrero Marxista, and began to put out another paper, *Revolución,* which continued to appear until 1948. In 1947 the Grupo Obrero Marxista changed its name to Partido Obrero Revolucionario (POR).[1] The Trotskyists were particularly bitter at this time in their attacks on the Communist Party. For example, in the issue for the second fortnight of June 1947, Jorge del Prado, Secretary-General of the Communist Party, was referred to as an "ex-Comrade" and "renegade."

The appearance of this Trotskyist group in Peru was greeted with interest by Trotskyists abroad. For instance, the dissident Trotskyist periodical *The*

157

*New International*, published in New York City, editorialized in its September 1947 issue: "If this group lacks influence over the masses, it nevertheless represents the outstanding school of Marxist theory in South America. It stands at the head of the Trotskyist movement in matters of theory and makes plain the tasks of the revolution."

This judgment was based principally on a manifesto issued by the Grupo Obrera Marxista, apparently soon after its establishment. The manifesto rejected the idea that the leadership of revolution in Peru or elsewhere in Latin America could come from any element of the bourgeoisie. It argued that "the fate of our weak-kneed national bourgeoisie is intimately bound up with the fate of the entire world capitalist system....The real big bourgeoisie is not in Peru but in Wall Street, that fierce enemy of democratic and national revolution." It added, "The petty bourgeois anti-imperialists of the 'twenties have been transformed into the bourgeois pro-imperialists of the 'forties," referring to the Aprista Party.

Therefore the manifesto argued that "the democratic revolution is the task of the proletarian revolution." It quoted with approval the statement by José Carlos Mariátegui, the precursor of the Peruvian Communist Party, that "the country's economic emancipation can be achieved only through the action of the proletarian masses in solidarity with the world anti-imperialist struggle." The Trotskyist bona fides of the manifesto were attested to by its quotation from Trotsky to the effect that "in the course of its development the democratic revolution passes into the socialist revolution, and thus constitutes itself the permanent revolution," and its addition that "the socialist revolution is international or is not socialist at all."

In 1952 the Partido Obrero Revolucionario recruited a young man who for a number of years was to be one of the leading figures in Peruvian Trotskyism. This was an eighteen-year-old student, Ismael Frías, who had first been active in the Aprista Party Youth but had become disillusioned with that group. Considering himself a Marxist, but hostile to the Communist Party, he joined the POR.[2]

In February of the following year the POR received sudden publicity when the dictatorship of General Manuel Odría accused the POR and the Communist Party of being chiefly responsible for a general strike which took place in the southern city of Arequipa. Documents seized by the police in raids and published in the daily press cast some interesting light on the Trotskyite movement of that time.

One of these documents was a program of the POR. According to the police report on the POR, it had been sent by Ismael Frías to Félix Zevallos Quesada and Carlos Howes Beas, members of the POR Central Committee. The program dealt first with the problems of political organizations; it called for an end to all repressive laws of the dictatorship, for the extension of suffrage to all those over eighteen years of age, for political rights for soldiers, and for freedom of trade unionization and "the labor press." The program called on the proletariat "to reconstitute the unions and central labor groups, including the CTP [Confederación de Trabajadores del Perú]," and urged the elimination of all control by "the bourgeois state" over trade-union organization; it then proceeded to list a number of "immediate demands of the workers." The program also advocated nationalization of the land, "that is to say, abolition of all private ownership of land." Large landholdings were to be confiscated and granted, with use-rights, to poor peasants. It also called for confiscation of large sugar and cotton haciendas along the coast and their conversion into state farms. The Indian communities were to be turned into cooperatives. Finally, the program demanded the expropriation without compensation "of public services and of the large industrial enterprises—mines, oil fields, transport, and more developed manufacturing industries."

The revolution advocated by the POR was to follow, in a general way, the model of the Bolshevik upheaval of 1917. The Program stated: "The cohesion of vast elements of the working population of the countryside, the organization of the workers of the cities, and the solid worker-peasant alliance, indispensable for the victory of the revolution, can only be carried out through local committees of workers, peasants, local residents, and garrison soldiers.... The destruction of the bureaucratic-military-police machinery of the bourgeois state, the expropriation of the expropriators, the repression of the attempts to restore the feudal-bourgeoisie and imperialism, require that the committees be converted into organs of the proletarian state. The Committees of Workers, Peasants, and Soldiers thus come to be the dictatorship of the proletariat supported by the poor peasants."

The police report on the POR said that many of its members were "former members of the Aprista Party" and that they were "much more active than many Stalinist Communists." The party was reported to have five local groups, three of them in Lima, one in Callao, and one in Arequipa. Another document disclosed at this time that the PORistas tended to have a somewhat exaggerated impression of their own importance. This document was said to be a report sent to the Central Committee of the party by Félix Zevallos, one of its members, during a visit to Bolivia. Zevallos talked about "our decision to mobilize APRA." He also mentioned the possibility of winning supporters from dissident elements in the Communist Party.[3]

These documents published in 1953 indicated that the POR was in more or less direct contact with the Fourth International, and that it submitted reports on party activities to the International. A letter in French from the International to the POR leaders said: "Your last letter...interested us enormously. Your activity, your aggressive and optimistic spirit, your comprehension of the real movement of the masses, makes us very happy. We are certain that your organization really represents the nucleus of a true revolutionary party of the Peruvian masses and that it is truly 'on the right road.' " But this letter also warns the Peruvian PORistas of "the effects of reaction" and warns: "Be careful, don't become too enthusiastic over your successes. It is necessary that the organization be consolidated; maintain your cohesion and function, even if it means giving up spectacular, immediate successes, since we have on a worldwide scale a long revolutionary period.''

In 1953 police claimed that a member of the Peruvian POR living in Paris, Francisco Abríl de Vivero Lestonnat, an ex-university student, was the principal contact of the party at the Paris headquarters of the Fourth International.[4] Later that year Ismael Frías was exiled from Peru by the Odría regime. He went to Mexico, where he lived until 1955; and is reported to have worked there, at least part of the time, as a secretary to Trotsky's widow, Natalia Sedova Trotsky. He returned to Peru in 1956.[5]

In spite of the scare publicity which the Odría dictatorship gave to these events of 1953, there was certainly no serious Trotskyist plot afoot; there were too few of them to make a plot significant in any case. Apparently the Odría regime chose to make the POR the scapegoat for an occurrence that rather seriously embarrassed the government. A student strike at the University of San Marcos in Lima coincided with a workers general strike in the city of Arequipa, and both workers and students were temporarily successful in their protests. Later, during a vacation period at the university, when most of the students were away, the police rounded up most of the more important student leaders, among whom there were a handful of Trotskyists. If proof were needed that there was no plot, it was to be found in the fact that the police found all of their documentation for the "plot," with suspicious ease, only when they arrested the students.[6]

## THE PABLO-POSADAS POR

The POR split in 1956 over two main issues: the division in the Fourth International, and disagreements on the political strategy the party should follow in Peru.

Internationally, one of the factions—both of them continued to call themselves Partido Obrero Revolucionario—aligned itself with the Michel Pablo branch of the Fourth International; the most important figure in this party was probably Ismael Frías. The other element, headed by Carlos Howes and Félix Zevallos, joined the forces of the International Committee of the Fourth International, of which the Socialist Workers Party of the United States was the leading party. Insofar as national politics was concerned, the pro-Pablo POR favored the sort of "entrism" policy which Pablo was preaching at that time, whereas the rival group was opposed to such a policy. The possibilities for "entrism" in Peru had increased considerably as a result of the events surrounding the end of General Odría's presidential term in 1956.

When the end of General Odría's term approached, his military colleagues would not permit him to continue in office, through elections or otherwise.

In the elections of June 1956, ex-President Manuel Prado was the victor as a result of the support he received from the underground organization of the outlawed Partido Aprista. Immediately upon assuming office, he legalized the Aprista party.

It was evident that the Aprista party was the only serious mass party in the country, but it was also obvious that there was a left wing in the organization which was unhappy with the old leadership and its policies. In this situation the pro-Pablo faction of the POR felt that the opportunity was ripe for the Trotskyists to enter the Partido Aprista, to try to assume leadership of this left-wing element and win it over to Trotskyist ideas.[7]

The position of the pro-Pablo group on this issue was presented in an article by Juan D. Leiva entitled "El Ascenso de Masas en Perú Después de las Elecciones," which appeared in the October 1956 issue of *Revista Marxista Latinoamericana*, the organ of the Pabloite Fourth International, in the following terms:

> The task of the Marxist revolutionary vanguard, of the Peruvian Trotskyists, organized in the Partido Obrero Revolucionario, is determined by this evolution and by the characteristics of the movement of the masses, the great majority of whom are passing through the channel of the APRA, and who develop their struggles and their politicalization in the bosom of that party. This fundamental task is to unite with the Aprista masses, within the organizational framework of the APRA, to stimulate the formation and the development in the midst of a working class left wing which is advancing toward revolutionary Marxist positions, as a means for developing the politicalization of the labor and Aprista masses for the formation of a mass labor party. A totally fundamental aspect of this task is the struggle to convert the CTP   [Confederación de Trabajadores del Perú ] into a mass central labor group which includes all workers, peasants, and poor petty bourgeoisie and which specially organizes and mobilizes   the great peasant masses in the struggle for the land. The CTP will also be one of the most powerful means for contributing to the development of the politicalization of the Peruvian masses and for accelerating its advance on the road to the construction of a mass labor party, a first step to forge a real revolutionary Marxist leadership of the great masses of Peru."[8]

Between 1956 and 1960, the Pabloite POR had some considerable trade-union influence in the city of Arequipa. It was also of some significance in the labor movement in the Lima area, and in 1959-60 helped to organize a city-wide labor group in opposition to the one affiliated with the CTP.[9] In Lima, the stronghold of the Pabloite POR's labor influence seems to have been in the union of workers employed by Fertisa, one of the country's principal chemical firms. The leaders of this union were arrested, along with Socrates García and Juan Palacios of the Central Committee of the POR, at a public meeting called by the POR to discuss the party's attitude toward the 1962 general election. The POR charged that the arrest of these leaders occurred when strongarm members of the Aprista Party attacked the POR meeting, at which point the police stepped in to arrest the Trotskyists and their friends. The POR issued a call for labor and peasant groups all over Latin America "to denounce this systematic oppression."[10]

The Pabloite POR also claimed in the early 1960's to have considerable influence in the important Miners Federation of the Central Region. They claimed credit for an open letter which the Federation sent in April 1962 to Fidel Castro expressing its "fervent proletarian salute ... to *The First Workers State of America and its Socialist Revolution*." This document ended with the slogan, "For Consolidation and Triumph of the Cuban Socialist Revolution; for the Proletarian Revolution of Latin America; for the Federation of Soviet Socialist States of Latin America."[11]

When most of the Latin American affiliates of the Pabloite Fourth International followed J. Posadas in launching still another version of that International, the Peruvian POR did likewise. Thus, the International Secretariat of the Posadas version of the Fourth International expressed its pleasure with the declaration of the Miners Federation of the Central Region by issuing a letter in June 1962 to the Latin American sections of the International. It claimed that this declaration showed "how our little parties can come to influence large mass organizations," and went on to argue that "it is possible to orient, direct, and influence that same process in the other countries of Latin America, and in a certain manner of Europe, Asia, and Africa."[12]

During the Prado regime, the Pabloite-Posadista POR had frequent difficulties with the government. Ismael Frías, who attended the Fifth World Congress of the Pabloite Fourth International in Italy in 1957, was indicted in 1958 for having "put in danger the international relations of the state" by making this trip and participating in hostile demonstrations against Vice-President Richard Nixon when he visited Lima in May 1958. Frías was jailed again for some time in 1959.[13]

Meanwhile, the Pabloite-Posadista POR had undergone a split. The dissident group, headed by Ismael Frías, broke away largely over the issue of Posadas' attempt to dominate the Peruvian party. Posadas first visited Peru in 1957 and at that time sought to dictate to the local party leaders. Frías' resistance to Posadas finally culminated in 1960 in Frías' withdrawing with his own followers to form still another POR.[14] The loss of Frías was a serious blow to the Pabloite-Posadas POR. He had been a member of both the Executive Committee and the Secretariat of the Pabloite Fourth International. Upon withdrawing, the Frías group began to publish its own periodical, *Obrero y Campesino*.[15]

The Frías POR soon dissolved, and by 1966 Frías no longer considered himself a Trotskyist. However, in 1968 he organized an independent left-wing group known as the Liga Socialista Revolucionaria. With the advent of the military regime of General Juan Velasco, the Liga threw its support behind the reforming efforts of the new government. By 1971 the Liga had ceased to function, but Frías had acquired a position of some influence in the military government. He wrote a column first in the newspaper *Expreso*, which the Velasco government had confiscated from its original owner, and then in *La Crónica,* another pro-government paper; in July 1971 he was named a member of the Secretariat of Social Mobilization, an institution established to rally mass support for the Velasco regime.[16]

The Posadista POR in the meantime had changed its name to Partido Obrero Revolucionario (Trotskista) and remained loyal to Posadas. By the early 1960's it had given up any attempt to penetrate the Apristas and had lost most of whatever influence it once had in the labor movement, although it still controlled the Fertisa union in Lima. In July 1962, when elections were called to pick President Prado's successor, the Aprista candidate, Víctor Raúl Haya de la Torre, won a plurality but failed to obtain the 33.3 per cent of the popular vote necessary to win. The military then overthrew the Prado government, and the Aprista-controlled CTP responded by calling a general strike against the military's usurpation of power. The Trotskyite controlled Fertisa union answered this call by adopting a resolution in which it said that "the CTP long ago ceased to be an organization in the service of the workers, and has been converted into an agency at the service of the employers." It added: "We are for the general strike, but not to return Prado to power, or to bring to power Belaúnde, Odría, or Haya de la Torre. We are with the general strike for the purpose of the workers taking power and establishing a Workers and Peasants Government—that is, a government of the workers of field and city."[17]

Shortly before the 1962 election, the POR(T) had issued a new party program, labeled The Socialist Program. It put particular stress on "revolutionary agrarian reform," which it stressed "must be carried out by the peasants themselves, through the occupation of the land of the oligarchs." This POR program also included a Workers Plan for Economic Development, which called for "nationalizing imperialist enterprises in petroleum, mines, transport, large factories, electricity, telephones, etc." for nationalizing banks, investment banks, and insurance companies, and establishing a single National Bank; for "control and self-administration of nationalized firms by their own workers"; for urban reform, which included "reducing rents, converting renters into proprietors, redistributing the population of the cities, eliminating the slums, and launching a national program of housing construction"; and for "trade with the U.S.S.R., China, and the People's Democracies, as well as receiving credit in those countries." Other demands of this program were "replacement of the bourgeois army by workers and peasant militias," and "establishment of a worker and peasant government."[18]

When the government of President Fernando Belaúnde Terry called municipal elections in November 1966, for the first time in forty years, the POR(T) participated in the election in the isolated rural area of Tumbes. There it

formed, together with the Peasants Union of Tumbes, which it apparently controlled, what it called the United Class Electoral Front, to run candidates in
the municipality. The Front called for voters to give "political intervention
through elections a progressive and revolutionary meaning—and independently
of whether the Electoral Front in Tumbes can solve such and such regional
or zonal problems, because the problem of the country, and wherever capitalism still exists in the world, is not to compete with it or reform it, *but to
overthrow it.*"

The Trotskyite-backed ticket received 79 votes in Tumbes, or 19 per cent
of the total, but the Posadista Fourth International treated this showing as a
major victory for Trotskyism. Its periodical *Revista Marxista Latinoamericana,*
in its issue of July 1967, proclaimed (page 306): "This showing in the elections has repercussions throughout Peru and in all Latin America, because
in spite of being a limited experience in a region of little importance, it
demonstrates how organizations of the peasantry, as well as the unions and
the proletariat, can and should be used. . . ." This same issue of the *Revista
Marxista Latinoamericana* noted that the POR(T) had published several
pamphlets by J. Posadas. It commented that "this intense activity of the
Peruvian section has immense repercussions in the struggles of the exploited
masses of Peru and constitutes a center of programmatic influence."[19]

The Trotskyite leadership of the Peasants Union of Tumbes won a victory
in May 1967; the union claimed to have forced the agrarian reform authorities
of the Belaúnde government to grant to them the land of the hacienda which
they worked. The POR(T) celebrated this with a proclamation ending "Viva
the Worker Peasant Alliance."[20] In 1967 the POR(T) also took advantage
of a general strike of teachers, which it claimed was lost, to denounce the
Communist Party for its "conciliation" during the walkout. The POR(T)
paper argued that instead of such "conciliation," the workers should have
expanded the strike to revolutionary proportions, because "the crisis of the
bourgeoisie favors a fundamental struggle."[21]

When the government of President Fernando Belaúnde Terry was overthrown
in October 1968 by a military coup which established an Army dictatorship
led by General Juan Velasco, which pictured itself as "revolutionary" and
took a number of nationalistic and reform measures, the POR(T) came out
strongly in support of the new regime. However, the Trotskyites of the POR(T)
criticized the government for not seeking to develop an organized civilian base.
An editorial in the party paper *Voz Obrera* for the second fortnight of October
1969 said: "The organism upon which [the government leaders] rest for support
is the army. Nothing more. That is the structure of the government: the army.
The state administration does not support them" The editorial concluded: "The
political base for this development is to stimulate the *Anti-Imperialist United
Front,* with an immediate program for supporting the progressive measures

of the nationalist government and at the same time struggling to advance and develop in an independent class and revolutionary form the struggle for socialism in the country.''

The POR(T) continued to support the Velasco government. An editorial in *Voz Obrera* for the second fortnight of May 1970 denounced "terrorism against the nationalist movement" and praised the move to establish Committees for Defense of the Revolution as an expression of "the immense desire of the masses to intervene, to be able to decide, to have influence and at the same time to organize—not against the nationalist movement, as the bourgeois, oligarchic, and imperialist press attempt to make it appear, but to push forward, develop, and stimulate the forces of the anti-imperialist nationalist movement." In its issue for the first fortnight of June 1971, *Voz Obrera* noted the "theoretical" basis of the Posadistas' support of the Velasco regime: it said that J. Posadas had pronounced the regime a "revolutionary state," together with Egypt, Mali, Bolivia, and Chile.

In 1971 the POR(T) of Peru was one of the few Latin American Trotskyite parties to have a national headquarters—an office in a building near the center of Lima, with a small bookshop selling pamphlets by J. Posadas and issues of *Voz Obrera*.

## THE ANTI-PABLO POR

The segment of Peruvian Trotskyism which broke with the Fourth International of Michel Pablo and was opposed to "entrism" held its first congress at the end of March 1957. After this meeting a congress of representatives of anti-Pablo groups from Peru, Chile, and Argentina was held; it established the Secretariado Latino Americano del Trotskismo Ortodoxo, which came to be known by its initials as SLATO.[22]

The anti-Pablo Peruvian POR was very small at its inception, with organized groups only in Lima and Arequipa. It sought to penetrate the trade-union movements in those two cities; it had some success in the Bank Workers Union, and cooperated in organizing opposition to the regional labor federations in the capital and Arequipa.[23] One of its first major efforts was to organize an Anti-Imperialist Front to protest the visit of Vice-President Richard Nixon to Lima in May 1958. One student of the career of Hugo Blanco has written of this effort: "The men of the POR worked day and night. They succeeded in establishing their Anti-Imperialist Front with the Communist Party, the Movimiento Social Progresista, and the POR(T)."[24] The success of the anti-Nixon efforts led to the arrest of several POR leaders.

In January 1959 the POR held a regional plenum for the Lima Department in Callao. It studied the party's future political line and expressed jubilation over the fall of the Cuban dictator Fulgencio Batista and the triumph of the revolutionary movement of Fidel Castro. A few months later POR members participated in a widespread protest, spearheaded by the Chauffers Federation, against an increase in the price of gasoline imposed by the government.[25]

By 1960 two men had emerged as the principal leaders of the POR. One was Hugo Blanco, a young man from Cuzco who had returned to his native city to undertake trade-union and party work among the peasants in that part of southern Peru. The other was Antonio Aragón, the head of the POR organization in the Lima region. There were local leaders of less significance in the two other areas in which the POR had organizations, Puno and Arequipa. During the next two years three foreigners were to play key roles in the leadership of the POR. Probably the most important was the Argentine Hugo Bressano, generally better known under his pseudonym Nahuel Moreno; he was the head of SLATO, the regional Trotskyist group which had been established in 1957. Another Argentine, Alberto Pereyra, and a Spaniard, José Martorell, were the other two.

In November 1960 a national congress of the POR was held in Arequipa. Víctor Villanueva has noted: "In this congress they studied insurrectional possibilities, the popular support which could be mustered for action in peasant organizations, the capacity of the membership, and other things that had to be studied if they were to adopt such a line as that which was adopted: the insurrectional line was approved unanimously. The insurrection was to be carried out through guerrilla war."[26]

Five months later, at the request of the Peruvian POR, a meeting of SLATO was held in Buenos Aires. Delegates were reported as attending from Chile, Peru, Argentina, Bolivia, Uruguay, and Venezuela, although it should be noted that there was no functioning Trotskyist group then existing in Venezuela. This meeting endorsed the Peruvians' decision to try to take the path of insurrection, and it promised a large sum of money to help the effort.[27]

## THE POR'S MONEY PROBLEM

As a result of the SLATO meeting's decision, Bressano, Pereyra, and Martorell arrived in Peru late in 1961. However, the money which the foreign Trotskyists had promised did not arrive with them. The SLATO conference had originally offered to provide eight to nine million Argentine pesos, then the equivalent of about $131,580. Upon arriving in Peru, Nahuel Moreno cut this offer by about 80 per cent, offering half a million Peruvian *soles*. Although he promised to deliver the money by March 1962, Moreno was unable or unwilling to do so.

When the POR leaders in Cuzco, desperately in need of funds for the insurrectional operation they were about to launch, demanded the immediate summoning of a national congress of the party to settle the money matter, and gave the national leadership in Lima forty-eight hours to agree to this, Moreno insisted that Hugo Blanco and several others be removed from their leadership positions. This was done, with the result that Blanco—who was later to be treated as a hero by all branches of international Trotskyism—was a mere rank-and-file member of the party when he carried out his famous uprising in the Valley of Convención.[28]

Unable to get money from abroad, the POR leaders organized two "expropriations" of funds from banks. The first of these occurred in December 1961, when 105,000 *soles* were stolen from an agency of the Banco Popular (of which the President of the Republic, Manuel Prado, was one of the principal stockholders);[29] the second took place on April 12, 1962, when 2,950,000 *soles* were taken from a branch of the Banco de Crédito in Miraflores, a Lima suburb.[30]

However, these stolen funds did the POR, and particularly Hugo Blanco, little good. Almost half of the money, 1,115,000 *soles*, was captured by the police when it was being taken by truck to Cuzco. The rest, which had been placed in the hands of Hernán Boggio Allende, an engineer, disappeared. Boggio Allende was finally expelled by the Trotskyists in May 1963.[31] However, it was never learned whether he had absconded with the funds or had invested them for the party's future benefit, a possibility suggested by Víctor Villanueva.

## THE DEBATE OVER THE NATURE OF THE "INSURRECTIONAL LINE"

With the arrival of Nahuel Moreno in Peru a controversy took place within the Trotskyist ranks over the correct method of carrying out an armed insurrection. The original resolution endorsing "the insurrectional road" at the POR's November 1960 Congress had apparently endorsed the idea of a guerrilla war, but Moreno had a different concept. It was his idea that under the leadership of the Trotskyists, the peasants, organized into unions, should seize control of their landlords' land, organize self-defense forces to back up their actions with arms, and thus establish throughout the rural parts of the country "a dual power," which, if the movement spread rapidly enough, could challenge the ability of the existing government to rule.

Moreno had put forth his ideas in a book, *La Revolución Latinoamericana,* in which he argued strongly against the guerrilla tactic. He wrote: "The peasantry is leading the revolutionary struggle, occupies land, and confronts the military forces of the oligarchy. On the other hand, the Cuban revolution triumphed through a guerrilla war. These two facts have made part of the revolutionary vanguard believe that the only correct strategy is to develop a guerrilla war." However, he added, "this concept is doubly wrong . . . because guerrilla war is not the only method of armed struggle, and because there are other methods, which in certain places and circumstances of Latin America are much more useful."

Elaborating upon these ideas, Moreno commented: *"Guerrilla warfare is not synonomous with insurrection.* The latter is the art of bringing the masses to power and the former is one form of struggle which may permit the insurrection in its final stages, but in no sense should it be suggested at its commencement. *Guerrilla actions are a tremendous waste of revolutionary forces before the seizure of power.* . . . The guerrilla war as a strategy is the opposite of the insurrection, exactly because it does not base itself on the organization and massive activity of the peasantry or the working class to free a zone or seize power, but depends only on their sympathy and support in order to survive. *It is a defensive strategy."* In contrast to the guerrilla strategy, Moreno suggested that the "backward peasant" be convinced "of the need to seize land and develop the dual power. The occupation of land signifies the dual power because it breaks with the legality of the bourgeoisie and establishes in the occupied terrain the mandate of the masses, with their unwritten laws." Finally, Moreno adds: "Without party there is no revolution; the party is everything, the masses are the tools in its hands."[32]

At first, Hugo Blanco seems to have supported the idea of a guerrilla war. However, as his actions in the La Convención Valley ultimately indicated, he was brought around to support of the strategy outlined by Nahuel Moreno.

## THE ESTABLISHMENT OF THE
## FRENTE DE IZQUIERDA REVOLUCIONARIA (FIR)

For several years, the POR had been seeking to arrange a broader alignment of forces in the Trotskyist camp in Peru. The party newspaper POR launched the slogan "A Single Party of the Peruvian Revolution," and in Cuzco the PORistas succeeded in bringing together some other small groups in a body called the Frente Revolucionario. The POR participated with a number of groups of the far left in the Frente Nacional de Defensa del Petroleo, which was dominated by the Communist Party. Finally, negotiations were begun looking toward the unification of a number of Trotskyite or semi-Trotskyite groups. These included the Partido Comunista Leninista (a splinter from the Communist Party), a group of independents who had organized the Agrupación Pro-Unificación de Izquierdas Revolucionarias (APUIR), the POR, and the POR(T).

At first, the POR, the POR(T), and the APUIR agreed to join forces in a single organization. The Partido Comunista Leninista held back because there was some opposition to a merger within their ranks. At the last moment the POR(T) thought better of the idea and withdrew from the unity negotiations.

As a result, the Frente de Izquierda Revolucionaria (FIR) was finally established in December 1961 by the unification of the POR and the Agrupación Pro-Unificación de Izquierdas Revolucionarias. It was not until early 1963 that the Partido Comunista Leninista finally decided to join forces with the FIR.[33] The FIR became the Peruvian affiliate of the anti-Pablo International Committee of the Fourth International, as the POR had been, and after the partial unification of the forces of international Trotskyism in 1963, of the United Secretariat of the Fourth International.

Gonzalo Añi Castillo has commented on the objectives sought in the formation of the FIR: "The immediate objective was complete fusion, but in fact for a time there was coexistence of the two organizations which maintained the FIR (the POR and the Leninistas). This caused some difficulties. How to treat the many comrades who had entered the FIR directly and before the Leninistas ... and those who entered afterwards if they didn't belong to either of the basic organizations."[34] In time, complete integration of the members of the various groups which had established the FIR seems to have been achieved. Whatever subsequent quarrels there were within the group had nothing to do with the past affiliation of the contestants.

The Pablo-Posadas Trotskyites, although their Peruvian affiliate had at first contemplated joining the FIR, did not look upon it with any friendship. The Latin American Bureau of the Pabloite Fourth International, in a resolution adopted May 16, 1962, argued that "the Moreno group," as they called the FIR, had "demonstrated themselves incapable of maintaining activity, policy, and revolutionary discipline, have no political perspective, do not have and cannot have any force or reason to undertake an action of the importance of that in which they now appear involved." The Latin American Bureau further accused "the Moreno group" of being "agents of imperialism and of the bourgeoisie," and denounced them for having usurped the name of Trotskyism and the Fourth International.[35]

## HUGO BLANCO AND THE PEASANT UNIONS OF LA CONVENCIÓN VALLEY

The outstanding figure in Peruvian Trotskyism has undoubtedly been Hugo Blanco. He was the only Trotskyist leader able to build up a mass following. He was the one who put into practice the FIR's "insurrectional line." After it failed and Blanco was arrested, the Fourth International of the United Secretariat organized a worldwide campaign on his behalf, which won support not only from the other two factions of international Trotskyism but also from distinguished intellectuals who had no connection with Trotskyism, and even from a few Communist parties.

Blanco, who was born in Cuzco, has been called by Víctor Villanueva a "typical provincial petty bourgeois." He studied at the National Science High School and as an adolescent read widely, particularly Indianist novels by such writers as Jorge Icaza and Ciro Alegría.[36] Upon graduating from secondary school, he went to Argentina and enrolled as an agronomy student in the University of La Plata, where he joined the Trotskyist movement. On the faculty of the University of La Plata was Hugo Bressano (Nahuel Moreno), who was the principal figure in the *Palabra Obrera* branch of Argentine Trotskyism. Upon returning home in 1956, Hugo Blanco joined the Partido Obrero Revolucionario faction, which like Moreno's group in Argentina was aligned with those opposed to "Pabloism."[37]

After spending a couple of years in Lima, where he was active in the POR, Blanco returned to his native Cuzco about the middle of 1958. Apparently not quite certain what to do with himself, he worked at various jobs in the city of Cuzco, and organized unions among such unlikely groups as newsboys and shoeshiners. As the result of his trade-union and party activities, he found himself in jail in Cuzco in the middle of 1959. There he became friendly with another prisoner, Andrés González, a tenant farmer from the Valley of La Convención, in the Department of Cuzco and some 90 miles from the city. When they were both released, González, whose confidence he had won, gave Blanco a job as a subtenant or "allegado," apparently with the agreement that they would both seek to extend unionization among the peasants of the Valley.

Peasant unions had begun to appear in the La Convención Valley in the early 1950's and the union movement had grown slowly during that decade. In 1958 eight unions had united to form the Federación Provincial de Compesinos de la Convención y Lares [Provincial Federation of Peasants of La Convención and Lares]. It had entered into friendly relations with the Federation of Workers of Cuzco, which among other things had frequently supplied lawyers to help the peasant unions press their suits against the landlords.[39] Although Blanco had been named representative of some of the peasant unions to the Federation of Workers of Cuzco, his credentials were challenged by the Communists, who controlled the federation. Blanco did not consider the issue worth quarreling over and decided instead to concentrate his efforts on organizational work in the Valley of La Convención.[40] He soon became the leading figure of the union on the Chaupimayo plantation and organized a Revolutionary Workers School there, which according to Julio Cotler and Felipe Portocarrero "diffused a new ideology and promoted massive invasions of the haciendas."[41]

In 1962 Hugo Blanco presented himself as a candidate for Secretary-General of the Federación Provincial de Campesinos de La Convención y Lares. When he was elected to that post, a number of the older peasant leaders refused to accept the fact, and representatives of twenty unions affiliated with the federation withdrew and chose their own slate of officers. The federation was thus split into two antagonistic groups.

Wesley W. Craig has commented on the position which Blanco was taking with regard to the peasant movement by the time he became the federation's Secretary-General: "Blanco, a confessed Trotskyist, was an advocate of much stronger measures than those espoused by the earlier leaders of the peasant union movement. He felt that the campesinos, in the final analysis, would have to resort to violence and possible guerrilla warfare in order to achieve the objective of land control. Ownership of the *parcelas* as a goal of the movement began to be expressed in 1960 and was formulated into a slogan of 'Tierra o Muerte' (Land or Death)."[42]

Hugo Blanco had formalized the movement of the peasants to seize the land by a "decree" which he had issued in his capacity as Secretary of Agrarian Reform of the federation. This document, which was widely distributed throughout the La Convención Valley, read as follows:

1. The General Assembly of each Sindicato [union] must name a Commission of Agrarian Reform from its membership.
2. The renters and sub-renters will be converted automatically into proprietors of the lands which they work.
3. The uncultivated lands will be distributed in parcels, commencing fundamentally with the poorest peasants.
4. The lands which have been planted for the landlord will remain in his possession if his behavior has been humane. Otherwise, those lands, and if it is possible the hacienda house with its installations which have passed under the control of the Sindicato on a collective basis, will be used for a school, a store, irrigation, and so on.
5. The authorities employed by the landlords cannot be allowed to intervene because the only people who know agrarian reality well are the peasants themselves."

Hugo Blanco himself has described how this decree was carried out by the unions: "In my capacity as agrarian reform secretary of the Department of Cuzco Peasant Federation, I issued a decree which was implemented on a hundred estates and gave the peasants more than the present agrarian reform law [1964] . . . . In a nutshell, the decree gave the land to those who worked it without their having to compensate the landlords in any way. Those who had no land, or very little, were given uncultivated areas on the sole condition that they put it under cultivation. On some estates, the peasant unions decided how much land would be left in the hands of the landowners. In cases like Chaupimayo, where the ranchers had been actual murderers, the unions expropriated the land, the houses, the buildings, etc., without compensation, and everything became collective property to be used for schools, health facilities, defense (ransom for imprisoned peasants, 'lawyers,' etc.). All, or almost all, the directors of this deep-going agrarian reform were imprisoned. Others died in the struggle."[44]

Blanco also moved on to the second step of the revolutionary process outlined by Nahuel Moreno. A pamphlet issued by the Trotskyist Young Socialist Alliance of the United States described this: "Blanco began to develop groups of defense for the unarmed peasants so they could protect their recovered lands. If gamonales [reactionary landowners] or police terrorized them, the Indians sent a message to Blanco on his union rounds. If possible, he sent an armed commission of peasants to investigate and cool down the police by letting them know the peasants were defended. The Federation began to acquire some arms, hoping to establish defense guards in each local."[45]

On November 13, 1962, Blanco and some of his peasant followers attacked the small police station of the militarized Guardia Civil at Pucyura. The only Guardia Civil policemen at the post was killed; Blanco and his friends left with three rifles, a revolver, munitions, and equipment; and Blanco became a fugitive from the law.[46] He found refuge, together with a few followers, among the peasantry of La Convención Valley. By the time he was captured in May 1963, most of the other Trotskyites of the Cuzco region had also been arrested by the police.[47]

With the removal of Hugo Blanco from the scene, whatever Trotskyist influence he had been able to generate in the La Convención Valley and in the Cuzco region apparently died out. Over the next few years the Peruvian government first abolished the semi-feudal "obligations" which the peasants had owed to the local landowners, and then gave the peasants ownership of the small pieces of land which the landlords had allowed the Indians to use for their own purposes; this did a great deal to undercut radical influence among the peasants of the area. When a group of guerrillas (not associated with the Trotskyites) sought to establish a base in the Valley in 1965, they received little or no support.[48]

## THE CAMPAIGN FOR HUGO BLANCO

With the collapse of Hugo Blanco's work in the Cuzco region, the POR abandoned, at least for the time being, its emphasis on "the insurrectional road." This was emphasized in a letter from José Martorell to Víctor Villanueva, which said: "Whatever is said now or will be said in the future, in 1961-62 it was insisted that the historical task of the moment was the realization of the Peruvian revolution through an insurrectional process in which armed struggle should occupy a preponderant position. . . . Since then all kinds of things have been said, but the truth is that in that moment, at the beginning of 1962, no one doubted the necessity of starting armed actions as soon as possible. . . . Later Hugo Bressano in Argentina, and after him the FIR and Hugo Blanco, modified their insurrectional position, converting it into an attempted mass movement, and in some cases adulterating past positions in order to accommodate them to new ones, to give an appearance of continuity."[49]

After Blanco and his closest associates were captured, much of the activity of the FIR and the Fourth International of the United Secretariat itself was taken up with conducting propaganda on his behalf. For example, the issue of the Fourth International's publication *Perspectiva Mundial* of January 2, 1967, was devoted almost entirely to the Blanco case.

The April 1967 issue of *Cuarta Internacional*, the Spanish-language journal of the International, carried a long article on "The worldwide campaign in defense of Hugo Blanco and all of the Peruvian political prisoners." This article noted that among those who had been recruited to send messages to the Peruvian government on behalf of Blanco were not only representatives of other revolutionary groups in Peru, including the pro-Castro ELN and MIR, but also the following : a United States Committee For Justice to Latin American Political Prisoners; Jean-Paul Sartre, three educational workers unions in France, a group of French Catholics, the writer Simone de Beauvoir, the French economist Charles Bettelheim, and a group of distinguished French intellectuals; a group of British politicians and journalists, including several members of parliament; Amnesty International, a group devoted particularly to fighting for political prisoners, with headquarters in London; various Italian politicians, including several leaders of the Communist Party; and the Communist Party of Mexico. Wherever the Trotskyites of the United Secretariat had any influence, meetings were held to protest against Blanco's trial and imprisonment. Typical was a meeting held by Canadian Trotskyists in Toronto on January 27, 1967, which was addressed by several university professors and by André Gunder Frank, a left-wing journalist and professor.[50]

Hugo Blanco remained in jail until August 1966, when he was brought before a military court sitting in Tacna, the southernmost city of Peru. Although the prosecutor asked for a death sentence, Blanco was finally sentenced to twenty-five years in jail. Several of his associates were given lesser sentences. He appealed this conviction, and the prosecutor asked once again for the death penalty; in 1968 this appeal to the Supreme Council of Military Justice was turned down, and the twenty-five-year sentence was confirmed.[51] Blanco was finally released from prison in an amnesty in January 1971.[52] Several months later he was deported to Mexico.[53]

## THE IDEOLOGY OF THE FRENTE DE IZQUIERDA REVOLUCIONARIA

The Peruvian Trotskyists affiliated with the United Secretary of the Fourth International developed an ideological position in the middle and late 1960's which had certain peculiarities. This ideology was based in large part upon the experience of Hugo Blanco and his associates in the La Convención Valley between 1958 and 1962.

The chief exponent of this ideological position was Hugo Blanco himself, who in spite of having been deprived of his leadership position in 1962, was after his capture regarded as the principal spokesman for the party. His point of view was extensively presented in a pamphlet entitled *El Camino de Nuestra Revolución* which was published by the Trotskyist publishing firm Ediciones Revolución Peruana in Lima in July 1964.

In this pamphlet, Hugo Blanco stresses the importance of the peasants in the development of the Peruvian revolution. He stresses the importance of the peasant unions as the incipient "dual power," comparable to the Soviets in the Russian Bolshevik Revolution. Quite obviously, his "model" for the Marxist-Leninist revolution in Peru is that of his own experience with peasant organizations in the La Convención area.

Blanco thus urges that primary attention be placed upon the development of the peasant union, but the peasant union as a very broad-gauged organization, which should in fact be considered the nucleus of the new society. Thus, among the tasks which he argues that the peasant union or sindicato should undertake are the administration of justice on the local level, the establishment and manning of schools in the rural regions, the organization of rudimentary health services, the establishment of cooperatives (for consumers, for credit, and so forth), and the organization of small-scale public works projects for particular communities. The sindicato should undertake the job of instructing the peasants in modern methods of cultivation and care for their crops; they should also establish local defense units for the peasants, and should organize the occupation of large landholdings. The local peasant sindicatos should be organized in regional federations and a national confederation, which should be the nucleus of power from which to challenge the country's traditional government.[54]

Although the model used by Hugo Blanco was his own experience with the peasants of the La Convención area, he recognized that this model was by no means perfect. He argued that the fundamental weakness of his own efforts in the early 1960's was the lack of a sufficiently well-organized and revolutionary political party. In an interview in 1968, he said: "The fundamental weakness of the guerrilla struggle in which I took part, and of the succeeding ones, was that it was not backed up by a party rooted in the masses on a national scale. I cannot complain of a lack of popular support for our armed action in 1962. But there was a lack of means for channeling this support, of transmission belts, of a party. Our great mistake was that we did not give fundamental importance to the factor of the party."[55]

Blanco's position would seem to be closer to the Maoist pattern of Marxist-Leninist revolution than to anything else, but by 1969 he reasserted the importance of the traditional role assigned by Marxist-Leninists to the proletariat. In an interview published early in 1969, he answered the question "What is the role of the peasantry in the revolutionary process?" as follows: "The peasantry in Peru today is the major revolutionary force, but in the long run once they obtain land, the peasants become bourgeois. The working class is the only guarantee in the long run of a socialist revolution. Our work was concentrated in the countryside, but only our limited resources prevented us from developing the struggle on a national basis—in the factories as well as in the fields."[56]

Blanco had profound disagreements with the "foco" theory espoused by the followers of Fidel Castro. In an interview early in 1969, when asked what he thought of Régis Debray's book *Revolution in the Revolution?*, Blanco commented: "My main criticism is that he lacks a conception of a party, he sees the *foco* as a panacea for all Latin America. There is no specific analysis of the conditions in each country. Peruvian revolutionary politics cannot be advised by such an arbitrary approach."[57] Almost a year later, Blanco added: "The Fidelista comrades confuse revolution with guerrilla warfare and they substitute guerrillas for the concept of the party. This is what has weakened them most noticeably. . . . They have some contradictory aspects. Without a deep analysis, their repudiation of the opportunism of the Communist Party led them to repudiate Marxism-Leninism in many fundamental aspects. They underestimate the importance of the party. They underestimate the importance of the mass movements. They overestimate and glorify isolated heroic acts."[58]

## THE FIR AND THE VELASCO REGIME

The Trotskyites of the FIR, affiliated with the United Secretariat of the Fourth International, were not as enthusiastic toward the nationalist military regime of General Juan Velasco as their counterparts in the Partido Obrero Revolucionario (Trotskista). They backed a number of the measures carried out by that government, but drew back from giving it the kind of general support which was offered by the leaders of the POR(T), let alone by ex-Trotskyist Ismael Frías.

Perhaps the most authoritative statement by the FIR concerning the Velasco government was that issued by the party on August 20, 1969. It noted that "sections of the left . . . are saying that the junta is revolutionary and nationalist," and added that "we orthodox Trotskyists of the FIR say that the junta is a bourgeois regime which wants to develop the country, but that it is not nationalist and still less revolutionary." The FIR statement continued in its definition of the Velasco government as follows: "From the beginning, we said that it was Bonapartist, that is, that it represents the interests of the exploiting sectors in general. Within the framework of this Bonapartism, within the framework of its general objective of saving the system, it has leaned toward the sector favoring economic development, that is, those capitalist sectors, both indigenous and foreign, which have an interest in industrial development of the country."[59]

Hugo Blanco himself commented on the Velasco regime's agrarian reform program, which was certainly the most fundamental reform decreed by the military government. In an interview which took place presumably in July 1969, he commented: "The positions the junta takes benefiting the exploited masses and in defense of the national sovereignty must be firmly supported. There can be no doubt about that. In the specific case of the agrarian reform law, we can say that this is an advanced piece of legislation and superior to the previous law in many respects. . . . But this law, like the previous one, does not propose confiscating the big estates without compensation, which is what the peasants want."[60] Blanco obviously wanted cooperative rather than individual farming to result from agrarian reform in Peru, but he professed not to believe in coercion as a means of bringing this about: "If at first the peasants divide their lands, the effect of another group of peasants holding the land in common—with higher yields—will turn them around. And that is what occurs, because the vanguard elements strive to organize themselves into cooperatives."[61]

After his release from prison Blanco presented an additional assessment of the Velasco government's agararian reform, as well as of its general reform program. He said, in part:

> Imperialism has an urgent need for more extensive markets for its manufactured goods and machinery. The purpose of this neocaptialist policy is suited by an agrarian reform that would create an extensive layer of small agricultural proprietors capable of absorbing the consumer goods exports of the imperialist countries.
>
> Industrialization of our countries also suits the purposes of this policy. In this way they can absorb the imperialists' machinery exports. This is true even if the industrial concerns that carry out this development in our country are not imperialist but national or even state-owned companies.
>
> The reforms instituted by the military junta . . . fit into the context of this general policy of imperialist neocapitalism. This is true not only of the specifically economic measures like the agrarian reform, which is aimed at creating layers of consumers of industrial products; or of the individual development law, which is aimed at promoting this development for the benefit of the bosses. It is also true of the educational reform. The purpose of this measure is to provide skilled workers, such as lathe operators for example, that is, industrial slaves instead of illiterate Indian serfs of the landlords.
>
> Besides these fundamental economic reasons for the government's reformist measures, there are political reasons. Not just the desarrollista (pro-development) sectors but the most astute elements of the exploiting sectors understand that the previous situation in our country could not be maintained, that the danger of a *genuine popular revolution* was imminent."

Blanco gave a capsule summation of his, and presumably his party's, view of the Velasco regime when, in reply to the question "What historical significance does the Peruvian process have in the context of the Latin American revolutionary ferment?" he replied: "It is one of the last desperate efforts of a condemned system to divert the people from making their real revolution."[62]

In the light of the Velasco government's agrarian reform, Blanco appealed to his supporters in the FIR to go into the countryside and work among the peasants. He particularly appealed to the students. In an article in the latter part of 1969, he wrote: "My position is as follows on the debate in the universities over whether or not passage of the agrarian reform act is an occasion for the students going in a massive way to the countryside. . . . I repeat my appeal to the students to make a mass turn toward the countryside. We must keep up our criticism of the agrarian reform but not stay in the cities to discuss it. He is a better revolutionist who goes into the countryside and promotes this reform, sincerely believing in it, than the one who stays on the campus and combats it from a 'doctrinaire' revolutionary position."[63]

The university section of the FIR seems to have followed Blanco's suggestion. It adopted a resolution in the middle of 1969 which in its operational paragraphs urged that "This academic year be devoted to the Peruvian peasants. Thus, there must be no classes. Rather, led by our student associations and federations, we must go into the countryside to unite with the peasants. . . . We must force implementation of a real agrarian reform and introduction of efficient organization and production, and participate actively in achieving all the requirements of these mobilizations."[64]

## THE VANGUARDIA REVOLUCIONARIA

In the latter half of the 1960's there appeared a new organization of semi-Trotskyist orientation in Peru. This was the Vanguardia Revolutionaria, with its principal support in the universities. It was established in 1965 after the defeat of the guerrilla movements sponsored by the Fidelista MIR and the pro-Chinese Communists. As S. López, writing in the periodical of the Ligue Communiste, the French member of the United Secretariat, commented, it tended to "polarize the radicalized sectors" because of the weakness of the FIR. However, López notes that it tended to be "eclectic and conciliatory" and that it tried to avoid discussion of "the ideological struggle within the international Communist movement." It even underestimated the role of Trotsky in forming the original program of the Communist International. But López did admit that it had a Trotskyist coloration.

The Vanguardia Revolucionaria grew rapidly in the nation's universities, largely displacing the Maoist and Fidelista groups from the leadership of student federations. By 1971, however, the heterogenous nature of the membership of Vanguardia Revolucionaria had taken its toll, and it had split into three rival groups, each using the name Vanguardia Revolucionaria. One of these splinters openly proclaimed itself to be Trotskyist, and the two others inclined in the direction of Maoism. There had not yet developed a close association of the admittedly Trotskyist element of the VR with either the FIR or the POR(T).[66]


## CONCLUSION

By 1971 the Trotskyite movement in Peru was divided into three different groups. Two of these had international affiliations, the POR(T) with the Posadista version of the Fourth International and the FIR with the United Secretariat. The Vanguardia Revolucionaria had not yet made any international connections.

During the quarter-century of its existence, Trotskyism in Peru has not been a serious contender for power. In the late 1950's it did begin to develop some influence in the labor movement, with the POR(T) being the main beneficiary. In the early 1960's the POR (and subsequently the FIR) attained a position of leadership among the peasant unions of the Department of Cuzco, although this influence seems to have disappeared after the principal Trotskyite leader, Hugo Blanco, was imprisoned and the government carried out an agrarian reform in the affected area. Trotskyism remains a relatively minor factor on the extreme left in Peru, and the extreme left itself is still only a minor element in the national political picture.

# —9—

# Leon Trotsky, Diego Rivera,
# and Mexican Trotskyism

Trotskyism in Mexico has been distinctive for several reasons. For one thing, Mexico was the only Latin American country in which Leon Trotsky actually lived, and the only one in which he had more or less close personal contact with his Latin American supporters. Second, the Trotskyist movement in Mexico was the only one in the Latin American region which was able, at least for a time, to count among its members and leaders such an internationally distinguished figure as Diego Rivera, the great mural painter, and among its sympathizers such other distinguished intellectual figures as the novelist José Revueltas and the musician Carlos Chávez. Finally, the Mexican Trotskyists were the Latin American group most directly influenced by the Trotskyist movement of the United States, and through it, by the Fourth International. On several occasions, U.S. Trotskyists intervened directly and sometimes peremptorily in the internal quarrels of their Mexican comrades.

## THE ORIGINS OF MEXICAN TROTSKYISM

As in the case of the Mexican Communist Party, the Trotskyist variant of Communism in Mexico owed its origins in large part to someone from the United States.[1] The first convert to Trotskyism there seems to have been Russell Blackwell, an American Communist who came to the country in the late 1920's to organize the "Pioneers," the Communists' childrens' organization.

Blackwell, who used the name Rosalio Negrete in Mexico, sympathized with those in the Communist Party of the United States who sided with Trotsky in his struggle with Stalin. With the establishment of the Communist League of America, he began to receive the League's newspaper, *The Militant*, and other Trotskyist literature. He also began to seek converts among Mexican

Communists. A former colleague of Blackwell's has written: "Russell sowed the protest of Trotskyism in Mexico, and seemed to be the enlightened man who sought to see the present (in the revolutionary organization) and the future, the human society which would give life to the creative free man. Himself creative, he projected the future, as Karl Marx had dreamed. His whole life was consumed as a flame in seeking this objective."[2]

Blackwell's first convert was Manuel Rodríguez. He was a young man of indefinite profession who in the early 1920's had become interested in Marxist philosophy, particularly in the *Anti-Duhring,* Friedrich Engels' famous philosophical polemic, and had subsequently become actively involved in left-wing politics as a participant in campaigns organized by the Mexican Communists in favor of Augusto Sandino, the Nicaraguan who was carrying on a guerrilla war against the United States Marines, who were occupying his country. Through these activites Rodríguez became involved in the Socorro Rojo (Red Aid), a Communist front organization ostensibly organized to raise money to defend Communist political prisoners in various parts of the world.

At first, Manuel Rodríguez was not trusted by the Communist leaders. They later told him that his great enthusiasm for all kinds of work, no matter how humble, made them suspect that he might be an agent provocateur. However, after he had been arrested several times, he gained their confidence. Although he never formally joined the Communist Party, he came to be trusted as if he were a member; the Central Committee met in his house on various occasions, and mail directed to the Communist Party was sent through him.

Meanwhile, Rodríguez began to participate in a pro-Trotskyite group organized by Russell Blackwell; it included Rodríguez's wife, José Revueltas (who later became a well-known novelist), and Pedro María Anaya Ibarra, who several decades later was to become editorial secretary of the government newspaper *El Nacional.* Blackwell was expelled from the Communist Party (and thoroughly beaten up by his ex-comrades), and soon afterwards was deported from Mexico as a dangerous radical, but the group he had founded went on. During 1933 it got out various mimeographed bulletins; one was called *Oposición,* another *Izquierda (Left).* They were joined by several other recruits, including Félix Ibarra, who was to play an important role in Trotskyist affairs in later years, and several of Ibarra's relatives.

In the meantime, Rodríguez was expelled from the several Communist front groups to which he belonged although for reasons having nothing to do with his Trotskyist sympathies; he was thrown out because he had sent out announcements of a meeting of the Central Committee of the Communist Party, to be held in his house, inserted in advertisements of the "capitalist" mercantile house for which he worked. After being expelled from the CP front groups, he openly proclaimed his adherence to Trotskyism, and took the lead in establishing a frankly Trotskyist organization in Mexico. His group was joined by several others who had recently been expelled from the Communist Party for their Trotskyist sympathies.[3]

Those expelled from the ranks of the Communist Party and its front organizations formed the Oposición Communista de Izquierda (Communist Left Opposition). During 1933 and 1934 they sought actively to establish contacts with the organized labor movement. Whenever an important strike broke out, the members of the OCI distributed propaganda to the striking workers, but they had little success at this time in recruiting them into their ranks.

## THE FERNÁNDEZ-GALICIA GROUP

The second group that was important to the birth of Mexican Trotskyism was headed by Luciano Galicia and Octavio Fernández, both of whom were teachers. Galicia came from Jalapa, in the state of Veracruz, where he became interested in Communist activities while a student at the local teachers college. He worked with the Communists for a number of years, doing the usual run-of-the-mill jobs—putting up posters, bringing people to meetings, and so on. Even there, he came across a proclamation of the Left Opposition published in New York City in Spanish for distribution in Latin America. He wrote those who had published it and began to receive Trotskyist material regularly.

Galicia moved to Mexico City in 1931, to attend the Instituto Pedagógico. There he met people with a great deal more ideological training than those he had known in Jalapa. He began to work in Socorro Rojo, the Liga de Escritores y Artistas Revolucionarios (a Communist front organization of writers and painters), and the Juventud Comunista, the Communist Party's youth organization. He finally decided to join the Communist Party late in 1933. During this time he kept up contacts with the Left Opposition, and propagated its ideas among the Communists of Mexico City. He soon became head of Socorro Rojo in the Federal District.[4]

The other principal figure in the second pioneer group in Mexican Trotskyism, Octavio Fernández, had become interested in the Trotskyist schism from Communism through the offices of Russell Blackwell, who he had come to know in 1932 when he, Fernández, was a student at the Instituto Pedagógico. Blackwell had put him in touch with A. González, a Mexican-American member of the Communist League of America, whose principal job was to establish contacts for Trotskyism in Latin America. He had also become acquainted with Galicia, and the two men, together with a third Instituto Pedagógico student, Benjamín Álvarez, decided to join the Communist Party in late 1933.

However, by March 1934 Galicia, Fernández, and Álvarez decided that there was little reason to remain in the Communist Party, which was itself very small, and that they might as well set up their own group. They resigned from the Communist Party, which did not recognize their right to do so and insisted on expelling them. Since it was then the Communist Party's custom to beat up those it expelled, the three normal school students went to their expulsion "trial" armed with revolvers, to make sure they would not receive the usual treatment.

Once out of the Communist Party, the prospective teachers joined forces with the group gathered around Manuel Rodríguez, with which they were put in contact through their mutual correspondents in New York. They joined the Oposición Comunista de Izquierda, which later in 1934 changed its name to Liga Comunista Internacionalista. The Liga's first endeavor was to get out a magazine, *Nueva Internacional*, which went through five issues.

Much of the first year's work of the new Trotskyist group was taken up with the publication of their magazine. They had sought help for financing it from the famous mural painter Diego Rivera, who had openly proclaimed his sympathy for Leon Trotsky's position; they also appealed to the musician Carlos Chávez, the novelist José Revueltas, and other intellectuals, and all of these contributed to financing *Nueva Internacional*.[5]

The first issue of *Nueva Internacional* (March 15, 1934) contained a political declaration issued by Galicia, Fernández, and Álvarez when they resigned from the Communist Party, and a reply to a violent attack made on the three by *El Machete*, the organ of the Mexican Communists, which labeled them "slanderers, provocateurs, splitters, counter-revolutionaries."[6]

Subsequent issues of *Nueva Internacional* carried several articles by Leon Trotsky himself, including "Syndicalism and Communism," "A Historical View of the United Front," and "Permanent Revolution." It also carried such pieces as Friedrich Engels' May Day Manifesto of 1890, reports on a congress of the international left opposition recently held in Paris, and an article entitled "How Industry is Distributed in Mexico."[7]

## EARLY ACTIVITIES OF THE LIGA COMUNISTA INTERNACIONALISTA

The Liga held a "regional" conference, which was in fact of national scope, in the middle of 1934; it elected an executive committee, approved statutes, and adopted theses on organized labor and various agrarian questions.[8] In August 1934 the Liga also undertook a fund-raising campaign. It issued appeal sheets on its stationery addressed "To Intellectuals, Students, Workers, and Peasants With Work," on which contributions were to be pledged. These sheets proclaimed that "We make a call to all revolutionaries to come to our aid, which is aid to the cause of the proletarian revolution."[9]

The Liga also undertook the establishment of a front organization, the Asociación de Estudios y Divulgación Marxista-Leninista (Association for Marxist-Leninist Studies and Propaganda). Diego Rivera was its Secretary-General, and four Liga members, including Luciano Galicia, were on its executive committee. A report on an Asociación meeting by Octavio Fernández commented:

The society organized Saturday the 23rd of last month a commemoration meeting for the anniversary of the death of the poet Gutierrez Oyus. We obtained the collaboration of the musicians Chávez and Revueltas, the meeting having come out much better than we expected. Diego, Manuel Rodríguez, and a worker spoke, there were revolutionary songs, and the people became very heated; there was a large proportion of workers who cheered Trotsky, the Liga, and the Fourth International. As you will know there has appeared here an organization, virtually fascist, called "Acción Revolucionaria Mexicanista," which has all of the characteristics of fascism in its initial development, that is, anti-semitic nationalism, struggles against Marxism, demagoguery about workers demands, etc. Well, these "gold shirts" here attempted to break up various revolutionary meetings and we foresaw that they would want to dissolve ours and we armed with clubs. When the meeting was about to start, a group of these gold shirts appeared and began to distribute their propaganda, but in the face of the hostility of the workers they had to retire. The political content of the meeting was very good. Rivera spoke attacking fascism and speaking of our tactic of the United Front. Rodríguez spoke on the danger of war and we succeeded in selling many copies of our periodical.[10]

The Trotskyist leaders in the United States were not entirely happy with this front organization of their Mexican comrades. They argued that it should not be organized as a mere legal arm of the Liga, but rather as an organization of sympathizers. They argued that its name was too closely associated with Trotskyism.[11] The Trotskyists were also seeking to gain influence in the organized labor movement; by early 1935 they had succeeded in organizing a small union of textile workers and were trying to build up a union of construction workers.[12]

During this early period of Mexican Trotskyism, its leaders and members were having difficulties with both the Communists and the Mexican government. Throughout 1934 the official Communist periodical *El Machete*, as well as the organs of various Communist front groups, violently attacked the Mexican followers of Leon Trotsky.[13] At the time the Trotskyist movement was officially launched in Mexico, the government was cracking down rather heavily on all left-wing dissidents. As a result, four of the Trotskyist leaders were arrested and deported to the Islas Marias in September 1934. This event moved A. González, of the United States Trotskyists, to say that he had for some time feared such a development, since it did not seem to him that the Mexican comrades were taking the precautions against possible police persecution which were required for an underground organization such as the Liga Comunista Internacionalista.[14]

## EARLY SPLITS IN THE LCI

Within less than a year after its establishment the Liga Comunista Internacionalista split into several quarreling groups. Although personal differences undoubtedly played a major role in these schisms, there were also questions of ideology and political tactics involved. One source of problems was the very close association which had developed between Manuel Rodríguez and the painter Diego Rivera. After a considerable period of unemployment, due largely to his political activities, and frequent "vacations" in jail, Rodríguez had become Rivera's secretary. There was apparently some feeling on the part of other members of the Liga that Rodríguez had in effect become "Rivera's man" in the organization, although Rodríguez consistently denied this.[15]

The ideological issues in the controversy arose from the famous "French turn" of the international Trotskyist movement. Upon the recommendation of Leon Trotsky himself, the French affiliate of the international left opposition had entered the French Socialist Party, to work as a fraction there and to gain recruits for Trotskyism. Similar moves were to be made subsequently by other national Trotskyist groups, culminating with the entry of the American Trotskyists into the Socialist Party of the United States early in 1936.

Manuel Rodríguez argued that the Mexican affiliate of the international left opposition ought to do the same thing as its French counterpart. He urged that the Liga Comunista Internacionalista members should enter the Partido Socialista de Izquierdas (PSI). This was a party which had arisen during the 1934 election campaign to support the presidential ambitions of Colonel Adelberto Tejeda, the left-wing Governor of Veracruz. The party persisted for some time after the election of President Lázaro Cárdenas, the nominee of the government's official party, the Partido Nacional Revolucionario. The PSI was a loosely organized group within which Rodríguez was convinced the Trotskyists could work and recruit new members.[16]

Another issue between Rodríguez and other LCI leaders was whether or not they should work closely with Vicente Lombardo Toledano, then head of the Confederación General de Obreros y Campesinos de México, and a strong opponent of the Communists. Early in 1934 Lombardo had attended a number of LCI meetings and apparently had even considered joining the LCI. He sought the help of the Trotskyists and suggested broad cooperation with them. Rodríguez was in favor of accepting this offer, but other members of the Liga, including Luciano Galicia and Octavio Fernández, opposed the idea.[17]

The upshot of these controversies was the split of the Liga Comunista Internacionalista into three rival bands. One of these was at first headed by Galicia and Fernández, a second by Rodríguez, and a third by S. De Anda, who earlier in 1934 had threatened a split because of what he alleged were the "Stalinist attitudes" of Fernández and Galicia, although these differences had subsequently been patched up, at least temporarily.[18]

This split persisted for more than a year. Although a document was signed on August 1, 1935, by Manuel Rodríguez and Félix Ibarra on the one hand, and Octavio Fernández on the other, apparently reuniting these two groups,[19] this did not put an end to the feuding among the Mexican adherents of the Fourth International.

Luciano Galicia, who had withdrawn from his association with Octavio Fernández early in 1935, was the principal leader of a new group, of which S. de Anda was also a member, known as the Comité Organizador de la Juventud Leninista. In December these people issued a manifesto denouncing "the group of Diego Rivera," apparently meaning the Rodríguez-Fernández element, and denying that it was Trotskyist. They also expressed their support for the idea of a Popular Front and for the newly organized Comité Nacional de Defensa Proletaria, which had been set up under Lombardo Toledano's leadership, in an attempt to unify all of the country's rival trade-union groups, and which a few months later patronized the establishment of the Confederación de Trabajadores de México. This manifesto called for the establishment of "a true Independent Revolutionary Workers Party in Mexico" and pledged its adherence to the movement for a Fourth International.[20]

## THE RECONSTITUTED LIGA COMUNISTA INTERNACIONALISTA

A certain degree of unity among Mexican Trotskyists was again established in the middle of 1936. Manuel Rodríguez dropped out of activity entirely, and S. de Anda maintained a small group of his own, which established some relationship with the Partido Obrero de Unificación Marxista (POUM) of Spain, and for a while published a periodical with the same name as that of the POUM, *La Batalla*. However, the forces headed by Luciano Galicia and Octavio Fernández joined once again under the old name Liga Comunista Internacionalista.[21]

The new Liga was led by a Political Bureau composed of Luciano Galicia, Octavio Fernández, Félix Ibarra, and Diego Rivera. Ibarra served for some time as Secretary-General, devoting his full time to the activities of the Liga. This was the first time that Diego Rivera formally appeared in the leadership of Mexican Trotskyism.[22]

The newly reconstituted Liga began to issue a newspaper, *IV Internacional*. Its first number was dated September 3, 1936, and it bore the subtitle "Órgano de la Liga Comunista Internacionalista (Bolchevique-Leninista), Sección Mexicana de la IV Internacional." Sixteen issues of the periodical appeared, the last one being dated December 1937, by which time the Liga had again split into quarreling factions.

*IV Internacional* was a lively newspaper. It was large in size, specialized in frequent mammoth headlines, and carried a wide variety of different material. This included a great deal of news about the Spanish Civil War, and particularly about the machinations of the Spanish and Russian Stalinists to suppress their opponents within the Spanish Republican forces; denunciations of the first Moscow trials; and frequent news and comment on Mexican politics and trade-union affairs. It also carried lengthy documents issued by the International Left Opposition and numerous articles by Leon Trotsky himself.

For the first time during this period, the Trotskyites began to have some real influence in the labor movement. There was a building boom in Mexico City and other towns, and the Trotskyists took the lead in organizing the Sindicato Único de la Construcción, which became one of the largest unions among this rapidly growing group of workers. They also had influence in the Casa del Pueblo, a bakers' union which offered hospitality in its headquarters to several other small workers groups. Diego Rivera had particularly close relations with the leaders of the Casa del Pueblo.[23]

## LEON TROTSKY AND MEXICAN TROTSKYISM

In the meantime, Leon Trotsky himself had taken up residence in Mexico. The idea of Trotsky seeking refuge in Mexico seems first to have been suggested in correspondence between Manuel Rodríguez and the Secretariat of the International Left Opposition. Rodríguez, who at the time was working for General Francisco Mujica, a member of President Cárdenas' cabinet, ascertained from Mujica that if the occasion should arise, the Cárdenas administration would be willing to entertain the idea.[24]

Somewhat later, in the summer of 1936, the Political Bureau of the Liga Comunista Internacionalista received a letter from the International Secretariat of the Fourth International inquiring what the climate would be for Trotsky's coming to Mexico, and the Liga began a propaganda campaign in favor of the idea, but by their own admission "without for a moment thinking that there existed any possibility, first that Trotsky would urgently need to come to the country, or second that the government of General Cárdenas would concede him asylum."

However, on November 21, 1936, Diego Rivera received a cable from New York saying that there was life-and-death urgency about discovering whether General Cárdenas would allow Trotsky to come to Mexico. The Political Bureau of the Liga decided immediately to dispatch Rivera and Octavio Fernández to the northern city of Torreón, where General Cárdenas was staying, to ask him about this. They left with two chauffeurs who drove steadily, stopping only for meals, until they got to Torreón.

The two Liga leaders had had the foresight to consult with General Mujica before they left Mexico City, and he had given them a letter of introduction to President Cárdenas which indicated that he supported the idea of admitting Trotsky. So they were almost immediately received by the President, who informed them on the spot that he would grant asylum to Trotsky, the only provision being that the Mexican Trotskyists not receive him in such a fashion as to arouse counter-demonstrations from local enemies of Trotsky. He told them to return to Mexico City, where the Minister of Foreign Affairs would be informed of his decision.

When they arrived in Mexico City they were informed by the Minister of Foreign Affairs that he was violently opposed to the idea of granting asylum to Trotsky, and that so long as he remained in the post, no such asylum would be granted. Several weeks passed, during which a struggle took place within the government between the Minister of Foreign Affairs on the one hand and General Mujica on the other.

Finally, the Liga decided on December 17 to send another delegation to General Cárdenas, who was still in Torreón, to press the issue with him, since there was grave danger that if he did not receive Mexican asylum soon, Trotsky might be handed over to the Soviet government by the Norwegians. This second delegation had reached Monterey when they read the welcome news that the Mexican government had agreed to grant Trotsky permission to come to Mexico to live. They continued on to Torreón, this time to thank the President for his action.[25]

In spite of General Cárdenas' statement during his first interview with the Liga leaders that he would impose no conditions upon Trotsky as the price for receiving asylum, there was one condition upon which he did insist—that Trotsky would not intervene in internal Mexican politics. Isaac Deutscher comments on this:

> In admitting Trotsky, at Rivera's request and on promptings from his own entourage, Cárdenas had acted from a sense of revolutionary solidarity. He declared that he had not merely granted Trotsky asylum, but invited him to stay in Mexico as the government's guest. From the outset he did his utmost to protect his guest's head against the storms of hatred gathering over it; and he was to go on doing this till the end. However, his own situation was rather delicate.... He asked Trotsky to pledge himself that he would not interfere in Mexico's domestic affairs. Trotsky gave this pledge at once, but, taught by his bitter Norwegian experience, he was on his guard and explicitly reserved his "moral right" to reply in public to any accusation or slanders. Cárdenas was satisfied with this. It never occurred to him to ask Trotsky to refrain from political activity; and he himself stood up for Trotsky's right to defend himself against Stalinist attacks.... Trotsky often expressed his gratitude and, strictly observing his pledge, never ventured to state any opinion on Mexican politics even in private, although his view of Cárdenas' policy, which did not go beyond the 'bourgeois stage' of the revolution, must have been critical to some extent.

This situation naturally created a somewhat strained relationship between Trotsky and his Mexican adherents. He did not feel himself free, except under the most unusual circumstances, to intervene directly in the affairs of the Mexican section of the international left opposition.

Trotsky's position was made clear almost immediately upon his arrival. In a letter to the Liga leaders, which was published in the February 1937 issue of *IV Internacional*, the first number of the paper to appear after Trotsky's arrival, he noted that they belonged to an organization which shared the ideas he represented, and thanked them for their friendly reception; but he went on to say, "I cannot take upon myself the least responsibility for your activities." The letter ended, "Our relations will remain personal and friendly, but not political."

There were at least two occasions, however, on which Trotsky did indicate displeasure with actions of the Liga. One of these was when, having lost control of the Sindicato Único de la Construcción, the Trotskyist leaders decided to go into a union meeting with arms and take back the union. Trotsky heard of these plans and informed his followers that this was not a revolutionary way of winning support from the working class.[27] The second instance came when Luciano Galicia issued a call, published in the May 1937 issue of *IV Internacional*, to "assault three or four large stores" and take other sabotage measures as "direct action" against the high cost of living. This call was issued at a time when Trotsky was under attack from the Kremlin for alleged efforts to organize sabotage and murder in the Soviet Union, and he immediately wrote a letter to his Mexican followers telling them that Galicia's attitude was wrong and under the circumstances bordered on treason to the movement.[28]

Another, and more serious, intervention in Mexican politics was being prepared by Trotsky, but it did not come to fruition before he died. After the attack on his house led by David Alfaro Siqueiros, the Communist painter, in May 1940, Trotsky worked feverishly on a book denouncing all those he felt were involved in this attack or were among its "intellectual authors." Some of this material was submitted to Mexican police and judicial authorities and other parts were sent to the press in Mexico and the United States. In general, it constituted an indictment of the Communist movement and its fellow travelers in Mexico, and their connections with the Soviet regime and the GPU (its secret police). The volume came out some months after Trotsky's death under the title *Los Gangsters de Stalin*.

Another intervention by Trotsky in Mexican affairs took place in connection with the Cárdenas government's decision to turn the administration of nationalized railroads over to the Railroad Workers Union. This move engendered controversy within the Confederation of Workers of Mexico (CTM), with Communist members of its executive being particularly vociferous in their opposition to the idea. Rodrigo García Treviño, Assistant Secretary of Technical Affairs of the National Committee of the CTM, was the principal supporter of workers control.

At one point in the controversy, García Treviño decided to solicit Trotsky's comments on the controversy. In their first interview, Trotsky quickly expressed his opinion that García Treviño was wrong and the Communists were right, that such union control of an industry was "anarcho-syndicalism" not Marxism. But when García Treviño insisted on pursuing the matter, Trotsky listened, and after several hours of discussion he informed his guest that he had changed his mind, that he had no decision on the issue and would have to study it further.

Several days later, García Treviño was again summoned to Trotsky's house in Coyoacán, and was handed a document which represented the distillation of Trotsky's ideas on the subject. After discussing at length the positive and negative aspects of workers' control, the document concluded:

> On balance, one can say that this new control of labor contains both the greatest possibilities and the greatest dangers. The dangers lie in the possibility that state capitalism may be able, through the unions, to maintain the workers in submission, exploit them cruelly, and paralyze their resistance. The revolutionary possibilities lie in the fact that by supporting their positions in exceptionally important branches of industry, the workers can mount an attack against all the strong points of capital and against the bourgeois state. Which of these possibilities will triumph? When? Naturally, it is impossible to say. Everything depends entirely on the struggle of various tendencies in the working class, on the experience of the workers themselves, and on the world situation. In any case, to use this new form of activity in the interest of the working class and not of the labor aristocracy and bureaucracy will only be possible under one condition: the existence of a revolutionary Marxist party which carefully studies the forms of activity of the working class, which criticizes all of its deviations, which educates and organizes the workers, which conquers influence in the unions, and which assures a revolutionary workers representation in the nationalized industry.''[29]

Trotsky told García Treviño that he could use this document for whatever internal purposes he might have within the Confederación de Trabajadores de México, but that it was not for publication. García Treviño did use it, although without notable success for the cause which he was supporting and he did not publish it until almost a dozen years after Leon Trotsky's death, when he did so with the approval of Trotsky's widow, Natalia Sedova Trotsky.[30]

One important function of the Mexican Trotskyists at this point was to provide guards for Trotsky's home. From the time of his arrival in Mexico, there was fear that agents of the Stalin regime would try to kill him, and so a regular system of round-the-clock guards was established to protect him and his family. The job of organizing this was given to Octavio Fernández, one of the principal Mexican Trotskyist leaders. He himself frequently stood guard duty, as did members of his family and other carefully selected members of the Liga Comunista Internacionalista.

After the split in the Liga at the end of 1937, however, the Trotskyists decided they should no longer depend exclusively on the Mexican comrades for this service. Members of the United States affiliate of the Fourth International and some German exile Trotskyists were brought in for the purpose, although a select group of Mexicans continued to work with these outsiders. Two attacks were eventually made on Trotsky—the second was fatal—and each time no Mexicans were on guard. Fernández believes that had Mexicans been there, the first attack would have resulted in casualites among the attackers, and the second, by Jacson-Monard, would not have occurred at all, because he would have been thoroughly searched before being admitted to see Trotsky.[31]

Trotsky developed friendly relationships with some of the Mexican Trotskyist leaders. Sra. de Fernández remembers a Christmas party at the Octavio Fernández house which was attended by the Trotskys; to the delight of his grandson, "the Old Man" participated in breaking the piñata, the traditional Mexican container for Christmas toys, and was an active participant in a game of "pin the tail on the donkey."[32]

## ANOTHER SPLIT IN THE LIGA COMUNISTA
## INTERNACIONALISTA

Within a year of Trotsky's arrival in Mexico, his followers in that country split again. The new division was in part a struggle for power and influence between Luciano Galicia and Octavio Fernández, but also in part centered on issues of tactics. As we have noted, Galicia tended increasingly to take an extremist position, advocating sabotage and other resorts to violence, and he also supported the idea of having Trotskyist-controlled unions withdraw from the main labor movement. Both attitudes were opposed by Trotsky himself, which embittered Galicia.

Since Trotsky himself was not in a position to try to patch up the differences among his Mexican followers, he called in the aid of his United States comrades. Early in 1938 the U.S. Socialist Workers Party sent to Mexico a highpowered delegation consisting of James Cannon, Max Shachtman, and Vincent R. Dunne. They conferred with members of both the Galicia and Fernández groups and spoke at a meeting organized in their honor by the leaders of the Casa del Pueblo. However, nothing concrete came of this quick visit, and it was decided to send a Socialist Workers Party representative for a longer period to try to reorganize Mexican Trotskyism.[33]

The person chosen for this task was Charles Curtiss, a Los Angeles member of the Socialist Workers Party, who had been in Mexico during 1933-34 and knew most of the leaders of Mexican Trotskyism. James P. Cannon, the principal leader of the SWP, wrote Curtiss a letter of instruction and sent him credentials from the All America-Pacific Bureau of the International Left Communist Opposition and from the Socialist Workers Party. He told Curtiss, "[You must not] allow yourself to be put in a position of an individual who contributes merely a personal opinion. You are the *representative* of the Bureau, charged with the task of *reconstituting* the Mexican section."

Cannon wrote, "In our judgment, the most pernicious factor in the situation is Galicia (Blanno) who impresses us more and more as a petty inner-party demagogue who was obviously educated too long in the Stalinist school." The Fernández group, he said, "are also intellectuals and partly responsible for the debacle of the League; but with different nuances. It is our impression that the Fernández brothers offer more possibilities for the future." Cannon urged his delegate to exercise "firmness" but "without truculence or needlessly antagonistic gestures." He said that he knew "very well that in this situation, as always, you will display the necessary diplomacy and tact and comradliness." And he told Curtiss that he "need not be in too big a hurry to reconstitute the section."[34]

After he had been in Mexico for some months, Curtiss reported on the success of his mission. This report indicated that the Galicia group consisted mainly of workers. He said that it had agreed to dissolve the dual union which its leaders had organized among the construction workers, and to merge this group into the construction group belonging to the Confederación de Trabajadores de México. He reported that Galicia had been unhappy about this move, but had gone along with it. He noted that the Fernández group consisted mainly of "either students or teachers." Its members did not seem as active as those of the Galicia faction, but they were exerting considerable pressure to be recognized as the official Mexican section of the International Left Opposition, feeling that their chances would be much improved by such recognition.

Curtiss also reported that the Casa del Pueblo leaders were demanding that all of the principal figures of Mexican Trotskyism be expelled, and that reestablishment of the Mexican section be limited to the trade-union leaders of the Casa. However, Curtiss reported that he did not think this a good idea, that he did "not think that all or even a minority of the old League members deserve such treatment." He reported that the Casa del Pueblo leaders were "essentially trade unionists first and Communists afterwards." Furthermore, they were opposed to liquidating the dual unionist policies sponsored by the Galicia group. Finally, Curtiss proposed a six-month program for reconstituting the Mexican section of international Trotskyism. This emphasized worker leadership of the rebuilt group, establishment of provincial branches if possible, indoctrination of the section's members, and establishment of a youth organization.[35]

The problems of the Mexican section were dealt with by the founding congress of the Fourth International, held in the Paris area in September 1938. It adopted a special resolution on the subject. This document, after denouncing various aberrations of the Mexican section, particularly the Galicia faction, authorized "Comrade C. to continue his efforts, under the direct supervision of the International Sub-Secretariat, to facilitate the reorganization of the Mexican section of the Fourth International." It authorized Curtiss ("Comrade C.") to admit both Luciano Galicia and Octavio Fernández, but "only on the basis that for a period of one year they shall not occupy any leading post in the organization. The new executive committee of the organization should be composed, above all, of serious and experienced proletarian elements." Insofar as Diego Rivera was concerned, the conference decided that "in view of the difficulties that have arisen in the past with this comrade in the internal relationships of the Mexican section, he shall not form part of the reconstituted organization, but his work and activity for the Fourth International shall remain under the direct control of the International Sub-Secretariat.''[36]

During this party struggle and the Curtiss negotiations, Galicia wrote a letter to Trotsky in which he denied the claims that he, Galicia, had been largely responsible for the Trotskyists' dual union policy. He denounced attacks on him by the Fernández faction and by Curtiss, and protested the decision of the Pan American and Pacific Bureau of the Fourth International that he should be eliminated from the Mexican section of the Fourth International. He blamed Trotsky personally for much of the opposition he had experienced within the International.[37]

A new Mexican section was finally constituted in January 1939. The reorganized Liga Comunista Internacionalista wrote to the Pan American Bureau of the Fourth International informing them of the event and asking for official recognition as the Mexican section of the International. This letter informed the Pan American Bureau that during January the Fernández and Galicia factions had each met with Charles Curtiss, and that two joint meetings had also been held, but that both sides had concluded that reunification was impossible.

As a result, Charles Curtiss issued a call to a meeting on January 31, 1939, of "All the comrades who wish to form the Mexican section of the Fourth International, belonging to and disciplined by this International." This letter set forth the requirements for attendance at the meeting and adherence to the International: All those participating would have to sign a document entitled "To the Militants of the Fourth International," which stated that any who joined the reorganized section of the Fourth International would have to accept the decisions of the Fourth International and the Pan American Bureau, including the decision to expel Luciano Galicia and P. González; that only active members could belong to the section; that they be willing to rejoin the organization once it was accepted by the Fourth International; that the cases of three comrades be investigated by the International before granting them admission to the section.

The meeting of January 31, 1939, was attended by twelve Mexicans and Curtiss; several others who were unable to attend had indicated their willingness to accept the decisions of the meeting. The agenda of the meeting included discussion of the tasks of the organization, election of committees and commissions, determination of regular meeting times, acquisition of a headquarters, educational work, and additional business. Félix Ibarra was elected Secretary-General, P. Toriz was chosen Secretary of Organization, and S. Langarica was named Treasurer.

The letter from Curtiss calling for the meeting noted that the Galicia opposition group was about equal in size to that which had met on January 31, and that it consisted largely of workers. It urged that efforts be made to gain the adherence of key working-class members of the rival group, which it noted was now led by a student, Carbajal, who was himself considered susceptible to being won over to the official Fourth Internationalist group.[38]

Aside from attempting to reestablish a Mexican Section of the Fourth International, Charles Curtiss had the task of launching a new publication in Mexico. This was *Clave (Key)*, which according to Octavio Fernández, who served as its manager, was designed largely as a vehicle for Leon Trotsky himself. Although it carried many articles by other people, as well as news of the Fourth International in various parts of the world, *Clave's* main purpose was to be an organ through which Trotsky could present articles in Spanish, which later might be translated into other languages and published throughout the world. The publication of articles concerning events and developments in various parts of the world in a Mexican periodical, ostensibly for local circulation, was conceived of as shielding Trotsky from allegations that he was interfering in the internal affairs of these countries.

Virtually every one of the fifteen issues of *Clave* published while Trotsky was still alive carried at least one article by him. These included his comments on problems in France, India, Spain, and the Soviet Union. They included obituaries of Karl Kautsky and Lenin's widow Krupskaya, comments on the Second World War, even book reviews. The magazine also carried proclamations of the Fourth International, including the documents of the founding congress, news on Trotskyist groups in other countries, articles on events in Mexico, and an article by George Novack on the elections of 1940 in the United States.

The editorial board of *Clave* consisted of Adolfo Zamora, a lawyer who was Trotsky's attorney while he lived in Mexico; José Ferrel, a young journalist; and Diego Rivera, until he left the Trotskyist ranks early in 1939. Octavio Fernández remained the manager of the periodical throughout its existence.

## DIEGO RIVERA AND THE MEXICAN TROTSKYISTS

During the period when *Clave* was being published, Diego Rivera broke his relations with the movement headed by Leon Trotsky. During the five years or more in which he had been associated with Trotskyism, he had been a problem for the leadership of the movement.

Diego Rivera had been one of the outstanding early members of the Mexican Communist Party. His services to the party were many and varied. He wrote several of the documents which it issued during the 1920's; he was head of its delegation to the celebration of the tenth anniversary of the Bolshevik Revolution in November 1927; He was chairman of its front group, the Anti-Imperialist League, president of the Workers and Peasants Bloc, and director of *El Libertador*, the organ of the Anti-Imperialist League of the Americas.[39] But Rivera was a much better artist than he was a politician. As early as 1924 Bertram Wolfe, then a member of the Central Committee of the Communist Party of Mexico (although a United States citizen), tried to persuade Rivera to resign from the Communist Party, reasoning that he could make his best contribution to the Communist cause through art rather than through political activity. Furthermore, he was not a very good Central Committee member, a post which he then occupied. According to Wolfe, "he was constantly forgetting what day of the week it was and what hour of the day, so absorbed in his painting that he missed committee meetings and even speaking dates."[40]

In 1927-28 Rivera spent several months in the Soviet Union. He was engaged to paint a mural on a wall of the Red Army Building, but various impediments were put in his way by jealous Soviet artists, with whom he engaged in extensive polemics. He did accept an invitation to make a sketch of Joseph Stalin, then approaching complete power as Secretary-General of the Soviet Communist Party, but according to Bertram Wolfe the sketch was uncomplimentary. In the middle of 1928, Rivera was ordered back to Mexico by his party and the Comintern, to perform his duties as president of the Workers and Peasant Bloc in the presidential elections of 1928.[41]

Diego Rivera was expelled from the Communist Party of Mexico in September 1928. Wolfe describes his expulsion as part of "a worldwide purge emanating from factional politics in the Soviet Union, involving in some countries the expulsion of whole parties, in others expulsion or resignation of the principal leaders and founders, spreading at last, in milder and more confused form, to the more backward lands." He notes that the charges against Rivera "were hastily trumped up and so palpably inadequate that the party busied itself inventing better ones." Both Rivera and the Communist leaders later said that he was expelled because of Trotskyist sympathies but Wolfe writes that "actually Diego did not become an adherent of Trotsky until after his expulsion and the charge did not figure at all in his trial and defense."[42]

Rivera's growing sympathy for Trotsky inevitably brought him into contact with the nascent Trotskyist movement of Mexico in the early 1930's and his fame made him its most important source of funds. However, he did not officially join the movement until the first reorganization of the Liga Comunista Internacionalista in 1936; indeed, both the Mexican and international Trotskyist leaders had reservations about admitting him to their ranks. For instance, A. González, the Mexican Trotskyists' contact in New York City, wrote Octavio Fernández in the middle of 1934 urging that the Mexicans be careful about how they handled Diego Rivera. He commented that Rivera could be very useful as a sympathizer, but that the Liga should not accept him as a member or put him forward to express its ideas. He said that the Communist Party had never known how to handle Rivera, and had lost him completely by allowing him to become a member in the first place; he urged the Trotskyists not to commit the same mistake.[43] Six months later, Russell Blackwell (by then back in the United States) wrote to Luciano Galicia and Octavio Fernández along the same lines. He advised that they not provoke any break with Rivera, but that they keep him as a sympathizer (not as a member) because of his national and international popularity. He suggested that they "isolate" him politically.[44]

These cautions were thrown to the wind, however, when the Liga Comunista Internacionalista was reorganized early in 1936. At that time, Diego Rivera was accepted as a member of the Liga and even named one of the four members of its Political Bureau, a post which he held for approximately a year.

We have already noted that after the 1937-38 split in the Liga Comunista Internacionalista, the Trotskyists resumed their cautious position on Rivera. At its founding congress the Fourth International resolved that in the reconstituted Mexican section of the International, Diego Rivera should not become a member, but should continue his political activities directly under the supervision of the Pan American and Pacific Bureau of the International. José López, the Secretary of the Bureau, officially informed Rivera of this decision, and told him that he "felt sure" Rivera would "support comrade Curtiss" in bringing about unity in the Mexican Trotskyist movement.[45]

Rivera cooperated in the establishment of *Clave* and became a member of its editorial board, but within a few months he wrote a letter to José Ferrel, one of his co-editors, resigning as a member of the board; he gave no reasons, and said "I remain in the most complete active sympathy with *CLAVE*." The two remaining members of the board, Ferrel and Adolfo Zamora, replied that they did not know the reasons for the resignation, since they shared "complete theoretical and political solidarity with Rivera. They "rejected the resignation and suggested instead that Rivera go on a leave of absence."[46]

However, in the following number of *Clave*, for April 1939, "Carlos Cortes" (probably Charles Curtiss) wrote that he had come to the conclusion that Diego Rivera's differences with *Clave* and the Trotskyists were "a basic divergence in theory and policy." This was shown, he said, by Rivera's participation in the formation of the Partido Revolucionario Obrero y Campesino, which had "a program and a membership very far from being Marxist." He supposed that Rivera was disillusioned with Marxism, was looking for a new theory, and had come up with "a mixture of anarchism, liberalism, and social democracy."

Rivera himself replied to the Trotskyists in a letter to Curtiss. He argued that the new party, the Partido Revolucionario Obrero y Campesino, was organized not by himself but by the Casa del Pueblo, which believed that the workers should have their own party to participate in the coming presidential election. He argued that there were differences between the various candidates for the government nomination for the presidency, and that it was important for the workers to make a choice between them. He added that since he had already resigned from Trotskyist ranks, he bore no responsibility to them, and they were in no way responsible for his own actions.[47]

Finally, on August 7, the Central Committee of the Mexican section of the Fourth International issued a declaration on Diego Rivera. It noted that he had issued a statement provisionally supporting General Juan Andreu Almazán (the principal opposition presidential candidate, generally considered to be rather right-wing), and that since Rivera had been considered a Trotskyist, it must speak out. It noted that he had ceased some months before to have any connection with the Trotskyists, "as a direct consequence of a series of opportunist deviations which brought him to break with the Fourth International."[48]

Undoubtedly one aspect of Diego Rivera's turn away from Trotskyism was his personal break with Leon Trotsky. Bertram Wolfe had written in his first biography of Rivera, which was published in 1939, that "there is not, however, as far as I have been able to ascertain, any truth in the rumours of fundamental political disagreement between them," and that "Trotsky has surely not changed Diego's penchant for political fantasy; yet however warm their discussions on secondary political matters may be, the painter has always deferred to the professional politician in basic matters in the latter's field." But this had already ceased to be the case by the time Wolfe's book appeared.[49]

Several who have known both Trotsky and Rivera well have commented that Trotsky was particularly tolerant of Rivera's political vagaries during the period in which they were comrades. He valued Rivera highly as a member of the Fourth International and felt that a man of his artistic talent and temperament should not be held to strict party discipline. He frequently urged other political colleagues to tolerate in Rivera's case actions they might not pardon in others.[50]

However, both men were temperamental, highly competent in their respective fields, and rather lacking in tolerance toward those with opinions differing from their own, and it was perhaps inevitable that they should clash sooner or later. By the time that Trotsky had been a guest in a house belonging to Diego Rivera and his wife for a year and a half, such a clash had apparently taken place. Charles Curtiss relates that when he returned to Mexico in the middle of 1938, Trotsky was insisting that he no longer wanted to be Rivera's "guest." He gave Curtiss 100 pesos which he asked him to deliver to Rivera as rent for the house he was occupying. Rivera was very annoyed at this, insisted that he was not a landlord, and refused the money. Several trips by Curtiss back and forth between the two men did not bring Rivera to accept the money, and certainly did not help to improve the relations between the artist and his house guest.

Rivera's break with Trotsky and the Trotskyites proved to be only the first step in a long and tortuous path back to the Communist Party, which he was allowed to rejoin shortly before his death. However, several people have suggested that Rivera was never serious in his support of Trotskyism, or even much concerned about his political career in general. Bertram Wolfe, for one, has argued that "no one, Diego least of all, had taken seriously" his adherence to Trotskyism.[51] Rodrigo García Treviño, a Mexican acquaintance of both Trotsky and Rivera although never himself a Trotskyist, has made the same point. He tells of a workers education meeting which he (García Treviño) addressed in the late 1930's, in his capacity as a leader of the Confederación de Trabajadores de México, at which Rivera was present. The artist challenged an answer García Treviño had given to a worker's question, and proceeded to speak for a quarter of an hour, claiming that he was giving a verbatim quotation from a passage in Marx's *Das Kapital*, but in fact completely improvising the quotation. When Rivera was finished, García Treviño replied by citing an equally lengthy and equally fictitious passage from a supposed work of Leon Trotsky. When the two men left the meeting, Rivera put his arm around García Treviño, and laughingly told him, "You are a scoundrel!" Whereupon both men roared with laughter. García Treviño insists that this incident was an apt commentary on Rivera's seriousness as a politician, and argues that he was largely a fraud.[52]

## THE PARTIDO OBRERO INTERNACIONALISTA

The Mexican section of the Fourth International was reconstituted early in 1939 under its old name, the Liga Comunista Internacionalista. For some months after its reestablishment, the LCI issued a mimeographed periodical, *El Bolchevique*; it first appeared as the *Bulletin of Organization* of the LCI, but starting with the issue of May 14, 1939, it bore the subtitle "Órgano Central de La Liga Comunista Internacionalista (S. Mexicana del P. Mundial de la Revolución Socialista) IV Internacional." The "responsible editor" of this periodical was listed as R. Tokto, and the manager was Salvador Langarica.

*El Bolchevique* regularly carried news on the Fourth International and its various national affiliates, as well as a page of "Marxist information," which sought to educate LCI members and other readers of *El Bolchevique* ideologically. It also carried news on general Mexican politics and developments in the trade-union movement.

On several occasions the LCI issued manifestoes which it published and apparently distributed as throwaways. One of these, entitled "Declaraciones de la Liga Comunista Internacionalista en Relación con Diego Rivera y la Actitud de Éste Hacia el Candidato Almazán," denounced Rivera's declaration of support for General Juan Andreu Almazán, the principal opposition candidate running against the government's nominee, General Manuel Ávila Camacho. Another, entitled "Frente a la Baja del Peso Mexicano," called for a series of measures by workers against the high cost of living caused by a depreciation of the national currency. Finally, in August 1939, the LCI issued a throwaway entitled "Stalin y Hitler," denouncing the Hitler-Stalin Pact which had just been signed but also indicating its opposition to "democratic imperialism."[53]

In September the Liga Comunista Internacionalista decided to change its name to Partido Obrero Internacionalista. The reason was explained in the first issue of the party's new organ, *Lucha Obrera,* dated September 20, 1939:

> The Fourth International, since its creation in the Constituent Congress of September 1938, has become the leader of the fighters for world socialism. Our group has been the only one which has demonstrated to the workers the revolutionary

way out. It has as a result the right to constitute itself and call itself the Revolutionary Party of the Mexican Proletariat.

Communism has become identified for the masses with Stalinism, a product of the stage of world reaction which began in 1923, which has brought humanity to fascism and the second imperialist war. As a result, without renouncing our objectives, which are those announced by Marx and Engels—the establishment of the world communist society—it is necessary to abandon the denomination Communist.

As a result, *The Liga Comunista Internacionalista* assumes as of today the name *Partido Obrero Internacionalista, Sección Mexicana de la Cuarta Internacional.*"[54]

The fact that the dissident faction headed by Luciano Galicia was also using the name Liga Comunista Internacionalista may also have had something to do with the change.

So long as Trotsky was alive, most of the energies and time of the members of the POI were taken up with putting out *Clave* and guarding Trotsky's house, but from time to time the group made political pronouncements. Thus on December 29, 1939, the party issued a "Resolution on the Character of the Soviet State, the Occupation of Poland, and the War of Finland," which appeared in the January 1940 issue of *Clave*. This document took the official line then being advocated by Leon Trotsky and his followers. It stated: "Our attitude toward the U.S.S.R. is determined by the necessity of conserving and developing a planned economy. This is, at the same time, the only form of revolutionary struggle against bureaucratic parasitism. The bourgeoisie is not interested in the struggle against the Soviet bureaucracy except to the degree that this can work against the revolution of October. In the war of Finland, it sees the possibility and extends aid to the 'attacked democracy.' The Bolshevik-Leninista must defend the Soviet Union, putting themselves at the head of the struggle for the proletarian revolution in Finland. To the cries of Stalin and his government of marionettes, the Finnish workers must respond: 'Not popular government but dictatorship of the proletariat based on democratic soviets of workers, peasants, and soldiers.' In Finland and occupied Poland, the struggle for the social revolution and independence is the best way of carrying to its ultimate consequence the defense of the U.S.S.R. against the world bourgeoisie and against the Thermidorist bureaucracy.''

# —10—

# Mexican Trotskyism After Trotsky

In the early 1940's Trotskyism had more influence in Mexico than ever before, or since. Its followers were also more unified. In 1940, for instance, Luciano Galicia, who had stood aside from the official Fourth Internationalist group for more than two years, joined the Partido Obrero Internacionalista and became one of its principal leaders; there was no major split in the group for the next five years. The POI's newspaper, *Lucha Obrera*, was published with some regularity from September 1939 until 1947, almost two years after the ranks of the Mexican Trotskyists split late in 1945; and during this period it reflected fairly accurately the interests and activities of the POI.

As might be expected, *Lucha Obrera* occasionally reprinted articles by Trotsky, particularly during the months before his death and in later issues commemorating the anniversary of his murder. They also carried official statements of the Fourth International from time to time, particularly after the progress of the war made it possible for the International to be reestablished in European territory and to function once again with some degree of normalcy. Throughout the war it carried articles opposing Mexican participation in the conflict and denouncing the war as imperialist. It also reflected official Fourth International policy in calling for "unconditional defense of the Soviet Union." These calls were usually accompanied by strong attacks on Stalin, blaming him for whatever difficulties the U.S.S.R. was having at the time.

*Lucha Obrera* also reflected the close association of the Mexican Trotskyists with their United States comrades; it carried frequent news about the Socialist Workers Party, and particularly about the Smith Act trials of SWP leaders which took place during the war—in several issues, it carried detailed biographies of those who had been tried and convicted. It also featured news about Trotskyist parties and groups elsewhere in Latin America, and about the revival of Trotskyism in various countries of Europe as the Germans were driven out.

The POI organ reflected the party's considerable involvement in the labor movement during these years. It consistently attacked the leadership of the largest central labor group, the Confederación de Trabajadores de México, and

199

carried extensive news on the activities of rival labor groups; for example, on March 10, 1942, it had a long article on the establishment of the Confederación Proletaria Nacional, and in the issue for the second fortnight of November 1944 it reported on the first congress of the Federación Libertaria de Obreros y Campesinos del Distrito Federal.

Finally, the Trotskyist paper took a consistently critical attitude toward the government. Almost equally unflattering references were made to the government candidate in the 1940 election, Manuel Ávila Camacho, and to his opponent, General Juan Andreu Almazán; the same was true in the 1946 election in the case of the official nominee Miguel Alemán and the major opposition candidate Ezequiel Padilla. The paper also attacked the Ávila Camacho government's announced intention to establish a social security system, which it called a means of taking money from the workers' pockets without returning anything to them.[1]

During this period, Mexican Trotskyism obtained a number of new recruits of considerable importance. These included Rafael Galván, an electrical worker and former member of the Communist Party who after passing through the Trotskyist movement became one of the most important trade-union leaders in Mexico; A. Yañez, who later became an official of several international organizations; and Francisco Alvarado, an official of a large bank at the time he joined the Trotskyist movement, who went on to become one of Mexico's principal bankers.[2]

## THE INFLUENCE OF TROTSKYISM IN ORGANIZED LABOR, 1939-45

The World War II period was the only epoch in which the Mexican Trotskyists had some significant influence in the organized labor movement. Members of the Partido Obrero Internacionalista worked actively with several of the groups which were seeking to establish rivals of the Confederación de Trabajadores de México (CTM), which was headed by Vicente Lombardo Toledano (then a Communist fellow-traveler), and in which the Stalinists had extensive influence. They supported the establishment of the Confederación Proletaria Nacional, a central labor group which was set up by dissidents from the formerly anarcho-syndicalist trade-union group, Confederación General de Trabajadores (CGT), and from the Confederación Regional de Obreros Mexicanos (CROM).[3] They also supported the establishment of the Federación Libertaria de Obreros y Campesinos, an affiliate in the Federal District of the Confederación Nacional de Trabajadores (CNT).[4]

Trotskyists were given representation in the leading bodies of these organizations. Thus they represented the construction and mosaic workers unions in the leading bodies of the Confederación Proletaria Nacional, and they obtained at least one position on the National Council of the CNT. They also tried to use their growing influence in these union groups to influence the political thinking of their members and leaders; thus Octavio Fernández was requested by the Federación Libertaria to organize a Marxist study group, which came to have forty workers in attendance.[5]

A major event involving the trade-union groups with which the Trotskyists were working took place in the Zócalo, the central square of Mexico City, on July 20, 1944. A meeting organized by the Frente Nacional Proletario—which consisted of the CGT, the Federación Libertaria, and until shortly before this meeting the Confederación Proletaria Nacional—protested control of the labor situation by the CTM and demanded changes in the proposed social security legislation introduced by the Ávila Camacho government. The demonstrators claimed that they were attacked by police and members and agents of the CTM, and there was bitter fighting in the square for several hours. Several people were killed in this clash, and fifty-six of the demonstrators were arrested.[6]

Some elements of the POI also tried to work within the Confederación de Trabajadores de México. *Lucha Obrera* from time to time publicized the efforts of some CTM leaders to free it from control of Lombardo Toledano and the Communists, and to "renovate" it. The issue of whether the Trotskyites should concentrate their efforts on trying to reform the CTM or on seeking to build up a rival to it was to play a role in the 1945-46 split in the Mexican Trotskyist movement.

But while it is true that the Trotskyist movement gained some significance among those who were seeking to challenge CTM control of organized labor, their influence should not be exaggerated. During these years the majority of the workers remained within the ranks of the CTM, and the minority central labor groups were controlled principally by ex-anarcho-syndicalists and other elements, with the Trotskyists remaining but a minority factor in their leadership.

## THE 1945-46 SPLIT IN MEXICAN TROTSKYISM

The possibility of Trotskyism acquiring a significant influence in Mexican organized labor, and perhaps even some influence in the country's general politics, was shattered by a new split in Trotskyist ranks. Although this division had been brewing for some time, it culminated in the last months of 1945.

Once again, the leaders of the two rival factions were Luciano Galicia and Octavio Fernández. In a long letter addressed to the Chilean Trotskyist leader Diego Henríquez, Octavio Fernández explained his version of the reasons for the split. He argued that the Galicia group had opposed the POI's cooperation with anti-CTM trade-union groups, favoring instead an attempt to "reform" the CTM. He insisted that the Galicia followers had taken virtually no active part in any Trotskyist labor activity, but rather had tended to criticize the work of the POI trade-union activists from the sidelines. Nor, according to him, had they carried their share of the burden of putting out *Lucha Obrera*, or doing other chores for the POI. Fernández also accused the Galicia group of wanting to soften the anti-Stalinist position of the Mexican Trotskyists.[7]

It is hard to say whether this letter gave a complete picture of the factors laying behind the split in the Trotskyist ranks, for there is no documentation from the Galicia side. It is certain only that a schism did take place in the Mexican Trotskyist group in October 1945; a dissident element led by Octavio Fernández withdrew from the POI to establish the Grupo Socialista Obrero (GSO), which began to issue a new periodical, *Tribuna Socialista*.

In a meeting of a Plenum of the Enlarged Central Committee of the GSO in October 1946, a year after the GSO was organized, Octavio Fernández reported that the group had "strong and decided support" from the Casa del Pueblo trade-union group, and had reestablished fraternal relations with the CNT, the Food Workers Federation, the Confederación General de Trabajadores, and the Confederación Proletaria Nacional.[8] The Casa del Pueblo had given the GSO space to carry on the publishing activities of *Tribuna Socialista*, whereas the GSO held its meetings in the headquarters of the linotype operators union.[9] Within a year *Tribuna Socialista* was reported to have a circulation of four thousand copies, a sizable proportion of which were distributed by unions sympathetic to the GSO.[10]

## THE END OF TROTSKYISM OF
## THE 1930'S AND 1940'S

For a while, both the Partido Obrero Internacionalista and the Grupo Socialista Obrero declared themselves to be "the Mexican section of the Fourth International." The International itself finally decided in favor of the POI, headed by Luciano Galicia. In December 1945, several months after his break with the POI, Octavio Fernández visited New York City, to renew contacts with the leaders of the Socialist Workers Party of the United States, and through them with the Fourth International. His expenses for the trip were paid in part by the SWP. At that time, he was accepted as the legitimate representative in Mexico of the Fourth Internationalist movement.[11]

In the early phases of the split the International Secretariat of the Fourth International informed Octavio Fernández that the International was very upset by the rift and could not, except for "profound political reasons," take sides in a case in which there were none. The International also indicated its willingness to cooperate in the distribution of *Tribuna Socialista* to other affiliates of the world organization.[12] But the International also indicated to the Fernández group that it was considered the "dissident" element within Mexican Trotskyism: A. Fer of the International wrote to Octavio Fernández from New York, "You must not forget the fact that, from the formal point of view, the LO group remains technically the Mexican section."[13]

However, as time went on, ideological differences developed between the GSO and the Fourth International. The principal divergence occurred over the key issue of the nature of the Soviet Union. The group led by Octavio Fernández, in its periodical *Tribuna Socialista*, began to refer to the U.S.S.R. as "totalitarian,"[14] and became increasingly unwilling to declare itself in favor of "unconditional defense of the Soviet Union," an attitude which aroused growing hostility from the leaders of the Fourth International.[15]

The GSO also undoubtedly aroused the enmity of the Socialist Workers Party and the Fourth International leaders because of its sympathetic attitude toward dissidents who were expelled from the SWP late in 1946. Felix Morrow, one of those expelled from the SWP, sent the Mexican GSO a copy of a letter he had written to the French affiliate of the Fourth International, asking for support in his struggle against the SWP leadership. As a result, Octavio Fernández wrote a letter to the International Secretariat of the International objecting to the expulsion of the minority group from the SWP, charging that this seemed like the action of a "monolithic" party rather than that of one practicing democratic centralism. He sent a copy of this letter to Morrow.[16]

In its *Internal Bulletin* the GSO also joined in objecting to the official Trotskyist position on the Soviet Union. In the first issue of this periodical it published an article by Daniel Logan, a member of the SWP minority, entitled "The Eruption of Bureaucratic Imperialism—A Contribution to the Discussion on the Russian Question."[17] This growing divergence between the GSO and the Fourth International reached the crisis point early in 1947. Charles Curtiss once more came to Mexico, and one of his tasks was to try to resolve the differences between the GSO and the POI. In effect he gave the GSO leaders directions to merge with the POI headed by Luciano Galicia, and to abandon their critical position on the Soviet system. Curtiss informed the GSO that it could no longer consider itself the Mexican section of the Fourth International, and was told in turn that the GSO had no intention of taking orders from the Fourth International.*

This break between the GSO and the Fourth International was reflected in the GSO periodical, *Tribuna Socialista*. In its issue of July 16, 1947, the newspaper editorialized: "The international directing organism of the Fourth International, without basing its procedure on any discussion, in an official resolution or in a report, without any criticism whatsoever of the position maintained by the GSO or by *Tribuna Socialista* . . . has been insisting recently that the Grupo Socialista Obrero is not the 'official Mexican section.' " Because

*Interview with Octavio Fernández, Mexico City, January 23, 1971. Charles Curtiss, in a letter to the author dated February 10, 1971, comments on the GSO version of the events given here: "I have to plead dimness of memory, and I have no documents to restore the events. I cannot recall the conversation with Fernández. I was asked to go to Mexico in 1947 to help Natalia with some problems concerning the house and her position in Mexico. I surely visited with Fernández, and such a conversation may have taken place. I would trust Fernández' recall more than my own... However I am very doubtful of the peremptory tone he says was used.... I am sure that I urged such unity between the two groups, but my certainty is not due to any recall of the specific exchange but as being consistent with general policy."

of this, the paper said, it would no longer use the subtitle identifying it with
the International.

Neither the GSO nor *Tribuna Socialista* long survived the break with the
Fourth International. By the end of 1947 both had passed out of existence.[18]
The rival Trotskyite group, the Partido Obrero Internacionalista, and its periodical, *Lucha Obrera*, also died by the end of 1947.[19] For all practical purposes,
the Trotskyist movement in Mexico ceased to exist, and it was not to be revived
in a regularly organized group for at least a decade.

## THE HIATUS OF THE 1950'S

By 1948 few pretended that there was a "party," "league," or "group"
affiliated with International Trotskyism in Mexico. Virtually all of those who
had been active in the movement during the previous decade and a half retired
from any avowedly Trotskyist activity, although several of them continued to
function as trade-union rank and filers and even leaders.

One of the most important of the ex-Trotskyist trade-union leaders was
Rafael Galván, a leading figure in the country's electrical workers' unions.
He was the only one who continued overtly Trotskyist activity into the early
1950's; in this work, he used the name Martin Arriaga.

Another ex-Trotskyist leader who continued extensive activity as a trade
unionist was Félix Ibarra. Until 1952 he was one of the principal leaders of
the telephone workers union, working with four or five others who had previously
been active Trotskyists. They lost control of the union in 1952 when officials
of the Ministry of Labor refused to recognize their union.[20]

It was Martín Arriaga who apparently took the lead, together with United
States Trotskyites, in the establishment of a new Trotskyist periodical, *¿Qué
Hacer? (What to Do?)*, which began publication late in 1953 and had the
subtitle "In Defense of the Workers and Peasants Interests." Although this
periodical did not hide its Trotskyist inclinations, it did not go out of the way
to stress them either; its analyses seemed to stress a general Marxist-Leninist
approach to affairs, rather than a specifically Trotskyist one.

*¿Qué Hacer?*, a monthly magazine of which about a dozen issues appeared,
paid particular attention to developments in the Mexican labor movement. It
vigorously attacked corruption in the unions, their subordination to the government, and the role of the Communists in them; it stressed the need for cleaning
up the labor movement. Other articles dealt with general political conditions
in Mexico at the time. They tended to stress the "bourgeois" nature of the
Mexican Revolution as it had developed so far, and the need for it to move
into a new "proletarian" phase. One article dealt specifically with devaluation
of the Mexican peso, and was entitled "Devaluation: Expropriation of the
Resources of the People for the Benefit of the Bourgeoisie."

The May 20, 1954, issue of *¿Qué Hacer?* carried a May Day manifesto.
It ended with a series of five slogans: "Viva the Social Revolution," "Viva
the Memory of the Heroes of the Working Class," "Viva the Example of

the Revolutionaries of all the World," "Viva the Lessons of the Russian Proletariat and of the Party of Lenin and Trotsky," and "Viva Mexico Renewed by Socialism and Democracy." However, this manifesto was not identified as being issued by any particular political group, and was ostensibly issued only by the individuals putting out the magazine. One passage commented in this regard: "In the Mexican Republic also, there must be struggle for the establishment of a revolutionary labor party of true Leninist and Trotskyist type. There is no directive more historically necessary than that of creating a Bolshevik group adequately equipped with the principles of Marx, Lenin, and Trotsky, which is the only key to getting out of the sinister labyrinth in which our country and all other peoples are prisoners."

It seems likely that Arriaga Galván and the other Mexicans involved in publishing *¿Qué Hacer?* received aid and encouragement from the Socialist Workers Party of the United States. The magazine carried several articles by James P. Cannon, the principal leader of the SWP, and one by Joseph Hanson, another prominent party figure.

Although during most of the 1950's there seems to have existed no Mexican affiliate of the Fourth International, a few of the ex-members of the one-time Mexican section continued to be active in politics. One of these was Fausto Dávila Solís, of the oil town of Poza Rica. He was elected mayor of Poza Rica in 1956, apparently on an "independent" ticket, but was never allowed by the government to take office.[21]

## THE REVIVAL OF MEXICAN TROTSKYISM

In the late 1950's there arose a new and active Trotskyist movement associated with the Fourth International. It consisted almost exclusively of students, and involved very few of those who had participated in Trotskyist activities in the late 1930's and 1940's. Even figures such as Luciano Galicia and Rafael Galván, who still considered themselves "more or less" Trotskyists, and who had some considerable influence in the electrical workers unions, were not recruited into the new Trotskyist movement of Mexico.

The new generation of adherents to the Fourth International was particularly concerned with doctrinal purity, and one senses that it tended to be suspicious of "anyone over thirty." For example, the well-known writer Víctor Rico Galán attended a number of Trotskyist meetings, and even spoke at one at which J. Posadas was the principal orator, and expressed interest in joining the movement. His overtures were apparently rejected after the young Trotskyist insisted on checking all of his writings to see whether they conformed with their concept of Fourth International orthodoxy.[22]

The revived Trotskyist movement in Mexico had its origins in the Juventud Socialista, an independent student group active in the late 1950's; the group gave support to the railroad strikes of 1958, which were broken by the government when they were converted by their leaders into an outright political challenge to the regime of President Adolfo Ruíz Cortines. The Juventud Socialista split in 1959. The majority group, which put particular emphasis on trade-union work, became the nucleus of the Partido Obrero Revolucionario (Trotskista), which was accepted in 1961 as the Mexican section of the Pabloite faction of the Fourth International, at its Sixth Congress. The second element of the former Juventud Socialista, composed principally of students, took the name Liga Estudiantil Marxista. It claimed to have become the principal rival of the Communist Youth in the university community. After fruitless negotiations for unity with the POR(T), which were broken off at the request of the latter, the Liga Estudiantil Marxista changed its name to Liga Obrera Marxista (LOM), and began to become interested in the anti-Pablo faction of international Trotskyism.

In 1961 a group of exiled Guatemalans who had been involved in guerrilla activities joined the LOM. However, at the beginning of 1962 they joined some Mexican colleagues in breaking away from the LOM to join the POR(T), thus establishing contacts between the POR(T) and the Guatemalan guerrilla movement which were later to become of considerable significance. At about the same time the POR(T) joined forces with the Posadas faction of the Fourth International.

## THE UNITED SECRETARIAT'S MEXICAN AFFILIATE

Meanwhile, the LOM declared its solidarity with those who were seeking to reunify the Fourth International. They were represented as a fraternal group at the "Reunification Congress" which merged elements of the Pablo and anti-Pablo factions and established the United Secretariat in 1963.

During 1964 and 1965 the LOM experienced a crisis, which arose from different points of view held by its student members and those who were active in the electrical workers unions. Reportedly, the student element was "much more dynamic and radicalized than the trade-union group." At this time, the university group claimed fifty members and was an important sector of the opposition to the Communist Party." The warring factions of the LOM were reunited temporarily as a consequence of the Eighth Congress of the Fourth International of the United Secretariat, at which the LOM was recognized as the Mexican section of that organization. What happened then has been described in the following terms:

> At the beginning of 1966 the LOM was a political group of some importance, with links in the student sector and in the working-class belt of the city of Mexico. Thus in the university strike of 1966 the Trotskyist faction carried out an important role, which put them in the headlines for the first time. In 1966 the LOM developed important contacts in certain sectors for the first time.
>
> But the LOM was unprepared for the new phase which was opened. Again it was faced with a different rhythm of development in its centers of action.

The student sector broke with the trade-union group, which in fact was not perfectly imbued with the revolutionary Marxist positions. The split of 1966 was lamentable but inevitable. The LOM was as a result reduced from more than eighty members to about two dozen.

After this split the LOM concentrated almost exclusively on work among the university students. It joined with a variety of other leftists—"Maoists, Guevarists, Debrayists, and Trotskyists"—to form the Committee for the Defense of Political Prisoners, in July 1967. This body called a National Congress of Revolutionary Students, out of which emerged the Unión Nacional de Estudiantes Revolucionarios. However, within a few months, this organization was captured by the Posadistas of the POR(T), and as a result was abandoned by most of the other groups, including the Trotskyists of the LOM.

The LOM then joined forces early in 1968 with the Liga Obrera Campesina to form the Juventud Marxista Revolucionaria (JMR). However, quarreling within this new group began almost immediately; some members wanted a "loose" form of organization, with memberships open to anyone who would declare his loyalty to its general statement of principles, whereas others favored a form of "democratic centralism." This factional struggle in the Juventud Marxista Revolucionaria had not yet reached its conclusion before the outbreak of the student strike movement of the middle of 1968. The JMR students, as well as those affiliated with the POR(T), played an important role in leading this strike, although more as individuals than as members of tightly organized groups. They spearheaded the element in the student leadership which deprived the Communist Party of any effective role in the movement.

It was from the Trotskyist participants in the student movement of 1968 that there emerged the latest group to be associated with the United Secretariat faction of the Fourth International, the Grupo Comunista Internationalista (GCI).[23] The new GCI began publishing two kinds of documents, both mimeographed. One of these was its *Boletín Interno,* designed to be read by members of the organization; the other was *La International,* apparently intended for wider distribution.

In addition to these periodicals intended for use in Mexico, the Mexican Trotskyists worked on putting out more or less official publications of the International of the United Secretariat. These included the Spanish language version of the basic periodical of the International, entitled *Cuarta Internacional,* which generally specialized in official pronouncements of the United Secretariat and in more heavily theoretical material; and *Perspectiva Mundial,* a livelier publication with more agitational and topical material.

Both of these publications were printed by the same man who put out the occasional periodical of the POR(T) group affiliated with the Posadas branch of international Trotskyism. Payment for printing the publications of the United Secretariat usually came on a regular basis from abroad; payment for the Posadista periodicals was made on a more sporadic basis. At one point, a foreign leader of the Posadas group was reported to have brought the printer over $30,000

(U.S.) in cash to be used for purchasing a press upon which the International's periodicals could be printed. [24]

Besides working with student groups and publishing national and international periodicals, the Mexican Trotskyists aligned with the United Secretariat of the Fourth International carried on a number of campaigns on other issues. For instance, after Fidel Castro's attack on Trotskyism in January 1966 the GCI issued an "Open Letter to Fidel Castro," which they published as a pamphlet. This document denied that the Posadistas whom Castro directly attacked were genuine Trotskyists, and argued that "Posadismo is a social phenomenon which should be considered as an ultra-leftist sectarian movement and not as an agency of imperialism." It also insisted that "the opportunism of the Communist parties" was the "principal impediment within the revolutionary movement."[25]

The faction of Mexican Trotskyism associated with the United Secretariat had virtually no members of the older generation of Trotskyists in its ranks. The only such persons who seem to have been associated with them were A. Camejo, who was principally responsible for putting together the material for the publications designed for international distribution by the Mexican Trotskyists; and Professor Nicolás Molina, who had had in his classes at the University of Mexico a number of the young students who made up the bulk of the membership of the group, and who collaborated in translating and publishing a volume of selected works of Leon Trotsky in this period.[26]

Another old-time Trotskyist who rekindled his sympathy for Trotskyism, and particularly for the United Secretariat version of the Fourth International (after having spent many years in the Communist Party), although he does not appear to have joined the International's Mexican affiliate, was the well-known writer José Revueltas. A world-famous novelist by the late 1960's, Revueltas sent a message to the Third Congress of the Fourth International After Reunification which was bursting with enthusiasm.[27]

As a result of the student disturbances of mid-1968, most of the leaders of the GCI, including Professor Molina, were jailed. The United Secretariat then began a worldwide campaign for their release, and widely publicized the conditions being suffered by the Trotskyists and other political prisoners being held in Mexican jails. This campaign finally bore some fruit early in February 1971, when the new Mexican President, Luis Echeverría, released Professor Molina and some other members of the GCI. Some of the other jailed Trotskyists, however, remained in prison, having been given long sentences.[28]

Apparently the release of several Trotskyists from jail made it possible for them to return to more or less regular political activity. The French Trotskyist weekly *Rouge* reported in its issue of July 1971 that on May 29-30, 1971, the GCI, "a sympathizing organization" of the United Secretariat's Fourth International, had held a national conference. This was attended by forty delegates and focused its attention on the problem of capitalizing on the growing influence of the GCI among university students. Right after this conference one of the

GCI, Carlos Sevilla, was sentenced to a sixteen-year jail term, after being held under "provisional arrest" since September 1968.

Meanwhile, one faction of the former Liga Obrera Marxista had kept alive an organization with that name. It has been described by Joseph Hansen of the Socialist Workers Party of the United States as "a small group in Mexico whose main activity has been to supply occasional articles for the *Workers Press,*" the organ of the Socialist Labor League of Great Britain. The LOM was accepted as a member of the Healyite International Committee of the Fourth International at a meeting of the committee held sometime in 1970.[29]

## THE ACTIVITIES OF THE PARTIDO OBRERO REVOLUCIONARIO (TROTSKISTA)

Many members of the POR(T) were also jailed as the result of the student demonstrations and strikes in 1966. Much of the subsequent effort of the remaining members of the group was spent on campaigning for the release of these prisoners. The Posadas Fourth International itself spent much time and energy on this same kind of agitation. Thus, the January 1967 issue of the *Bolétin de Información del Secretariado Internacional de la IV Internacional* was devoted entirely to an exchange of letters between the Mexican POR(T) prisoners and J. Posadas. Other PORistas were picked up by the police after the 1968 student uprising. In May 1969 a number of these, including the Argentine journalist Adolfo Gilly, were given heavy jail sentences, ranging up to eight years, for "criminal activity," "inciting to subversion," "conspiracy," and other charges.[30]

In spite of persecution by the Mexican authorities, the POR was able to carry on other activities. For example, in July 1967 the party held a conference and leadership training school. It is reported to have lasted nine days, and to have had members present from all units of the party (although no mention is made of how many units there were). This meeting elected a new Central Committee and Political Bureau and laid plans for expanding party activities.

As in all affiliates of the Posadas version of the Fourth International, the Mexican POR has given much of its time to absorbing the ideas of Posadas and disseminating them. For instance, the report on the conference and leadership training school noted the need "to assimilate collectively and individually all the teachings of the struggle of Posadas in the construction and formation of the conception, the centralized spirit of the Fourth International."[31]

The POR had among its members a few men of an earlier generation. One of these was Fausto Dávila Solís, who had been active in the Trotskyist movement in the 1940's, and had been elected but not seated as Mayor of Poza Rica in 1956.[32] Others included Galván (not to be confused with the electrical workers union leader), and F. Vidal; Galván had been an active Trotskyist in the 1940's, and Vidal had been a member of the Communist Party of Mexico until after Nikita Khrushchev's speech to the Twentieth Congress of the Communist Party of the Soviet Union and the Soviet invasion of Hungary in 1956, when he had broken with the Communist Party and had begun to cooperate in the effort to revive Trotskyism in Mexico.[33]

## MEXICAN POSADISTA INTERVENTION IN GUATEMALAN GUERRILLA ACTIVITIES

Certainly the most spectacular and perhaps the most important activity undertaken by the Trotskyists of the Mexican POR(T) was its participation in the guerrilla movement led by Lt. Marco Antonio Yon Sosa in the neighboring republic of Guatemala. Although this activity did not result in the establishment of any Trotskyist group in Guatemala, it did gain worldwide attention when Fidel Castro violently denounced the Yon Sosa movement for alleged "Trotskyism."

Carlos Manuel Pellecer, a former leader of the Guatemalan Communist Party, has given the author extensive details on the activities of the Posadista Trotskyists of Mexico in his native country. He reports that the antecedents of their work in Guatemala go back to the spring of 1962, when Fidel Castro decided to support scattered guerrilla efforts and bring together competing guerrilla groups.

Castro chose as his intermediary with the Guatemalan guerrillas one Francisco Amado, a Guatemalan businessman living in Mexico, whose business activities gave him a useful "cover" for establishing contacts with and passing money to the guerrillas. Amado began traveling to Guatemala, Venezuela, and Colombia as Castro's courier and paymaster. His first contacts in his native country were with certain leaders of the orthodox Communist Party, known locally as the Partido Guatemalteco del Trabajo. He became a secret member of the PGT and succeeded in involving the party in the guerrilla movement for some time.

However, Castro soon broke with Amado, and the latter turned to a guerrilla group led by Marco Antonio Yon Sosa and known as MR-13, which had maintained a certain degree of independence from both Castro and the Guatemalan Communists. Amado also sought the help of some Mexican Posadas Trotskyists whom he had known at the university, where sometime before he had studied in the Social Science School. With their help, he began publishing in Guatemala a periodical entitled *Revolución Socialista*, which took a strong Posadista Trotskyist line. In addition, one of these Trotskyists, Galván, became the principal agent of the Yon Sosa group in purchasing arms and smuggling them into Guatemala.

Galván was finally captured by agents of the Guatemalan government, which also seized a sizable quantity of arms which Galván had with him. He was kept in prison in Guatemala until after the death in March 1966 of Francisco Amado, who was captured and executed with a number of other guerrilla leaders. At that time, Galván was freed and deported to Mexico.[34] Meanwhile, Castro had thrown his support behind the rival guerrilla movement led by another ex-Army officer, Luis Turcios. Fidel used the meeting of the Tricontinental Conference in Havana in January 1966 as the occasion to denounce the Yon Sosa movement, using its connections with the Posadas Trotskyists as his principal argument.[35]

A final break between the Yon Sosa guerrilla group and the Mexican Posadista Trotskyists took place in April 1966. At that time three Posadistas were "tried" by a revolutionary tribunal of the MR-13, presided over by Yon Sosa himself. The charges against them were: "(a) that in the month of November 1965, the MR-13 carried out a forcible collection of taxes from the bourgeoisie, an operation which produced various thousands of quetzales, destined to cover the necessary costs of establishing in power and developing the Socialist revolution in Guatemala; (b) however, all this money was divided between the Fourth International and the MR-13, without previous consultation and approval of Comandante Marco Antonio Yon Sosa; (c) that this division of funds was decided upon and carried out by Francisco Amado Granados (a former member of the Political Bureau) and the members of the Fourth International, whose pseudonyms were Tury, Evaristo, Tomás, and Roberto; (d) that this distribution was the culmination of a plan which had been conceived and decided upon almost a year ago by the International Secretariat (CI) of the Fourth International, a plan which those now being submitted to trial quickly carried out."

It was reported that "Evaristo, Tomás, and Roberto did not contradict, refute, or essentially alter the evidence offered, limiting themselves to political comments that were never raised by the tribunal. They argued that the money was being used in all of the sections of the Fourth International and that they never took any of it for their personal use." The decision of the revolutionary tribunal was clear: "First: To expel Evaristo, Tomás, and Roberto from MR-13. Second: To break all connections with the Fourth International."[37]

This decision ended the incursion of the Mexican Posadista Trotskyists into the guerrilla conflict in Guatemala. Subsequently, the rival United Secretariat of the Fourth International expressed its "unconditional solidarity" with the action of the Yon Sosa group, taking advantage of the opportunity to deny the Trotskyist authenticity of the Posadas group.[37]

## RELATIONS OF MEXICAN TROTSKYISTS TO THEIR UNITED STATES COUNTERPARTS

Throughout the long and rather turbulent history of Trotskyism in Mexico, there has been a close relationship between the Mexican adherents of the Fourth International and their comrades in the United States. We have already referred to the specific cases of intervention by United States Trotskyist leaders in the affairs of Mexican Trotskyism, but it will be useful here to outline the full scope of these relations.

Trotskyism received its start in Mexico as a result of the contacts of some members of the Communist Party and Communist front groups with the new Trotskyist movement in the United States. The direct agent for this contact was Russell Blackwell, a United States Communist, who was won over to Trotskyism as soon as it began to appear as an international movement, and was an early if not a founding member of the U.S. Communist League of America. Through him, Mexican Communists and fellow-travelers who were interested were put in direct correspondence with people in the League who were assigned to the development of relations with sympathizers in Latin America. Most important in this regard was A. González, a Mexican of long residence in the United States, who was for fifteen years the principal member of the United States Trotskyist movement charged with Latin American relations.

In these early days, González, as well as Blackwell (who used the name Rosalio Negrete in his relations with the Mexicans) and Arne Swabeck were constantly giving the Mexican Trotskyites advice on organizational problems. They were also seeking to ground them more thoroughly in Trotskyist ideas, particularly the criticisms of Stalin and Stalinism made by the International Left Opposition.

During the first decade of the existence of Trotskyism in Mexico, undoubtedly the single most important United States Trotskyist who intervened in Mexican affairs was Charles Curtiss. Then a young man belonging to the Los Angeles branch of the Trotskyist movement, he had an advantage over most of his North American colleagues in his ability to speak and write Spanish. For some months in 1933-34 he had lived in Mexico City, where he had not only helped teach his Mexican comrades the ideas of the International Left Opposition, but had also done a great deal of "Jimmy Higgins work"—day-to-day jobs such as getting out literature, organizing meetings, and trying to win converts through personal persuasion.

He was thus the logical person for the United States Trotskyists to send to Mexico when a new split developed in Mexican Trotskyist ranks in 1938. He was given credentials both from the International Secretariat and the Socialist Workers Party of the United States and was given a broad mandate to reorganize the demoralized ranks of Mexican Trotskyism. This power extended to deciding which of the quarreling factions was most nearly "right," and who might be excluded from or readmitted to a reorganized group.

Curtiss had a certain talent for diplomacy as well as a good deal of "political muscle" insofar as International Trotskyism was concerned. He was therefore able to put together once again a Mexican affiliate of the Fourth International, which survived without major disruption for more than half a decade. Of course, in his activities in Mexico, Curtiss did not act with complete autonomy. He made frequent and regular reports to the Socialist Workers Party headquarters in New York, and through them to the Fourth International. However, there is no indication that the SWP and Fourth International ever seriously questioned his judgment or overruled any of his significant recommendations.

When storms of dissension once again broke over Mexican Trotskyism after World War II, an extensive correspondence was carried on between New York City and the vying factions. Finally, New York once again sent Charles Curtiss to decide what should be done about the quarreling Mexican comrades. Although he recommended the more orthodox Luciano Galicia group over the somewhat heterodox Octavio Fernández faction, all of his efforts were not sufficient to keep the quarrel from resulting in the temporary demise of Mexican Trotskyism. The only important Trotskyist activity in Mexico during the early 1950's seems to have been stimulated from New York City, specifically the publication *¿Qué Hacer?* for about a year.

In the 1960's there was again close contact between the Mexican Trotskyists, particularly those aligned with the United Secretariat of the Fourth International, and their United States colleagues. With financial help and documentary material from New York City, the Mexicans published, on behalf of the International, periodicals in Spanish intended for distribution not only in Mexico but elsewhere in Latin America. We have not, however, come across any evidence that there was the kind of direct intervention in factional quarrels among the latter-day Mexican Trotskyists which took place in an earlier period.

There certainly is no other case in which a Latin American Trotskyist movement has been so closely supervised by the United States movement. Although there was some intervention by correspondence with the Cuban Party, and for a short while in the early 1940's there was a direct personal intervention by Terence Phelan in the Argentine and Chilean parties and groups, this interference was not as frequent or continuous as in the Mexican case.

## CONCLUSION

All Mexican Trotskyist factions were severely hurt by the roundup of left-wing political opponents made by the Government of President Gustavo Díaz Ordaz during and after the student uprising of the middle of 1968. Most of the leaders of these groups were jailed and remained in prison two and a half years later. The issuance of the publications of the Grupo Comunista Internacionalista, except in mimeographed form, was suspended. The POR(T) was still putting out *Voz Obrera* at least as late as the first fortnight of March 1969—as usual, the issue of that date was filled with the writings of J. Posadas himself. However, the activities of those members of the POR and GCI remaining out of prison were severely circumscribed.

In any case, the Mexican Trotskyist movement of the 1960's was only a pale reflection of the earlier phase of Mexican Trotskyism. Neither the POR(T) nor the GCI had any influence in the organized labor movement, and trade-union leaders who continued to have more or less Trotskyist sympathies, such as Rafael Galván and Luciano Galicia, did not affiliate with either group. Although the Trotskyists of both groups did have some influence in the very active student movement of the late 1960's, they seem to have been at least as active in internal squabbles and factional fighting between the two branches of international Trotskyism as they were in proselytizing among the unconverted.

# Cuban Trotskyism, the Fourth International, and the Castro Revolution

Cuban Trotskyism and the whole Fourth Internationalist movement have felt the impact of the revolution led by Fidel Castro, as has virtually every political group of the left in Latin America and the world revolutionary movement in general. At the same time, Castro's revolution has been to some degree influenced by Trotskyism.

Within the island itself, the Castro revolution resulted in the suppression of the only organized Trotskyist group which had been functioning in the country, the one aligned with the Posadista faction of the Fourth International. However, disagreements over the way in which the Trotskyists should be handled were the cause of at least some controversy among those leading the revolution. Finally, the Castro regime served as a major source of dispute between the leaders of the various factions into which the Fourth Internationalists were divided.

## THE ORIGINS OF CUBAN TROTSKYISM

One name stands out particularly among the founders of Trotskyism in Cuba, that of Sandalio Junco. He was one of the major trade-union figures in the Communist Party in the late 1920's, and was the party's most important Negro leader at that time. A powerful orator with a magnetic personality, Junco had become the International Secretary of the Communist-controlled Confederación Nacional Obrera de Cuba (CNOC).[1]

In 1928 Sandalio Junco fled abroad as the result of the growing persecution of all sectors of the opposition by the dictatorship of President Gerardo Machado. He first went to Mexico, where he worked with the local Communists, and along with Julio Antonio Mella, Aureliano Sánchez Arango, and various others he helped found the Asocación de Nuevos Emigrados Revolucionarios de Cuba (Association of New Revolutionary Émigrés of Cuba, ANERC).[2]

In the following year, in his capacity as an official of the CNOC, Junco attended the conference of leaders of Latin American Communist trade-union groups in Montevideo which established the Confederación Sindical Latino Americana (CSLA). He may also have attended the conference of Latin American Communist parties held in Buenos Aires the month after the trade-union meeting. He then proceeded to Europe and to the Soviet Union. By this time, he was already beginning to question the line of the Communist International under Stalin's leadership. One of the legends about him, which may or may not be true, is that in an interview with Stalin he aroused the Soviet leader's wrath by expressing sympathy for Trotsky's position.[3]

Junco finally returned to Cuba in 1932 and almost immediately took steps to establish a Communist opposition. He wrote a memorandum to the Communist International objecting to its analysis of the situation in Cuba. He argued that there was no alliance in the island republic between a traditional landlord oligarchy and imperialism, as postulated by the Comintern, because such an old-type oligarchy did not exist—it had been destroyed in the first Cuban War of Independence from 1868 to 1878. He also brought to the Comintern's attention the size and importance of the middle class in Cuba, noting that it was not the traditional European type of middle class, but one made up of the bureaucracy. He stressed the importance of involving this middle class in the Cuban revolution, and emphasized its willingness to resort to violent and even terrorist methods.

This memorandum had little effect on the Comintern, but as a result of it Junco withdrew or was expelled from the Communist Party late in 1932, before the fall of the Machado government. He took the lead in forming the Oposición Comunista, which soon took the name Partido Bolchevique-Leninista. The official Communist explanation for the expulsion of Sandalio Junco and his associates was scurrilous rather than analytical. The Comintern's official publication *International Press Correspondence* reported on June 15, 1934, that the Junco group "held the counter-revolutionary theory of the impossibility of a revolution in Cuba without a proletarian revolution in the United States.This has worked out in practice as a constant collaboration of the Trotskyists with the government which followed Machado, in their carrying out a role of strike-breaking." Later, in the October 10, 1935, issue of the same periodical, it was reported that "at the very first stages of its development, this opposition began to obstruct the change of front of the party toward the masses, and subsequently it adopted a clear-cut, counter-revolutionary Trotskyist position."

Sandalio Junco's influence lay primarily among the country's trade unionists, but there was also a student element which participated in the establishment of the Oposición Comunista. This group came out of the so-called Ala Izquierda (Left Wing) of the student movement which was opposing the Machado dictatorship. Communists and other left-wing elements were in the Ala Izquierda, which was the principal opposition in university circles to the dominant Directorio Estudiantil, which was a group with a rather vague ideology and a preference for resorting to terrorist methods in its struggle against the Machado dictatorship.

Elements in the Ala Izquierda who were opposed to the influence of the Communists cooperated with Junco and his trade-union associates in organizing the Oposición Comunista. The principal student figure was Charles Simeon.

The Oposición Comunista aligned itself with the International Left Opposition led by Leon Trotsky. However, the members of the group were by no means all orthodox Trotskyists. Some were perhaps not much more radical than Social Democrats; others, including Eusebio Mujal, were more or less aligned with Joaquín Maurín, a Spanish Marxist who maintained a political position somewhere between that of the Communist Party and that of the Trotskyists.

Sandalio Junco himself had had considerable contact during his stay in Europe with Andrés Nin, a Spanish leader of the Red International of Labor Unions, who became the founder of Trotskyism in Spain. Subsequently, Junco and others received and read a good deal of the literature put out by the Spanish Trotskyists, particularly Andrés Nin and Juan Andrade; finding themselves generally in agreement with the positions taken by the Spanish Trotskyists, the Cubans decided to adhere to the International Left Opposition.[4]

Mario Riera Hernández, in an appendix to his history of Cuban organized labor, provides a list of members of the Partido Bolchevique-Leninista as of 1934. He names Urbano Armesto, Luis M. Busquets, Roberto Fontanillas, Marcos García Villarreal, Joaquín Gasso, Carlos González Palacios, Sandalio Junco, Armando Machado, Carlos Padrón, Fermín Sanchez, and Charles Simeon. This list is certainly incomplete. Eusebio Mujal, who years later was to succeed Sandalio Junco as the principal trade-union leader of the Auténtico Party, certainly belonged to the PBL, and it seems likely that Pablo Balbuena and Samuel Powell, who also were to become leading Autentico trade unionists in later years, did as well. Perhaps Riera Hernández was listing the Executive Committee of the Partido Bolchevique-Leninista, which at the time was claiming several hundred members. By the time of the overthrow of the Machado dictatorship in August 1933, the Oposición Comunista was firmly established. Its trade-union influence was considerable, and it controlled the Federación Obrera de La Habaña, a major labor federation in the region of the national capital.

## WAS JULIO ANTONIO MELLA A TROTSKYIST?

One of the most interesting questions concerning this formative period of Cuban Trotskyism concerns the attitude of Julio Antonio Mella toward Trotsky and his quarrel with official Communism. One of the founders of the Communist Party of Cuba in 1925,[5] Mella came to be regarded after his death as one of the patron saints of Cuban Communism; but there are grounds for asking whether Mella had not become a Trotskyist, in his thinking at least, by the time of his murder.

Mella had been a student leader in the University of Havana, and had led the campaign for university reform right after World War I. In January

1923, he organized the Popular University José Martí, and in 1924-25 he helped organize the Cuban section of the All American Anti-Imperialist League. He was arrested several times and was finally deported by the Machado government. After some time spent in Guatemala, where he worked with the local Communist Party, he finally went to Mexico. There he became active in the Mexican Communist Party, was a member of its Central Committee, and edited *El Libertador,* the organ of the All America Anti-Imperialist League.[6]

There seems little question that during his last months, Mella had growing disagreements with the Communist Party of Mexico and with Stalinism. He was in contact with those Mexican Communists and fellow travelers who were inclining toward the Trotskyist opposition.[7] He had had a serious quarrel at a meeting of the Political Bureau of the Mexican Communist Party with the Italian Comintern agent Vittorio Vidali, who under the name of Carlos Contreras was then one of the leaders of the Mexican party. Julián Gorkin in his book *Como Asesinó Stalin a Trotski,* reports that Contreras attacked Mella, saying "oppositionists like you deserve only death."[8] Víctor Alba notes that in January 1929 "it appears that the definite decision had been taken to expel him."[9]

Mella was assassinated in the streets of Mexico City in January 1929. The Communists immediately charged that he was murdered by agents of the Machado government, but Gorkin has summed up the opposing evidence thus: "A series of subsequent revelations have led to the conclusion that the real assassin of Mella was the sinister agent of the GPU (Contreras)."[10] It would probably be too much to argue that Julio Antonio Mella was the most distinguished Cuban recruit to the cause of Trotskyism. However, there is some reason to believe that before he died he had developed a certain sympathy for the positions of the outcast Soviet leader, and that this may have had much to do with his assassination.

## THE TROTSKYISTS AND THE FEDERACIÓN OBRERA DE LA HABAÑA

Upon returning from Europe, Sandalio Junco threw himself not only into the political activities of the Oposición Comunista but also into work in the labor movement. A leader of the bakers union, he quickly emerged as one of the principal figures in the Federación Obrera de La Habaña, one of the country's oldest labor groups, having been established in 1920.[11] The major political groups with followings in this labor unit were the Oposición Comunista, the new Aprista Party of Cuba, and the Socialists. The federación had a strong counterpart in the eastern city of Santiago, and it was also under the influence of these same political groups. These two regional federations were the major opponents in the organized labor movement of the Communist-controlled Confederación Nacional Obrera Cubana (CNOC).

During the radical nationalist government of President Ramón Grau San Martín, which seized power on September 4, 1933, as the result of a conspiracy between students and professors of the university and non-commissioned army officers led by Sergeant Fulgencio Batista, the Federación Obrera de La Habaña threw its support behind the government.[12] This was in sharp contrast with the position of the CNOC and the Communist Party (which had tried to "call off" the general strike which overthrew Machado); they accused the Grau regime of being "social fascist" and called for the establishment of "soviets" throughout the island.[13]

Because of the turbulence engendered by the Communists and the blind opposition of the United States government, the Grau San Martín regime was ousted in January 1934, by the same Fulgencio Batista, by then a colonel. In the months that followed, the Federación Obrera, under Junco's leadership, organized a number of strikes, among construction workers, among employees of downtown Havana department stores, including Woolworth's, and among various other groups. At the same time, it carried on a bitter conflict with the Communist unions of the CNOC. The struggle between the Trotskyist-led Federación Obrera and the Communist-dominated CNOC reached a high point on August 27, 1934. On that evening, a group of armed Communists gathered at the headquarters of the CNOC and went from there to the building of the Federación Obrera, which they assaulted. In the fighting, one person was killed and various others were wounded.[14]

By 1934 the Partido Bolchevique-Leninista (PBL), the name which the Oposición Comunista had by then assumed, had what was for a Latin American Trotskyist group a considerable membership. A. González, the Mexican-American charged with maintaining relations between the United States Trotskyists and their Latin American counterparts, reported to a Mexican correspondent that in the middle of 1934 the Cuban party had over six hundred members.[15]

The Cuban Trotskyists were very optimistic in this period about their future prospects. Thus, M. García Villarreal, one of the principal leaders of the PBL, wrote in the New York Trotskyist newspaper *The Militant* of April 28, 1934, that "the abnegation, vigor, and tenacity demonstrated by the Bolshevik-Leninists in the recent months, their wholehearted consecration to the proletarian cause, make it possible to predict that we shall be able with the aid, especially, of the proletariat of North and South America, to guide the broad Cuban masses, correctly and surely, toward the conquest of political power."

## THE TROTSKYISTS AND THE 1935 GENERAL STRIKE

The elements which had supported the Grau San Martín regime were busy during 1934 and the first months of 1935 in planning a movement to oust the government of Colonel Carlos Mendieta, which Colonel Batista had put in power in place of the revolutionary Grau administration. In the forefront of these conspiracies was the Partido Bolchevique-Leninista (PBL). The Trotskyists were plotting particularly with the organization Joven Cuba. This was a group organized by Antonio Guiteras, the most left-wing of the members of the Grau San Martín government. Joven Cuba had considerable support among the students and also some influence in labor circles. It was a rival to, but maintained friendly relations with, the Partido Revolucionario Cubano (Auténtico), which had been established by Grau San Martín himself in February 1934.[16]

In October and November 1934 the PBL issued two proclamations setting forth its position. One of these was entitled "Resolution on the Present Political Situation and Our Task in It," and the other was called "Program of Action." The first of these called for a "democratic anti-imperialist revolution of the workers and peasants." The second set forth a government program agreed upon by the PBL and Joven Cuba, to be put into execution once they succeeded in seizing power.

These proclamations brought some anguished protests from the United States Trotskyists, then organized in the Workers Party. A. J. Muste, the National Secretary of that party, wrote the Partido Bolchevique-Leninista leaders objecting to the PBL's slogan of a "democratic anti-imperialist revolution of the workers and peasants," fearing that if such a revolution were successful it would result in the establishment of a regime similar to the Kuomintang government of China, and suggesting instead that the Bolchevique-Leninistas should support a "democratic anti-imperialist insurrection, with whatever power of coalition that might last for a short while, solely as the agrarian anti-imperialist phase of a single revolution, the workers' revolution."

A. J. Muste also indicated that the United States Trotskyists felt that there was too much discussion of conspiracy with Joven Cuba, and too much time spent in elaborating a government program. Instead, the Cuban Trotskyists, according to Muste, ought to "deepen" their agitation, "expanding the revolutionary ferment to ever wider groups," and the "Partido Bolchevique-Leninista should convert itself into the authentic party of the Cuban working masses." It should present a "program of immediate struggle" instead of a proposed governmental program. Finally, Muste urged that the unity committee formed by the PBL and Joven Cuba should be expanded to include other groups, "even including the Stalinists."[17]

The conspiracies against the Mendieta government culminated in a general strike in March 1935, which Mario Riera Hernández says was called for the purpose "of installing a new order in the republic."[18] García Montes and Alonso Ávila, in their history of the Cuban Communist Party, comment thus on this walkout: "The revolutionary strike was set for the ninth of March. It was not a secret to anyone. The strike committees worked indefatigably. The cafes were converted into centers of conspiracy. The explosion of bombs and other petards was unpredictable in time and place. Their detonations seemed like thunder that announced the storm. As the days passed, the situation became increasingly obscure."[19]

The strike was supported by the Federación Obrera de La Habaña, the Trotskyists, Joven Cuba, the Auténticos, the Apristas, and even the ABC, a group often called "fascist" by its opponents.[20] However, the Communists refused to join the Committee of Proletarian Defense, which had originally launched the strike and in which Joven Cuba and the PBL had strong influence. The Communist Party, "in the desire to maintain its own hegemony, called for a strike separately from the Committee."[21]

The general strike was met by terror on the part of the Batista-dominated government. Colonel Pedraza, the military governor of Havana, declared virtual martial law. García Montes and Alsonso Ávila have described what happened: "In Havana, Colonel Pedraza took charge of the situation. He resolved it with one stroke. He dictated an order to break the strike, and prohibited anyone from going out after nine at night. Those who defied the order were to be retained, and if they resisted the order was to kill. They closed all political and trade-union groups. The repression was violent. Panic prevailed. The terror was indescribable."[22]

The Trotskyists themselves attributed the failure of the March 1935 revolutionary general strike to something more than the repression of the government. R. S. de la Torre, writing in the October 1935 issue of the United States Trotskyist journal *New International*, commented that "the strike, for lack of the central leadership which the Bolshevik-Leninist party sought to give it, was unable to resist the formidable attack of the reaction, and terminated in failure."

## THE DETERIORATION OF THE PARTIDO BOLCHEVIQUE-LENINISTA

Cuban Trotskyist activities dropped off sharply after the March 1935 insurrectional attempt. Most of those who had established the PBL abandoned its ranks, and those who remained had relatively little influence in organized labor or in the general politics of the island. However, the situation which existed in the months following the defeat of the general strike did not seem to be disadvantageous from the Trotskyists' own point of view. For one thing, within about two months after the collapse of the walkout, Antonio Guiteras was killed by the police of the Mendieta-Batista regime, and the road seemed open for the Trotskyists to win over his followers to their cause. For another, the bloody suppression of the strike aroused widespread hatred of the government in power, and seemed to create circumstances which would be propitious to the growth of the Bolchevique-Leninistas, who were among the most dedicated and determined of the opponents of the regime.

The guardedly optimistic attitude of the Trotskyists in the wake of the defeat of the March 1935 strike was reflected in an article by R. S. de la Torre in the October 1935 issue of *New International*, which we have already mentioned. He notes that the death of Guiteras "created a different situation on the Cuban political scene. Our penetration into the ranks of Young Cuba, the sympathy that its members have for our party, open up good perspectives for our organization. The petty bourgeoisie does not want to call a halt to its insurrectionary intentions. It is a question of life or death for it. Here is offered a brilliant opportunity to the proletarian party to demonstrate its abilities of leadership. On the one side, in the terrible situation in which it finds itself, the Cuban proletariat will draw the petty bourgeoisie in its train in whatever insurrectionary movement may come. If our party knows how to mobilize its forces and to take on the form of a vanguard whose voice is heard by the masses, then we shall be able to say that the revolution will be saved."

De la Torre added: "The work is difficult. Our party is lacking in financial resources, cannot publish its press legally, can conduct no legal campaign for collecting funds, and must address itself to the proletariat of other countries with the immediate request to come to its assistance. This appeal is addressed in particular to the North American proletariat with which we are united by common patterns of exploitation."

For a short while, the Cuban Trotskyists joined with a wide range of other groups, including even the Communists and the CNOC, to rally support in Cuba and abroad for those who had been arrested during the March 1933 strike. The United States Trotskyist Felix Morrow, in a letter in the October 19, 1935, issue of the *Socialist Call* (the organ of the left wing of the Socialist Party of the United States), said of the National Committee for Amnesty for Social and Political Prisoners: "It includes thirty-one political and working-class organizations, ranging from the Communist Party to the National Revolutionary Party of former President Grau San Martín, and including the Bolshevik-Leninists of Cuba, the Workers Aid of Cuba, the Havana Federation of Labor ... the Commercial Employees Union, Joven Cuba, etc."

However, the principal problems of the Cuban Trotskyists did not come from the persecution of the Mendieta-Batista government but rather from internal developments. The fact was that instead of the Bolshevik-Leninists taking over Joven Cuba and converting it into a vehicle for Trotskyism in the republic, most of the Trotskyist leaders joined Joven Cuba and themselves became lost to Trotskyism.

Charles Simeon had already abandoned the PBL for the Partido Auténtico of ex-President Grau San Martín, in 1934, and had taken a lead in organizing its youth group, the Juventud Auténtica. Soon after the death of Antonio Guiteras, various Bolshevik-Leninist leaders, including Sandalio Junco and Eusebio Mujal, joined Joven Cuba; they virtually took it over, and Junco became Labor Secretary of the group.[23]

Later the ex-Trotskyists of Joven Cuba became part of the Auténtico Party led by ex-President Ramón Grau San Martín. On August 15, 1937, a meeting was held in Havana, of representatives of the Partido Auténtico, Joven Cuba, the Izquierda Revolucionaria, the Radical Party, and various independent individuals, at which a reconstituted Partido Revolucionario Cubano (Auténtico) was established.[24] The ex-Trotskyists played a major role in the reorganized Partido Auténtico. Sandalio Junco and Eusebio Mujal established the Comisión Obrera (Labor Commission) of ex-President Grau San Martín's party, which offered the principal opposition to the Communists within the country's organized labor movement.

Other original Trotskyists evolved politically in other directions. For instance, one of them, Emilio Tró, took the lead in organizing a terrorist student group, the Unión Insurreccional Revolucionario (UIR). The UIR continued for a decade or more to have some influence in student circles, and it was in this organization that a young student, Fidel Castro, had his first political experience while at the University of Havana in the late 1940's.[25]

Sandalio Junco and his former Trotskyist associates organized the principal group opposed to the predominant influence of the Communists in Cuban organized labor. The Comisión Obrera of the Auténtico Party worked on much the same basis as the Communist Party, establishing cells in as many unions as possible throughout the island. Ultimately, this work was to pay off by giving the Auténticos control of the Confederación de Trabajadores de Cuba in 1947, three years after the party had won control of the government.

Meanwhile, Sandalio Junco had been assassinated by the Communists in 1942. The Mayor of Sancti Spiritus, a member of the Auténtico Party, had organized a meeting in that city to commemorate the anniversary of the death of Antonio Guiteras. The Comisión Obrera of the party strongly supported this meeting, and Sandalio Junco was announced as the principal speaker. The Communist daily newspaper, *Hoy*, denounced the coming meeting to commemorate Guiteras; it called Junco a "fifth columnist" and called on "the workers" to oppose the meeting. The upshot was that after the singing of the national anthem and a short speech of welcome by the Mayor, Charles Simeon began his speech, at which point a group of Communists burst into the hall, began firing at those on the platform, and succeeded in killing Sandalio Junco. In all, three people in the hall were murdered and several others were wounded.

The assassination of Junco aroused a wave of protest throughout the island. The Communists responded by accusing the Auténticos of having killed their own leader. However, within the Political Bureau, Joaquín Ordoqui, who had apparently been in general charge of the attack on the Auténtico meeting, was reported to have accused the leader of the Communist Party in Sancti Spiritus of having gone beyond his instructions by actually murdering Junco.[26]

## THE PARTIDO BOLCHEVIQUE-LENINISTA
## AFTER THE DEPARTURE OF JUNCO

With the departure of Sandalio Junco and most of the other founders of Cuban Trotskyism, the PBL became a very minor factor in the organized labor movement and an element of absolutely no significance in the country's general politics. However, it continued to exist and was occasionally able to publish some sort of periodical; in March 1939, for instance, the Mexican Trotskyist periodical *Clave* reported that the Cuban Trotskyists were putting out an organ named *Rayo y Divisa*. One of the principal remaining leaders of the Trotskyists was Juan Ramón Brea. He played a leading role in Cuban Trotskyism and was also active in the movement in other countries, including Spain, where he spent some time during the Civil War of the late 1930's. He died in May 1941.[27]

The PBL joined the Fourth International when it was formally established in September 1938, but it had some disagreements with the leaders of the International, and particularly with the United States Trotskyist leaders. Thus, when a crisis developed in the Trotskyist Liga Comunista Internacionalista, and Charles Curtiss of the United States Socialist Workers Party was dispatched to attempt to reorganize it, the PBL of Cuba supported the Luciano Galicia faction, which was eliminated from the group by Curtiss in the reorganization of Mexican Trotskyism. Although Curtiss and the international leadership considered the LCI dissolved in 1938, the PBL of Cuba declared that "for us the Liga continues to be a section of the Fourth International."[28]

In the years following the abandonment of their ranks by Junco and his associates, the Trotskyists continued to be active in the ranks of organized labor. In the early 1940's they were reported to have had their principal strength in the Guantánamo region of eastern Cuba, particularly among the workers of the Guantánamo Railroad, organized in Delegation Number 10 of the Railroad Brotherhood.[29]

The Trotskyists sought what influence they could obtain within the Confederación de Trabajadores de Cuba (CTC), which was established under Communist influence late in 1938, and they opposed Stalinist influence in the organization. According to a report in the United States Trotskyist periodical *Fourth International*, the Partido Obrero Revolucionario, the name which the Partido Bolchevique-Leninista had taken a few years before, made a "strong showing" in the CTC Congress of 1943.[30]

When the struggle for control of the CTC between the Communists and the Auténticos began to reach crisis proportions after the election of President Ramón Grau San Martín in 1944, the Trotskyists took a position in favor of maintaining the unity of the Confederación. They called for a continuation of the struggle not only against Communist control of the CTC but also against the general idea of government domination of the labor movement, which it argued had been characteristic ever since 1936, and which the Auténtico government was trying to continue, or so the Trotskyists claimed.[31]

However, when the actual split between the Auténticos and Communists in the Confederación de Trabajadores de Cuba came in 1947, the Trotskyists played no significant role in this schism. The struggle was between the followers of Grau San Martín, the Communists, and a group of "independent" trade unionists in the maritime, telephone, and electrical workers unions, none of whose leaders was Trotskyist.

In May 1941 the Partido Obrero Revolucionario began publishing a newspaper, *Revolución Proletaria*. It was still appearing five years later, although it had not come out every month, as it was presumably scheduled to do. The editor of the newspaper was Pablo Díaz González.

From time to time the Trotskyists participated in elections. During the 1944 campaign, when Ramón Grau San Martín ran as the Auténtico candidate against a hand-picked nominee of outgoing President Fulgencio Batista, the Partido Obrero Revolucionario (POR) threw its support behind Grau, and also urged its supporters to vote for trade unionists who were running for legislative offices on the ticket of Grau's Partido Revolucionario Cubano (Auténtico).

However, two years later, when congressional and municipal elections again took place, the POR took another position. In the Guantánamo region they organized a "front party," the Vanguardia Revolucionaria, which nominated candidates for local offices. However, when the electoral tribunal refused to grant official recognition to this party, the POR called upon its supporters to abstain from voting. It argued that the "Cubanism" of the Auténticos had been discredited, and that it had been demonstrated that the workers who were elected on the Auténtico ticket were no better than those Auténtico candidates who were not workers, insofar as working-class interests were concerned.[32]

When the split in the Fourth International between the Pablo and anti-Pablo forces took place in 1953-54, the Cuban POR remained with the Pablo faction, and affiliated with the Latin American Bureau of that group, headed by J. Posadas. With the further split in the Pablo ranks in the early 1960's, the POR became aligned with the Posadas version of the Fourth International.

The anti-Pablo faction, and subsequently the United Secretariat, does not seem to have had any organization in Cuba, although they may have had individual members there. This is indicated in a report for the Political Committee of the Socialist Workers Party of the United States made by Joseph Hansen on January 14, 1961. In discussing the emergence of the Cuban revolutionary regime, Hansen commented: "But we're still left with the question how are we to explain this victory in Cuba in the absence of a party like the Socialist Workers Party. Let me explain that. There's no Socialist Workers Party in Cuba."[33] A bit later on, Hansen asked the rhetorical question "Where would the Cuban Trotskyists have been in Cuba?" His answer, "They would have been in the CP, wouldn't they?", further suggests that in fact the Trotskyist international group with which the SWP was affiliated had no organized counterpart in the island.

## THE PARTIDO OBRERO REVOLUCIONARIO
## (TROTSKISTA) AND THE CASTRO REVOLUTION

The Partido Obrero Revolucionario (Trotskista), the Posadista group in Cuba fully supported the Castro revolution. It reportedly had members fighting with Fidel's guerrilla forces in the Sierra Maestra, and after 1959 they strongly backed the movement of the revolution in a Marxist-Leninist direction. Members of the POR(T) enthusiastically joined the militia which the regime recruited to defend itself from the menace of external attack and the growing internal dissidence of 1960-61.[34]

Until 1961 the POR(T) was allowed to function more or less without interference from the regime. However, even during the first two years of the revolution, the orthodox Communist Party of Cuba (still known then as the Partido Socialista Popular) furiously denounced the Trotskyists and did its utmost to discredit them and have them suppressed.

One such maneuver by the old-line Communists took place at the First Conference of Latin American Youth, which met in Havana in 1960. Carlos Manuel Pellecer, a former leader of the Guatemalan Communist Party, in an article intitled "Del Doctor Wertheim al Doctor Polcano," described what went on at that meeting: "It should be remembered that at that time, Fidel Castro did not yet appear committed to Communism and pictured his revolution as having the broadest scope. That conference was a decisive battle for the Communists. The Cubans, allied with delegates from other nationalities, began brutally to accuse the non-Communist participants, and in particular the Trotskyists, who like the Communists acted as an organized faction. The Uruguayan and Mexican delegations, who expressed themselves with frankness, were more or less imprisoned in their respective hotels until the time came to leave the country. The Communists appeared victorious 'against a Trotskyist conspiracy' which was attempting to take over the Cuban revolution and liquidate Castro, and on July 26 in Santiago Castro spoke in violent passages against the 'Trotskyist conspirators, enemies of the revolution and of the Cuban people.''

In May 1961 the government officially moved against the POR(T). It suppressed the party's paper, *Voz Proletaria,* and destroyed the plates for printing Trotsky's *Permanent Revolution,* which the party was about to publish. At the same time, the Ministry of Labor took over the print shop in which the Trotskyists' paper had been printed.[35] The government later refused to allow the POR(T) to obtain the newsprint it needed to publish its newspaper, or any other printed matter. This was done in spite of the fact that *Voz Proletaria,* according to the Trotskyists, had been "the first to publicly propose the socialist transformation of our revolution in 1960."[36]

The POR(T) again ran into trouble with the Castro government in August 1962. On August 18 two party leaders, Idalberto and Juan León Ferrera Ramírez, were arrested while distributing a leaflet containing a message from the party's Political Bureau to a congress of cane cooperatives. Two days later a meeting called by the POR(T) regional group in Guantánamo to commemorate the anniversary of the murder of Leon Trotsky was banned by the police "because they had not received a permit fourteen days in advance."

As a result of these actions, the Political Bureau of the POR(T) sent a letter to the revolutionary government on August 22. It was signed by Idalberto Ferrera Acosta, and "protested the repression against the party, which violates our revolutionary legality and all the principles of proletarian democracy, and asked for the release of the detained comrades and the cessation of all administrative hindrances to our functioning." On August 30, police came to the headquarters of the POR(T), "carrying in their hands copies of our publications, in which appeared the address of this headquarters ... and detained Comrades Idalberto Ferrera Acosta and José Lungarzo." This time, however, the Trotskyist leaders were not held for long; all those in jail were released on September 1, 1962.

Meanwhile, on August 24, 25, and 26 the POR(T) had held its Second National Conference in Havana. Opening with homage to Trotsky and his recently deceased widow Natalis Sedova, the meeting went on to discuss five major subjects, on each of which a report was given. J. Lozada delivered the report on the international situation; E. Molina the report on the Extraordinary Conference of the Fourth International (which established the Posadas version of the International); R. Carvajal on the U.S.S.R. and other workers states; Carvajal also on the situation and prospects for the revolution and the Cuban workers state and the tasks of the Trotskyists; and I. Ferrera on party activity and organization. This conference of the POR(T) "made its own the conclusions and resolutions of the Extraordinary Conference of the Fourth International, held in April 1962," the meeting which had formally established the Posadas branch of international Trotskyism. It also resolved to hold a congress of the POR(T) sometime before the Seventh World Congress of the Posadas Fourth International scheduled for March 1963. [38]

The reasons why elements in the Castro regime were annoyed by the POR(T) were shown in the "Manifesto of the POR(T) of Cuba to the Congress of Cane Cooperatives." Although this document endorsed the idea for which the congress was called, to transform the sugar cooperatives into state farms, it contained several implied if not explicit criticisms of the way in which the sugar enterprises were operating under the Castro regime. It suggested, for instance, that "it is necessary that the new unions which are organized —as well as the existing ones—function in a more democratic manner." It urged that "their leadership be elected democratically by the workers, without imposition of a single list, and if the workers consider it necessary, that they have the right to present more than one list."

Dealing with the more general problems of the organization of the Cuban "workers state," the manifesto stated: "to assure the democratic, proletarian, and revolutionary functioning of all our workers state, it is necessary to organize councils of workers and peasants, elected by the masses in their centers of work, to be directing bodies which name all of the functionaries of the workers state, and through which the masses make their voice heard, discuss, approve, reject, and decide all the problems of the state. The POR(T) proposes that there should be a Soviet Constituent Assembly to organize the workers state on this basis, as Lenin suggested in *State and Revolution*."[39]

In late 1963 the Castro government moved definitively to outlaw and crush the handful of Posadista Cuban Trotskyists. The most extensive report we have seen on this action began as follows: "The arrests began in November 1963, when Andrés Alfonso, a mechanic at the Interprovincial Bus Repair Shop, was arbitrarily ordered arrested by the administrator of the shop, Manuel Yero, after distributing copies of *Voz Proletaria* among his fellow workers. (The Trotskyists' newspaper consisted of several mimeographed pages, all they have been allowed to print since the seizure of their printing presses in May 1961 and the smashing of the type of a Spanish edition of L. Trotsky's *Permanent Revolution*.)"

Andrés Alfonso had on several previous occasions been dismissed from his job and jailed for short periods. After his final arrest he was taken to the dreaded La Cabaña fortress in Havana, where many of the regime's political prisoners were incarcerated. This action against him was taken in spite of the fact that he was a militia man, had been mobilized at the time of the October 1962 missile crisis, and was a member of the Committee for the Defense of the Revolution (CDR), the "block system" of espionage established by the Castro regime.

Alfonso's wife was also arrested a few days after her husband. On December 2, a similar fate befell Ricardo Ferrara when he went to the local CDR to inquire about the fate of Sra. de Alfonso. Ferrara had fought in the guerrilla war against Batista, was also a member of the militia and the CDR, and had won recognition as a "vanguard worker" in his place of employment. Shortly before his arrest he had returned from voluntary coffee picking following hurricane Flora. Roberto Tejera, another POR(T) member, was later jailed for asking about what had happened to his comrades. Subsequently, Idalberto Ferrera, General Secretary of the POR(T) and editor of *Voz Proletaria*, suffered a similar fate, and the party's small office was ransacked by the police.

All of these Trotskyist leaders were sentenced in secret trials to terms in jail ranging from two to nine years. The charges against them were "(1) distributing an illegal paper; (2) advocating the overthrow of the Cuban government; and (3) being critical of Fidel Castro."

That this persecution of the POR(T) was not a merely local phenomenon, but was intended as a break with the Posadas Fourth International if not the whole of international Trotskyism, was indicated by other actions taken by the Castro regime at about the same time. The residence permit of the representative of the Posadas Fourth International was suddenly cancelled, and no Cuban was allowed to leave the island to participate in the world meeting of the Posadas International, which was scheduled to be held early in 1964.[40]

## THE CASTRO GOVERNMENT'S LEADERS AND TROTSKYISM

It is not remarkable that the POR(T) was ultimately suppressed, since all other political groups except the regime's own party were outlawed. The government party was formed in 1962 through a merger of Castro's own 26th of July Movement, the old Communist Party (Partido Socialista Popular), and the Directorio Revolucionario, another group which had participated in the struggle against Batista. What was more surprising than the suppression of POR(T), perhaps, was the fact that it was allowed to function as long as it did. This fact raises some questions about the attitude of the leaders of the Castro revolution toward Trotskyism.

We have already noted that Fidel Castro received his first political training, such as it was, in the Unión Insurreccional Revolucionaria, which was founded by people who had once been Trotskyists. This should not have prejudiced him against Trotskyism. By his own admission, he was only a Marxist of the vaguest sort when he rode into Havana as the leader of the victorious revolution in January 1959, and there is no reason to believe that there was anything in his background at that time to prejudice him particularly against Trotskyism.

It was not until January 1966 that Fidel Castro pronounced himself a declared enemy of Trotskyism. The occasion was the Tricontinental Congress, and the immediate victim of Fidel's wrath was a group of Mexican Posadista Trotskyists who had been cooperating with the Yon Sosa guerrilla bands in Guatemala. But Castro extended his indictment of Trotskyism considerably beyond this limited target. In a long tirade, he engaged in several generalizations about Trotskyism. At one point, he spoke of "this discredited thing, this anti-historical thing, this fraudulent thing which emanates from elements so clearly at the service of Yankee imperialism, which is the program of the Fourth International." A bit later on, he said: "If at one time Trotskyism represented a mistaken position, but a position within the field of political ideas, Trotskyism was converted in later years into a vulgar instrument of imperialism and of reaction."

It should be noted, however, that in the details of his indictment, Castro was referring to the Posadista faction of the Fourth International. He cites an article from the publication of its Italian affiliate, as well as statements by a Mexican Posadista and by Adolf Gilly (whom he refers to as Adolfo Guil), an Argentine member of the group. Fidel was apparently particularly upset by three aspects of Posadista Trotskyism. These were the insistence by the Posadistas at that time that Ernesto Guevara had been either killed or jailed by the Castro regime; that the Castro government had not given the support it should  have to the "constitutionalists" of the Dominican Republic during the civil war in that country during 1965; and that the Mexican Trotskyists associated with the Yon Sosa guerrilla group in Guatemala had succeeded in getting that movement to adopt a Trotskyist program.

Nevertheless, it should also be observed that Castro did not draw any distinction between the Posadistas and other Trotskyists. Whether this was because he was ignorant of the divisions among them, or simply wanted to put himself on record as being against Trotskyism in general, is by no means clear. The fact remains that on the only occasion on which he saw fit to deal at some length with Trotskyism, his treatment was a general indictment of this branch of Marxism-Leninism.[41]

Two other major leaders of the revolution apparently took a more favorable view of Trotskyism although neither could be called an outright supporter of Fourth Internationalism, and both were gone from the Cuban scene by early 1965. They were Camilo Cienfuegos and Ernesto Guevara.

Cienfuegos was one of the principal military leaders of the Castro revolution, and during the first few months after its victory was commander of the rebel army. He made little secret of his opposition to the Partido Socialista Popular (the orthodox Stalinist Communist Party) and was reported at one point to have banned party members from distributing their newspaper *Hoy* in Camp Columbia, the major military base near Havana where he had his headquarters. There is some reason to believe that Cienfuegos was a sympathizer with the Trotskyists in his adolescent years, if not actually a member of the POR. Although there is no way of confirming this, it might explain his antipathy toward the Cuban Stalinists. In any case, Camilo Cienfuegos disappeared under somewhat mysterious circumstances in late October 1959.[42]

Perhaps more important is the discussion which has taken place concerning the attitude of Ernesto "Ché" Guevara. During the six years in which he played a major role in Cuban affairs, Guevara expressed conflicting views with regard to them. Joseph Hansen, one of the leaders of the Socialist Workers Party of the United States, gave one example of these conflicting attitudes: "On one occasion, Guevara attacked the newspaper of the Cuban Trotskyists over TV. News of this attack was quickly disseminated, since there are many forces, including Stalinist-minded, who are interested in driving a wedge between the Cuban Revolution and Trotskyism. Only months later did we learn accidentally that on TV, the very next night after this episode, Guevara apologized to the 'Trotskyist comrades' for the misrepresentation of their views and said that he had been mistaken in his interpretation of what they had said." Hansen also noted that at the time of Ché Guevara's attendance at the Punta del Este conference, which established the Alliance for Progress, he met with "leading representatives of the Posadas group."[43]

Ché Guevara's general international line would also seem to fit in more with Trotskyist ideology than with that of most other revolutionary groups. Guevara insisted that the revolution could not hesitate, could not be "stabilized," but rather would have to continue advancing, or it would retreat. Thus, he denounced efforts to stimulate workers' output by "material" incentives, and argued that "moral" incentives were appropriate to the period of "socialism," which according to Marxist-Leninist theory is the anteroom to "Communism," because only by the use of such moral incentives could the "new Communist man," appropriate to the subsequent historical period, be forged. Although Leon Trotsky certainly never argued along these lines, they would certainly seem to have some consistency with his "permanent revolution" argument.

However, there is evidence that Guevara's attitude toward Trotskyism and the Trotskyists had hardened by his last months of association with the Castro regime. When he was asked by a member of a group of United States students which visited the island in the summer of 1964 whether or not "political criticism in the framework of unconditional support and defense of the revolution should be handled politically rather than by suppression of views," Guevara is reported to have replied: "I agree with your statement, but the Cuban Trotskyists are not inside the revolution, but only 'divisionists.' I did not see them in any mountains. I did not see them dead in any city battle. They appeared after the revolution was over giving instructions about Guantánamo, and so on. I won't say they are CIA agents—we don't know. *They have no history of support to the revolution.* They say there is a right-wing formed by the Stalinists and we (Guevara) are the left-wing.''[44]

## THE FOURTH INTERNATIONALS AND THE CASTRO REVOLUTION

Disagreements over the nature of the Castro regime have long been part of the factional politics of the Fourth International. The faction led by the United Secretariat, with which the Socialist Workers Party of the United States was associated, arrived fairly quickly at the conclusion that the Castro regime was a "workers state." Joseph Hansen, one of the major figures in the SWP, has stated this position in a strong fashion. As early as November 20, 1962, he wrote: "Once you see Cuba for what it is, a workers state and the opening stage of the socialist revolution in the Western Hemisphere ... then it is quite clear why it plays such a spectacular role. The extension of the October 1917 Revolution into the Western Hemisphere is a *revolutionary action* far more decisive in the scales than the weight of Cuba's economy in North and South America." Hansen adds: "This is not all. By bringing forward a leadership of non-Stalinist origin, the Cuban revolution has visibly hastened the eventual closing of the whole chapter of Stalinism."[45]

The United Secretariat version of the Fourth International continued to support the Castro regime in an "unqualified" way, although it offered Fidel's government unsolicited advice from time to time concerning its "errors." Near the end of a long analysis of the aftermath of the Cuban government's unsuccessful campaign to achieve a ten-million-ton sugar crop in 1970, Livio Maitan, an Italian spokesman for the United Secretariat's view, wrote in the November 30, 1970, issue of *Intercontinental Press*: "The Fourth International has never subordinated its analysis of the workers states and their evolution to any tactical considerations. This is why today we are attempting a criticism of the tendencies operative in Cuba, and point out—along with positive aspects—a series of alarming elements. Cuba remains a rampart of the world revolution. The existence of revolutionary Cuba represents an unceasing source of weakness for American imperialism and an element objectively assisting the Latin American revolution as a whole. All indications are that the Cuban leaders will be on the side of any revolutionary movement that develops, because they have not forgotten that their revolution in the last analysis depends on that of the continental revolution."

The United Secretariat was upset by the Heberto Padilla case early in 1971. Padilla, a poet whose works had received prizes from the Castro government's Casa de las Américas, was arrested and released only after making a humiliating "confession" of his errors. Concerning this, Jean-Pierre Beauvais wrote in the May 10, 1971, issue of *Rouge*, the organ of the United Secretariat's French affiliate: "In Moscow, in Prague, in Warsaw, this is normal. There the use of terror is the only thing that occurs to the haughty, imbecile bureaucrats, who are essentially preoccupied with preserving order. It doesn't astonish us. In Havana, the thing is new. It is grave, very grave." Then, after noting the consistent support of the United Secretariat Trotskyists for the Cuban revolution, Beauvais says: "Thus, the aggravation in recent years of a series of bureaucratic deformations, the errors which these have imposed on the economic plan, certain international positions such as the support of the invasion of Czechoslovakia, or the support of Latin American revolutionaries passing to secondary rank in the priority list of the Cuban leadership, have been for us subjects for worry and material for criticism.... It is in this context that the Padilla affair appears in all its gravity."

The July 1971 issue of *Quatrième Internationale* carried a further commentary by Livio Maitan on the Castro revolution, under the title "Cuba: A Necessary Balance Sheet." Written in two parts—one completed in February and a postscript written in June, after the Padilla incident—this article reflects concern over the Padilla question but indicates that the United Secretariat's position on Cuba has not changed. In the earlier part of the article, Maitan says: "We are convinced that the Cuban revolution has not yet expressed all of its potentialities," and that Latin American revolutionaries are inspired by consciousness "of their duty to defend by their anti-imperialist actions the Cuban workers state, which has not ceased to represent the most audacious defiance and the most noxious annoyance to the most powerful imperialism in the history of capitalism." In his postscript, Maitan concludes: "The essential elements of the problem- –and of the balance sheet which we have drawn—have not had any qualitative change."

The Posadista faction of the Fourth International has also regarded the Castro regime as a "workers state" since the early 1960's. We have already noted that the criticisms of the functioning of the regime made by its Cuban affiliate, the Partido Obrero Revolucionario (Trotskista), were stated in terms of trying to improve the Cuban workers state. The International likewise took this same stand.

The political resolution of the Seventh World Congress of the Posadas Fourth International contained a section headed "The Influence of the Cuban Revolution." This document began with a reference to "The Cuban Socialist Revolution," and subsequently noted that "the activity of the Trotskyists in Cuba, as in the whole world, is one of unconditional defense of the workers state." However, it also commented that the condemnation of the Cuban Trotskyists by the Castro government "indicates a serious beginning of a process of bureaucratization." This posture of "unconditional support" together with criticism of details of the functioning of the Castro regime continued to be the position of the Posadista faction throughout the 1960's.

The only element of Fourth Internationalism which frankly condemned the Castro regime, and argued that the Trotskyists should have nothing to do with it, was the Healyite International Committee of the Fourth International. At its Third Conference in London in April 1966 it adopted a "Manifesto of the International Committee of the Fourth International," which commented as follows on the nature of the Castro regime: "The petty bourgeois Bonapartist cliques are collapsing. Their political role, which gave them an apparent independence in relation to imperialism, consisted essentially in canalizing the mass movements. The most radical of them, however far they may have gone with their split from imperialism, have finally remained under its domination."

The manifesto then went on to apply this generalization specifically to the Cuban case: "The most extreme example—Cuba—is no exception to the rule. U.S. imperialism forced the Cuban petty bourgeoisie to go so far as to expropriate the American firms and to call on the Cuban worker and peasant masses to support its measures. But no matter how far Fidel Castro and the 26th of July Movement may have gone, the social nature of the regime remained bourgeois. In its struggle against U.S. imperialism, its main support could only be the Kremlin bureaucracy, and this made it its prisoner."

Finally, the manifesto predicted a sorry end to the Castro revolution: "The offers to negotiate compensation for nationalized imperialist property, the struggle against the 'lefts,' the trials of the original leaders of the Castro movement, the discovery of plots against Fidel Castro, the anti-Trotskyist attacks, are so many symptoms showing that the Cuban revolution is reaching a critical stage. Under the petty bourgeois Castroite leadership the contradictions of the regime grow. In the absence of a revolutionary workers' party, they will lead to the decay of the regime to the benefit of imperialism, whatever may be the personal destiny of Fidel Castro and his petty bourgeois entourage."[46]

The Healyites have not changed in their attitude since then. Thus, in the process of reviewing a biography of Ernesto Guevara by Andrew Sinclair, in the March 6, 1970, issue of the *Workers Press*, the organ of the Socialist Labor League, Tony Short commented: "Total concentration in the hands of a few men of power, based on the apparatus of the bourgeois state, army, and police, is at best Bonapartism and at worst fascism. The cult of violence and war as creators of virtue in men is also reminiscent of fascist ideology."

Later in the same year, after the failure of the ten-million-ton sugar crop in Cuba, *Workers Press* carried an article entitled "Cuban Crisis Grows." It said in part: "Castroism—and all those who have tried to present it as a revolutionary alternative to Stalinism—is going into a deep crisis that will have its repercussions not only in Cuba and Latin America but throughout the world— and essentially in the ranks of the ex-Trotskyist renegades of the United Secretariat.... This Pabloite group has based practically its entire political perspective on the emergence of a Castroite 'third force' between imperialism and Stalinism.... It now shows itself tied to both, confirming everything we have said about the Castro variety of petty-bourgeois nationalism since its emergence in the early 1960's.[47]


CONCLUSION

Although Cuban Trotskyism had considerable influence in organized labor in the early 1930's, it declined sharply when its principal leaders withdrew to join what was for a quarter of a century the "mainstream" of national politics. Throughout the 1940's and 1950's, the Trotskyists continued to be a very minor factor in organized labor, and their main support was confined to the area of Guantánamo at the eastern tip of the island.

The Partido Obrero Revolucionario (Trotskista) enthusiastically supported the Cuban revolution, both before and after Castro's assumption of power, but its "unconditional support" of the regime was not sufficient to save it from persecution and final suppression by Castro's government. There was no place in Cuba for a second revolutionary party, even such a miniscule one as the POR(T); after 1961 there was only one legal political party, the one which four years later took the name Partido Comunista de Cuba, with Fidel Castro as its Secretary-General.

The various factions of International Trotskyism have taken different attitudes toward the Castro regime. In spite of the suppression of its own affiliate in Cuba, the Posadista International has insisted that the Castro regime is a workers state and should be supported, although it has also insisted on the need to keep Trotskyism alive in Cuba and has been highly critical of some of the actions of the regime. The United Secretariat has been most enthusiastic in its support of Castro (although it has offered him frequent advice and has been perturbed by such events as his endorsement of the invasion of Czechoslovakia and the "confession" of Padilla); it has had its few Cuban followers join Castro's party. The Healyites, finally, have been uncompromisingly hostile toward the Castro regime from the beginning, and have attacked groups, such as the United Secretariat, who have supported it.

# —12—

# Trotskyism in Other Latin
# American Countries

In previous chapters we have discussed the most significant and long-lasting Latin American affiliates of international Trotskyism, those in Argentina, Brazil, Chile, Bolivia, Peru, Mexico, and Cuba. But Uruguayan Trotskyism was also of some significance, particularly in the country's labor movement; and Trotskyist movements have appeared briefly, particularly in Trotskyism's formative years as a Left Communist tendency, in Ecuador, Panama, Puerto Rico, and Colombia. The Uruguayan movement and these short-lived groups will be dealt with in this chapter.

## URUGUAY

During most of the first half of the twentieth century, Uruguay was unique among Latin American countries. Under the influence of José Batlle y Ordoñez, a nationalist and socially oriented program brought large segments of the economy under the state ownership, made primary education virtually universal, and produced extensive labor legislation and an oversized social security system.

Largely as a result of Batlle's program, the traditional Colorado and Nacionalista parties continued to hold the loyalty of most Uruguayans. The Colorados were the principal representative of urban interests and the Nacionalistas were backed by rural dwellers, particularly the large landholding groups and others opposed to Batlle's reform program. Most workers tended to vote for the Batllista faction of the Partido Colorado, which was known from the time of the First World War as the Partido Colorado Batllista. An idiosyncratic electoral system made it possible for the Colorado and Nacionalista parties to put up a common front against one another and against other political groups, in spite of large-scale factionalism within each of these parties.

All of the minor parties together represented no more than 15 to 20 per

236

cent of the vote in Uruguay. During most of the first sixty years of the century, these parties were the Catholic Unión Cívica, the Partido Socialista, and the Partido Comunista. The Unión Cívica normally received about half of the total vote for the minor parties; the Socialists and Communists usually divided the rest, with the Partido Socialista tending to gain as the Communists lost, and vice versa. Within this general political schema, the Trotskyists never came to represent more than a tiny fraction of the rather small minority of the population that did not support the two traditional major parties. Its influence in organized labor was for some time noticeable but not substantial; from time to time it has had a certain following among politically active students.

## THE LIGA OBRERA REVOLUCIONARIA

Trotskyism appeared in Uruguay soon after it made its appearance as a worldwide schism in international Communism. Esteban Kikích, a Yugoslav-Uruguayan, had corresponded since 1926 with James Cannon, who later became one of the principal leaders of the Trotskyist movement in the United States; he, another Yugoslav, and a Bulgarian withdrew from the Uruguayan Communist Party in 1929 at about the same time Cannon and his followers were expelled from the Communist Party of the United States. However, it was not until 1937 that a formal Trotskyist organization, the Liga Obrera Revolucionaria, was established in Uruguay. This delay was said to be due principally to the fact that Trotskyism found its principal supporters among the foreign-born workers in Uruguay.

The Trotskyists had some influence in the labor movement. Esteban Kikích took the lead in 1940 in establishing the Sindicato Único de la Industrial Metalúrgica, to which most of the metalworkers of Montevideo came to belong. This union joined the Unión General de Trabajadores (UGT), at that time the chief central labor organization in the country. However, the UGT was under Communist domination, and the new union soon also came under the control of the Communist Party. As a result, Kikích, who had been a member of the union's executive committee, was finally forced to withdraw from this post and from the union itself in 1942.

Upon being forced out of the Sindicato Único de la Industria Metalúrgica, Kikích and his associates concentrated on building up an independent union in the Ragusci and Voulminot shipbuilding and repair firm in Montevideo. By the middle 1940's this became one of the strongest unions in the city, obtaining a union shop and gaining sizable wage increases for its members.

As a result of a revolt of various political tendencies within the UGT against Communist domination of that organization, the Unión General de Trabajadores began to fall apart in 1942. As a result, there were three principal central labor bodies functioning by the end of World War II: the UGT, under Communist control; the Comité de Relaciones Sindicales, largely Socialist-dominated; and the Comité de Enlace de Sindicatos Autónomos. The Comité de Enlace de Sindicatos Autónomos was under the joint control of Anarchists and Trotskyists. Esteban Kikích was its outstanding figure, and it included within its ranks the bakers union, the plumbers union, and two shipyard workers organizations.

In the meantime, the Uruguayan Trotskyists had felt the impact of the split which had taken place in the United States Trotskyist movement in 1940, when Max Shachtman had led his followers out of the Socialist Workers Party after a bitter argument, with the rest of the SWP leadership and with Leon Trotsky himself, over the nature of government in the Soviet Union, and in particular over Trotsky's support of the Soviet invasion of Finland at the end of 1939. Esteban Kikích and other Uruguayan Trotskyist leaders sympathized with Shachtman's position on these issues, but they did not break with those in the Liga Obrera Revolucionaria who took the opposite point of view. Since Shachtman and his followers made little effort at that time to establish a rival to the Fourth International headed by Trotsky, there was no occasion for the Uruguayan Trotskyists to have to choose between rival international bodies, a choice which might have provoked a schism within the Uruguayan Trotskyist movement.[1]

In the middle of 1944 the Liga Obrera Revolucionaria received nationwide attention when the Minister of Interior attacked the organization violently during a legislative debate in the Chamber of Deputies. The minister was urging passage of a bill providing for the establishment of compulsory committees of conciliation and arbitration for handling labor disputes, and one of his major arguments in favor of this legislation, which would have virtually banned strikes, was his assertion that the Trotskyists "use the strike as a revolutionary training school." The Trotskyists replied, "We do not use 'the strike as a revolutionary training school,' but we do affirm and maintain that the strike is the only arm which the workers possess to obtain their demands and that it must be defended by all means." They urged the formation of a "united class front to defend the right to strike and trade-union liberties," and urged workers "to demand that every union mobilize in defense of those liberties and begin a joint campaign with other workers organizations against the repression of the labor movement."[2]

For some years the Trotskyists were able to publish a newspaper occasionally. It was first called *Acción Socialista*, but starting in 1942 it took the name *Contra la Corriente (Against the Current)*. It was a lively paper containing a variety of news stories, ideas, and propaganda. Denunciations of the Stalinists, both in other countries (particularly the Soviet Union) and in Uruguay itself, were frequent. It paid special attention to events in the Uruguayan labor movement, notably the situation among the metallurgical workers; it also attacked the "betrayal" of trade-union leaders of various political tendencies in the Packing House Workers Federation, the single most important labor organization in Uruguay at the time. International events were dealt with extensively in *Contra la Corriente*. The civil war in Greece, the "Truman Plan" for strengthening economic relations between Latin America and the United States, and the establishment of the United Nations were among the events discussed.

Much attention was paid to the activities of Trotskyists in other countries. The success of the French Fourth Internationalists in winning 60,000 votes in the first postwar elections was noted in the November 1946 issue; the struggle of the Greek Trotskyists against the regime then in power was discussed in the October 1946 issue; and the problems of the Bolivian Partido Obrero Revolucionario were dealt with in several numbers of the paper. In its June 1946 issue there was an extensive article on the Fourth International conference which had been held shortly before in Belgium; the article does not say whether the Uruguayan group was represented directly at this meeting.

*Contra la Corriente* carried a number of articles designed to present the doctrine of the Fourth Internationalists to its readers. Thus, the November 1946 issue published the "five fundamental decrees" made by the Bolshevik government late in 1917 and early in 1918. Several numbers dealt with the problem of agrarian reform, underscoring the Trotskyists' opinion that it was essential in Uruguay, and outlining the kind of land redistribution program which they favored.

On the occasion of a packinghouse workers strike late in 1946, the Trotskyists, who had little or no influence among that key group of workers, issued a throwaway entitled *Viva la Huelga de los Obreros de los Frigoríficos!* (*Long Live the Strike of the Packinghouse Workers*), in which it warned the workers against "a deal between the bourgeoisie and traitorous labor leaders." It also urged the strikers not to be satisfied with any promise that the workers' demands would be resolved through a bipartite wage council, a procedure which the government was then using extensively to deal with various labor crises.

The Liga Obrera Revolucionaria did not participate actively in elections. The November 1946 issue of *Contra la Corriente* called on workers to boycott the general election scheduled for that month. The Liga apparently did not offer candidates of its own, and argued that the workers' interests were not to be served by their voting for the nominees of any other party. The paper also argued that the referendum which was on the ballot, on the issue of establishing a new nine-man "colegiado" in the place of the President of the Republic, was of no concern to the country's workers. The next issue of the LOR's paper bore the banner headline "More than half a million votes do not change the asphyxiating poverty of the people."

By 1952 the Liga Obrera Revolucionaria had changed the name of its newspaper to *Frente Obrero*. The July 1952 issue of this periodical gave some indications of the Liga's activities at that time. It carried a major article against a proposed military treaty with the United States. This article criticized those who were conducting most of the agitation against this treaty as being under the control of "organs dominated by the bourgeoisie." It called for a "great national movement for the unity of action of the masses against the treaty" and for a national plebiscite on the issue.

This number of *Frente Obrero* also carried news on Trotskyite activities in Argentina and Ceylon, and a reply to an attack on the Uruguayan Trotskyites by *Clase Obrera*, the organ of a schismatic left-wing group of the Socialist Party, the Agrupación Socialista Obrera. This editorial, entitled "The Fundamentals of a Labor Party," stressed the need for a new labor party in Uruguay, which would be Marxist-Leninist in ideology. But it commented: "A Marxist-Leninist party does not arise by spontaneous generation. Rather, it arises on the basis of the acquisitions of Marxism-Leninism for the international labor movement…. We offer to the revolutionary vanguard," it asserted, "the Marxism-Leninism developed by Trotskyism and the Fourth International in the struggle for the new Party."

By the early 1950's, the Trotskyists had lost most of the influence they had acquired in the labor movement five years earlier. The Comité de Enlace de Sindicatos Autónomos, the group which had been under Trotskyist and Anarchist leadership right after World War II, had disappeared, and most of the labor movement was consolidated in either the Unión General de Trabajadores, led by the Communists, or the Confederación Sindical Uruguaya, then the larger of the two groups, which had members of the Socialist Party, Independent Nationalist Party, and Batllista Colorado Party among its leaders. There is no indication in *Frente Obrero* of any direct Trotskyist activity in the labor movement, although the paper did call for unification of the two central labor groups.

With the split of the Fourth International in 1953-54, the Uruguayan Trotskyists remained with the faction led by Michel Pablo. They also changed the name of their organization to Partido Obrero Revolucionario (IV Internacional). It became one of the first Trotskyist parties outside of Argentina to come under the influence of J. Posadas.

## THE TROTSKYISTS AND THE
## GROWING URUGUAYAN CRISIS

During the years following World War II, it became increasingly obvious to many that the economy and society of Uruguay were entering a profound crisis. The solutions which Batlle had offered several decades before were no longer sufficient. The traditional grazing sector of the national economy, which had provided most of the country's foreign exchange, had entered a period of serious decline. Industrialization, which all governments since Batlle had favored, had advanced about as far as was possible without a basic change in orientation. A system whereby large numbers of workers held part-time jobs in both government and private employment had expanded and to a growing degree was devoid of all economic sense. The social security system was increasingly inefficient and expensive.

However, the political leaders of the post-World War II period did little to come to grips with any of these problems. As a result in 1958, for the first time in over ninety years, the Partido Colorado was defeated and an eight-year period of rule by the Partido Nacional began. At the same time, discontent was mounting against both of the traditional parties, and it was a discontent which did not seem to find a viable outlet in any of the existing minor parties.

At this juncture, the Partido Obrero Revolucionario (IV Internacional) sought to provide an alternative, at least for those on the extreme left of national politics. It held a national congress soon after the victory of the Partido Nacional, and subsequently issued as a pamphlet a resolution of a July 1959 meeting of its Central Committee, which set forth the party's position on national political problems.

The Trotskyites argued strongly for reunification of the divided labor movement: "The unified central labor organization and the Proletarian United Front appear as the instruments necessary for acting against the class enemy, and advancing the political maturity of the masses, and for deepening, through action and the party program, the crisis within the Socialist and Communist parties, and for giving it a progressive solution."[3]

The PORistas argued that there were severe crises within both the Socialist and Communist parties, and felt that the Trotskyists could take advantage of these. The Central Committee resolution argued: "The working class and its struggles on the one hand, and the conscientious action of our party through all means, on the other, are the decisive elements for the development of an ample Socialist left tendency which will thus appear as a possible alternative leadership within the Socialist Party. Our party has the right and revolutionary duty to push for a progressive outcome to the crisis in the Socialist Party.[4]

Insofar as the Communist Party was concerned, the POR saw growing disenchantment with the party's national leadership on the part of lower-ranking leaders and the rank and file. "In these conditions," it added, "the organization of a tendency within the Communist Party presents itself not only as something to be pushed and encouraged, but as the path toward a progressive solution to the crisis in the Communist Party."[5]

The July 1959 resolution of the POR Central Committee ended with the presentation of an extensive program. Among the things it called for were "a workers program of industrialization," "establishment of industries in the interior, nationalized and under workers control," "a plan of housing in accord with popular necessities," and "the occupation in the meantime of all edifices and houses available—summerhouses, apartment houses, hotels." In addition, it called for an agrarian reform, including "the expropriation without compensation of latifundia," and "the extension of all social conquests to the countryside." The program urged "commerce with the Workers States," and "accords and joint planning with other Latin American countries.[6]

However, this program was not sufficient to win the Partido Obrero Revolucionario (IV Internacional) any substantial influence either within the labor movement or in the general political spectrum. Although the crisis in the Socialist Party, which the Trotskyists had analyzed so extensively, did lead to a rapid decline in the fortunes of that party, the **POR** (IV Internacional) was not able to capitalize on this. The crisis in the Communist Party ranks which the Trotskyists had predicted did not in fact take place; the party extended its influence considerably during the 1960's, coming to control all but a small fraction of the labor movement and substantially increasing its representation in Congress. Meanwhile, the POR remained a marginal group in Uruguayan affairs.

## THE RECENT HISTORY OF POR(T)

With the new attempts to unify the Fourth International in 1962-63, which resulted in the emergence of three organizations each using the same name, the Uruguayan Trotskyists joined the predominantly Latin American faction of the Fourth International headed by J. Posadas. Furthermore, because of the relatively democratic atmosphere in Uruguay, that country became the de facto seat of the Posadas Fourth International and Posadas himself spent most of his time there.

Nonetheless, this situation did not serve to enhance the fortunes of the Uruguayan Trotskyists. Their lack of influence was underscored by the fact that the candidates they offered to the electorate in the 1962 general election received a total of only 213 votes. The Trotskyists did not participate in the next election, in 1966.[7]

Like the rest of the groups affiliated with the Posadista Fourth International, the Partido Obrero Revolucionario (IV Internacional) supported the Cuban revolution of Fidel Castro. Luis Eduardo Naguil Moratorio, a member of the party's Political Bureau, was reported to have attended a Cuban Solidarity Congress in Havana in 1963.[8]

In the late 1960's, the Trotskyist group, which was by then called the Partido Obrero Revolucionario (Trotskista), came to be severely persecuted by the government. The Colorado Party returned to power in the presidential and congressional election of 1966, which brought retired General Oscar Gestido to the presidency. He died late in 1967 and was succeeded by his Vice-President, Jorge Pacheco. Pacheco's new government undertook a serious program to deal with the country's rampant inflation (moving at the rate of over 100 per cent a year), began a serious reform of the social security system, and drafted a long-range economic development policy.

This program was greeted by a strong outcry from the labor movement and the political left. During 1968 strikes were prevalent, and the terrorist activities of the Castroite Tupamaros group, which had been a feature of national life for several years, were intensified. However, terrorism was repudiated by the orthodox Communist Party, and there was reason to believe that that party, which by this time largely dominated the labor movement, was acting as a moderating influence within the trade unions.

In the face of this situation, the Pacheco government—unable to deal adequately with the Tupamaros—appears to have made the miniscule Trotskyite group its scapegoat. In October 1968 the police raided a meeting of the POR(T), breaking up what the police claimed was a meeting of the Posadas Fourth International. This event received a good deal of publicity in the daily press of Montevideo, and *El Popular*, the newspaper of the Communist Party, insisted that one of those who was arrested, the Argentine Homero Rómulo Cristali, was in fact the famous J. Posadas. The Trotskyites denied this, and even went so far as to insist that there was no such actual person as Posadas, but the Communists were correct in their identification of Cristali-Posadas. His picture appeared in the papers the next day.

This persecution of the Trotskyists aroused a good deal of sympathy for them both inside Uruguay and abroad. Even the Communist paper, a few days after identifying Posadas, protested against the imprisonment of POR(T) leaders, saying that it was "a violation of the right to ideas, an attack on ideas, a persecution of revolutionary ideas." Even the President of the Chamber of Deputies protested, and the Uruguayan government received letters from groups in several Latin American countries urging the release of the Trotskyists.

For their part, the Trotskyist prisoners did not make life easy for their jailers. They insisted on singing revolutionary songs with great vehemence, and absolutely refused to answer any questions when they were interrogated. They spent much of their time in political discussions, which seem to have been led—or dominated—by Posadas. It is interesting to note that much of the attention of the other prisoners was concentrated on trying to prevent any misfortune from overtaking a man who was identified in Trotskyist documents only as "N", but was apparently Posadas. The Uruguayans among the prisoners were finally released; the foreigners were deported to Italy, after Chile refused to accept them, and several other Latin American countries informed the Uruguayan government that they would not allow the group to land within their frontiers.[9]

This incident was not the end of the persecution of the POR(T). During the first weeks of March 1969, the police raided houses and apartments in various parts of Montevideo and a number of Trotskyists, including several foreigners, were arrested.[10] Finally, on March 15, 1969, the Pacheco government issued a decree dissolving the Partido Obrero Revolucionario (Trotskista) and suppressing its newspaper, *Frente Obrero*. In the preamble of the decree, the President noted the capture by the government of "abundant manifestos, proclamations, resolutions, ideas, harangues, programs of the party, etc., which in large part advocate a world revolutionary struggle, violence, and the use of arms as effective methods of taking power after the destruction of existing regimes in our country and other countries of the world."[11]

In spite of this assessment of the nature of POR(T) propaganda, which was reasonably accurate, there is no evidence that the Uruguayan Trotskyites ever seriously tried to overthrow the government. Nor is there any evidence, in particular, of their having had any association with the Tupamaro urban guerrilla group.

In the election of November 1971, the POR(T) threw its meager support to the retired General Liber Segnini, the candidate of the Frente Amplio (Wide Front), in an unsuccessful attempt to establish the kind of victorious coalition which had brought Salvador Allende to the presidency of Chile in 1970. The Frente Amplio was composed chiefly of the Communist, Socialist, and Christian Democratic parties, and dissident factions of the two major parties, the Colorados and Nacionalistas.

## THE PARTIDO REVOLUCIONARIO DE LOS TRABAJADORES

In 1969 another Trotskyist party was established as a rival to the POR(T). This was the Partido Revolucionario de los Trabajadores (PRT), which was identified by *Intercontinental Press* on March 1, 1971, as "adhering to the Fourth International," meaning the United Secretariat faction. The PRT was said to be "doing its utmost to extend its proletarian bases by actively participating in the country's political process," and was said to believe that "only armed struggle growing out of a mass working-class movement can achieve final victory." According to this report, the PRT had been established by "both students and workers," although there is no indication of what their previous political affiliation, if any, may have been. Although forced to function underground, the party brought out on a more or less regular basis a newspaper entitled *Tendencia Revolucionaria*.

In spite of the identification of the PRT by *Intercontinental Press* as "adhering to the Fourth International," the United Secretariat issued a statement dated March 22, 1971, which seemed to deny this. This statement was published in *Intercontinental Press* on April 12, 1971, and stated categorically that "there is no section of the Fourth International in Uruguay." This United Secretariat statement also strongly opposed the Frente Amplio, which was then being organized. It stated that the United Secretariat was "totally opposed, as it has always been, to any kind of collaboration whatsoever by revolutionary Marxist forces in Popular Fronts, i.e., with bourgeois forces, whenever and wherever they happen to exist."

In spite of the United Secretariat's position, the Partido Revolucionario de los Trabajadores, which *Intercontinental Press* of December 13, 1971, identified as "a Trotskyist grouping that has proclaimed its adherence to the Fourth International but that has not yet been accepted as a section," became part of the Frente Amplio. After trying unsuccessfully to get the leaders of the Frente Amplio to agree to allow the PRT to run its own candidates for president and vice-president under the Frente Amplio banner, which would have been technically possible under the peculiar Uruguayan reform laws, the party carried the names of the Frente's official presidential and vice-presidential nominees at the head of its slate, which was called the Lista Obrera (Labor List). However, it ran a number of its own candidates for lesser posts. So far as is known, none of its nominees was elected.

## CONCLUSIONS CONCERNING
## URUGUAYAN TROTSKYISM

Although a Trotskyite movement has existed in Uruguay for almost three and a half decades, it has never become a really influential element either in the labor movement or in the country's left-wing politics, let alone in the wider national political scene. Although they had some influence in organized labor in the 1940's, the Trotskyites lost virtually all of this during the next decade. The party had a significant opportunity to take advantage of the crisis which gripped the Socialist Party in the late 1950's and early 1960's, but it was not able to capitalize on it. Even the presence in the country of the headquarters of the Posadas faction of the Fourth International during the middle 1960's did not expand the POR(T)'s influence, or even its prestige, in national political life. Uruguayan Trotskyism never became more than a miniscule left-wing faction.

## TROTSKYISM IN OTHER
## LATIN AMERICAN COUNTRIES

In the early days of the emergence of Trotskyism as an international movement, the Communist League of America, of the United States, corresponded extensively with individuals and groups in various Latin American countries which expressed interest in the positions being taken by the International Left Opposition. In some cases, as we have seen, this exchange of letters, information, and propaganda material contributed in at least some degree to the emergence of fairly substantial national Trotskyist parties or groups.

However, in several instances, the hopes which this correspondence aroused among international Trotskyist leaders proved to be misplaced. The Trotskyist groups which emerged in several Latin American nations proved to be short-lived. For instance, A. González, the Mexican-American in charge of Latin American relations for the Communist League of America, reported in the middle of 1934: "We have received a letter from an Ecuadorean comrade, in which he informs us that they also have a group formed in that country."[12] The name of this group is not even recorded, and it seems to have disappeared without a trace.

It was not until 1971 that there was again some indication of the existence of a Trotskyist group in Ecuador. The issue of *Voz Obrera*, the organ of the Posadista POR(T) of Peru, for the second fortnight of March 1971 carries news of an exchange of telegrams between the Partido Comunista Revolucionario (Trotskista) of Ecuador and the President of the Republic, Dr. José María

Velasco Ibarra. The party wired the President to congratulate him on his demand that the United States withdraw its military mission in Ecuador. The telegram also said "we call for the anti-imperialist united front, the government, the nationalist military, and the masses of the country to expropriate imperialism and the oligarchy," and ended with the slogan, "for federation and economic and political planning in Chile, Bolivia, Peru, and Ecuador."

The editors of *Voz Obrera* added a note saying that their party "salutes with immense revolutionary joy this event and this triumph of the Ecuadorean section." This note also commented on the existence of *Lucha Comunista*, the official organ of the Partido Comunista Revolucionario (Trotskista), and urged the Ecuadorean comrades to work hard to publish the paper on a regular basis. Finally, it commented: "The texts of Comrade Posadas, of the International Secretariat of the Fourth International, which the last number of the periodical of the Ecuadorean section publishes, are indispensable to the construction of revolutionary leadership, and to the advancement and maturation of the nationalist tendency which seeks to move forward in a united front with the Ecuadorean masses along the Socialist path."

The early Trotskyist group in Panama proved to be somewhat less ephemeral than its counterpart in Ecuador. The first notice we have of this Panamanian element again comes from A. González. He writes to a Mexican correspondent: "We have established contact with a distinguished element of the Panamanian Communist movement who is working for the formation of one of our sections in that country. In his latest he tells us that he now has a homogeneous group formed and hopes that in the near future they will be able to formally constitute one of our sections."[13]

By the early months of 1935, the Panamanian Trotskyists were firmly organized in the Partido Obrero Marxista-Leninista, which was putting out a newspaper, *Organización*. The leader of the new party was a young man named Diógenes de la Rosa, who was active in the country's trade-union movement. He was described by A. González as being "one of the most distinguished elements of the Panamanian revolutionary movement."[14]

However, the Partido Obrero Marxista-Leninista went out of existence in late 1935. Its members entered the Socialist Party of Panama, which was then fighting the Communists for control of the organized labor movement. It is not clear whether this move had any relationship to the so-called "French turn," which at about the same time was bringing various Trotskyist groups to enter their respective nations' Socialist Parties. In any case, it does not appear that the Trotskyites did any serious "boring from within" in the Panamanian Socialist Party. Rather, Diógenes de la Rosa emerged as one of the principal Socialist leaders, served as a member of the National Legislative Assembly in the middle 1940's, and in 1948 left the Socialist Party in a struggle for power within it which had nothing to do with Trotskyism, which he regarded by then as a relic of the past. In the 1950's and 1960's, de la Rosa served for some years as one of his country's more distinguished diplomats.[15]

The Trotskyist movement of Puerto Rico seems to have been of somewhat longer duration than those of Ecuador and Panama, but it apparently disappeared about the time of the outbreak of World War II. The circumstances surrounding the formation of the Puerto Rican group were described in a letter to A. González from Luis Vergne Ortíz, of the Organizing Committee of the Partido Comunista Independente de Puerto Rico, dated January 16, 1935. Vergne Ortíz notes that until September 6, 1934, the local Communist Party had remained united. However, after Alberto Sánchez and two or three other "Stalinists" were sent to Puerto Rico by the Communist Party of the United States, along with a representative of the Young Communist League, difficulties had arisen. Sánchez (himself a Puerto Rican) and the others had reportedly been sent without any consultation with the Puerto Rican leaders, and apparently they had been given broad powers to control the autonomous Puerto Rican Communist Party.

Vergne Ortíz reported to González that those who had split away from the Communist Party as a result of Sánchez' activities had been working on the formation of a purely local party, but that world events—including the Soviet entry into the League of Nations, terrorism in the Soviet Union in the wake of the assassination of Kirov (the leader of the Leningrad Communist Party, whose death began the process leading to the great Soviet purges of 1936-39), and inaction of the Spanish Communist Party during the Socialist uprising in October 1934—had led these Puerto Rican leaders to feel that a new Fourth International was necessary. Therefore, Vergne Ortíz said, the Partido Comunista Independente leaders had concluded that they should align their new party with the Trotskyists.

Although Vergne Ortíz said that an alignment with the Fourth Internationalist forces was not yet "definitive," action to make it so would be taken once an unemployment demonstration being organized by the party had taken place. He concluded by asking for material in Spanish on the Fourth Internationalist movement.[16] The Puerto Rican Trotskyists received little or no publicity in the international organs of the movement after their initial organization, although the March 1939 issue of the Mexican Trotskyist magazine *Clave* noted that the Puerto Rican comrades were putting out a publication entitled *Chispa (Spark)*.

A Trotskyist group apparently existed for a while in Colombia. The Mexican Trotskyist periodical *Bolchevique* noted in its issue of May 21, 1939, that "the internationalist Socialist Party of Colombia, the Colombian section of the Fourth International, has issued a call to the Colombian proletariat to join its ranks in the struggle for revolutionary Marxism." Nothing more is known about this group. In neighboring Venezuela, no Trotskyist group appeared until 1971. The January 10, 1972, issue of *Intercontinental Press* noted that a party of United Secretariat orientation had recently been established in Venezuela. However, it did not indicate the name of the group.

Finally, mention might be made of the recent appearance for the first time of a Trotskyist group in the French Antilles. In its issue of July 1971, *Quatrième Internationale*, the organ of the United Secretariat, noted the establishment of a Trotskyist newspaper, *Combat Ouvrier*, by a local group closely associated with the *Lutte Ouvrière* group in France, which in turn maintained friendly relations with the United Secretariat. The local governments in Guadeloupe and Martinique were reported to be taking steps to suppress this new Trotskyist publication.

# Postscript

Although it has never been a major factor in Latin American politics, Trotskyism has been a persistent stream of thought and action on the extreme Left for more than four decades. Trotskyism parties or groups have existed, at one time or another, in twelve of the twenty Latin American republics, as well as in Puerto Rico and the French Antilles. They have had a continuous existence for several decades in eight of these countries.

In a few countries Trotskyites have been, at least briefly, a force of considerable significance in left-wing politics. This was true in Chile and Cuba in the middle 1930's and in Bolivia in the early 1950's. The Mexican Fourth Internationalists gained particular prominence during the late 1930's by the fact of Leon Trotsky's presence in their country, and after Trotsky's death they exercised noticeable influence in the nation's trade-union movement for several years. But with the possible exception of the Bolivian Partido Obrero Revolucionario, no Latin American Trotskyist party has been a serious competitor for power. In most countries the Trotskyists have never been more than a part of a small and seldom effective Marxist-Leninist Left.

Latin American Trotskyites have often been highly dogmatic and prone to engage in intense personal rivalry; these qualities have produced frequent and often disastrous factional struggles, which in most cases have led to the formation of two or more Trotskyist groups in the same country. Those Trotskyist leaders of a less dogmatic turn of mind, such as the founders of Trotskyism in Chile and Cuba, have generally tended to abandon the Fourth Internationalists after a brief flirtation with Trotsky, his associates, and his heirs.

Trotskyist parties and groups from Latin America have accounted for a large proportion of the membership of international Trotskyism. Perhaps because of their distance from Europe and New York, and their relative poverty as groups, they have seldom played leadership roles consonant with their numerical importance in the activities of the Fourth International. The one exception to this generalization is the faction of Trotskyism represented by the Fourth International of J. Posadas, an Argentine who organized his group on the basis of the Latin American Bureau of the Pabloite International and has completely dominated it. Whatever it is, the credit or blame for it belongs to him. However, when splits within the International itself have taken place, the leaders of its opposing factions have assiduously sought the support of the various Latin American parties. Schisms in the International have also been a significant source of factionalism within the Latin American parties themselves, with rival International factions seeking to win away friendly elements from parties affiliated with rival segments of the Fourth International.

The Fourth International has interfered to some degree in the international affairs of many of its Latin American affiliates. Such interference has been most frequent in Mexico, where the International has several times tried to reorganize the local movement. It has also been of some importance in Argentina and in Bolivia, where the International has occasionally thrown its weight behind one or another of the quarreling local factions.

It is hard to imagine any of the Latin American Trotskyist groups ever coming to power on its own; their small size, extreme dogmatism, and penchant for witch-hunting would seem to preclude this. What does seem certain is that Trotskyite parties and groups will continue to exist in Latin America, occasionally acting as gadflies to more powerful elements of the extreme left. And it is not impossible that someday, somewhere in Latin America, a Trotskyist group will participate in a regime representing a broader spectrum of the far Left.

# NOTES

## 1: THE RISE AND DEVELOPMENT OF INTERNATIONAL TROTSKYISM

1. James P. Cannon, *The History of American Trotskyism: Report of a Participant* (1944), p. 40.
2. *Ibid.*, p. 43.
3. *Ibid.*, p. 49.
4. Letter from Max Shachtman to Robert J. Alexander, December 7, 1970.
5. C. L. R. James, *World Revolution, 1917-1934: The Rise and Fall of the Communist International* (1937), pp. 200-201.
6. Issac Deutscher, *The Prophet Outcast: Trotsky, 1929-1940* (1963), p. 45.
7. *Ibid.*, p. 53.
8. *Ibid.*, p. 58.
9. Letter from Max Shachtman to Robert J. Alexander, December 7, 1970.
10. Deutscher, *The Prophet Outcast*, p. 59.
11. *Ibid.*, p. 43.
12. *Ibid.*, p. 44.
13. *Ibid.*, pp. 200-201.
14. *The Militant*, New York City, April 21, 1934.
15. Deutscher, *The Prophet Outcast*, p. 273.
16. *Ibid.*, p. 419.
17. *Ibid.*, p. 420.
18. *Ibid.*, p. 421.
19. *Ibid.*, p. 422.
20. *Ibid.*, p. 423.
21. *Ibid.*, p. 471.
22. *Ibid.*, p. 471.
22. *Ibid.*, p. 473.
23. *Ibid.*, p. 477.
24. Letter from Max Shachtman to Robert J. Alexander, December 7, 1970.
25. *Intercontinental Press*, New York, April 27, 1970.
26. *Fourth International*, New York, June 24, 1946, p. 184.
27. *Ibid.*, p. 183.
28. *Ibid.*, p. 178.

29. Interview with Max Shachtman, New York, June 21, 1970.

30. Max Shachtman, "The Congress of the Fourth International," *The New International*, September 1948.

31. "Comrade Tito and the Fourth International," *The New International*, September 1948.

32. Interview with Max Shachtman, New York, June 21, 1970.

33. All of the foregoing quotations from *Labor Action*, New York, June 2, 1952.

34. *Ibid.*

35. Gerald Healy, *Problems of the Fourth International*, newsletter, London, n.d.but 1966, p. 6.

36. *The Militant*, New York, April 14, 1954.

37. *Intercontinental Press*, New York, April 27, 1970.

38. *The Militant*, New York, July 10, 1963.

39. *Ibid.*

40. *Intercontinental Press*, New York, November 22, 1971.

41. *International Socialist Review*, New York, Spring 1966, p. 48.

42. *Ibid.*, p. 36.

43. *Ibid.*, p. 42.

44. For an exposition of Régis Debray's theories see Régis Debray, *Revolution in the Revolution?*, Monthly Review Press, London and New York, 1967.

45. *International Socialist Review*, New York, Spring 1966, p. 74.

46. *Perspectiva Mundial*, Mexico, October 7, 1966, p. 23.

47. *Quatrième Internationale* (United Secretariat), Paris, May 1969, pp. 61-62.

48. *Fourth International*, London, August 1966, p. 104.

49. *Ibid.*, p. 111.

50. *Ibid.*, p. 116.

51. *Ibid.*, p. 111.

52. *Ibid.*, p. 112.

53. *Fourth International*, London, Winter 1968–69, p. 113.

54. *Intercontinental Press*, November 22, 1971, p. 1016.

55. Interview with N.M. Pereira, leader of Lanka Sama Samaja, in New York, September 21, 1971.

56. Fernand Charlier, *Le Posadisme: Un Rapport d'Autopsie*, unpublished article.

57. *Cuarta Internacional* (Posadista), September 1962, p. 12.

58. *Ibid.*, p. 13.

59. *Cuarta Internacional* (Posadista), July 1964, pp.18 and 1920.

60. *Ibid.*, p. 20.

61. *Revista Marxista Latinoamericana* (Posadista), August 1966, pp. 34 and 195.

62. *Ibid.*, p. 171.

63. *Ibid.*, p. 136.

64. *Ibid.*, p. 37.

65. *Revista Marxista Latinoamericana* (Posadista), July 1967, p. 175.

66. *Voz Obrera*, Lima, Peru, second fortnight of May 1970.

67. J. Posadas, *La Desagregación Mundial del Capitalismo* (1968), p. 93.

68. *Revista Marxista Latinoamericana* (Posadista), July 1967, p. 62.

69. *Cuarta Internacional* (United Secretariat), August 1966, p. 42.

70. Letter of Natalia Sedova Trotsky to "Comité Ejecutivo de la IV Internacional" and to "Comité Político del Socialist Workers Party," dated May 9, 1951.

## 2: FOURTH INTERNATIONALISM IN LATIN AMERICA

1. *Clave,* Mexico City, October 1, 1938 and November 1, 1938.
2. Octavio Fernández Archives (hereafter referred to as OFA), letter from José Santiago, Secretary-General of Partido Obrero Revolucionario of Chile, to "Secciones y Grupos de la IV Internacional," dated November 1946.
3. More extensive information on the activities of SLATO may be found in Chapter Eight, "Peruvian Trotskyism."

## 3: TROTSKYISM, PERONISMO, AND THE NATIONAL REVOLUTION IN ARGENTINA

1. For a discussion of the Partido Comunista de la República Argentina, see Robert J. Alexander, *Communism in Latin America* (1957), p. 161.
2. Liborio Justo, *Breve Reseña Cronológica del Movimiento Cuartainternacionalista Argentino (1941), p. 2.*
3. *Ibid.,* p. 3.
4. Data from *Boletín Interno de la I.C.A.,* republished in Liborio Justo, *Breva Reseña Cronológica,* pp. 2-5.
5. Anonymous, *Memorandum on Argentine Trotskyism,* p. 7.
6. Liborio Justo, *Breve Reseña Cronológica,* p. 9.
7. *Ibid.,* pp. 5-8.
8. For Liborio Justo's autobiography and an account of his intellectual evolution, see Justo, *Prontuario: Una Autobiografía* (1956).
9. Liborio Justo, *Como Salir del Pantano: Hacia la Formación de la Sección Argentina del Partido Mundial de la Revolución Socialista (4a Internacional)* (1939), p. 12.
10. Liborio Justo, *Breve Reseña Cronológica,* p. 11.
11. *Ibid.,* pp. 12-14.
12. Liborio Justo, *Centrismo, Oportunismo y Bolchevismo: El Grupo Obrero Revolucionario y la Lucha por el Marxismo Leninismo en la Argentina y en la América del Sur* (1940), p. 8.
13. Liborio Justo, *Estrategia Revolucionaria: Lucha por la Unidad y por la Liberación Nacional y Social de la América Latina* (1956), p. 76.
14. *Ibid.,*pp. 28-29.
15. Letter from Terence Phelan to Charles Curtiss, dated Sierras de Córdoba, Argentina, October 28, 1941.
16. Interview with Joseph Hansen, New York City, January 28, 1970.
17. Cited in Liborio Justo, *Estrategia Revolucionaria,* p. 108.
18. *Ibid.,*p. 184.
19. Letter from Terence Phelan to Charles Curtiss, October 28, 1941.
20. See Liborio Justo, *Estrategia Revolucionaria,* pp. 105-110.
21. Letter from Terence Phelan to Charles Curtiss, Oct. 28, 1941.
22. Liborio Justo, *Estrategia Revolucionaria,* pp. 90-91.
23. *Ibid.,* p. 127.
24. *Ibid.,* p. 126.
25. *Ibid.,* p. 115.
26. *Ibid.,* pp. 128-219.
27. *Ibid.,* p. 130.

28. Niceto Andrés, *La Política Nacional del Trotskismo en América Latina (Centralismo y Revolución* (1949), p. 15.

29. "V. G." in *Octubre*, No. 3, cited in Niceto Andrés, *La Política Nacional*, p. 13.

30. *El Militante*, Buenos Aires, November 1, 1946.

31. Ezequiel Reyes: *Qué es la Izquierda (Respuesta a los Compañeros Comunistas)* (1961), p. 31.

32. *Ibid.*, p. 26.

33. *Ibid.*, p. 27.

34. Interview with Joseph Hansen, New York City, January 28, 1970.

35. *The Militant*, New York, April 12, 1965.

36. *World Outlook*, New York, February 9, 1968.

37. *Cuarta Internacional* (United Secretariat), April 1967, p. 72.

38. *Ibid.*, p. 83.

39. *Perspectiva Mundial*, Mexico, May 1967, p. 28.

40. Cited in *Rouge*, Paris, October 13, 1969.

41. *Quatrième Internationale* (United Secretariat), Paris, September 1969, p. 19.

42. *Rouge*, Paris, June 7, 1971.

43. *Ibid.*, March 15, 1971.

44. Jorge Abelardo Ramos, *La lucha por un Partido Revolucionario* (1964), p. 138.

45. José Luis Madariaga, *¿Qué es la Izquierda Nacional? Manual del Socialismo Revolucionario* (1969). p. 69.

46. *Izquierda Nacional*, Buenos Aires, June 1971, page 10.

47. *Ibid.*, p. 9.

48. J. Posadas, *El Papel de la Vanguardia Peronista on la Organización de la Lucha por el Gobierno Obrero y Campesino en la Argentina* (1965), p. 27.

49. *Revista Marxista Latinoamericana* (Pabloite), October 1956, p. 105.

50. *Revista Marxista Latinoamericana* (Posadista), July 1967, pp. 259-60.

51. *Voz Proletaria*, Buenos Aires, first fortnight of August 1959.

52. *Cuarta Internacional* (Posadista), September 1962, pp. 174-75.

53. *Revista Marxista Latinoamericana* (Posadista), July 1967, p. 307.

54. *Frente Obrero*, Montevideo, January 10, 1969.

## 4: BRAZILIAN TROTSKYISM, GETULIO VARGAS, AND LUÍZ CARLOS PRESTES

1. Interview with Hilcar Leite, Río de Janeiro, June 11, 1953.

2. Interview with Aristides Lobo, São Paulo, June 17, 1953.

3. Interview with Astrogildo Pereira, Río de Janeiro, October 19, 1965.

4. Leoncio Basbaum, *Historia Sincera da Republica* (1968), Vol. 2, pp. 274-77.

5. Interview with Aristides Lobo, São Paulo, June 17, 1953.

6. Abguar Bastos, *Luíz Carlos Prestes e A Revolucão Social* (1946), p. 264.

7. Interview with Plinio Melo, São Paulo, June 16, 1953.

8. Bastos, *Luíz Carlos Prestes*, p. 248.

9. Interview with Plinio Melo, São Paulo, June 16, 1953.

10. *R.I.L.U. Magazine*, August 1, 1931, p. 12.

11. Interview with Hilcar Leite, Río de Janeiro, June 11, 1953.

12. *Vanguarda Socialista,* Río de Janeiro, October 26, 1945.

13. F. Lacerda, "The Fascist Coup d'etat in Brazil," *The Communist International,* London, January 1938.

14. Article by Mario Podrosa in *Vanguarda Socialista,* Río de Janeiro, October 12, 1945.

15. *International Press Correspondence,* February 6, 1937.

16. Interview with Hilcar Leite, Río de Janeiro, June 11, 1953.

17. *International Press Correspondence,* February 6, 1937.

18. For Agildo Barata's account of the November 1935 uprising, see Agildo Barata, *Vido de Um Revolucionario (Memorias)* (n.d.), Chapter 9.

19. Interview with Roberto Sisson, Río de Janeiro, September 8, 1965.

20. Interview with Hilcar Leite, Río de Janeiro, June 11, 1953.

21. *New International,* New York, October 1939.

22. Interview with Max Shachtman, Floral Park, Long Island, January 16, 1970.

23. Interview with Mario Pedrosa, Río de Janeiro, August 14, 1946.

24. Interview with Febus Gikovate, São Paulo, June 17, 1953.

25. Interview with Herminio Saccheta São Paulo, June 16, 1953.

26. *Lucha Obrera,* Mexico City, November 7, 1939.

27. *Clave,* Mexico City, February 1939.

28. *Lucha Obrera,* Mexico City, November 7, 1939.

29. Interview with Herminio Saccheta, São Paulo, June 16, 1953.

30. Liborio Justo, *Estrategia Revolucionaria: Lucha por la Unidad y por la Liberación Nacional y Social de la América Latina* (1956), p. 123.

31. *Vanguarda Socialista,* Río de Janeiro, September 28, 1945.

32. *Ibid.,* January 18, 1946.

33. *Inquerito Policial Militar No. 709: O Comunismo no Brasil,* Vol. 3, (1965), p. 442.

34. Cynthia Hewitt, *An Introduction to the Rural Labor Movement of Pernambuco* (1965), p. 18.

35. Cynthia Hewitt, "Brazil: The Peasant Movement of Pernambuco, 1961-1964," in Landsberger, *Latin American Peasant Movements* (1969), p. 385.

36. *Cuarta Internacional* (Posadista), October 1963, pp. 90-92.

37. Cited in *Ibid.,* p. 93.

38. "Le Contradizioni Interborghesi e l'Organizacione della prossime lotte per il potere operaio in Brasile," in *Lotta Operaia,* Rome, August 10, 1964, p. 5.

39. Ronald Chilcote, *"The Brazilian Communist Party"* (manuscript).

40. *El Terrorismo, La Represión Contra el POR (Trotskista), el Desarrollo de las Condiciones Revolucionarias en Brasil* (1970).

41. Letter from Joseph Hansen to Robert J. Alexander, December 24, 1970.

42. Eurico Mendes, "O Crescimento do Movimento Operario e as Tarefas da Vanda," *Política Operaria,* Number 6.

43. Resolution on "Movimento Operario" in *Politica Operaria,* Number 6, p. 14.

44. Resolution on "Movimento Campones" in *Política Operaria,* Number 6, p. 17.

45. *Política Operaria,* October 1962, p. 3.

46. *Política Operaria,* Number 6, mid-1963.

47. *Política Operaria,* Numbers 14 and 15, June and September 1965.

48. *Politica Operaria, Informe Nacional,* No. 14, February 5, 1966.

49. *Política Operaria*, Number 15, September 1965.
50. Política Operaria, *Por Qué Anular o Voto nas Eleiccões no Estado da Guanabara* (n.d.).
51. *Perspectiva Mundial*, Mexico City, May 1967, p. 14.
52. *Intercontinental Press*, New York, May 26, 1969.
53. From *Quatrième Internationale* (United Secretariat), republished in *Intercontinental Press*, New York, May 5, 1969.
54. *Ibid.*

## 5: CHILEAN TROTSKYISM

1. For a discussion of the origins and history of the Chilean Communist Party, see Robert J. Alexander, *Communism in Latin America* (1957), Chapter 10.
2. Interview with Manuel Hidalgo, Santiago, Chile, December 17, 1946.
3. Partido Comunista de Chile (Trotskyist faction), *En Defensa de la Revolución: Informes, Tesis y Documentos Presentados al Congreso Nacional del Partido Comunista a Verificarse el 19 de Marzo de 1933* (1933), p. 14.
4. *Ibid.*, p. 15.
5. *Ibid.*
6. *Ibid.*
7. *Ibid.*, p. 16.
8. *Ibid.*, p. 17.
9. *Ibid.*, p. 18.
10. *Ibid.*, pp. 19-21.
11. Interview with Oscar Waiss, Santiago, Chile, March 17, 1947.
12. Partido Comunista de Chile, *En Defensa de la Revolución*, pp. 133-35.
13. *Ibid.*, p. 19.
14. *Ibid.*, p. 137.
15. *Ibid.*, p. 22.
16. *Ibid.*, p. 45.
17. Manuel Hidalgo Plaza, *La Rebelión de la Armada: Discurso del Senador Comunista Manuel Hidalgo P. en el senado, el 16 de Septiembre de 1931* (1931).
18. Partido Comunista de Chile, *En Defensa de la Revolución*, p. 47.
19. *Ibid.*, p. 16.
20. Partido Comunista de Chile (Stalinist faction), *Hacia la Formación de Un Verdadero Partido de Clase—Resoluciones de la Conferencia Nacional del Partido Comunista realizada en Julio de 1933* (1933), p. 26.
21. *Ibid.*, p. 27.
22. *Ibid.*, p. 24.
23. Partido Comunista de Chile, *En Defensa de la Revolución*, p. 51.
24. *Ibid.*, p. 50.
25. *Ibid.*, p. 111.
26. *Ibid.*, pp. 114-16.
27. *La Junta del Gobierno al Pais*, proclamation distributed by Grove government of the Socialist Republic of Chile (1932).
28. *Los 30 Puntos*, proclamation distributed by Grove government of Socialist Republic of Chile (1932).

29. Interview with Oscar Waiss, Santiago, Chile, March 17, 1947.
30. Partido Comunista de Chile, *En Defensa de la Revolución*, pp. 54-57.
31. *Ibid.*, pp. 57-58.
32. Interview with Oscar Waiss, Santiago, Chile, March 17, 1947.
33. Partido Comunista de Chile, *En Defensa de la Revolución*, pp. 61-62.
34. *Ibid.*, p. 149.
35. *Ibid.*, p. 68.
36. *Ibid.*, p. 66.
37. *Ibid.*, p. 30.
38. *Ibid.*, p. 9.
39. *Ibid.*, p. 94.
40. *Ibid.*, p. 99.
41. *Ibid.*, p. 103.
42. *Ibid.*, p. 110.
43. For a discussion of Chilean labor legislation, see Robert J. Alexander, *Labor Relations in Argentina, Brazil, and Chile* (1962).
44. Alfredo Bowen Herrera, *Ensayo Sobre el Movimiento Sindical y el Sindicalismo Agrícola* (1934), p. 78.
45. Interview with Oscar Waiss, Santiago, Chile, March 17, 1947.
46. Juan Díaz Martínez, *Treinta Meses de Acción en Favor del Proletariado de Chile—Memoria del Consejo Directivo Nacional al 1er Congreso Ordinario, 26 al 30 de Julio de 1939 (CTCh)* (1939), p. 23.
47. Stephen Naft, *Labor Movements in Latin America* (n.d.), p. 7.
48. Partido Comunista de Chile, *En Defensa de la Revolución*, p. 49.
49. *Ibid.*, p. 68.
50. René León Echaiz, *Evolución Histórica de los Partidos Políticos Chilenes* (1939), p. 188.
51. Liborio Justo, *Centrismo, Oportunismo y Bolchevismo: El Grupo Obrero Revolucionario y la Lucha por el Marxismo Leninismo en la Argentina y en la América del Sur* (1940), p. 12.
52. Galo González Díaz, *El Congreso de la Victoria—Resumen de los Informes, Discusiones y Resoluciones, X Congreso Nacional del Partido Comunista de Chile*, (1938), p. 43.
53. Partido Socialista de Trabajadores, *El Camino del Pueblo—Resoluciones del Tercer Congreso General del Partido Socialista de Trabajadores, Santiago, 1 al 3 de Mayo de 1942*, (1942), p. 15.
54. Partido Socialista (Departamento Nacional de Propaganda), *El Libro Negro del Partido Comunista*, (1941), pp. 29-30.
55. Partido Socialista de Trabajadores, *El Camino del Pueblo*, p. 73.
56. Interview with José Santiago and Humberto Valenzuela, Santiago, Chile, December 18, 1946.
57. Liborio Justo, *Centrismo, Oportunismo y Bolchevismo*, p. 12.
58. Letter from Liborio Justo to Diego Henriquez, cited in Liborio Justo, *Estrategia Revolucionaria: Lucha por la Unidad y por la Liberación Nacional y Social de la América Latina* (1956), p. 181.
59. *Clave*, Mexico City, June 1939.
60. Liborio Justo, *Centrismo, Oportunismo y Bolchevismo*, p. 13.
61. Liborio Justo, *Estrategia Revolucionaria*, p. 182.

62. *Ibid.*, p.182.
63. Interview with José Santiago and Humberto Valenzuela, December 28, 1946.
64. Interview with Eduardo Ibarra, head of Municipal Workers Union, Santiago, April 12, 1947.
65. Interview with José Santiago and Humberto Valenzuela, December 28, 1946.
66. *Ibid.*
67. *Boletín Leninista,* Santiago, April-May 1943.
68. Octavio Fernández Archives [OFA], letter from José Santiago to "All Sections and Groups of the Fourth International in Latin America," October 11, 1946.
69. Interview with Manuel Narranjo, Secretary-General of Acción Sindical Chilena, Santiago, July 1, 1953.
70. Cited in *Intercontinental Press,* New York, July 28, 1969.
71. *International Socialist Review,* New York, Summer 1964.
72. Ernst Halperin, *Nationalism and Communism in Chile* (1965), p. 246.
73. Intreview with Oscar Waiss, Santiago, July 3, 1968.
74. *International Socialist Review,* New York, Summer 1964.
75. *Intercontinental Press,* New York, July 28, 1969.
76. *Cuarta Internacional* (Posadista), September 1962, p. 176.

6: THE BEGINNINGS OF BOLIVIAN TROTSKYISM

1. For a study of the early days of Ceylonese Trotskyism, see George J. Lerski, *Origins of Trotskyism in Ceylon* (1968).
2. Interview with Tristán Marof, La Paz, May 26, 1947.
3. Interview with Nicolas Sánchez, La Paz, June 3, 1947.
4. Liborio Justo, *Bolivia: La Revolución Derrotada* (1967), p. 101.
5. Interview with Lucio Mendívil, La Paz, May 28, 1947.
6. Liborio Justo, *Bolivia*, p. 102.
7. *Ibid.*, p. 102.
8. *Ibid.*, p. 103.
9. Interview with Nicolas Sánchez, La Paz, June 3, 1947.
10. Interview with Hernán Sánchez Fernández, La Paz, May 28, 1947.
11. Cited in Liborio Justo, *Bolivia*, p. 103.
12. Interview with Hernán Sánchez Fernández, La Paz, May 28, 1947.
13. Liborio Justo, *Bolivia*, p. 104.
14. Interview with Hernán Sánchez Fernández, La Paz, May 28, 1947.
15. Interview with Carlos Salazar, La Paz, May 29, 1947.
16. *Batalla*, La Paz, December 28, 1946.
17. *Ibid.*
18. *Ibid.*, January 18, 1947.
19. *Ibid.*, January 11, 1947.
20. Interview with Lucio Mendívil, La Paz, May 28, 1947.
21. *Batalla*, La Paz, February 8, 1947.
22. Interview with Tristán Marof, La Paz, May 26, 1947.
23. Liborio Justo, *Bolivia*, p. 137.
24. Alberto Corneje, *Programas Políticos de Bolivia* (1949), p. 359.

25. Liborio Justo, *Bolivia*, p. 104.
26. Cornejo, *Programas Políticos*, p. 359.
27. *Ibid.*, p. 365.
28. *Ibid.*, p. 366.
29. *Ibid.*, p. 368.
30. *Ibid.*, p. 369.
31. *Ibid.*, p. 371.
32. *Ibid.*, p. 377.
33. *Ibid.*, p. 381.
34. *Ibid.*, pp. 372-73.
35. *Ibid.*, p. 382.
36. *Ibid.*, p. 383.
37. *Ibid.*, pp. 383-92.
38. Liborio Justo, *Bolivia*, p. 105.
39. *Ibid.*
40. Interview with Hernán Sánchez Fernández, La Paz, May 28, 1947.
41. Interview with Guillermo Lora, La Paz, June 2, 1947.
42. Liborio Justo, *Estrategia Revolucionaria: Lucha por la Unidad y por la Liberación Nacional y Social de la América Latina* (1956), p. 174.
43. Interview with Guillermo Lora, La Paz, June 2, 1947.
44. For more extensive treatment of the Movimiento Nacionalista Revolucionario and its role in the miners union, see Robert J. Alexander, *The Bolivian National Revolution* (1958). James Malloy's *Bolivia: The Uncompleted Revolution* (1970) deals with the same problem, but we feel overemphasizes the role and influence of the POR.
45. Cornejo, p. 362.
46. *El Militante* of Buenos Aires, cited in Liborio Justo: *Bolivia: La Revolución Derrotada*, op. cit., page 122.
47. Cornejo, *Programas Políticos*, p. 361.
48. Interview with Guillermo Lora, La Paz, June 2, 1947.
49. Interview with Juan Lechín, La Paz, May 28, 1947.
50. Interview with Irineo Pimentel, New Brunswick, New Jersey, March 14, 1954.
51. Cornejo, *Programas Políticos*, p. 314.
52. *Ibid.*, pp. 314-15.
53. *Ibid.*, p. 319.
54. *Ibid.*, p. 321.
55. *Ibid.*, pp. 315-16.
56. *Ibid.*, p. 317.
57. *Ibid.*, p. 318.
58. *Ibid.*, p. 319.
59. *Ibid.*, pp. 335-40.
60. Interview with Juan Lechín, La Paz, May 28, 1947.
61. Interview with Lucio Mendívil, La Paz, May 28, 1947.
62. Liborio Justo, *Bolivia*, p. 141.
63. *Ibid.*, p. 140.
64. Interview with Edwin Moller, La Paz, July 10, 1953.
65. Liborio Justo, *Bolivia*, p. 141.
66. Cited in *ibid.*, p. 139.

67. *The Militant*, New York, April 30, 1951.
68. *Ibid.*
69. Liborio Justo, *Bolivia*, p. 141.
70. Quoted in *ibid.*, p. 137.
71. Cited in *ibid.*, p. 141.
72. *Labor Action*, New York, April 7, 1952.
73. Alipio Valencia Vega, *Desarrollo del Pensamiento Político en Bolivia* (1953), p. 112.

## 7: TROTSKYISM AND THE BOLIVIAN NATIONAL REVOLUTION

1. For descriptions of the events of the April 1952 revolution, see Liborio Justo, *Bolivia: La Revolución Derrotada* (1967), pp. 143-48; and José Fellmann Velarde, *Víctor Paz Estenssoro: El Hombre y la Revolución* (1955), pp. 263-80.
2. For discussions of the Bolivian national revolution, see Robert J. Alexander, *The Bolivian National Revolution* (1958), and James Malloy, *Bolivia: The Uncompleted Revolution* (1970).
3. *The Militant*, New York, April 28, 1952.
4. *Labor Action*, New York, April 28, 1952.
5. Liborio Justo, *Bolivia*, p. 142.
6. Reprinted in *The Militant*, New York, May 12, 1952.
7. Reprinted in *The Militant*, New York, May 19, 1952.
8. Interview with Jorge Salazar, La Paz, August 13, 1952.
9. *Lucha Obrera*, La Paz, June 12, 1952.
10. *Lucha Obrera*, La Paz, June 1, 1952.
11. Quoted in Liborio Justo, *Bolivia*, pp. 151-52.
12. *The Militant*, New York, October 20, 1952.
13. *The Militant*, New York, May 19, 1952.
14. Interview with Edwin Moller, La Paz, July 10, 1953.
15. Interview with Bernabé Villarreal, La Paz, August 14, 1952.
16. *Rebelión*, La Paz, May 1, 1952.
17. *Labor Action*, New York, October 27, 1952.
18. *Ibid.*, November 3, 1952.
19. *Ibid.*, December 22, 1952.
20. Interview with Edwin Moller, La Paz, July 10, 1953.
21. Interview with Oscar Barrientos, Cochabamba, July 26, 1954.
22. Interview with Edwin Moller, La Paz, July 20, 1957.
23. *The Militant*, New York, January 5, 1953.
24. *Ibid.*, March 2, 1953.
25. *Ibid.*, February 9, 1953.
26. *Ibid.*, January 4, 1954.
27. José Bonetti, "Llamado de Apoyo a la Revolución Boliviana," *Revista Marxista*, May 1954.
28. A report on the Central Obrera Boliviana's congress appeared in the International Labor Office's periodical, *Industry and Labour*, Geneva, May 15, 1955.
29. *Labor Action*, New York, January 10, 1955.

30. Liborio Justo, *Bolivia*, p. 233.
31. *Ibid.*, p. 234.
32. Interview with Edwin Moller, La Paz, July 30, 1954.
33. Liborio Justo, *Bolivia*, p. 227.
34. *Ibid.* p. 229.
35. *Masas*, La Paz, August 18, 1956.
36. Quoted in Liborio Justo, *Bolivia*, pp. 227-28.
37. *Ibid.*, p. 229.
38. *Ibid.*, p. 230.
39. Interview with Edwin Moller, La Paz, August 22, 1956.
40. Liborio Justo, *Bolivia*, p. 238.
41. *Ibid.*, p. 239.
42. For an extensive discussion of the stabilization effort of the Siles government, see George Eder, *Inflation and Development in Latin America, a Case History of Inflation and Stabilization in Bolivia* (1968).
43. Interviews with Edwin Moller, July 20, 1957, and Genaro Linares, July 23, 1957.
44. Interview with Mario Montenegro, Washington, D.C., May 28, 1960.
45. *Lucha Obrera*, La Paz, July 25, 1957.
46. *Masas*, La Paz, August 1957.
47. *Lucha Obrera*, La Paz, July 25, 1957.
48. *Masas*, La Paz, August 1957.
49. *Cuarta Internacional* (Posadista), October 1963, pp. 87-88.
50. *Cuarta Internacional* (United Secretariat), August 1966, pp. 158-60.
51. *Ibid.*, April 1967.
52. Interview with Mario Montenegro, La Paz, April 7, 1962.
53. *Intercontinental Press*, New York, December 15, 1969.
54. *Viertel Jahres Berichte*, Bonn, September 1969, p. 321.
55. *Ibid.*
56. *Intercontinental Press*, New York, December 15, 1969.
57. *Ibid.*, March 2, 1970.
58. *Presencia*, La Paz, February 16, 1970.
59. Cited in *Octubre*, La Paz, January, 1970.
60. Talk by June Nash, North American anthropologist, Rutgers University, New Brunswick, New Jersey, March 31, 1971.
61. Reported in *Informations Ouvrières*, Paris, March 4-11, 1970.
62. *Intercontinental Press*, New York, November 22, 1971, p. 1023.
63. Extensive discussion of the controversy over the behavior of Guillermo Lora's POR can be found in *Intercontinental Press*, New York, October 18 and November 22, 1971; this quote from *Intercontinental Press*, November 22, 1971, p. 1023.
64. *The Militant*, New York, December 7, 1964.
65. *International Socialist Review*, New York, Winter 1965.
66. *Perspectiva Mundial*, Mexico City, April 16, 1967, pp. 11 and 31.
67. *Entwicklung-politische Activitaten Kommunistischer Lander*, Bonn-Bad Godesberg, February 1970, p. 77.
68. Hugo González Moscoso, ''The Cuban Revolution and Its Lessons,'' *International Socialist Review*, New York, March-April 1968.
69. See Jay Mallin, *''Ché'' Guevara on Revolution* (1969), for a list of those participating in Guevara's guerrilla column.

70. *Intercontinental Press*, New York September 22, 1969.
71. *Ibid.*, November 24, 1969.
72. *Ibid.*, December 15, 1969.
73. *Ibid.*, April 13, 1970.
74. *Ibid.*, July 13, 1970.
75. *Ibid.*, November 23, 1970.
76. *Ibid.*, April 13, 1970.
77. *Entwicklung-politische Activitaten Kommunistischer Lander*, February 1970, p. 79.
78. *Viertel Jahres Berichte*, September 1969, p. 321.
79. *Intercontinental Press*, New York, April 13, 1970.

8: PERUVIAN TROTSKYISM

1. Interview with Ismael Frías, Lima, Peru, July 13, 1971.
2. *Ibid.*
3. *El Comercio*, Lima, February 4, 1953.
4. *Ibid.*, February 3, 1953.
5. *La Prensa*, Lima, April 26, 1970.
6. Interview with Ismael Frías, July 13, 1971.
7. *Ibid.*
8. Juan D. Leiva, "El Ascenso de Masas en Peru Después de las Elecciones," *Revista Marxista Latinoamericana* (Pabloite), October 1956.
9. Interview with Ismael Frías, Lima, July 13, 1971.
10. *Quatrième Internationale* (Pabloite), November 1961, p. 92.
11. *Cuarta Internacional* (Posadista), September 1962, p. 169.
12. *Ibid.*, p. 170.
13. *La Prensa*, Lima, April 26, 1970.
14. Interview with Ismael Frías, Lima, July 13, 1971.
15. *La Prensa*, Lima, April 26, 1970.
16. Interview with Ismael Frías, Lima, July 13, 1971.
17. *Cuarta Internacional* (Posadista), September 1962, p. 172.
18. *La Prensa*, Lima, April 26, 1970.
19. *Revista Marxista Latinoamericana* (Posadista), July 1967, p. 307.
20. *Voz Obrera*, second fortnight of June 1967.
21. *Ibid.*
22. Gonzálo Añí Castillo, *Historia Secreta de las Guerrillas* (1967), p. 14.
23. *Ibid.*, p. 29.
24. *Ibid.*, p. 30.
25. *Ibid.*, p. 33.
26. Víctor Villanueva, *Hugo Blanco y la Rebelión Campesina* (1967), p. 79.
27. *Ibid.*, p. 81.
28. *Ibid.*, p. 94.
29. The POR robbery of the Banco Popular is discussed at some length in Villanueva, *Hugo Blanco*, pp. 92-93, and in Añí Castillo, *Historia Secreta*, pp. 59-68.
30. The Banco de Crédito robbery is discussed by Villanueva, *Hugo Blanco*, pp. 97-98, and in Añí Castillo, *Historia Secreta*, pp. 77-104.
31. Añí Castillo, *Historia Secreta*, p. 142.
32. Villanueva, *Hugo Blanco*, pp. 103-4.

33. Añí Castillo, *Historia Secreta*, pp. 124-26.

34. *Ibid.*, p. 126.

35. *Cuarta Internacional* (Posadista), September 1962, p. 173.

36. Villanueva, *Hugo Blanco*, p. 72.

37. Ibid., p. 75.

38. Both Villanueva, p. 75, and Añí Castillo, p. 34, give this explanation of how Blanco became a "peasant." Wesley Craig in his chapter "Peru: The Peasant Movement of La Convención," in Landsberger (ed.), *Latin American Peasant Movements* (1969), p. 288, says that Blanco got his post as "allegado" through his father-in-law, who was a lawyer for one of the peasant unions in the Valley. We have opted for the explanation we give here.

39. Wesley Craig, "The Peasant Movement," p. 287.

40. Añí Castillo, *Historia Secreta*, p. 34.

41. Julio Cotler and Felipe Portocarrero, chapter on "Peru: Peasant Movements," in Landsberger, *Latin American Peasant Movements*, p. 315.

42. Wesley Craig, "The Peasant Movement," p. 289.

43. Villanueva, *Hugo Blanco*, p. 127.

44. *Intercontinental Press*, New York, September 29, 1969.

45. Young Socialist Alliance, *Land or Death* (1967), p. 12.

46. Villanueva, *Hugo Blanco*, p. 139; and Añí Castillo, *Historia Secreta*, pp. 136-38.

47. Villanueva, *Hugo Blanco*, p. 150.

48. Wesley Craig, "The Peasant Movement," p. 292.

49. Villanueva, *Hugo Blanco*, p. 155.

50. André Gunder Frank, *Hugo Blanco Must Not Die* (1965).

51. *Intercontinental Press*, New York, September 16, 1968.

52. *Ibid.*, January 11, 1971.

53. *Ibid.*, September 27, 1971.

54. Hugo Blanco, *El Camino de Nuestra Revolución* (1964).

55. *Intercontinental Press*, New York, September 30, 1968.

56. *Ibid.*, March 3, 1969.

57. *Ibid.*

58. *Ibid.*, February 23, 1970.

59. *Ibid.*, October 20, 1969.

60. *Ibid.*, September 29, 1969.

61. *Ibid.*

62. *Ibid.*, February 8, 1971.

63. Hugo Blanco, "The Mobilization of the Peasants," *Intercontinental Press*, New York, October 13, 1969.

64. *Intercontinental Press*, New York, September 22, 1969.

65. *Rouge*, Paris, May 10, 1971.

66. Interview with Adolfo Venegas, Lima, July 12, 1971.

9: LEON TROTSKY, DIEGO RIVERA, AND MEXICAN TROTSKYISM

1. For a discussion of the origins of the Mexican Communist Party, see Robert J. Alexander, *Communism in Latin America* (1957), Chapter 15.

2. Letter from Manuel Rodríguez to Robert J. Alexander, March 1971.

3. Interview with Manuel Rodríguez, Mexico City, January 22, 1971.

4. Interview with Luciano Galicia, Mexico City, January 22, 1971.

5. Interview with Octavio Fernández, Mexico City, January 21, 1971.

6. *El Machete*, Mexico City, March 20, 1934.

7. *Nueva Internacional*, Mexico City, March 15, April, and May 1934.

8. Octavio Fernández Archives (hereafter referred to as OFA), letter from Octavio Fernández to A. González, July 3, 1934.

9. OFA, fund appeal of Liga Comunista Internacionalista, August 15, 1934.

10. OFA, letter from Octavio Fernández to A. González, July 3, 1934.

11. OFA, Letter from A. González to Octavio Fernández, July 19, 1934.

12. OFA, letter from Luis Gutiérrez (Octavio Fernández) to A. González, February 4, 1935.

13. OFA, letter from A. González to Octavio Fernández, June 3, 1934, and from Octavio Fernández to A. González, July 3, 1934.

14. OFA, letter from A. González to Octavio Fernández, September 22, 1934.

15. Interview with Manuel Rodríguez, Mexico City, January 22, 1971.

16. *Ibid.*

17. Interview with Octavio Fernández, Mexico City, January 21, 1971.

18. OFA, letter from Octavio Fernández to A. González, June 3, 1934; A. González to Octavio Fernández, July 19, 1934; and Octavio Fernández to A. González, September 22, 1934.

19. OFA, "Resolución Tomada por los Representantes de los Grupos Colonia Obrera y Santa Julia de la Sección Mexicana de la Liga Comunista Internacional, Sobre los Problemas de la Sección Existente y Sobre la Unificación de los Mismos," August 1, 1935.

20. OFA, "Manfiesto de los Trotskistas de México a los Trabajadores," December 1935.

21. Interview with Octavio Fernández, Mexico City, January 21, 1971.

22. Interview with Félix Ibarra, Mexico City, January 20, 1971.

23. *Ibid.*

24. Interview with Manuel Rodríguez, Mexico City, January 22, 1971.

25. This information from "Así Se Obtuvo el Asilo Para Leon Trotsky," *Lucha Obrera*, Mexico City, August 21, 1943.

26. Isaac Deutscher, *The Prophet Outcast: Trotsky, 1929-1940* (1963), pp. 357-58.

27. Interview with Félix Ibarra, Mexico City, January 20, 1971.

28. Interview with Octavio Fernández, Mexico City, January 21, 1971.

29. Rodrigo García Treviño, "Un Artículo Inédito de Trotski Sobre México: Las Administraciones Obreras de las Industrias," *Programa*, Mexico City, January 20, 1971.

30. Interview with Rodrigo García Treviño, Mexico City, January 20, 1971.

31. Interview with Octavio Fernández, Mexico City, January 21, 1971.

32. Interview with Sra. de Fernández, Mexico City, January 21, 1971.

33. Interview with Max Shachtman, Floral Park, Long Island, January 16, 1970.

34. Letter from James P. Cannon to Charles Curtiss, June 21, 1938.

35. Letter from Charles Curtiss to Latin American Department, Socialist Workers Party, September 2, 1938.

36. Socialist Workers Party, *The Founding Conference of the Fourth International (World Party of the Socialist Revolution), Program and Resolutions* (1939), pp. 117-18.

37. Letter from Luciano Galicia to Leon Trotsky, December 20, 1938.

38. Letter from Liga Comunista Internacionalista to Buro Panamericana de la IV Internacional, February 10, 1939.

39. Bertram Wolfe, *The Fabulous Life of Diego Rivera* (1963), p. 229.
40. *Ibid.*, p. 226.
41. *Ibid.*, pp. 214-24.
42. *Ibid.*, p. 233.
43. OFA, letter from A. González to Octavio Fernández, July 19, 1934.
44. OFA, letter from Rosario Negrete (Russell Blackwell) to Luciano Galicia and Octavio Fernández, January 5, 1937.
45. Letter of J. López to Diego Rivera, October 21, 1938.
46. *Clave*, Mexico City, March 1939.
47. Letter from Diego Rivera to Charles Curtiss, March 20, 1939.
48. *Clave*, Mexico City, July 1939.
49. Bertram Wolfe, *Diego Rivera: His Life and Times* (1939), p. 263.
50. In interviews with the author both Charles Curtiss and Max Shachtman have emphasized Trotsky's lenient attitude toward Diego Rivera.
51. Bertram Wolfe, *The Fabulous Life of Diego Rivera*, p. 385.
52. Interview with Rodrigo García Treviño, Mexico City, January 20, 1971.
53. OFA, *Stalin y Hitler*, a throwaway of the Liga Comunista Internacionalista, dated August 1939.
54. *Lucha Obrera*, Mexico City, September 20, 1939.

## 10: MEXICAN TROTSKYISM AFTER TROTSKY

1. *Lucha Obrera*, Mexico City, first fortnight, February 1945.
2. Interview with Octavio Fernández, Mexico City, January 23, 1971.
3. Interview with Enrique Rangel, Mexico City, August 23, 1948.
4. Interview with Eucario León, Mexico City, August 20, 1951.
5. OFA, L. Red (Octavio Fernández) to Diego Henríquez, January 18, 1946.
6. *Lucha Obrera*, Mexico City, second fortnight, August 1944.
7. OFA, Letter from L. Red (Octavio Fernández) to Diego Henríquez, January 18, 1946.
8. OFA, "Reunión del Comité Central Ampleado del Grupo Socialista Obrero, 9 de Octubre de 1946."
9. OFA, letter from L. Red (Octavio Fernández) to Diego Henríquez, January 18, 1946.
10. OFA: "Reunión del Comité Central Ampleado."
11. Interview with Octavio Fernández, Mexico City, January 23, 1971.
12. OFA, letter of "Pilar" to L. Red (Octavio Fernández), December 16, 1946.
13. OFA: Letter of "A. Fer" to L. Red (Octavio Fernández), September 22, 1946.
14. *Tribuna Socialista*, Mexico City, November 17, 1946.
15. Interview with Octavio Fernández, Mexico City, January 23, 1971.
16. OFA, letter from Felix Morrow to Parti Communiste Internationale, November 23, 1946; L. Red (Octavio Fernández) to International Secretariat of Fourth International, December 20, 1946; and L. Red to Felix Morrow, December 27, 1946.
17. *Boletín de Información y Discusión* of Grupo Socialista Obrero, Mexico City, August 1946.
18. Interview with Octavio Fernández, Mexico City, January 21, 1971.
19. Interview with Luciano Galicia, Mexico City, January 22, 1971.
20. Interview with Félix Ibarra, Mexico City, January 22, 1971.

21. Interview with Félix Ibarra, Mexico City, January 22, 1971.

22. Interview with Arturo Martínez, Mexico City, January 20, 1971.

23. All of the foregoing from "Hacia la Construcción del Partido Revolucionario," in *Boletín Interno* of Grupo Comunista Internacionalista, undated.

24. This information comes from a Mexican Trotskyist source which wishes to remain unidentified.

25. Grupo Comunista Internacionalista, *Carta Abierta a Fidel Castro: Respuesta de los Trotskistas Mexicanos*, Mexico City, January 1966.

26. Interview with Arturo Martínez, Mexico City, January 20, 1971.

27. *Intercontinental Press*, July 28, 1969.

28. *Ibid.*, June 21, 1971.

29. *Ibid.*, November 22, 1971.

30. *Bulletin*, New York, May 19, 1969.

31. *Revista Marxista Latinoamericana* (Posadista), July 1967, p. 295.

32. Interview with Félix Ibarra, Mexico City, January 22, 1971.

33. Interview with Arturo Martínez, Mexico City, January 20, 1971.

34. Letter from Carlos Manuel Pellecer to Robert J. Alexander, March 14, 1969.

35. *Cuba Socialista*, Havana, February 1966, pp. 88-97.

36. The foregoing is from *Cuarta Internacional* (United Secretariat), August 1966, pp. 138-40.

37. *Ibid.*, pp. 141-42.

11: CUBAN TROTSKYISM, THE FOURTH INTERNATIONAL, AND THE CASTRO REVOLUTION

1. Interview with Charles Simeon, Union City, New Jersey, April 12, 1970.

2. Mario Riera Hernández, *Historial Obrero Cubano, 1574-1965* (1965), p. 281.

3. Letter from Antonio Alonso Ávila to Robert J. Alexander, March 21, 1970.

4. Interview with Charles Simeon, Union City, N.J., April 12, 1970.

5. Riera Hernández, *Historial Obrero Cubano*, p. 280.

6. *International Press Correspondence*, February 1, 1929.

7. *Lucha Obrera*, Mexico City, January 20, 1941.

8. Jorge García Montes and Antonio Alonso Ávila, *Historia del Partido Comunista de Cuba* (1970), p. 94.

9. Víctor Alba, *Esquema Histórico del Comunismo en Iberamérica* (1960), p. 96.

10. Cited in Garcia Montes and Alonso Ávila, *Historia*, p. 95.

11. Riera Hernández, *Historial Obrero Cubano*, p. 98.

12. The foregoing from an interview with Charles Simeon, Union City, N.J., April 12, 1970.

13. For a discussion of the Communist attitude toward the Grau San Martín government, see García Montes and Alonso Ávila, *Historia*, p. 139; and K. S. Karol; *Guerrillas in Power: The Course of the Cuban Revolution* (1970), pp. 74-77.

14. García Montes and Alonso Ávila, *Historia*, p. 164.

15. OFA, letter of A. González to Octavio Fernández, June 3, 1934.

16. Riera Hernández, *Historial Obrero Cubano*, p. 104.

17. OFA, letter from A. J. Muste to the Central Committee of Partido Bolchevique Leninista, January 6, 1935.

18. Riera Hernández, *Historial Obrero Cubano*, p. 102.

19. García Montes and Alonso Ávila, *Historia*, p. 171.

20. Riera Hernández, *Historial Obrero Cubano*, p. 102.

21. R. S. de la Torre, "The Situation in Cuba," *New International*, October 1935.

22. García Montes and Alonso Ávila, *Historia*, p. 171.

23. Interview with Charles Simeon, Guttenberg, New Jersey, April 12, 1970.

24. *Bohemia*, Havana, August 15, 1937, p. 34.

25. Letter from Antonio Alonso Ávila to Robert J. Alexander, March 21, 1970; and K.S. Karol, *Guerrillas in Power*, pp. 116-21.

26. García Montes and Alonso Ávila, *Historia*, pp. 288-89.

27. *Revolución Proletaria*, Havana, May 1946.

28. Cited in Liborio Justo, *Estrategia Revolucionaria: Lucha por la Unidad y por la Liberación Nacional y Social de la América Latina* (1954), p. 193.

29. Interview with Raúl Valdivia, Mexico City, January 20, 1971.

30. J. B. Stuard, "Cuba's Elections: Background and Analysis," *Fourth International*, July 1944.

31. *Revolución Proletaria*, Havana, May 1946.

32. *Ibid.*

33. Socialist Workers Party, *The Nature of the Cuban Revolution* (1968), p. 19.

34. "Manifiesto del Buro Político al Congreso de Cooperativas Cañeras, Agosto 1962," *Cuarta Internacional* (Posadista), September 1962, p. 165.

35. *New America*, New York, September 22, 1961.

36. "Manifiesto del Buro Político."

37. "Resolución del Buro Político del POR/T," dated September 22, 1962, in *Cuarta Internacional* (Posadista), September 1962, p. 167.

38. "Comunicado" of POR/T, published in *Cuarta Internacional* (Posadista), September 1962, p. 164.

39. *Cuarta Internacional* (Posadista), September 1962, p. 164.

40. All of the foregoing is from *Spartacist*, New York, January-February 1965.

41. See Fidel Castro's closing speech to the Tricontinental Congress, published in *Cuba Socialista*, Havana, February 1966, particularly pp. 88-97.

42. This information on the previous political affiliation and sympathies of Camilo Cienfuegos comes from an interview with a Cuban trade-union leader who may still be in the island, and so must remain anonymous.

43. Socialist Workers Party, *The Nature of the Cuban Revolution*, p. 28.

44. Cited in *Spartacist*, New York, January-February 1965.

45. Socialist Workers Party, *The Nature of the Cuban Revolution*, p. 25.

46. *Fourth International* (Healyite), London, August 1966, pp. 129-30.

47. *Workers Press*, London, July 30, 1970.

## 12: TROTSKYISM IN OTHER LATIN AMERICAN COUNTRIES

1. The foregoing from an interview with Esteban Kikích, in Montevideo, Uruguay, October 10 and October 17, 1946.

2. *Trabajadores del Uruguay: Peligran Nuestras Libertades Gremiales*, throwaway dated June 12, 1944.

3. Partido Obrero Revolucionario (IV Internacional), *La Situación Nacional: Perspectivas y Tareas del Proletariado, Resolución Política del Comité Central del Partido Obrero Revolucionario, Julio de 1959* (1959), p. 10.

4. *Ibid.*, p. 12.

5. *Ibid.*, p. 13.

6. *Ibid.*, pp. 15-16.

7. Anonymous diplomatic source, the Revolutionary Workers Party (POR/T), March 1969.

8. Anonymous diplomatic source, the Revolutionary Workers Party, Trotskyist (POR/T), March 1967.

9. This information is from Francisco Canas, *Relato del 1/12/68, Balance y Conclusiones*, an internal bulletin of the POR(T), mimeographed, n.d.

10. *El País*, Montevideo, March 11, 1969.

11. *La Mañana*, Montevideo, March 16, 1969.

12. OFA, letter from A. González to Octavio Fernández, June 3, 1934.

13. *Ibid.*

14. OFA, letter from A. González to Luis Gutiérrez (Octavio Fernández), March 12, 1935.

15. Interview with Diógenes de la Rosa, Panama City, July 26, 1948.

16. OFA, letter from Luis Vergne Ortíz to A. González, January 16, 1935.

# Bibliography

Information on Trotskyism in Latin America is widely dispersed and difficult to piece together. My sources have included interviews with leaders and former leaders of the movement, as well as with other persons who have been able to observe Trotskyism in action in one or more of the countries involved, even though they themselves have not been Trotskyists. Also useful have been copies of periodicals published by various Latin American Trotskyite parties and groups, by the Fourth International and its various factions, and by a few European and North American Trotskyist organizations. In only a few instances have I had access to a complete file of any of these. I have also examined passing references in books not principally concerned with Trotskyism, as well as pamphlets and a handful of books concerned mainly with Trotskyism in individual countries. The available material has likewise included scattered references to Trotskyist activities made in publications of the political opponents of the Fourth Internationalists. Finally, I have had the good fortune of having access to correspondence and other internal documentation made available to me by friends and acquaintances. For what use it may be to students of this subject, I have divided the following bibliography into eight categories; all sources cited in my notes are here given in full.

## BOOKS AND PAMPHLETS

Alba, Víctor. Esquema Histórico del Comunismo en Iberoamérica. Mexico: Ediciones Occidentales, 1960.

Alexander, Robert J. Communism in Latin America. New Brunswick: Rutgers University Press, 1957.

————— . Labor Relations in Argentina, Brazil, and Chile. New York: McGraw-Hill, 1962.

————— . The Bolivian National Revolution. New Brunswick: Rutgers University Press, 1958.

Andrés, Niceto. La Política Nacional del Trotskismo en América Latina (Centralismo y Revolución). Buenos Aires: Ediciones Nuevo Curso, 1949.

Añí Castillo, Gonzalo. Historia Secreta de las Guerrillas. Lima: Ediciones Masalla, 1967.

Barata, Agildo. Vida de Um Revolucionario (Memorias). Río de Janeiro: Editorial Melso, n.d.

Bastos, Abguar. Luíz Carlos Prestes e A Revolucão Social. Río de Janeiro: Editorial Calvino, Limitada, 1946.

Basbaum, Leoncio. Historia Sincera da Republica. Río de Janeiro: Editor Pulgor, Ltda., 1968.

Belloni, Alberto. Del Anarquismo al Peronismo: Historia del Movimiento Obrero. Buenos Aires: A. Peña Lallo Editor, 1960.

Blanco, Hugo. El Camino de Nuestra Revolución. Lima: Ediciones Revolución Peruana, 1964.

Bowen Herrera, Alfredo. Ensayo Sobre el Movimiento Sindical y el Sindicalismo Agrícola. Santiago: Imprenta "La Fama," 1934.

Cannon, James P. The History of American Trotskyism: Report of a Participant. New York: Pioneer Publishers, 1944.

Cornejo, Alberto. Programmas Políticos de Bolivia. Cochabamba: Imprenta Universitaria, 1949.

Deutscher, Isaac. The Prophet Outcast: Trotsky, 1929-1940. New York: Oxford University Press, 1963.

Echaiz, René León. Evolución Historica de los Partidos Políticos Chilenos. Santiago: Editorial Ercilla, 1939.

Eder, George. Inflation and Development in Latin America, A Case History of Inflation and Stabilization in Bolivia. Ann Arbor: University of Michigan, 1968.

El Terrorismo, La Represión Contra El POR (Trotskista), El Desarrollo de las Condiciones Revolucionarias en Brasil. Lima: Ediciones Voz Obrera, 1970.

Fellmann Velarde, José. Víctor Paz Estenssoro: El Hombre y la Revolución. La Paz: Empresa Industrial Gráfica, 1955.

González Díaz, Galo. El Congreso de la Victoria; Resumen de los Informes, Discusiones y Resoluciones, X Congreso Nacional del Partido Comunista de Chile. Santiago, 1938.

Gunder Frank, André. Hugo Blanco Must Not Die. Toronto: Robert McCarthy, 1965.

García Montes, Jorge, and Antonio Alonso Ávila. Historia del Partido Comunista de Cuba. Miami: Ediciones Universal, 1970.

Grupo Comunista Internacionalista. Carta Abierta a Fidel Castro: Respuesta de los Trotskistas Mexicanos. Mexico, January 1966.

Halperin, Ernst. Nationalism and Communism in Chile. Cambridge, Mass.: The M.I.T. Press, 1965.

Healy, Gerald. Problems of the Fourth International. London, n.d. (1966). Newsletter.

Hewitt, Cynthia. An Introduction to the Rural Labor Movement of Pernambuco. Columbia University: Institute of Latin American Studies, September 1965. Mimeographed.

Hidalgo Plaza, Manuel. La Rebelión de la Armada: Discurso del Senador Comunista Manuel Hidalgo P., en el senado, el 16 de Septiembre de 1931, Valparaíso: Editorial Europa, 1931.

Inquérito Policial Militar No. 709: O Comunismo no Brasil, Volume 3. Río de Janeiro: Biblioteca do Exercito Editora, 1967.

James, C. L. R.: World Revolution 1917-1936: The Rise and Fall of the Communist International. New York: Pioneer Publishers, 1937.

Justo, Liborio [Quebracho]. Bolivia: La Revolución Derrotada. Cochabamba, Bolivia: Editorial Serrano Hnos., Ltda., 1967.

_____ . Breve Reseña Cronológica del Movimiento Cuartainternacionalista Argentino. Liga Obrera Revolucionaria (La Internacional), República Argentina, 1941.

_____ . Centrismo, Oportunismo y Bolchevismo: El Grupo Obrero Revolucionario y la Lucha por el Marxismo-Leninismo en la Argentina y en la América del Sur. Buenos Aires: 1940.

————— . Como Salir del Pantano: Hacia la Formación de la Sección Argentina del Partido Mundial de la Revolución Socialista (4a Internacional). Buenos Aires: n.d.

————— . Estrategia Revolucionaria: Lucha por la Unidad y por la Liberación Nacional y Social de la América Latina. "Fragua", Buenos Aires: 1956.

————— . Frente al Momento del Mundo: Qué Quiere la Cuarta Internacional. Buenos Aires: 1939.

————— . Leon Trotsky y Wall Street: Como el Líder de la Cuarta Internacional se puso al Servicio del Imperialismo Yanqui en México. Buenos Aires: Ediciones Badajo, 1959.

————— . Prontuario: Una Autobiografía, 2nd Edition. Buenos Aires: Ediciones Cure, 1956.

Karol, K. S. Guerrillas in Power: The Course of the Cuban Revolution. New York: Hill & Wang, 1970.

Landsberger, Henry. Latin American Peasant Movements. Ithaca N.Y.: Cornell University Press, 1969.

Lerski, Geoíge J. Origins of Trotskyism in Ceylon. Stanford, Ca.: The Hoover Institution, 1968.

Madariaga, José Luis. ¿Qué es la Izquierda Nacional? Manual del Socialismo Revolucionario. Buenos Aires: Ediciones In, 1969.

Mallin, Jay. "Che" Guevara on Revolution. Miami: University of Miami Press, 1969.

Malloy, James. Bolivia: The Uncompleted Revolution. Pittsburgh: The University of Pittsburgh Press, 1970.

Partido Obrero Revolucionario (IV Internacional). La Situación Nacional: Perspectivas y Tareas del Proletariado, Resolución Política del Comité Central del Partido Obrero Revolucionario Julio de 1959. Montevideo: 1959.

Partido Socialista, Departamento Nacional de Propaganda. El Libro Negro del Partido Comunista. Santiago: 1941.

Peñaloza, Juan Ramón. Trotsky Ante la Revolución Nacional Lationoamericana. Buenos Aires: Editorial Indoamerica, 1953.

Posadas, J. El Papel de la Vanguardia Peronista en la Organización de la Lucha por el Gobierno Obrero y Campesino en la Argentina. Buenos Aires: Editorial Present, 1965.

————— . La Desagregación Mundial del Capitalismo, de la Burocracia de los Estados Obreros y de los Partidos Comunistas, el Avance Incontenible de las Luchas Revolucionarias y del Sentimiento Comunista de las Masas del Mundo y la Fusión de la Vanguardia Comunista Mundial con los Objetivos, con la Política, con el Programa de la Cuarta Internacional. Montevideo: Ediciones Revista Marxista Latinoamericana, 1968.

Ramos, Jorge Abelardo. La Lucha por un Partido Revolucionario. Buenos Aires: Ediciones Pampa y Cielo, 1964.

————— . La Revolución Nacional en Latinamérica: Manuel Ugarte y la Lucha Antiimperialista. Buenos Aires: Editorial Indoamerica, 1952.

Reyes, Ezequiel. Qué es la Izquierda (Respuesta a los Companeros Comunistas). Buenos Aires: Andes Editora, 1961.

Riera Hernández, Mario. Historial Obrero Cubano, 1574-1965. Miami: Rema Press, 1965.

Socialist Workers Party. The Founding Conference of the Fourth International (World

Party of the Socialist Revolution), Program and Resolutions. New York: 1939.
_____ . The Nature of the Cuban Revolution. New York: April 1968.
Trotsky, Leon. Los Gangsters de Estalin. Mexico: Editorial América, 1940.
Valencia Vega, Alipio. Desarrollo del Pensamiento Político en Bolivia. La Paz: 1953.
Villanueva, Víctor. Hugo Blanco y la Rebelión Campesina. Lima: Editorial Juan Mejia
    Paca, 1967.
Wolfe, Bertram D. Diego Rivera: His Life and Times. New York: Alfred A. Knopf,
    1939.
_____ . The Fabulous Life of Diego Rivera. New York: Stein & Day, 1963. Young
    Socialist Alliance. Land or Death. New York: 1967.

## PARTY AND TRADE-UNION CONGRESS REPORTS

Díaz Martínez, Juan. Treinta Meses de Acción en Favor del Proletariado de
    Chile—Memoria del Consejo Directivo Nacional al 1er Congreso Ordinario, 26 al
    30 de Julio de 1939 (CTCh). Santiago: 1939.
Partido Comunista de Chile [Trotskyist faction]. En Defensa de la revolución: Informes,
    Tesis y Documentos Presentados al Congreso Nacional del Partido Comunista a
    Verificarse el 19 de Marzo de 1933. Santiago: Ediciones Lucha de Clases, 1933.
Partido Comunista de Chile [Stalinist faction]. Hacia la Formación de un Verdadero
    Partido de Clase—Resoluciones de la Conferencia Nacional del Partido Comunista
    Realizada en Julio de 1933. Santiago: Gutenberg Press, 1933.
Partido Socialista de Trabajadores. El Camino del Pueblo—Resoluciones del Tercer
    Congreso General del Partido Socialista de Trabajadores, Santiago, 1 at 3 de Mayo
    de 1942. Santiago: 1942.

## TROTSKYIST PERIODICALS

*Batalla.* Organ of Partido Socialista Obrero de Bolivia, La Paz, late 1940's.
*Boletín de Información del Secretariado Internacional de la IV Internacional.* Mimeo-
    graphed publication of Posadas International Secretariat of the Fourth International,
    Montevideo, 1967.
*Boletín de Información y Discusión.* Mimeographed internal organ of Grupo Socialista
    Obrero, dissident Trotskyist group in Mexico, 1945-46.
*Boletín Interno.* Mimeographed internal bulletin of Grupo Comunista Internacionalista,
    Mexico, 1969.
*Boletín Interno del POR/T.* Mimeographed organ of Partido Obrero Revolucionario
    (Trotskista) of Uruguay, Montevideo, 1968.
*Boletín Leninista.* Edited by Central Provisional Committee for the Formation of a
    Revolutionary Vanguard, Chilean Section of the Fourth International, Year 1, Number
    1.
*Bulletin.* Organ of Workers League, United States affiliate of International Committee
    of Fourth International (Healyite), New York City, 1960's.
*Clave.* Trotskyist monthly magazine published in Mexico from October 1938 to May
    1941.
*Contra la Corriente.* Newspaper of Liga Obrera Revolucionaria of Uruguay in the 1940's.

*Cuarta Internacional*. Organ of Executive Committee of Fourth International (Posadista faction of international Trotskyism), after 1962.

*Cuarta Internacional*. Spanish language organ of International Executive Committee of the Fourth International (United Secretariat), 1963 and thereafter.

*IV Internacional*. Newspaper of Liga Comunista Internacionalista, Mexico City, 1936-37.

*El Bolchevique*. Mimeographed periodical of Liga Comunista Internacionalista, Mexico, 1939.

*El Militante*. Paper published by old-time Trotskyist Mateo Fossa, Buenos Aires, 1946-47.

*Fourth International*. Organ of Healyite International Committee of Fourth International, London, 1960's and 1970's.

*Fourth International*. Quarterly organ of Socialist Workers Party of United States, New York City, 1940's and 1950's.

*Frente Obrero*. Organ of Liga Obrera Revolucionaria of Uruguay in 1950's, subsequently of Partido Obrero Revolucionario (IV Internacional) and Partido Obrero Revolucionario (Trotskista), Montevideo.

*Frente Operaria*. Organ of Partido Operario Revolucionario (Trotskista) of Brazil, São Paulo, 1960's (Posadista).

*Informations Ouvrières*. Organ of Organization Communiste Internationaliste, Healyite French Affiliate, Paris, 1960's and 1970's.

*Informe Nacional*. Weekly mimeographed bulletin of Organizacão Revolucionaria Marxista Politíca Operaria, 1966-68, and subsequently of Partido Operario Comunista of Brazil, Río de Janeiro.

*Intercontinental Press*. International news weekly published unofficially by the Socialist Workers Party of United States, New York, 1960's and 1970's. Originally called *World Outlook*.

*International Socialist Review*. Quarterly review of Socialist Workers Party of the United States, New York, 1960's and 1970's.

*Izquierda Nacional*. Organ of Partido Socialista de la Izquierda Nacional (Jorge Abelardo Ramos), Buenos Aires, 1960's and 1970's.

*Labor Action*. Weekly paper of dissident (Shachtmanite), United States Trotskyist faction, first the Workers Party but later the Independent Socialist League, 1940's and 1950's.

*La Internacional*. Mimeographed periodical of Grupo Comunista Internacionalista of Mexico, 1969-70.

*Lotta Operaia*. Organ of Partido Comunista Rivoluzionario (Trotskista), Italian affiliate of Posadista Fourth International, Rome, 1960's.

*Lucha Obrera*. Organ of Partido Obrero Internacionalista of Mexico, 1939-47, Mexico.

*Lucha Obrera*. Organ of Partido Obrero Revolucionario of Bolivia, La Paz, 1940's and early 1950's.

*Lucha Obrera*. Organ of Hugo González Moscoso faction of Partido Obrero Revolucionario of Bolivia, after POR split in 1956-57, La Paz.

*Lucha Obrera*. Organ of Partido Obrero Revolucionario (Trotskista), Posadista party in Chile, Santiago, 1960's and early 1970's.

*Masas*. Organ of Guillermo Lora faction of POR of Bolivia after 1956-57 split, La Paz.

*New International*. "Theoretical" organ of Communist League of America; then of Workers Party, in early 1930's; then of Socialist Workers Party, New York, 1937-40.

*New International.* "Theoretical" organ of Shachtmanite faction of Trotskyism in the United States, New York, 1940 to 1958.

*Nueva Internacional.* Organ of Liga Comunista Internacionalista of Mexico, 1934-35, Mexico.

*Perspectiva Mundial.* Periodical of international news published by Mexican Trotskyists associated with United Secretariat, Mexico, 1967 and thereafter.

*Política Obrera.* Organ of Movimiento Política Obrera, Argentine affiliate of United Secretariat of Fourth International in 1960's, Buenos Aires.

*Política Operaria.* Organ of Organizacão Revolucionaria Marxista Política Operaria, group sympathetic to United Secretariat of Fourth International, Rio de Janeiro, 1960's.

*Programa Para los Estados Unidos Socialista de América Latina.* Alberto Belloni, publisher, Buenos Aires, 1964 and afterwards.

*¿Qué Hacer?* Trotskyist magazine in Mexico, subtitled "En Defense of los Intereses Obreros y Campesinos," Mexico, 1954-55.

*Revista Marxista.* Chilean Trotskyist publication, Santiago, middle 1960's.

*Revista Marxista Latinoamericana.* Until 1963 the Latin American regional publication of the Pabloite faction of International Trotskyism; thereafter "Organ of the International Secretariat of the Fourth International," the Posadas faction of the Fourth International.

*Revolución.* Fortnightly newspaper of Grupo Obrero Marxista, first Trotskyite group in Peru, Lima, late 1940's.

*Revolución Proletaria.* Organ of Cuban Trotskyists, Havana, early 1940's.

*Rouge.* Organ of Ligue Communiste, United Secretariat's French affiliate, Paris, September 1968 to present.

*Spartacist.* Organ of dissident Trotskyist group, Spartacist League, New York, 1960's and 1970's.

*The Militant.* Weekly newspaper of Communist League of America in 1930's and of Socialist Workers Party of United States from late 1930's into 1970's, New York.

*Tribuna Socialista.* Organ of Grupo Socialista Obrero, dissident Trotskyist group in Mexico, published 1945-47, Mexico.

*Vanguard Newsletter.* Mimeographed monthly published by dissidents from Spartacist League, New York, late 1960's and 1970's.

*Voz Obrera.* Mimeographed organ of Partido Obrero Revolucionario (Trotskista), Bolivian affiliate of Posadista Fourth International, La Paz, 1969 to present.

*Voz Obrera.* Organ of Partido Obrero Revolucionario (Trotskista), Posadista party in Mexico, in 1960's, Mexico.

*Voz Obrera.* Fortnightly newspaper of Partido Obrero Revolucionario (Trotskista) of Peru, Posadista affiliate, Lima, 1960's and 1970's.

*Voz Proletaria.* Organ of Partido Obrero (Trotskista), Posadista faction of Argentine Trotskyism, Buenos Aires, 1950's into 1970's.

*Workers Press.* Daily newspaper of Socialist Labor League, British affiliate of Healyite Fourth International, London, 1969 to present.

*World Outlook.* Unofficial international news weekly published by Socialist Workers Party; in middle 1960's renamed *Intercontinental Press.* New York.

## NON-TROTSKYIST NEWSPAPERS AND PERIODICALS

*Cuba Socialista*. ''Theoretical organ'' of government party of Castro's Cuba, 1961-67, Havana.

*El Comercio*. Daily newspaper in Lima, Peru, exceedingly conservative, owned by Miro Quesada family.

*El Machete*. Newspaper of Communist Party of Mexico in 1920's and early 1930's, Mexico.

*El País*. Daily newspaper representing Independent Nationalist Party of Uruguay, Montevideo.

*El Trabajador Latino Americano*. Organ of Communist-controlled Latin American trade-union confederation, Confederación Sindical Latino Americana, 1929-35, Montevideo.

*Entwicklung-politische Activitaten Komunistischer Lander*. Mimeographed periodical of Friedrich Ebert Foundation, devoted to activities of Communist nations in under-developed countries, Bonn-Bad Godesburg, German Federal Republic, 1960's and 1970's.

*Expreso*. Daily newspaper of Lima, Peru, taken over by Velasco government in 1969 and turned into a workers cooperative.

*Gramma*. Newspaper of Partido Comunista de Cuba after 1965, Havana.

*Industry and Labour*. Publication of International Labor Organization, Geneva.

*International Press Correspondence*. Weekly clipsheet of Communist International, 1920's and 1930's.

*La Mañana*. Daily newspaper, Montevideo.

*La Prensa*. Daily newspaper in Lima, Peru, conservative, owned by Pedro Beltrán.

*New America*. Organ of Socialist Party of United States, late 1950's into 1970's, New York.

*New York Herald Tribune*. Daily newspaper in New York, 1920's to 1960's.

*Octubre*. Organ of Centro de Integración Revolucionaria 'Sergio Almaraz Paz,' left-wing nationalist group supporting Ovando regime, 1969-70, La Paz.

*Presencia*. Bolivian newspaper of Christian Democratic orientation, 1950's-1970's, La Paz.

*Programa–Revista de Doctrina Socialista*. Organ of Grupo de Estudios Socialistas en México, early 1950's (Rodrigo García Treviño, editor), Mexico.

*Rebelión*. Organ of Central Obrera Bolivana, 1952 and thereafter, La Paz.

*R.I.L.U. Magazine*. Organ of Red International of Labor Unions, international trade-union organization of Stalinist Communists, late 1920's and early 1930's.

*Socialist Call*. Organ of ''Militant'' faction of Socialist Party of United States, and then official organ of the party, 1935-60, New York.

*The Communist International*. Organ of Communist International, published in Great Britain.

*Vanguarda Socialista*. Democratic Socialist Weekly, 1945-48 (Mario Pedrosa, editor), Río de Janeiro.

*Viertel Jahres Berichte*. Mimeographed publication of Friedrich Ebert Foundation, 1960's into 1970's, Bonn-Bad Godesburg, German Federal Republic.

## THROWAWAYS

*La Junta del Gobierno al País*. Proclamation distributed by Grove government of the Socialist Republic of Chile, June 1932, Santiago.

Liga Obrera Revolucionaria. *Trabajadores del Uruguay: Peligran Nuestras Libertades Gremiales*, June 12, 1944, Montevideo.

Liga Obrera Revolucionaria. *Viva la Huelga de los Obreros de los Frigorificos*, undated but 1946, Montevideo.

*Los 30 Puntos*. Proclamation distributed by Grove government of Socialist Republic of Chile, listing program of the government, June 1932, Talcahuano.

Política Operaria. *Por Qué Anular o Voto Nas Eleicões no Estado da Guanabara*. Denunciation of state elections in Guanabara, Brazil, undated but 1965.

## LETTERS

Antonio Alonso Ávila, historian of Cuban Communist movement, to Robert J. Alexander, March 21, 1970.

James P. Cannon to Charles Curtiss, June 21, 1938.

Charles Curtiss to Robert J. Alexander, February 10, 1971.

Luciano Galicia to Leon Trotsky, December 20, 1938.

Joseph Hansen to Robert J. Alexander, December 24, 1970.

Liga Comunista Internacionalista of Mexico to Buro Panamericana de la IV Internacional, February 10, 1939.

José López, Secretary of Pan American and Pacific Bureau of Fourth International to Diego Rivera, October 21, 1938.

Carlos Manuel Pellecer to Robert J. Alexander, March 14, 1969.

Terence Phelan to Charles Curtiss, from Sierra de Córdoba, Argentina, October 28, 1941.

Diego Rivera to Charles Curtiss, March 20, 1939.

Manuel Rodriguez to Robert J. Alexander, March 1971.

Max Shachtman, former leader of Socialist Workers Party and of dissident Trotskyist group, to Robert J. Alexander, December 7, 1970.

Natalia Sedova Trotsky to "Comité Ejecutivo de la IV Internacional" and to "Comité Político del Socialist Workers Party," May 9, 1951.

## OTHER UNPUBLISHED MATERIAL

Anonymous. "Memorandum on Argentine Trotskyism." Provided to author by former Argentine Trotskyist leader who wishes to remain anonymous.

Anonymous Diplomatic Source. "Revolutionary Workers Party—Trotskyite (POR/T)," March 1967.

Anonymous Diplomatic Source. "The Revolutionary Workers Party (POR/T)," March 1969.

Charlier, Fernand. "Le Posadisme: Un Rapport d'Autopsie." Unpublished article.

Chilcote, Ronald. "The Brazilian Communist Party." Manuscript.

Octavio Fernandez. Archives (referred to as OFA in text). Documentation on Trotskyist movement of Mexico, 1930's and 1940's, in possession of former Mexican Trotskyist leader Octavio Fernández.

Naft, Stephen. "Labor Movements in Latin America." Undated manuscript.

Pellecer, Carlos Manuel. Del Doctor Wetheim al Doctor Polcano. Typed article, undated.

## INTERVIEWS

Oscar Barrientos, leader of Partido Obrero Revolucionario in the Cochabamba region, in Cochabamba, Bolivia, July 26, 1954.

Germán Butrón, Executive Secretary of Confederación General de Trabajadores Fabriles, in La Paz, July 11, 1953.

Charles Curtiss, one-time Fourth International delegate in Mexico, in Piscataway, New Jersey, August 8, 1970.

Diógenes de la Rosa, founder of Partido Obrero Marxista-Leninista of Panama, later a leader of Socialist Party, in Panama City, July 26, 1948.

Octavio Fernández, one-time leader of Liga Comunista Internacionalista, Partido Obrero Internacionalista and Grupo Socialista Obrero of Mexico, in Mexico City, January 21 and 23, 1971.

Sra. de Fernández, wife of ex-Trotskyist leader Octavio Fernández, in Mexico City, January 21, 1971.

Ismael Frías, ex-leader of Pabloite faction of Partido Obrero Revolucionario of Peru, in Lima, July 13, 1971.

Luciano Galicia, one-time leader of Liga Comunista Internacionalista and of Partido Obrero Internacionalista of Mexico, in Mexico City, January 22, 1971.

Rodrigo García Treviño, one-time Assistant Secretary of Technical Affairs of Confederación de Trabajadores de Mexico; one-time Secretary-General of Grupo de Socialistas Mexicanos, in Mexico City, January 20, 1971.

Febus Gikovate, former Trotskyite, a São Paulo leader of Partido Socialista Brasileiro, in São Paulo, June 17, 1953.

Joseph Hansen, editor of *Intercontinental Press*, a major leader of Socialist Workers Party of United States, in New York City, January 28, 1970.

Manuel Hidalgo, former head of Izquierda Comunista of Chile, in Santiago, December 17, 1946.

Eduardo Ibarra, President of Unión de Obreros Municipales de Chile, in Santiago, April 17, 1947.

Félix Ibarra, one-time Secretary-General of Liga Comunista Internacionalista of Mexico, in Mexico City, January 20 and 22, 1971.

Esteban Kikích, member of Comité de Enlace de Sindicatos Autónomos, leader of Liga Obrera Revolucionaria of Uruguay, in Montevideo, October 10 and 17, 1946.

Juan Lechín, Executive Secretary of the Federación Sindical de Trabajadores Mìneros de Bolivia, in La Paz, May 28, 1947, August 14, 1952, and July 30, 1957.

Hilcar Leite, former Brazilian Trotskyist leader in Río de Janeiro, June 11, 1953.

Eucario León, President of Confederación Nacional del Trabajo of Mexico, in Mexico City, August 20, 1951.

Guillermo Limpias Villegas, head of Bank Workers Union of Bolivia, in La Paz, July 11, 1953.

Genaro Linares, Secretary-General of Federación Nacional de Gastronómicos, in La Paz, July 23, 1957.

Aristides Lobo, former Brazilian Trotskyist leader, in São Paulo, June 17, 1953.

Guillermo Lora, principal leader of Partido Obrero Revolucionario of Bolivia, in La Paz, June 2, 1947.

Arturo Martínez, former leader of Liga Comunista Internacionalista of Mexico, in Mexico City, January 20, 1971.

Plinio Melo, former Brazilian Trotskyist leader, São Paulo leader of Partido Socialista Brasileiro, in São Paulo, June 16, 1953.

Lucio Mendívil, leader of Partido Obrero Revolucionario of Bolivia, and Senator, in La Paz, May 28, 1947.

Edwin Moller, principal Trotskyite leader in Central Obrera Boliviana, subsequently deputy for MNR, in La Paz, July 10, 1953, July 20, 1954, August 22, 1956, and July 20, 1957.

Mario Montenegro, son of Carlos Montenegro, founder of MNR, himself a Movimientista, in La Paz, April 7, 1962, and Washington, D.C., May 28, 1960.

Manuel Naranjo, Secretary-General of Acción Sindical Chilena, in Santiago, July 1, 1953.

June Nash, United States anthropologist, in New Brunswick, New Jersey, March 31, 1971.

Gustavo Navarro (Tristán Marof), founder of Partido Obrero Revolucionario and of Partido Socialista Obrero de Bolivia, in La Paz, May 26, 1947.

Mario Pedrosa, former Brazilian Trotskyite leader, editor of *Vanguarda Socialista*, in Río de Janeiro, August 14, 1946.

Víctor Paz Estenssoro, ex-President of Bolivia, leader of Movimiento Nacionalista Revolucionario, in Lima, Peru, July 10, 1971.

Astrogildo Pereira, former leader in Brazilian Communist Party, in Río de Janeiro, October 19, 1965.

N. M. Pereira, leader of Lanka Sama Samaja Party of Ceylon, Minister of Finance, in New York City, September 21, 1971.

Irineo Pimentel, a leader of Federación Sindical de Trabajadores Mineros de Bolivia, MNR member, in New Brunswick, New Jersey, March 14, 1954.

Enrique Rangel, President of Confederación Proletaria Nacional of Mexico, in Mexico City, August 23, 1948.

Manuel Rodríguez, a founder of Mexican Trotskyism, in Mexico City, January 22, 1971.

Hermínio Saccheta, former leader of Partido Socialista Revolucionario of Brazil, in São Paulo, June 16, 1953.

Carlos Salazar, member of Executive of Partido Socialista Obrero de Bolivia, editor óf *Batalla,* in La Paz, May 29, 1947.

Jorge Salazar, a leader of Partido Obrero Revolucionario, Manager of Caja de Ferroviarios, in La Paz, May 28, 1947 and August 13, 1952.

Nicolas Sánchez, a leader of Partido Obrero Revolucionario faction in the miners federation, in La Paz, May 26, 1947.

Hernán Sánchez Fernández, member of Executive Committee of Partido Socialista Obrero de Bolivia, early leader of Miners Federation of Bolivia, in La Paz, May 28, 1947.

José Santiago, Secretary-General, and Humberto Valenzuela, member of Executive Committee of Partido Obrero Revolucionario, in Santiago, Chile, December 28, 1946.

Max Shachtman, former leader of Socialist Workers Party, former member of Executive Committee of Fourth International, in Floral Park, Long Island, January 16, 1970, and in New York City, June 21, 1970.

Charles Simeon, one of founders of Trotskyist movement of Cuba, in Union City, New Jersey, April 12, 1970.

Roberto Sisson, former Secretary of Aliança Nacional Libertadora, in Río de Janeiro, September 8, 1965.

Raúl Valdivia, former Auténtico leader in Sugar Workers Federation of Cuba, in Mexico City, January 20, 1971.

Adolfo Venegas, member of Discipline Commission of Partido Aprista Peruano, ex-secretary of Univeristy Command of Aprista party, in Lima, Peru, July 12,1971.

Bernabé Villarreal, Secretary-General of La Paz Chauffeurs Union, member of Executive Committee of Confederación Sindical de Trabajadores Bolivianos, in La Paz, August 14, 1952.

Oscar Waiss, a former leader of Chilean Trotskyists, in Santiago, Chile, March 17, 1947, July 3, 1968, and June 19, 1971.

José Zegada, Recording Secretary of Central Obrera Bolivia, in La Paz, July 29, 1954.

# Index

Ação Integralista Brasileira, 74
Ação Popular, 87
Acción Democrática, 35
Acción Revolucionaria, Mexicanista, 183
Acción Socialista, Chile, 102
*Acción Socialista*, Uruguay, 238
Acuña, Carlos, 92, 104
Agrupación de Propaganda Marxista, Argentina, 50
Agrupación Pro-Unificación de Izquierdas Revolucionarias, Peru, 168, 169
Agrupación Socialista Obrera, Uruguay, 240
Aguirre Cerda, Pedro, 104, 105
Aguirre Gainsborg, Jose, 112, 117
Ala Izquierda, Cuba, 216, 217
Alba, Victor, 218
Alberto, João, 73
Aldaña, Eliseo, 152
Alegría, Ciro, 170
Alemán, Miguel, 200
Alfaro Siqueiros, David, 188
Alessandri, Arturo, 94, 95, 101
Alfonso, Andrés, 228
Alfonso, Sra. de, 228
Aliança Nacional Libertadora, Brazil, 74, 75, 76
*Alianza Obrera*, Chile, 105
Alianza Socialista Revolucionaria, Chile, 98, 103
All American Anti-Imperialist League, 218
All America Pacific Bureau of International Left Communist Opposition, 190
Allende, Salvador, 108, 109, 110, 244
Almaráz, Sergio, 136
Almazán, General Juan Andreu, 195, 197, 200
Alonso Avila, Antonio, 220, 221
*A Luta de Classe*, 77
Alvarado, Francisco, 200
Alvarez, Benjamín, 181
Alvarez Plata, Julio, 134
Amado Granados, Francisco, 210, 211
*América Libre*, Argentina, 50, 112
American Federation of Labor, 126
Américo, José, 76, 77
Ampuero, Raúl, 109
Anaya, Ricardo, 112
Anaya Ibarra, Pedro María, 180

281

Anda, S. de, 185
Andrade, Juan, 217
Añi Castillo, Gerardo, 169
Anti-Duhring, 180
Aprista Party, Cuba, 218
Aprista Party, Peru; See Partido Aprista Peruano
Aprista Party Youth, 158
Araes, Miguel, 80
Aragón, Antonio, 166
Araya, M., 90, 91
Arce Loureiro, Eduardo, 112
Arnesto, Urbano, 217
Arriaga, Martín; See Rafael Galván
Arze, José Antonio, 118
Asociación de Estudios y Divulgación Marxista-Leninista, Mexico, 182
Asociación de Nuevos Emigrados de Cuba, 215
Autenticos; See Partido Revolucionario Cubano (Autentico)
Ávila Camacho, General Manuel, 197, 200, 201
Ayala Mercado, Ernesto, 112


Balbuena, Pablo, 217
Baldivieso, Enrique, 112
Ballivián, Hugo, 124
Bandarinike, Mrs. S., 24, 30
Bank Workers Union, Bolivia, 135
Bank Workers Union, Peru, 165
Banzer, Hugo, 148
Barrata, Agildo, 75
Barrenechea, J., 132
Barrientos, General René, 145, 148, 149, 150
Barrios, D., 90
Barros, Adhemar de, 81
Barros, Luiz de, 72, 73
Basbaum, Leoncio, 71
Bascuñan, Jose R., 89, 90, 91
Batalla, Bolivia, 114
Batista, Fulgencio, 36, 165, 219, 221, 222, 225
Batlle y Ordoñez, Jose, 236
Batllista Colorado Party; See Partido Colorado Batllista
Beauvoir, Simone de, 173
Beauvais, Jean-Pierre, 232
Belloni Alberto, 66
Ben Bella, 31
Bernal; See Liborio Justo
Bestfalling, Emilio Adolfo, 157
Bettelheim, Charles, 173

Blackwell, Russell, 179, 180, 181, 194, 212
Blanco, Hugo, 22, 38, 165, 166, 167, 168, 169, 170, 171, 172, 173, 174, 175, 176, 177, 178
Blest, Clotario, 108
Bloc de Izquierda, Chile, 103
Bloque de Izquierda Boliviana, 112
Boggio Allende, Hernan, 167
*Bolchevique*, Mexico, 247
*Boletín de Información*, Argentina, 51
*Boletín de Información del Secretariado Internacional de la IV Internacional*, Posadista, 209
*Boletín Interno*, GCI, Mexico, 207
*Boletín Leninista*, Chile, 106
*Boletín Sudamericano*, Argentina, 58
Bolshevik-Leninist Group, Brazil; See Grupo Bolchevique-Leninista
Bolshevik Party, Russia, 4, 32, 155
Bonetti, Jose, 138
Brandão, Octavio, 72, 73
Brandler, Heinrich, 3
Bravo, Carlos María, 61
Bravo, Fernando, 138, 143
Brea Ramón, 224
Bressano, Hugo; See Nahuel Moreno
Brezhnev, Leonid, 35
Brizola, Leonel, 82, 84, 86
Bueno, Leoncio, 157
Bukharin, Nikolai, 3, 5, 32
*Bulletin*, Liga Comunista Internacionalista, Argentina, 50
*Bulletin Oppositsii;* See *International Bulletin of the Left Opposition*
*Bulletin of Organization*, Mexico, 197
Burnham, James, 12
Busch, Colonel German, 113, 114, 118, 120
Busquets, Luis M., 217
Bustos, C., 151
Butrón, Germán, 132, 134, 135, 136


Cáceres, D., 90
Canejo, A., 208
Canejo, Daniel, 22
Cannon, James, 6, 7, 12, 190, 191, 205, 237
Capelino, Nelson, 119
*Capital*, 197
*Cara y Sello*, 157
Carbajal, 192
Carbajal, V.: See A. Narvaja
Cárdenas, Lázaro, 6, 184, 186, 187, 188

Carmona Enrique: See Santiago Escobar
Cartel Socialista, Chile, 99
Carvajal, R., 227
Casa del Pueblo, Mexico, 186, 190, 191, 195
Castelo Branco, Humberto A., 81, 82, 85
Castro, Fidel, 20, 21, 24, 35, 36, 41, 42, 146, 162, 166, 175, 208, 210, 211,
    215, 223, 226, 227, 229, 230, 231, 232, 233, 234, 242
Cavalcanti, Claudio, 80, 81
Central Construction Workers Committee, Chile: See Comite Unico de la
    Construccion, Chile
Central Obrera Boliviana, 123, 129, 130, 131, 133, 134, 135, 136, 137, 138,
    141, 142, 143, 149, 154, 155, 156
Central Provisional Committee for the Formation of a Revolutionary
    Vanguard, 106
Central Unica de Trabajadores de Chile, 107, 108, 109
*Centrismo, Oportunismo y Bolchevismo*, 55
Centro Obrero Revolucionario, 118
Chacón, J., 90
Chadwick, Tomás, 98
Chamudez, 100
Chávez, Carlos, 179, 182, 183
Chávez, Ñuflo, 132, 135, 136, 138
Chilcote, Ronald, 82
*Chispa*, Puerto Rico, 247
Christian Democrats, 35
Christian Democratic Party, Uruguay, 244
Cienfuegos, Camilo, 230
*Claridad*, Argentina, 51, 57
*Clarté*, France, 69
*Clase Obrera*, Uruguay, 240
*Class Struggle*, Brazil; See *A Luta de Classe*
*Clave*, Mexico, 32, 77, 193, 195, 198, 224, 247
Cochabamba Departmental Federation of Labor, Bolivia, 133
*Combat Ouvrier*, French Antilles, 248
Comintern; See Communist International
Comisión Obrera of PRC(A), 223
Comité Comunista de Oposición, Argentina, 46
Comité de Enlace de Sindicatos Autonomos, Uruguay, 238, 240
Comité de Relaciones Sindicales, Uruguay, 238
Comité Nacional de Defensa Proletaria, Mexico, 185
Comité Organizador de la Juventud Leninista, Mexico, 185
Comité Unico de la Construcción, Chile, 95, 102
Commercial Employees Union, Cuba, 222
Committee for Proletarian Defense, Cuba 221
Committees for the Defense of the Revolution (CDR), Cuba, 228
Communist International, 3, 5, 6, 7, 8, 9, 10, 35, 37, 69, 70, 72, 74, 89, 100,
    111, 117, 216

Communist League of America (Opposition), 9, 179, 212, 245
Communist Parties, 14, 16, 17, 21, 35, 37, 42, 43, 44
Communist Party, Argentina, 45, 47, 50, 51
Communist Party, Bolivia, 135, 138, 149
Communist Party, Brazil, 69, 71, 75, 77
Communist Party, Chile; See Partido Comunista de Chile
Communist Party, China, 5, 23, 36
Communist Party, Cuba; See Partido Comunista de Cuba
Communist Party, Germany, 10
Communist Party, Guatemala, 218, 226
Communist Party, Italy, 173
Communist Party, Leningrad, 247
Communist Party, Mexico, 173, 180, 181, 182, 193, 196, 200, 207, 209, 210, 212, 218
Communist Party, Peru, 157, 158, 164, 165, 168, 170
Communist Party, Puerto Rico, 247
Communist Party, Soviet Union, 3, 5, 6, 23, 36, 100, 194, 200
Communist Party, Spain, 247
Communist Party, United States, 3, 179, 237, 247
Communist Party, Uruguay; See Partido Comunista, Uruguay
Communist Party, Yugoslavia, 16
*Communist Tribune*, Argentina, 46
Communist Youth, Mexico, 206
*Como Salir del Pantano*, 52
Confederación General de Obreros y Campesinos de Mexico, 184
Confederación General del Trabajo, Argentina, 62, 63, 67, 68
Confederación General de Trabajadores, Chile, 102
Confederación General de Trabajadores, Mexico, 200, 201
Confederación General de Trabajadores Fabriles, Bolivia, 136
Confederación Nacional de Trabajadores, Mexico, 200, 201
Confederación Nacional Obrera de Cuba, 215, 216, 218, 219, 222
Confederación Nacional de Sindicatos Legales, Chile, 102
Confederación de Trabajadores de América Latina, 126
Confederación de Trabajadores de Chile, 102, 104
Confederación de Trabajadores de Cuba, 223, 224, 225
Confederación de Trabajadores de México, 185, 188, 189, 191, 196, 199, 200, 201
Confederación de Trabajadores del Peru, 159, 161, 163
Confederación de Trabajadores Particulares, Bolivia, 142
Confederación Proletaria Nacional, 200, 201
Confederación Regional Obrera Mexicana, 200
Confederación Sindical de Trabajadores Bolivianos, 113, 114, 122, 123, 133, 142
Confederación Sindical Latino Americana, 216
Confederación Sindical Uruguaya, 240
Confederation of White Collar Workers, Bolivia, 155
Congress of Industrial Organizations (CIO), USA, 126

Conservative Party, Argentina, 49
*Contra la Corriente*, Uruguay, 238, 239
Contreras, Carlos; See Vittorio Vidali
Contreras Labarca, Carlos, 91, 96, 100
Contreras, M., 90
Córdova, Víctor, 151
Cornejo, Alberto, 115, 119
Costa, L., 26
Cotler, Julio, 170
Council of Construction Workers, Chile, 96
Council of Unemployed Workers, Chile, 96
Coutinho, Rodolfo, 70
CPSU—See Communist Party, Soviet Union
Craig, Wesley, 171
Crespo, Paulo, 80
*Cronica*, Peru, 163
Cruz, Luis, 91
*Cuarta Internacional*, Posadista, 109
*Cuarta Internacional*, United Secretariat, 173, 207
*IV Internacional*, Mexico, 185, 187, 188
Cuban Solidarity Conference, 242
Curtiss, Charles, 191, 192, 193, 195, 196, 203, 204, 212, 213, 224
Cuzco Peasant Federation, 171


Dávila, Carlos, 97, 98, 99
Dávila Solís, Fausto, 205, 209
Debray, Régis, 20, 21, 36, 86, 146, 151, 175, 207
de la Rosa, Diogenes, 246
de la Torre, R.S., 221, 222
*Democrácia*, Argentina, 65
Deutscher, Isaac, 9, 11, 187
Díaz González, Pablo, 225
Díaz Ordaz, Gustavo, 213
Dickman, Enrique, 61
Directorio Estudiantil, Cuba, 216
Directorio Revolucionario, Cuba, 229
Dominguez, Eliodoro, 98
Donoso, 89
Dunne, Vincent R., 190


Echeverría, Luis, 208
Ejercito de Liberación Nacional, Bolivia, 50, 147
Ejercito de Liberación Nacional, Peru, 173
Ejercito Revolucionario del Pueblo, Argentina, 63, 64
*El Bolchevique*, Mexico, 197

*El Camino de Nuestra Revolución*, Peru, 174
*El Clarín*, Chile, 108
*El Combatiente*, Argentina, 62, 64
*El Ingenio Continente Americano*, 111
*El Libertador*, Mexico, 193, 218
*El Machete*, Mexico, 182, 183
*El Militante*, Argentina, 60, 61
*El Nacional*, Mexico, 180
*El Trabajador Latino Americano*, 96
Engels, Frederick, 180, 182, 198
Escobar Filemón, 145
Escobar, Santiago, 59
*España Obrera*, Argentina, 51
*Essay in Marxist Interpretation of the September Movement*, 49
*Estrategia*, Argentina, 62
*Estrategia Revolucionaria*, 55
Etkin, E., 57
*Expreso*, Peru, 163


Factory Workers Union, Bolivia; See Unión de Fabriles
Falange Socialista Boliviana, 138, 140
Federação Operaria de Sao Paulo, 74
Federación de Empleados Particulares, Bolivia, 133
Federación Libertaria de Obreros y Campesinos del Distrito Federal,
    Mexico, 200, 201
Federación Obrera de Chile (FOCh), 88, 96, 102
Federación Obrera de La Habana, 217, 218, 219, 221, 222
Federación Provincial de Campesinos de la Convención y Lares, 170, 172
Federación Sindical de Trabajadores Mineros, 113, 118, 119, 120, 121, 123,
    137, 145, 147, 155
Federation of Workers of Cuzco, 170
Fernández, Octavio, 181, 182, 184, 185, 186, 189, 190, 191, 192, 193, 194,
    202, 203, 204, 213
Fernández, Sra. de, 190
Ferrel, Jose, 193, 195
Ferrera, Ricardo, 228
Ferrera Acosta, Idalberto, 227, 228
Ferrera Ramirez, Juan Leon, 227
Fertisa Union, Peru, 163
Figueroa, H., 90, 91
First Conference of Latin American Youth, 226
Foley, Gerry, 145
Fontanillas, Roberto, 217
Fossa, Mateo, 58, 60
Fourth International, 3, 10, 11, 12, 13, 14, 16, 17, 18, 19, 20, 22, 23, 24, 25,
    26, 27, 28, 29, 30, 31, 33, 34, 35, 36, 37, 38, 39, 40, 41, 42, 43, 44, 50, 53,

55, 56, 57, 58, 59, 61, 66, 67, 75, 77, 78, 80, 82, 103, 106, 110, 111, 115,
118, 125, 129, 139, 140, 144, 154, 159, 160, 161, 164, 173, 179, 185, 186,
189, 191, 192, 193, 195, 197, 199, 203, 204, 205, 206, 209, 211, 212, 213,
215, 224, 225, 227, 228, 229, 230, 231, 232, 233, 243, 245
*Fourth International*, USA, 224
Franco, Cid, 84
Franco, Francisco, 26
Frank, André Gunder, 173
French Fourth Internationalists, 239
*Frente al Momento del Mundo—Que Quiere La Cuarta Internacional*, 55
Frente Amplio, Uruguay, 244
Frente de Izquierda Revolucionaria, Peru, 168, 169, 172, 173, 175, 177, 178
Frente Nacional de Defensa del Petroleo, Peru, 168
Frente Nacional Proletario, Mexico, 201
*Frente Obrero*, Argentina, 57, 59, 64
*Frente Obrero*, Uruguay, 239, 240, 243
*Frente Operaria*, 79, 80, 81
Frente Popular de Libertação, 82
*Frente Proletario*, Argentina, 51
Frente Revolucionario, Peru, 168
Frente Revolucionario Indoamericano Popular, Argentina, 62
Frías, Ismael, 158, 160, 162, 163
Frigerio, R.; See J. Lagos
Frondizi, Arturo, 68


Galdames, Maclovio, 91
Galicia, Luciano, 181, 182, 184, 185, 188, 190, 191, 192, 194, 198, 201, 202
Gallo, Antonio, 46, 47, 48, 49, 50, 52, 53, 55
Galván, 209, 210
Galván, Rafael, 200, 204, 205, 213
García, Socrates, 161
García Montes, Jorge, 220, 221
García Treviño, Rodrigo, 188, 189, 196, 197
García Villarreal, Marcos, 217, 219
Garmendia, A., 50, 51, 52
Gasso, Joaquín, 217
General Confederation of Labor, Brazil, 73, 74
Gestido, General Oscar, 242
Ghioldi, Rodolfo, 92
Gilly, Adolfo, 209, 229
Godoy, H, 90, 91
Godoy Urrutia, César, 104
Gomes, Eduardo, 78
González, A., Chilean, 90
González, A., USA, 183, 194, 212, 219, 245, 246, 247
González, Abel, 109

González, Andrés, 170
González, Manuel, 96
González, P., 192
González Díaz, Galo, 91, 104
González Moscoso, Hugo, 137, 138, 139, 140, 141, 143, 144, 145, 146, 148, 149, 150, 151, 152, 153
González Palacios, Carlos, 217
González Videla, Gabriel, 36
Gorkín, Julián, 218
Goulart, João, 80, 81, 82, 84, 85
GPU, 188, 218
Grandizo Muñiz, 13
Grau San Martín, Ramón, 219, 220, 223, 224, 225
Greek Trotskyists, 239
Grove, Marmaduque, 89, 97, 98, 99, 103, 105
Grupo Bolchevique-Leninista, Brazil, 75
Grupo Bolchevique-Leninista, Chile, 105
Grupo Comunista Internacionalista, Mexico, 207, 208, 213
Grupo Comunista Leninista, Brazil, 70
Grupo Internacionalista Obrero, Chile, 105
Grupo Obrero Marxista, Peru, 157, 158
Grupo Obrero Revolucionario, Argentina, 52, 53
Grupo Socialista Obrero, Mexico, 202, 203, 204
Grupo Tupac Amaru, Bolivia, 112
Grupos Libertarios, Brazil, 74
Guevara, Ernesto, 20, 21, 36, 145, 146, 150, 151, 153, 207, 230, 231, 234
Guevara Arce, Walter, 132
Guil, Adolfo; See Adolfo Gilly
Guinney, Juana, 48
Guinney, M., 45, 48
Guinney, Roberto, 45, 47
Guiteras, Antonio, 220, 221, 222
Gutierrez, Oyas, 183
Gwarkey, Tomas, 112


Hansen, Joseph, 15, 32, 39, 40, 205, 209, 225, 230, 231
Hansen, Olavo, 82
Havana Federation of Labor; See Federación Obrera de La Habana
Haya de la Torre, Víctor Raúl, 157, 163
Healy, Gerald, 19, 22, 24, 30, 40, 41, 145, 146, 209, 233, 234, 235
Hegel, G.W.H., 48
Henríquez, Diego, 107, 201
Hernández Arregui, J.J., 66
Hertzog, Enrique, 115, 120, 123
Hewitt, Cynthia, 39
Hidalgo, Manuel, 88, 89, 90, 91, 92, 94, 95, 96, 97, 98, 99, 101, 102, 104, 110

Hitler, Adolf, 7, 9, 12, 197
Homero; See J. Posadas
Horacio, 30
Howes Beas, Carlos, 158, 160
*Hoy*, Cuba, 223


Ibabaca, Ramón, 109
Ibañez, Carlos, 88, 89, 90, 91, 94, 95, 101, 102, 106
Ibarra, Eduardo, 106
Ibarra, Felix, 180, 184, 185, 192, 204
Icaza, Jorge, 170
Independent Revolutionary Workers Party, Mexico, 185
Independent Socialist League, USA, 13
Independent Socialist Party, Netherlands, 10
*Informations Ouvrières*, France, 146, 147
*Informe Nacional*, Brazil, 85, 86
*Inicial*, Argentina, 52, 53, 54
Iñiguez, 138
Integralistas; See Ação Integralista Brasileira
*Intercontinental Press*, USA, 145, 146, 150, 232, 244, 247
*Internal Bulletin*, Fourth International, 125
*Internal Bulletin*, GSO, Mexico, 203
*Internal Bulletin*, Izquierda Comunista Argentina, 47, 48
*International Bulletin of the Left Opposition*, 9
International Committee of Fourth International, 18, 19, 22, 24, 39, 40, 148,
    209, 233
International Communist Opposition, 3, 5
International Executive Committee of Fourth International, 14, 16, 38, 76
International Executive Committee of Fourth International, Pabloite, 18, 40
International Executive Committee of Fourth International, Posadista, 19, 25,
    26, 39, 62
*International Press Correspondence*, 75, 216
International Secretariat of Fourth International, 38, 203, 212
International Secretariat of Fourth International, Posadista, 26, 27, 80, 144
    162, 211
*International Socialist Review*, USA, 19, 20
Internationalist Proletarian Faction, Bolivia, 140
Internationalist Socialist Party, Colombia, 247
Iriarte, 89
Irigoyen, Hipolito, 46
Islas, Eduardo; See Pedro Milesi
IWW, Chile, 105
*Izquierda*, Argentina, 51, 64
*Izquierda*, Mexico, 180
Izquierda Boliviana, 12
Izquierda Comunista, Chile, 101, 102, 103, 104, 105, 109, 110

Izquierda Comunista Argentina, 46, 47, 48, 61
Izquierda Nacional, Argentina, 65
*Izquierda Nacional*, Argentina, 65
Izquierda Revolucionaria, Cuba, 223


Jacson-Monard, 190
James, C.L.R., 7, 13
Joven Cuba, 220, 221, 222, 223
Julião, Francisco, 80
Junco, Sandalio, 215, 216, 217, 218, 222, 223, 224
Juventud Autentica, 222
Juventud Comunista, Mexico, 181
Juventud Marxista Revolucionaria, Mexico, 207
Juventud Socialista, Chile, 109
Juventud Socialista, Mexico, 205, 206
Justo Agustín P., 49, 51
Justo Liborio, 46, 48, 49, 51, 52, 53, 54, 55, 57, 59, 78, 106, 117, 118,
    124, 154


Kautsky, Karl, 193
Kerensky, Alexander, 132, 155
Khrushev, Nikita, 35, 46, 210
Kikich, Esteban, 237, 238
Kirov, Serge, 247
Koiffman, L., 50, 55
Krupskaya, 193
Kuomintang, 5, 220


*La Batalla*, Mexico, 185
*Labor Action*, USA, 17, 125, 129, 133
Labor Party, Great Britain, 21
Labour Federation of São Paulo, 73
Lacerda, Carlos, 81
Lacerda, Fernando, 75
Lacerda, Mauricio, 71
Lafferte, Elias, 88, 89, 91, 94, 95, 96, 99, 100, 101, 102
Lagos, J.; See Jorge Abelardo Ramos
*La Internacional*, Argentina, 53, 54
*La Internacional*, Mexico, 207
*La Nación*, Chile, 97
Landau, K., 8
Langarica, Salvador, 192, 197
Lanka Sama Samaja, Ceylon, 17, 24, 30
*La Nueva Internacional*, Argentina, 53, 54

Lanusse, General Alejandro, 65
Lara, Juan, 138
*La Razón*, Bolivia, 119
*La Revolución Latinamericana*, 167
Latin American Bureau, Fourth International, 19, 25, 26, 29, 39, 40, 139, 162
Latin American Bureau, Fourth International, Pabloite, 140, 144, 225, 249
*La Verdad*, Argentina, 1930's, 46, 47
*La Verdad*, Argentina, 1960's, 61, 62
*La Verité*, France, 130
Lavín, Jorge; See Humberto Mendoza
Leão, Josias Carneiro, 72, 73
Leather Workers Federation, Chile, 106
Lechín, Juan, 119, 120, 121, 123, 128, 129, 132, 133, 134, 135, 136, 138,
        142, 143, 145, 149, 155
Left Bloc; See Bloc de Izquierda
Legión de Ex-Combatientes, Bolivia, 120
Leite, Hilcar, 69, 77
Lenin, Vladimir Ilyich, 3, 4, 33, 46, 67, 115, 117, 148, 205, 228
Leninist Workers Faction, Bolivia, 140
*León Trotsky y Wall Street*, 59
Levía, Juan D., 161
Liacho, C., 50, 51, 52, 55
Liga Comunista Internacional, Seccion Argentina, 48
Liga Comunista Internacionalista, Argentina, 48, 49, 50, 52, 53
Liga Comunista Internacionalista, Brazil, 74, 75, 77
Liga Comunista Internacionalista, Mexico, 182, 183, 184, 185, 186, 188, 189,
        192, 194, 195, 197, 224
Liga de Escritores y Artistas Revolucionarios, Mexico, 181
Liga dos Comunistas, 70
Liga Estudiantil Marxista, Mexico, 206
Liga Obrera Campesina, Mexico, 207
Liga Obrera Leninista, Chile, 107
Liga Obrera Marxista, Chile, 118
Liga Obrera Marxista, Mexico, 206, 207, 209
Liga Obrera Revolucionaria, Argentina, 53, 54, 55, 56, 57, 58, 59, 106
Liga Obrera Revolucionaria, Uruguay, 237, 238, 239
Liga Obrera Socialista, Argentina, 53, 54, 56
Ligue Comuniste, France, 153, 177
Lima, Luis Alberto Días, 82
Limpias Villegas, Guillermo, 135
Lista Obrera, Uruguay, 245
Lobo, Aristides, 69, 70, 71, 72
Logan, Daniel, 203
Lombardo Toledano, Vicente, 184, 185, 200, 201
López, Camilo, 45, 47
López, Pablo, 89, 96
López, Pedro, 98

López, S., 177
López Avila, Hugo, 136
López Cáceres, Luis, 95
Lora, Cesar, 145
Lora, Guillermo, 19, 39, 40, 113, 115, 118, 119, 121, 123, 125, 129, 130, 131,
     139, 140, 141, 143, 144, 145, 146, 147, 148, 155
Lora, Miguel, 149
Loris, Marc, 57
*Los Gangsters de Stalin*, 188
*Los Tiempos*, Bolivia, 119
Lott, General Henrique Teixeira, 85
Lovestone, Jay, 3
Lozada, J., 227
*Lucha Comunista*, Ecuador, 246
*Lucha Obrera*, Argentina, Posadista, 65
*Lucha Obrera*, Argentina, Liborio Justo, 58
*Lucha Obrera*, Bolivia, 131, 137, 138, 140, 143, 144
*Lucha Obrera*, Chile, 109, 110
*Lucha Obrera*, Mexico, 197, 199, 201, 202, 203
Lungarzo, Jose, 227
*Lutte Ouvrière*, France, 248


Machado, Armando, 217
Machado, Gerardo, 215, 216, 218
Maciel, P.; See Pedro Milesi
Madariaga, José Luis, 65
Maitán, Livio, 149, 232, 233
Mangan, Sherry, 55, 56, 57, 106, 213
Mao Tse-tung, 138, 174, 207
Mariategui, Jose Carlos, 158
Marof, Tristan, 50, 111, 112, 113, 114, 115, 118
Martí, Jose, 218
Martínez, Francisco, 96
Martorell, Jose, 166, 172
Marx, Karl, 48, 180, 197, 198, 205
*Marxismo*, Argentina, 51
*Marxist Review*, Posadista; See Revista Marxista
Marxist Socialist Party, Chile; See Partido Socialista Marxista
*Masas*, Bolivia, 144, 147
Matheus, João, 74
Matte, Eugenio, 97, 103
Mattos, J., 87
Maurín, Joaquín, 217
Mella, Julio Antonio, 215, 217, 218
Melo, Antonio, 80
Melo, Plinio, 72, 73

Méndez Dorch, Rafael, 157
Mendieta, Colonel Carlos, 219, 220, 221, 222
Mendivil, Lucio, 112, 114, 123
Mendoza, Humberto, 90, 91, 92, 93, 103
Menshevik Party, Russia, 4
Miguel, 57
Milesi, Pedro, 47, 48, 49, 51, 52, 53, 55
*Militant*, USA, 18, 46, 57, 62, 107, 129, 138, 148, 149, 179, 219
Mill, 8
Miners Federation, Bolivia; See Federación Sindical de Trabajadores Mineros
Miners Federation of the Central Region, Peru, 162
Molina, E., 227
Molina, Nicolás, 208
Moller, Edwin, 123, 133, 135, 136, 137, 139, 140, 142, 143, 155
Monroy Block, Germán, 119
Montarroyos, Carlos, 80, 81
Montero, Juan Esteban, 94
Moreno, Antonio, 151
Moreno, Nahuel, 38, 57, 59, 61, 67, 166, 167, 168, 169, 170, 172
Moreno, O., 90
Morrow, Felix, 56, 203, 222
Movimiento de Agrupaciones Obreras, Argentina, 61
Movimiento de Izquierda Revolucionaria, Chile, 21, 40, 108, 109, 110
Movimiento de Izquierda Revolucionaria, Peru, 173
Movimiento de Unidad y Coordenación Sindical (MUCS), 68
Movimiento Nacionalista Revolucionario, Bolivia, 112, 114, 119, 120, 122, 123,
    124, 125, 126, 127, 128, 130, 134, 135, 137, 138, 139, 140, 141, 142, 143,
    145, 149, 150, 154, 155, 156
Movimiento Politica Obrera, 66
Movimiento Revolucionario Comunista, 108
Movimiento Revolucionario Tiradentes, 85
Movimiento Social Progresista, 165
MR-13 revolutionary movement, Guatemala, 210, 211
Mujal, Eusebio, 217, 222, 223
Mujica, General Francisco, 186, 187
Municipal Workers Union, Chile; See Unión de Obreros Municipales
Muriel, Jesús, 143
Muste, A.J., 220


Naft, Stephen, 102
Naguil Moratorio, Luis Eduardo, 242
Narvaja, A., 21, 57, 59
National Committee for Amnesty of Social and Political Prisoners, Cuba, 222
National Liberation Alliance; See Aliança Nacional Libertadora
National Revolutionary Party, Cuba; See Partido Revolucionario
    Cubano (Autentico)

Nationalist Party, China; See Kuomintang
Nationalist Party, Uruguay; See Partido Nacional, Uruguay
Navarro, Gustavo; See Tristan Marof
Naville, Pierre, 8
Nazi Party, 9, 10
Negrete, Rosalio; See Russell Blackwell
*New International*, USA, 61, 158, 221, 222
Nin, Andrés, 8, 49, 217
Nixon, Richard, 162, 165
Norte, Jorge, 100
*Norte Revolucionario,* Argentina, 62
Novack, George, 193
*Nuestras Perspectivas Politicas*, 55
Nueva Accion Politica, 97, 102
*Nueva Etapa*, Argentina, 49, 50, 53
*Nueva Internacional*, Mexico, 182
*Nuevo Curso*, Argentina, 52


Obstrobsky, C.C., 48
*Obrero y Campesino*, Peru, 162
Odría, Manuel, 158, 160, 163
*O Estado de São Paulo,* Brazil, 80
Ongañía, Juan Carlos, 62, 63
Ontiveros, A.; See Antonio Gallo
*Oposición*, Mexico, 180
Oposición Comunista, Cuba, 216, 217, 218, 219
Oposición Comunista de Izquierda, Mexico, 181, 182
Opposition Communist Party, Chile, 97, 99
Orden Socialista, Chile, 99, 102
Ordoqui, Joaquín, 223
Organização Revolucionaria Marxista Politica Operaria; See Politica Operaria
*Organización*, Panama, 246
Organización Latino Americana de Solidaridad (OLAS), 42
Organización Regional Inter Americana de Trabajadores (ORIT), 126
Organizatión Comuniste Internationaliste, France, 19, 25, 148
Oscar; See Miguel
Ovando, General Alfredo, 147, 148, 151, 152, 153, 154
Overseas News Agency, 57


Pablo, Michel, 16, 17, 18, 19, 22, 23, 24, 26, 31, 36, 39, 40, 62, 67, 79, 108,
    139, 141, 144, 148, 160, 161, 162, 165, 169, 206, 225, 234, 240
Pacheco, Jorge, 242, 243
Packinghouse Workers Federation, Uruguay, 238
Padilla, Ezequiel, 200
Padilla, Heriberto, 232, 235

Padrón, Carlos, 217
Painters Union, Chile, 96, 106
*Palabra Obrera*, Argentina, 61, 62, 170
Palacios, Juan, 161
Pan American and Pacific Bureau of Fourth International, 37, 192, 195
Partido Aprista Peruano, 157, 159, 161, 162
Partido Bolchevique-Leninista, Cuba, 216, 217, 219, 220, 221, 222, 224
Partido Colorado, Uruguay, 236, 241, 242
Partido Colorado Batllista, Uruguay, 35, 236, 240
Partido Comunista, Uruguay, 237, 241, 242, 243, 244
Partido Comunista Brasileiro, 80, 82, 84, 86
Partido Comunista de Bolivia, pro-Moscow, 150
Partido Comunista de Bolivia, pro-Peking, 150
Partido Comunista de Chile, 88, 89, 91, 92, 104, 108, 110
Partido Comunista de Cuba, pre-Castro, 215, 217, 219, 221, 222, 223, 224,
     225, 229, 230
Partido Comunista de Cuba, Fidelista, 21, 40, 41, 225, 234
Partido Comunista de la Republica Argentina, 45, 46
Partido Comunista do Brasil, 73, 74, 76
Partido Comunista do Brasil, pro-Chinese, 80, 82, 85
Partido Comunista Independiente, Puerto Rico, 247
Partido Comunista Leninista, Peru, 164, 169
Partido Comunista Revolucionario (Trotskista), Ecuador, 245, 246
Partido de Izquierda Revolucionaria, Bolivia, 114, 118, 120, 123, 124, 133,
     135, 142, 155
Partido Democratico, Chile, 103, 104
Partido Guatemalteco del Trabajo, 210
Partido Laborista, Chile, 102
Partido Leninista Operario, 75, 76, 77
Partido Liberal, Bolivia, 120
Partido Nacional, Uruguay, 236, 240, 241
Partido Nacional Revolucionario, Mexico, 184
Partido Obrero, Argentina, 50, 61
Partido Obrero de la Revolución Socialista, Argentina, 57, 58, 59
Partido Obrero de Unificación Marxista, Spain, 185
Partido Obrero Internacionalista, Chile, 105, 106
Partido Obrero Internacionalista, Mexico, 197, 198, 199, 200, 201, 202,
     203, 206
Partido Obrero Marxista-Leninista, Panama, 246
Partido Obrero Revolucionario, Argentina, 61
Partido Obrero Revolucionario, Bolivia, 40, 42, 112, 113, 114, 115, 118, 119
     120, 122, 123, 124, 125, 126, 127, 129, 130, 131, 132, 133, 136, 137, 138,
     139, 140, 141, 142, 143, 144, 145, 146, 147, 148, 149, 150, 151, 152, 154,
     155, 156, 239
Partido Obrero Revolucionario, Chile, 37, 104, 105, 106, 107, 108
Partido Obrero Revolucionario, Cuba, 144, 223, 224, 230
Partido Obrero Revolucionario, Peru, 157, 158, 160, 161, 162, 165, 166,
     168, 170

Partido Obrero Revolucionario, (IV Internacional), Uruguay, 240, 241, 242
Partido Obrero Revolucionario (Trotskista), Bolivia, 138, 143, 144, 153
Partido Obrero Revolucionario (Trotskista), Chile, 108, 109
Partido Obrero Revolucionario (Trotskista), Cuba, 41, 226, 227, 228, 229, 233, 234
Partido Obrero Revolucionario (Trotskista), Mexico, 207, 209, 210, 213
Partido Obrero Revolucionario (Trotskista), Peru, 163, 164, 165, 168, 169, 175, 178, 245
Partido Obrero Revolucionario (Trotskista), Uruguay, 242, 243, 244
Partido Obrero (Trotskyista), Argentina, 66, 67, 68
Partido Operario Comunista, 79, 86, 87
Partido Operario Revolucionario (Trotskyista), 79, 80, 81, 82
Partido Radical Socialista, Chile, 99, 103, 104
Partido Revolucionario Cubano (Autentico), 217, 220, 222, 223, 225
Partido Revolucionario de la Izquierda Nacionalista, Bolivia, 143, 149
Partido Revolucionario Obrero y Campesino, Mexico, 195
Partido Revolucionario de Trabajadores, Argentina, 62, 63
Partido Revolucionario de Trabajadores, Uruguay, 244
Partido Social Democrata, Chile, 102
Partido Social Republicano, Chile, 102
Partido Socialista, Argentina, 50, 61
Partido Socialista, Bolivia, 111, 113
Partido Socialista, Brazil, 74, 80, 84, 85
Partido Socialista, Uruguay, 237, 238, 241, 244, 245
Partido Socialista de Chile, 98, 102, 103, 104, 105, 109, 110
Partido Socialista de Izquierdas, Mexico, 184
Partido Socialista de la Izquierda Nacional, Argentina, 65, 66
Partido Socialista de la Revolución Nacional, Argentina, 61, 65
Partido Socialista de Trabajadores, Chile, 104, 109
Partido Socialista del Estado, Bolivia, 112
Partido Socialista Internacional, Chile, 102
Partido Socialista Marxista, Chile, 94, 98
Partido Socialista Obrero, Argentina, 50, 51, 52
Partido Socialista Obrero Boliviano, 113, 114, 115, 116, 117, 118
Partido Socialista Popular, Chile, 107, 108, 109
Partido Socialista Popular, Cuba; See Partido Comunista de Cuba, pre-Castro
Partido Socialista Revolucionario, Brazil, 77, 78, 79
Partido Socialista Unificado, Chile, 99, 102
Partido Trabalhista Brasileiro, 84
Partido Unión Republicana Socialista, 120
Paz Estenssoro, Victor, 124, 128, 132, 134, 135, 137, 138, 139, 142, 148, 155
Peasants Union of Tumbes, Peru, 164
Pedraza, Colonel, 221
Pedrosa, Mario, 11, 13, 38, 69, 74, 75, 76, 78, 118
Pellecer, Carlos Manuel, 210, 226
Peña, Braulio León, 91
Peña, Luís, 91
Peñaloza, Juan Ramón; See Enrique Rivera

Peñaloza, Luís, 112
Peñaranda, General Enrique, 114, 118
Penelón, Jose, 45
Peredi, Inti, 151
Pereira, Astrogildo, 71, 72, 73
Pereira, José, 136
Perelman, A., 66
Pereyra, Alberto, 166
Pérez Baz, René, 109
*Permanent Revolution*, 226
Perón, Juan, 59, 60, 61, 67, 68, 142
*Perspectiva Mundial*, 150, 173, 207
Phelan, Terence; See Sherry Mangan
Pinheiro, Eduardo, 87
Pinto, Paulo Roberto, 80
Pinto, Roberto, 92, 96
*Piquete*, Argentina, 51
*Polemica*, Chile, 108
*Politica*, Argentina, 64
*Politica Obrera*, Argentina, 66
Politica Operaria, 79, 82, 83, 84, 85, 86, 87
*Politica Operaria*, 82, 83, 84, 85, 86
Popular Assembly, Bolivia, 148, 153
Popular Front, Chile, 104, 105
Popular Front, Mexico, 185
Popular Unity, Chile, 109
Portocarrero, Felipe, 170
Posadas, J., 19, 22, 24, 25, 26, 27, 28, 29, 30, 38, 39, 40, 41, 42, 44, 53, 54, 57,
    61, 66, 67, 68, 79, 81, 82, 108, 141, 144, 153, 162, 163, 164, 165, 169,
    205, 207, 209, 210, 211, 215, 225, 226, 227, 228, 229, 230, 233, 234, 240,
    242, 243, 245, 246, 249
Powell, Samuel, 217
Prado, Jorge del, 157
Prado, Manuel, 161, 162, 163, 167
Prestes, Luiz Carlos, 69, 70, 71, 72, 76
Proletarian Front, Bolivia, 114
*Pucara*, Bolivia, 18


*Quatrième Internationale*, 1930's, 13
*Quatrième Internationale*, United Secretariat, 87, 232, 247
Quebracho; See Liborio Justo
*Qué Es La Izquierda Nacional?*, 65
*Qué Hacer?*, Mexico, 204, 205, 213


Radical Party, Argentina, 49

Radical Party, Cuba, 223
Radical Socialist Party, Chile; See Partido Radical Socialista
Railroad Brotherhood, Cuba, 224
Railroad Workers Union, Mexico, 188
Rámos, Jorge Abelardo, 50, 56, 57, 64, 65, 66, 142
Rámos López, J., 47
Raurich, R., 46, 47, 48, 49, 50, 55
*Rayo y Divisa*, Cuba, 224
*Rebelión*, Bolivia, 134, 142
Recabarren, Luis Emilio, 88, 89
Red International of Labor Unions, 217
*Revista Marxista*, Posadista, 27
*Revista Marxista Latinoamericana*, Pabloite, 161, 164
*Revolución*, Peru, 157
*Revolución en la Revolución?*, 175
*Revolución Proletaria*, Cuba, 225
*Revolución Socialista*, Guatemala, 210
Revolutionary Committee of the Workers United Front, Chile, 94
Revolutionary Council of Workers, Peasants and Soldiers, Chile, 98
Revolutionary Lanka Sama Samaja Party, Ceylon, 24
Revolutionary League, Brazil, 70
Revolutionary Military Committee, Russia, 4
Revolutionary Socialist Party, Netherlands, 10
Revolutionary Workers Party, 29
Revueltas, José, 179, 180, 182, 183, 208
Rey Esteban, 57
Rey, Juan, 125, 126, 129, 133, 135, 138
Riera Hernández, Mario, 217, 220
Right Opposition; See International Communist Opposition
*RILU Magazine*, 73
Rios, Juan Antonio, 106
Rivas Rooney, O., 52
Rivera, Diego, 27, 43, 52, 179, 182, 183, 184, 185, 186, 191, 193, 194, 195, 196, 197
Rivera, E., 57
Rivera, Enrique, 64, 142
Roca, Blas, 32
Rocha, Laudo Reginaldo, 76
Rodríguez, L., 78
Rodriguez, Manuel, 180, 182, 183, 184, 185, 186
Rosas, R., 89, 90, 91, 100
Rosmer, Alfred, 7, 8, 11
*Rouge*, France, 153, 208, 232
Ruíz Cortines, Adolfo, 206
Russian Left Opposition, 6
Rykov, Andrei, 3

Sa, Aybire, 80, 81
Saenz, Alberto, 146, 147
Salazar, Carlos, 114
Salazar, Jorge, 130
Sánchez, Alberto, 247
Sánchez, E., 152
Sánchez, Fermin, 217
Sánchez Arango, Aureliano, 215
Sánchez Fernandez, Hernan, 113
Sandino, Augusto, 180
Santiago, Jose, 104
São Paulo State Trade Union Reorganization Committee, 73
Sartre, Jean-Paul, 173
Second International, 9, 11
Secretariado Latino Americano del Trotskismo Ortodoxo, 38, 165, 166
Sedov, Leon, 8
Segnini, General Liber, 244
Selemé, General Antonio, 128
Sepulveda Leal, Ramón, 104
Sevilla, Carlos, 22, 209
Shachtman, Max, 8, 11, 12, 13, 14, 15, 16, 31, 32, 76, 190, 238
Short, Tony, 234
Siburu, D., 51, 52
Siles, Hernan, 124, 128, 132, 138, 142, 143, 149
Siles, Luis Adolfo, 149
Silva, 107
Simeon, Charles, 217, 222, 223
Sinclair, Andrew, 234
Sindicato Unico de la Construcción, Mexico, 184, 188
Sindicato Unico de la Industrial Metalurgica, Uruguay, 237
Siqueira Campos, 71
Sisson, Roberto, 75
Sob Nova Bandeira, Brazil, 77
Social Democratic Party, Bolivia, 149
Social Democratic Party, Brazil, 85
Social Democratic Party, Germany, 10
Social Democratic Party, Switzerland, 3
Socialist Call, USA, 222
Socialist Freedom Party, Denmark, 21
Socialist Labor League, Great Britain, 17, 19, 22, 23, 30, 31, 146, 209, 234
Socialist Parties, 11, 14, 16, 17, 21, 35, 102
Socialist Party, Argentina; See Partido Socialista Argentino
Socialist Party, Austria, 21
Socialist Party, Bolivia; See Partido Socialista, Bolivia
Socialist Party, Brazil; See Partido Socialista, Brazil
Socialist Party, Chile; See Partido Socialista de Chile
Socialist Party, France, 115, 184

Socialist Party, Panama, 246
Socialist Party, USA, 13, 76, 184, 232
Socialist Party, Uruguay; See Partido Socialista, Uruguay
Socialist Workers Party (SAP), Germany, 10
Socialist Workers Party, USA, 11, 12, 15, 17, 18, 19, 31, 32, 56, 59, 62, 67, 76,
    107, 108, 139, 140, 144, 145, 146, 160, 190, 199, 202, 203, 205, 209, 212,
    224, 225, 230, 231, 238
Socialists, Cuba, 218
Socorro Rojo, 180, 181
Solís Solís, Luis, 102
Sosa, Victor, 149
Sotelo, 91
South American Secretariat, Comintern, 71, 72, 88, 89, 90, 91, 92, 99
Souzo, 8
Spanish Trotskyites, 46, 100
Stalin, Joseph, 4, 5, 6, 12, 16, 32, 70, 74, 99, 100, 102, 120, 179, 189, 194,
    197, 224, 234
*State and Revolution*, 228
Steinfeld, Kurt, 57
Suarez, Ismael, 107
Sun Yat Sen, 5


Tamayo, Jose, 112
Tavora, Juarez, 71
Tejeda, Colonel Adelberto, 184
Tejera, Roberto, 228
*Tendencia*, Argentina, 61
Tenentes, Brazil, 70, 71
*Terra e Socialismo*, Brazil, 80
Thalheimer, August, 3
Third International; See Communist International
Thomas, Norman, 76
Tito, Josip Broz, 16
Tokto, R., 197
Tomsky, Mikhail, 3
Toriz, P., 192
Toro, David, 112, 113
Torres, E., 90
Torres, General Juan José, 25, 148, 152, 153
Torres, Mario, 133, 134
Trabalhista Party, Brazil, 85
*Transición*, Argentina, 50
*Tribuna Leninista*, Argentina, 49, 50
*Tribuna Socialista*, Mexico, 202, 203
Tricontinental Congress, 211, 229
Tro, Emilio, 223

Trolley Car Workers Union, Chile, 96
Trotsky, Leon, 3, 4, 5, 6, 7, 8, 9, 10, 11, 12, 13, 22, 24, 31, 32, 33, 34, 45, 46,
   47, 48, 49, 50, 51, 59, 64, 67, 70, 77, 100, 112, 118, 148, 160, 179, 180,
   182, 183, 184, 185, 186, 187, 188, 189, 190, 192, 193, 194, 196, 197, 198,
   199, 200, 205, 216, 217, 226, 227, 228, 231, 238
Trotsky, Natalia Sedova, 33, 160, 189
Tupamaros, Uruguay, 242
Turcios, Luis, 211
26th of July Movement, Cuba, 229


Ugarte, Manuel, 64
*Unidad Obrera*, Argentina, 61
Unified Construction Committee, Chile, 97
Unión Civica, Uruguay, 237
Unión de Fabriles, Bolivia, 123, 133, 155
Unión de Obreros Municipales, Chile, 106, 107
Unión General de Trabajadores, Uruguay, 237, 240
Unión Insurrectional Revolucionaria, Cuba, 223, 229
Unión Nacional de Estudiantes Revolucionarios, Mexico, 207
United Class Electoral Front, Peru, 164
United Secretariat, Fourth International, 18, 19, 20, 21, 22, 23, 24, 30, 31, 40,
   67, 79, 146, 148, 149, 153, 169, 173, 175, 177, 178, 206, 207, 208, 213,
   225, 230, 233, 244, 247, 248
Urriolagoitia, Mamerto, 123


Valdés, G., 90
Valencia Vega, Alipio, 112, 114
Valenzuela, Humberto, 106
*Vanguarda Socialista*, Brazil, 78
Vanguardia Popular Socialista, 105
Vanguardia Revolucionaria, Cuba, 225
Vanguardia Revolucionaria, Peru, 177, 178
Varela, P., 58
Vargas, Amadeo, 153
Vargas, Getulio, 69, 70, 71, 72, 74, 75, 76, 77, 78, 81
Vazquez, Elio, 151
Vazquez, Felipe, 151
Vega, José, 91
Velasco, General Juan, 162, 163, 165, 175, 176, 177
Velasco Ibarra, José María, 36, 246
Venezuelan Trotskyites, 247
Vergne Ortiz, Luis, 247
Vidal, F., 209
Vidali, Vittorio, 218
Videla, Carlos, 104

Villanueva, Victor, 166, 167, 170, 172
Villarroel, Major Gualberto, 114, 115, 118, 119, 120, 122, 125, 127, 155
*Visión*, Argentina, 50
Vitale, Luís, 108, 109
*Viva la Huelga de los Frigoríficos!*, Uruguay, 239
Vivero, Francisco Abril de, 157, 160
*Voz Obrera*, Bolivia, 153
*Voz Obrera*, Mexico, 213
*Voz Obrera*, Peru, 164, 165, 245, 246
*Voz Proletaria*, Argentina, 67
*Voz Proletaria*, Cuba, 226, 228


Waiss, Oscar, 98, 102, 109
Wilkinson, 7
Wolfe, Bertram, 193, 194, 196
Workers and Peasants Bloc, Mexico, 194
Workers League, USA, 24
Workers Party, USA, 13, 15, 76, 220
*Workers Press*, Great Britain, 31, 234


Xavier, Livio, 69


Yañez, A., 200
Yero, Manuel, 228
Yon Sosa, Marco Antonio, 42, 210, 211, 229, 230
Young Communist League, USA, 247
Young Cuba; See Joven Cuba
Young Socialist Alliance, USA, 31, 172


Zamora, Adolfo, 193, 195
Zamora, Oscar, 150
Zapata, Emilio, 96, 99, 104
Zavala, J.S., 89, 90
Zegada, José, 133
Zevallos Quesadas, Félix, 157, 158, 159, 160
Zinoviev, G.E., 6